TEACHER'S EDITION

WorldView 2

SERIES EDITOR: MICHAEL ROST

Kristin Sherman

Longman

WorldView Teacher's Edition 2

Authorized adaptation from the United Kingdom edition entitled *Language to Go*, First Edition, published by Pearson Education Limited publishing under its Longman imprint.
Copyright © 2002 by Pearson Education Limited

American English adaptation published by Pearson Education, Inc.
Copyright © 2005.

Pearson Education, 10 Bank Street, White Plains, NY 10606

Editorial director: Pamela Fishman
Project manager: Irene Frankel
Senior aquisitions editor: Virginia L. Blanford
Senior development editors: Karen Davy, Stella Reilly
Vice president, director of design and production: Rhea Banker
Executive managing editor: Linda Moser
Associate managing editor: Mike Kemper
Production editor: Michael Mone
Art director: Elizabeth Carlson
Vice president, director of international marketing: Bruno Paul
Senior manufacturing buyer: Edie Pullman
Text and cover design: Elizabeth Carlson
Photo research: Aerin Csigay
Text composition: Word and Image Design
Text font: 10.5/13pt Utopia and 10/12pt Frutiger Bold

ISBN: 0-13-184002-9

Printed in the United States of America
2 3 4 5 6 7 8 9 10–BAM–09 08 07 06 05 04

Text Credits

Page 21 "River Deep, Mountain High." Jeff Barry, Ellie Greenwich and Phil Spector. © 1966, 1967 Trio Music Co., Inc., Mother Bertha Music, Inc. and Universal — Songs of Polygram International, Inc. (BMI). Copyrights renewed. All rights on behalf of Mother Bertha Music, Inc. administered by ABKCO Music, Inc. All rights reserved. Used by permission of Warner Bros. Publications. 59 "Wonderful Tonight." Words and Music by Eric Clapton. © 1977 by Eric Patrick Clapton. All rights in the U.S.A. Administered by Unichappell Music Inc. All rights reserved. Used by permission of Warner Bros. Publications. 97 "Matter Of Time." Written by David Hidalgo and Louis Perez. © 1984 Los Lobos Music (BMI) Administered by BUG. All rights reserved. Used by permission. 135 "This Used To Be My Playground." Words and music by Madonna Ciccone and Shep Pettibone. © 1992 WB Music Corp., Webo Girl Publishing, Inc., Universal—MCA Music Publishing, a division of Universal Studios, Inc. and Shepsongs, Inc. All rights for Webo Girl Publishing, Inc. administered by WB Music Corp. All rights for Shepsongs, Inc. administered by Universal — MCA Music Publishing, a division of Universal Studios, Inc. All rights reserved. Used by permission of Warner Bros. Publications.

Illustration Credits

Steve Attoe, pp. 80, 104, 112, 116; Pierre Berthiaume, pp. 38, 57, 132, 138, 141; Kasia Charko, pp. 64, 67; François Escalmel, p. 31; Stephen Harris, pp. 63, 140, 142; Paul McCusker, pp. 18-19, 46-47, 85, 95; NSV Productions, pp. 83, 138, 141; Stephen Quinlan, pp. 33, 83, 95, 137, 139; Steve Schulman, p. 82.

Photo Credits

Page 3 *(top)* Doug Menuez/Getty Images, *(middle)* Cosmo Condina/Getty Images, *(bottom)* The Stock Market; 8 AbleStock/Index Stock Imagery; 10 Spencer Platt/Newsmakers/Getty Images; 11 *(top)* Aquarius Library, *(bottom)* Rex Features/SIPA; 12 Richard Smith/Corbis; 15 *(top right)* Stone/Stewart Cohen, *(middle left)* Stone/David Ball, *(middle right)* Pictor International, *(bottom left)* Ulli Seer/Getty Images, *(bottom right)* John W. Banagan/Getty Images; 16 *(top)* Peter Adams/Getty Images, *(bottom)* Stone/Lori Adamski Peek; 19 Arlene Sandler/SuperStock; 20 B.D.V./Corbis; 23 Ryan McVay/Getty Images; 26 *(top)* Graham Porter, *(middle)* Walter Hodges/Getty Images, *(bottom)* Getty Images; 27 Network Photographers; 28 Laurence Monneret/Getty Images; 30 *(left & right)* Ryan McVay/Getty Images; 31 *(left)* Amos Morgan/Getty Images, *(right)* Dorling Kindersley Media Library; 32 *(bottom)* Erik Dreyer/Getty Images; 34 *(A)* Danjaq/Eon/UA/The Kobal Collection, *(B)* Universal/The Kobal Collection/Bruce McBroom, *(C)* Moviestore Collection; 35 Moviestore Collection; 36 G.D.T./Getty Images; 39 Touchstone/The Kobal Collection; 40 Getty Images; 41 Tom Paiva/Getty Images; 44 *(A)* Hutchinson Library, *(B)* Science Photo Library, *(C)* Science Photo Library, *(D)* Corbis, *(E)* Science Photo Library, *(F)* Art Directors & Trip, *(G)* Katz Pictures; 48 *(top)* Getty Images, *(middle)* Getty Images, *(bottom)* Robert Harding Picture Library; 49 Getty Images; 50 Jose Luis Pelaez, Inc./Corbis; 52 Robert Harding Picture Library; 53 Getty Images; 54 Getty Images; 58 *(top)* Neal Preston/Corbis, *(left)* RubberBall Productions/Getty Images, *(middle)* Ryan McVay/Getty Images, *(right)* Digital Vision/Getty Images; 60 *(A)* Steve Cole/Getty Images, *(B)* Dorling Kindersley Media Library, *(C)* Barry Rosenthal/Getty Images, *(D)* Dorling Kindersley Media Library, *(E)* Getty Images, *(F)* Getty Images, *(G)* Liz McAulay/ Dorling Kindersley Media Library, *(H)* Dorling Kindersley Media Library, *(I)* Stephen Oliver/Dorling Kindersley Media Library, *(J)* Steve Gorton/Dorling Kindersley Media Library; 62 Dorling Kindersley Media Library; 66 Adam Smith/Getty Images; 68 *(A)* Getty Images, *(B)* Corbis, *(C)* William R. Sallaz/Getty Images, *(D)* Getty Images, *(E)* Allsport, *(F)* Allsport; 70 Mark Adams/Getty Images; 72 Trevor Clifford, *(bottom)* Philippe Gelot/Telegraph Colour Library; 73 Trevor Clifford; 76 *(top)* Dorling Kindersley Media Library, *(bottom)* Dorling Kindersley Media Library; 77 *(top)* Getty Images, *(middle)* Richard Price/Getty Images, *(middle inset)* Getty Images, *(bottom)* Getty Images; 78 Stone/Zigy Kaluzny; 86 *(A)* Robert W. Ginn/PhotoEdit, *(B)* Daily Mail, *(C)* Bill Aron/PhotoEdit; 87 *(D)* Daily Mail, *(E)* Daily Mail, *(F)* Corbis, *(G)* Daily Mail; 88 Ryan McVay/Getty Images; 90 Pictorial Press; 91 Niall MacLeod/Corbis; 93 Mirisch-7 Arts/United Artists/Kobal Collection; 96 Philip Gould/Corbis; 98 *(top)* Redferns, *(middle)* Christine Cheney Putnam c/o ITA Hall of Fame Archives at the McCormack-Nagelsen Tennis Center in Williamsburg VA, *(bottom)* Corbis; 100 Dave King/Dorling Kindersley Media Library; 103 *(top)* The Image Bank/Barros & Barros, *(middle)* Stone/Kalvzny/Thatcher, *(bottom left)* Stone/Stewart Cohen, *(bottom right)* The Image Bank/Ghislain & Marie David de Lossy; 109 *(top left)* Mary Evans Picture Library, *(top right)* Hulton Deutsch, *(bottom left)* Hulton Deutsch, *(bottom right)* Topham Picturepoint; 110 *(A)* Richard Price/Telegraph Picture Library, *(D)* ActionPlus/Steve Bardens, *(E)* Stone/David Madison, *(F)* Popperfoto/Simon Bruty; 111 *(C)* Index Stock, *(G)* Robert Holland/Getty Images, *(H)* Allsport Concepts/Getty Images, *(I)* Murry Sill/Index Stock Imagery, *(J)* Getty Images; 113 ActionPlus/Steve Bardens; 114 *(top)* Rob Francis/Robert Harding World Imagery, *(bottom)* Corbis; 116 Camera Press, London (RING/RBO); 117 *(left)* EPS/Derek Santini, *(right)* Chika; 121 Jon Feingersh/Corbis; 126 Royalty-Free/Corbis; 128 *(top left)* Stone/John Beatty, *(top right)* Steve McAlister Productions/Getty Images, *(middle)* The Photographers Library, *(bottom left)* The Image Bank/Sparky, *(bottom middle)* Telegraph Colour Library/V.C.L., *(bottom right)* Britstock-IFA/West Stock Fotopic; 133 *(left)* RubberBall Productions/Getty Images, *(middle)* Michael Newman/PhotoEdit, *(right)* Getty Images; 134 Corbis, *(background)* Michael Matisse/Getty Images.

Acknowledgments

The authors and series editor wish to acknowledge with gratitude the following reviewers, consultants, and piloters for their thoughtful contributions to the development of *WorldView*.

BRAZIL: São Paulo: Sérgio Gabriel, **FMU/Cultura Inglesa, Jundiaí;** Heloísa Helena Medeiros Ramos, **Kiddy and Teen;** Zaina Nunes, Márcia Mathias Pinto, Angelita Goulvea Quevedo, **Pontifícia Universidade Católica;** Rosa Laquimia Souza, **FMU-FIAM;** Élcio Camilo Alves de Souza, **Associação Alumni;** Maria Antonieta Gagliardi, Marie Adele Ryan, **Centro Britânico;** Chris Ritchie, **Sevenidiomas;** Joacyr Oliveira, Debora Schisler, **FMU;** Maria Thereza Garrelhas Gentil, **Colégio Mackenzie;** Carlos Renato Lopes, **Uni-Santana;** Yara M. Bannwart Rago, Jacqueline Zilberman, **Instituto King's Cross;** Vera Lúcia Cardoso Berk, **Talkative Idioms Center;** Ana Paula Hoepers, **Instituto Winners;** Carlos C.S. de Celis, Daniel Martins Neto, **CEL-LEP;** Maria Carmen Castellani, **União Cultural Brasil Estados Unidos;** Kátia Martins P. de Moraes Leme, **Colégio Pueri Domus;** Luciene Martins Farias, **Aliança Brasil Estados Unidos;** Neide Aparecida Silva, **Cultura Inglesa;** Áurea Shinto, **Santos:** Maria Lúcia Bastos, **Instituto Four Seasons. Curitiba:** Marila de Carvalho Hanech. **COLOMBIA: Bogota:** Sergio Monguí, Rafael Díaz Morales, **Universidad de la Salle;** Yecid Ortega Páez, Yojanna Ruiz G., **Universidad Javeriana;** Merry García Metzger, **Universidad Minuto de Dios;** Maria Caterina Barbosa, **Coninglés;** Nelson Martínez R., **Asesorías Académicas;** Eduardo Martínez, Stella Lozano Vega, **Universidad Santo Tomás de Aquino;** Kenneth McIntyre, **ABC English Institute.**
JAPAN: Tokyo: Peter Bellars, **Obirin University;** Michael Kenning, **Takushoku University;** Martin Meldrum, **Takushoku University;** Carol Ann Moritz, **New International School;** Mary Sandkamp, **Musashi Sakai;** Dan Thompson, **Yachiyo Chiba-ken/American Language Institute;** Carol Vaughn, **Kanto Kokusai High School. Osaka:** Lance Burrows, **Osaka Prefecture Settsu High School;** Bonnie Carpenter, **Mukogawa Joshi Daigaku/ Hannan Daigaku;** Josh Glaser, Richard Roy, **Human International University/Osaka Jogakuin Junior College;** Gregg Kennerly, **Osaka YMCA;** Ted Ostis, **Otemon University;** Chris Page, **ECC Language Institute;** Leon Pinsky, **Kwansei Gakuin University;** Chris Ruddenklau, **Kinki University;** John Smith, **Osaka International University. Saitama:** Marie Cosgrove, **Surugadai University. Kobe:** Donna Fujimoto, **Kobe University of Commerce. KOREA: Seoul:** Adrienne Edwards-Daugherty, Min Hee Kang, James Kirkmeyer, Paula Reynolds, Warren Weappa, Matthew Williams, **YBM ELS Shinchon;** Brian Cook, Jack Scott, Russell Tandy, **Hanseoung College. MEXICO: Mexico City:** Alberto Hern, **Instituto Anglo Americano de Idiomas;** Eugenia Carbonell, **Universidad Interamericana;** Cecilia Rey Gutiérrez, María del Rosario Escalada Ruiz, **Universidad Motolinia;** Raquel Márquez Colin,

Universidad St. John's; Francisco Castillo, Carlos René Malacara Ramos, **CELE – UNAM/Mascarones;** Belem Saint Martin, **Preparatoria ISEC;** María Guadalupe Aguirre Hernández, **Comunidad Educativa Montessori;** Isel Vargas Ruelas, Patricia Contreras, **Centro Universitario Oparin;** Gabriela Juárez Hernández, Arturo Vergara Esteban Juan, **English Fast Center;** Jesús Armando Martínez Salgado, **Preparatoria Leon Tolstoi;** Regina Peña Martínez, **Centro Escolar Anahuac;** Guadalupe Buenrostro, **Colegio Partenon;** Rosendo Rivera Sánchez, **Colegio Anglo Español;** María Rosario Hernández Reyes, **Escuela Preparatoria Monte Albán;** Fernanda Cruzado, **Instituto Tecnológico del Sur;** Janet Harris M., **Colegio Anglo Español;** Rosalba Pérez Contreras, **Centro Lingüístico Empresarial. Ecatepec:** Diana Patricia Ordaz García, **Comunidad Educativa Montessori;** Leticia Ricart P., **Colegio Holandés;** Samuel Hernández B. **Instituto Cultural Renacimiento. Tlalpan:** Ana María Cortés, **Centro Educativo José P. Cacho. San Luis Potosi:** Sigi Orta Hernández, María de Guadalupe Barrientos J., **Instituto Hispano Inglés;** Antonieta Raya Z., **Instituto Potosino;** Gloria Carpizo, **Seminario Mayor Arquidiocesano de San Luis Potosí;** Susana Prieto Noyola, Silvia Yolanda Ortiz Romo **Universidad Politécnica de San Luis Potosí;** Rosa Arrendondo Flores, **Instituto Potosino/Universidad Champagnat;** María Cristina Carmillo, María Carmen García Leos, **Departamento Universitario de Inglés, UASLP;** María Gloria Candia Castro, **Universidad Tecnológica SLP;** Bertha Guadalupe Garza Treviño, **Centro de Idiomas, UASLP. Guadalajara:** Nancy Patricia Gómez Ley, **Escuela Técnica Palmares;** Gabriela Michel Vázquez, **Colegio Cervantes Costa Rica;** Abraham Barbosa Martínez, **Colegio Enrique de Osso;** Ana Cristina Plascencia Haro, Joaquín Limón Ramos, **Centro Educativo Tlaquepaque III;** Lucía Huerta Cervantes, Paulina Cervantes Fernández, Audrey Lizaola López, **Colegio Enrique de Osso,** Rocío de Miguel, **Colegio La Paz;** Jim Nixon, **Colegio Cervantes Costa Rica;** Hilda Delgado Parga, **Colegio D'Monaco;** Claudia Rodríguez, **English Key. León:** Laura Montes de la Serna, **Colegio Británico A.C.;** Antoinette Marie Hernández, **"The Place 4U2 Learn" Language School;** Delia Zavala Torres, Verónica Medellín Urbina, **EPCA Sur;** María Eugenia Gutiérrez Mena, Ana Paulina Suárez Cervantes, **Universidad la Salle;** Herlinda Rodríguez Hernández, **Instituto Mundo Verde,** María Rosario Torres Neri, **Instituto Jassa. Aguascalientes:** María Dolores Jiménez Chávez, **ECA – Universidad Autónoma de Aguascalientes;** María Aguirre Hernández, **ECA – Proyecto Start;** Fernando Xavier Goúrey O., **UAA – IEA "Keep On";** Felisia Guadalupe García Ruiz, **Universidad Tecnológica;** Margarita Zapiain B, Martha Ayala de la Concordia, Fernando Xavier Gomez Orenday, **Universidad Autónoma de Aguascalientes;** Gloria Aguirre Hernández, **Escuela de la Ciudad de Aguascalientes;** Hector Arturo Moreno Diaz, **Universidad Bonaterra.**

Contents

Scope and Sequence

GRAMMAR FOCUS	PRONUNCIATION	SPEAKING	WRITING
Verbs for likes/dislikes + noun/verb + -ing	Stress to compare and contrast ideas	Talking about sports you like doing	Explain why you like or dislike a sport
Quantifiers + count/ non-count nouns	Vowel sounds: /u/ (food) and /ʊ/ (cookies)	Talking about what you eat	Explain which foods are good and bad to eat, and why
Modals: have to/had to for present and past necessity	Weak and strong forms: to	Talking about obligations	Write to an American friend about business practices in your country
Simple past and past continuous	Weak forms: was and were	Describing activities in the past	Describe a memorable event in your life
because, for, and infinitives of purpose	Stress in compound words	Giving reasons	Write an article about your favorite stores or restaurants and explain why you like to go there
a/an, the	a, an, the in connected speech	Talking about the theater	Summarize the story of the musical West Side Story
Present perfect: how long/for/since	Voiced and voiceless /ð/and /θ/	Talking about how long you have done something	Write an article that gives interesting facts about a person
Modals for requests and offers	Weak forms and blending: can, could, should, would	Making and responding to requests and offers	Write an email asking your job partner to do some tasks and offering to do others
used to/didn't use to	used to/ use to (useta)	Talking about past customs	Compare your life when you were a child with your life now
Present perfect vs. simple past	Word stress	Talking about experiences	Describe your experience with adventure sports to complete an application
could and be good at for past ability	Weak and strong forms: could and couldn't	Talking about abilities in the past	Describe a sport or other activity that you could do in the past
Present perfect: yet, already	Contracted forms of have and has	Saying what you've done so far	Describe what you have already done and what you haven't done yet to reach a goal
Present factual conditional (If + simple present + simple present)	Vowel sounds: /ɪ/ (give) and /ɛ/ (empty)	Talking about consequences	Describe your behavior in a situation and explain why you behave that way
like + verb + -ing; would like + infinitive	The sound /ɚ/ (work, earn)	Talking about job and career preferences	Write a want ad for a job you would like to have

WorldView
An introduction to the course
by Michael Rost

Welcome to *WorldView*, a four-level English course for adults and young adults. *WorldView* builds fluency by letting students explore and talk about a wide range of compelling topics presented from an international perspective. *Worldview's* trademark two-page lesson design, with clear and attainable language goals, ensures that students feel a sense of accomplishment and increased self-confidence in every class.

WorldView's approach to language learning follows a simple and proven **M.A.P.**:

☆ **M**otivate learning through stimulating content and achievable learning goals

☆ **A**nchor language production with strong, focused language presentations

☆ **P**ersonalize learning through engaging and communicative speaking activities

Course components

- **Student Book with Student Audio CD**

- The **Student Book** contains 28, four-page units, seven Review Units (one after every four units), four World of Music Units, Information for pair and group work, a Vocabulary list, and a Grammar reference section.

- The **Student Audio CD** includes tracks for all pronunciation exercises and listening extracts (or reading extracts, in selected units) in the *Student Book*. The *Student Audio CD* can be used with the *Student Book* for self-study and also coordinates with the *Workbook* listening and pronunciation exercises.

- The interleaved **Teacher's Edition** provides step-by-step procedures and exercise answer keys for each activity in the *Student Book* as well as a wealth of teacher support: unit Warm-ups, Optional Activities, Extensions, Culture Notes, Background Information, Teaching Tips, Wrap-ups, and extensive Language Notes. In addition, the *Teacher's Edition* includes a Course Orientation Guide, Audio Scripts, and the *Workbook* Answer Key.

- The **Workbook** has 28, three-page units that correspond to each of the *Student Book* units. The *Workbook* provides abundant review and practice activities for vocabulary, grammar, listening, and pronunciation (listening and pronunciation exercises are done in conjunction with the *Student Audio CD*). In addition, the *Workbook* includes self-quizzes after every four units. A Learning Strategies section at the beginning of the *Workbook* helps students to be active learners.

- The **Class Audio Program** is available in either CD or cassette format and contains all the recorded material for in-class use.

- The **Teacher's Resource Book** (with **Testing Audio CD** and **TestGen Software**) has three sections of reproducible material: extra communication activities for in-class use, model writing passages for each *Student Book* writing assignment, and a complete testing program: seven quizzes and two tests, along with scoring guides and answer keys. Also included are an audio CD and an easy-to-use TestGen software CD for customizing the tests.

- For each level of the course, the **WorldView Video** presents seven, five-minute authentic video segments connected to *Student Book* topics. Notes to the Teacher are available in the *Video* package, and Student Activity Sheets can be downloaded from the *WorldView* Companion Website.

- The **WorldView Companion Website** (www.longman.com/worldview) provides a variety of teaching support and includes Video Activity Sheets and supplemental reading material.

Unit contents

Each of the 28 units in *WorldView* has seven closely linked sections:

- **Getting started:** a communicative opening exercise that introduces target vocabulary

- **Listening/Reading:** a functional conversation or thematic passage that introduces target grammar

- **Grammar focus:** an exercise sequence that allows students to focus on the grammar point that has been introduced in the reading and listening extracts and to solidify their learning

- **Pronunciation:** stress, rhythm, and intonation practice based on the target vocabulary and grammar

- **Speaking:** an interactive speaking task focused on student production of target vocabulary, grammar, and functional language

- **Writing:** a personalized writing activity that stimulates student production of target vocabulary and grammar

- **Conversation to go**: a concise reminder of the functional language introduced in each unit

Course length

With its flexible format and course components, *WorldView* responds to a variety of course needs. *WorldView* is suitable for 70 to 90 hours of classroom instruction. Each unit can be easily expanded by using bonus activities from the *Teacher's Edition*, reproducible activities available in the *Teacher's Resource Book*, linked lessons from the *WorldView Video* program, and supplementary reading assignments in the *WorldView Companion Website*.

The *WorldView Student Book with Student Audio CD* and the *Workbook* are also available in split editions.

Teaching Principles in *WorldView*

WorldView approaches language learning from a belief in three fundamental principles: motivate, anchor, and personalize.

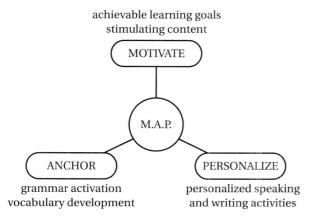

achievable learning goals
stimulating content

MOTIVATE

M.A.P.

ANCHOR   PERSONALIZE

grammar activation
vocabulary development

personalized speaking
and writing activities

Motivate

Motivate learning through stimulating content and achievable learning goals

At all levels of proficiency, language students learn better when they are given stimulating content and activities. The topics chosen for *WorldView* are international in scope, compelling, and engaging, and the activities designed around them promote student participation and active learning.

Each unit in *WorldView* is made up of 2, two-page lessons that set clear, achievable goals. By working through short, goal-oriented activities—for vocabulary, listening, reading, grammar, pronunciation, speaking, and writing—students feel both a sense of accomplishment and increased self-confidence.

Anchor

Anchor language production with strong, focused language presentations of vocabulary and grammar

Anchoring knowledge—planting it firmly—is the basis for systematic progress in language learning. *WorldView* features a strong vocabulary and grammar syllabus that anchors each unit.

Vocabulary is presented in various formats in the *Getting started* section of each unit, allowing students to gain mastery of specific lexical sets. Students interact with the new words in a series of activities before they encounter them in reading or listening texts.

Grammar is introduced in the listening and reading texts so that students are first exposed to the grammar receptively. Students are then given examples of the target structure to study, with their attention directed to specific aspects of the language. They then complete grammar charts, which allows them to focus on the way the language works. Once they have worked with the grammar examples and charts, students use the grammar in structured exercises to help the new grammar concepts take root.

Personalize

Personalize learning through engaging and communicative speaking and writing activities

In every *WorldView* unit, the central goal is fluent self-expression. This goal is achieved through a careful sequence of activities, each building toward personalized speaking and writing tasks.

Personalization is the basis for making language learning memorable—and enjoyable. *WorldView* provides opportunities for students to personalize what they learn throughout the unit: *Getting started* elicits students' ideas; the *Reading* and *Listening* sections draw out students' views and opinions; and the *Speaking* and *Writing* sections allow students to express their own thoughts, plans, preferences, and experiences.

The *WorldView* Teaching Plan

Teaching from *WorldView* is easy because each unit of the *Student Book* is based on a carefully planned flow of activities. Each four-page unit is designed as a complete instructional cycle that focuses on all key language areas—vocabulary, grammar, and pronunciation—and links the skills of listening, speaking, reading, and writing in an integrated, reinforcing fashion. Within each unit are two lessons: Lesson A builds comprehension, and Lesson B builds fluency.

The two lessons include the following:

- **Getting started:** Designed to get students interacting from the start, this opening activity introduces and contextualizes the target vocabulary of the unit. Vocabulary sets are always semantically related and include useful expressions and collocations. *Getting started* allows you to check what students already know and to teach words and phrases that may not be familiar. As students learn the meaning and pronunciation of the words and expressions, engaging follow-up activities encourage them to use and extend their new vocabulary.

- **Listening** or **Reading:** This section presents a realistic listening extract—conversations, interviews, talk shows, etc.—or an authentically based reading passage, such as a magazine article, an ad, or a website—that is related to the unit theme. Each high-interest listening or reading passage incorporates the target vocabulary and models the grammar in context. In keeping with principles of authenticity, the listening extracts are recorded at natural speed and the reading selections contain idiomatic expressions beyond the students' production capacity. Students are not expected to understand every word of the passages; rather, students are given multiple opportunities to work with the same passage for different purposes, which serves to deepen their comprehension skills and their confidence in dealing with authentic language.

- **Grammar focus:** In this pivotal section of the unit, students work with practical examples of the target structures—all previously featured in the Reading or Listening extracts—and notice the rules for themselves. Students get actively involved in grammar discovery, an approach that anchors their learning of the language. Once students have formulated the grammar rules, they use the target grammar in contextualized practice exercises. An enhanced Grammar Reference section for each unit is included at the back of the book so students have full grammar paradigms and explanations at their fingertips.

- **Pronunciation:** Brief pronunciation activities in every unit target word and sentence stress, rhythm, intonation, linking, and problematic sounds through clear, contextualized examples based on the target vocabulary or grammar of the unit. The pronunciation activity prepares the students for the upcoming speaking activity by providing useful models for communication.

- **Speaking:** This interactive task builds upon the Listening or Reading theme and incorporates the target vocabulary, grammar, and pronunciation, giving students the opportunity to use this language creatively to build fluency. Students are encouraged to share opinions, exchange information about themselves, and discuss ideas with their classmates.

- **Writing:** The final activity in each unit encourages further personal expression by students, who are directed to write about their own ideas and experiences in a guided, communicative assignment. This activity, which may be done in class or as homework, encourages personalized writing that can be shared with the class as an idea exchange, and be used by the teacher as evidence of the students' control of targeted grammar and vocabulary.

- **Conversation to go:** A brief conversation to remind students of the key communicative function and grammar appears at the end of each unit. Students can act out the conversation, or extend it to create their own "conversations to go."

Review Units

Review Units appear after every four units to help both students and teachers to revisit key presentations. Review Units incorporate an audio model (found in the *Class Audio Program*) to give students another opportunity to use the language of each unit in a productive, engaging speaking activity. The Review Units can be used as reinforcement or for an assessment of students' progress.

World of Music Units

Four World of Music units in each *Student Book* build a stimulating class activity around a popular song, using music from the past few decades. Structured as selective listening activities, the World of Music units encourage students to activate vocabulary and grammar before they listen, and conclude with a sing-along option (contained in the *Class Audio Program*).

Teaching Tips

You will find a range of Teaching Tips in this *Teacher's Edition* to give you specific suggestions for adding learning value to individual activities in the *WorldView Student Book*. The specific tips revolve around the following general teaching principles: **keep your class active, extend your students' learning strategies, make it easy for students to participate,** and **help students with specific skills**. These principles are demonstrated below, with general suggestions that can be implemented throughout the *WorldView* course.

- **Keep your class active**

  o Make sure students participate actively. The key is finding the right balance between "teacher-fronted" instruction and "student-centered" instruction. In communicative classes, it is important to direct your instruction time toward brief demonstrations and explanations, support for tasks, and feedback. Aim to maximize the time that students use the language.

  o Vary the groups. Most activities call for students to work with a partner or in a small group. Try various groupings of students. Working with new partners can often inject new energy into the class and help the class develop a larger sense of community. Particularly if you have students of mixed levels, it will be important to try different groupings so that students have an opportunity to work with partners of differing levels.

  o When possible, offer students alternate ways of doing an activity. You will find suggestions in the unit notes in this *Teacher's Edition* as well as on the *WorldView* companion website.

- **Extend students' learning**

  o Look for opportunities to introduce learning strategies. (You can consult the list of strategies at the beginning of the *WorldView Workbook*, or look through the Teaching Tips in the *Teacher's Edition*.) Take advantage of the times in class—for example, when a student needs to ask a clarification question—to call students' attention to a particular strategy. If you introduce and reinforce learning strategies on a regular basis, you will encourage learning beyond the classroom.

  o Provide at-home assignments for students. Giving sufficient homework is important to reinforce in-class learning. Homework can easily be assigned from the *Workbook*, and additional homework ideas are given in the *Teacher's Edition*. Spend just a short time in each class checking homework, having students work in pairs and small groups to compare answers. Take notice of how students have done, and provide brief mini-lessons to address any common errors.

  o Monitor your students' progress and provide feedback to them, verbally and through regular quizzes and tests.

- **Make it easy for students to participate in class**
  - Aim to create a comfortable environment in the classroom. You want your students to feel relaxed enough to talk to you and to each other in English. Students who feel relaxed will be more likely to take risks in their language learning and will gain confidence more rapidly.
  - Insure that each student has an opportunity to contribute ideas, opinions, and experiences in every class meeting. One way to do so is by fully utilizing the steps in activities that encourage comparing ideas and sharing answers, as well as by having students work in pairs and small groups.
  - Let the students do the talking. In communicative classes, it is important that students have ample time to talk, to each other in pairs and small groups, and to the whole class. Don't be too eager to correct. Generally, it is best to respond to meaning first in communication activities. Let the students know when you understand their ideas and when you don't. When they know you are interested in their ideas and not just their English ability, they will become more relaxed.
  - Keep your classroom activities in English. Although it is natural for you and your students to use their first language from time to time, aim to keep all classroom activities in English, including your instructions. Teach clarification expressions (such as "Could you say that again?") and information questions ("Whose turn is it now?") that will help your students stay in English. Make agreements with the students about when their first language can be used in class. The consistent use of English in the classroom will eventually make the classroom more comfortable for your students.

- **Help students with specific skills**

  Although most students will make progress through the use of models, participation in classroom activities, and feedback on their classwork and homework, many students will need specific help with one or more skills.

  - **Help students become better listeners**

    The recordings in *WorldView* are at natural speed, and students need to be reassured that they can do the listening activities successfully without understanding every word. Listening ability develops gradually by having students work with the same listening material in a number of ways. The listening exercises in *WorldView* use both "bottom up" and "top down" methods. *Bottom-up processing* refers to hearing the exact words and grammatical structures that the speaker uses, even if these are reduced or ellipted. Bottom-up activities include dictation (full dictation or cloze dictation), pre-teaching of vocabulary and structures used in a listening extract, and targeted listening for a specific item. *Top-down processing* refers to using expectations in order to infer what the speaker means, even if the speaker's message is incomplete or unclear. Top-down activities include selective listening for given information, answering questions (and guessing unknown answers), and summarizing.

    Another listening skill that students need to develop is interactive listening, which is the ability to understand live conversation, give feedback, ask for clarification, and respond in real time. This aspect of listening can improve dramatically through the guided interaction tasks (like information gaps) provided in *WorldView*, especially if supplemented with instruction on how to give feedback (such as using comprehension signals like "Oh" and "Um-hmm") and ask clarification questions (such as "What do you mean?").

  - **Help students improve their pronunciation**

    Pronunciation is an important skill and most students can make and sustain improvements in their pronunciation with a concerted effort. Most students can improve their pronunciation both on a segmental level (the individual sounds of words) and on a suprasegmental level (the overriding rhythm and intonation of a whole utterance).

    The majority of pronunciation exercises in *WorldView* focus on the suprasegmentals because this is the area of pronunciation that most influences communication. Encourage your students to work through these lessons carefully and to practice with the *WorldView Student Audio CD*.

    In addition, provide focused feedback to students. When you really don't understand a student because of a pronunciation problem, ask him or her to repeat it so you do understand—and then point out the pronunciation issue for him or her to work on in the future. (For individual sounds of words, see the Pronunciation table on page T188.) Focused feedback helps students identify a small number of pronunciation points that will truly boost their speaking ability.

  - **Help students develop fluency**

    Most students want to become fluent speakers of English, the essence of which is staying focused and assuring that their communicative goal is reached. As students begin to accomplish communicative goals, they will begin to speak more smoothly and effortlessly.

    There are three specific ways of developing fluency in communication tasks, all of which have been incorporated into *WorldView*. The first way is *pre-task planning*. This means having an overview of the communication task in advance, knowing how the procedures work, and what the outcome will be. This kind of planning allows for an internal rehearsal of the communication process, which generally improves fluency. The second way is to *preview vocabulary* that is needed in the task. Knowing what vocabulary to use in advance is like having stepping stones through the task, and this obviously increases the smoothness of the communication. The third way to improve fluency is *authentic repetition*. Communicative tasks that involve real personal information and ideas can be done again with new partners, without a feeling of mechanical repetition. Having students repeat tasks with new partners, or recycling tasks later in the course, or using parallel tasks (as is done in the *WorldView* Review Units) will all help students gain genuine fluency.

○ **Help students become better writers**

The most direct way to help students become better writers is to give them ample opportunities for extended, communicative writing. In addition to helping learners consolidate their learning of grammar and vocabulary, writing provides an avenue for creativity and self-expression that many learners value.

A few simple guidelines can help your class get the most out of writing tasks:

Have students write multiple drafts and revisions of an assignment whenever possible. In the first draft of an assignment, encourage them to write freely and not worry about mistakes. Give at least one round of feedback before students produce the "final product."

Use models of the completed writing assignment (from the *Teacher's Resource Book*) to provide your students with a "macrostructure" for their work. Models can motivate students to raise their expectations and provide guidance for homework assignments.

Give feedback on content as well as form. Because students are writing for a communicative purpose, it is important to let them know what they have communicated to their audience.

Be selective when offering corrections. For most writing assignments, you will not want to correct every error. Concentrate on those that get in the way of communication.

Present a simple "key" or code for corrections (like *v* for vocabulary problem, *t* for verb tense problem). This will enable you to respond more quickly to students' writing.

Have your students keep all their written work and create a portfolio. Review the students' portfolio at the end of the course. This will build confidence for your students and give you a sense of satisfaction as well!

If time allows, have students share their writing in class with a partner. Partners can give feedback on specific aspects of the writing—for example, on the content, the organization, or the choice of words.

• **Correcting errors**

In both meaning-focused and form-focused activities, students will make errors, and many errors will seem to persist. Your attitude and approach to feedback and error correction should be related to the purpose of the activity and what you think your students are ready to learn.

One error-correction method is to note commonly occurring errors in the class and give a short presentation for the whole class at the end of an activity. For instance, you may note frequent errors in verb tenses during one speaking activity, and provide a short review of the problematic points before going on to the next activity. This focused feedback, provided at regular times during the flow of classroom activities, seems to be more effective for most learners than simply being corrected for every grammatical error they make.

Another method that works well is *recasting* an utterance that has contained an error. For instance, a student may say, "Yesterday, I don't come to class," and you recast it as, "Oh, you didn't come to class yesterday?" In this process, it is important for the student to "notice" the error and then restate the correct utterance, as in, "Right. I didn't come to class yesterday." This process is effective because the student has the opportunity to self-correct an error that is still in short-term memory.

When students notice and recast their own errors, they are more likely to remember the correction. For instance, you might ask students to look at their own writing assignment and circle all uses of a particular tense and then to rewrite any parts with errors that they notice. Or you may ask students to make their own audio recording of a short conversation or speech and then transcribe exactly what they said in one column and make grammatical improvements in another column.

How to Get the Most From This *Teacher's Edition*

In each of the interleaved units of this *Teacher's Edition*, you'll find notes for how to proceed with each exercise, as well as answer keys, if appropriate. You will also find the following types of teaching ideas and information:

(Lesson A) Warm-up: a brief activity to get the students involved in the topic of the unit at its outset

(Lesson B) Warm-up: a brief activity recommended for when time has passed between doing Lesson A and B. Since Lesson B begins with the *Grammar focus* section, and the grammar has been modeled in the Listening or Reading done in Lesson A, this activity involves playing the audio for the Listening (or Reading, which has been recorded for this purpose), so that students can hear the grammar in context before they begin their work on the grammar.

Vocabulary Preview: a brief, optional activity that allows you to pre-teach the vocabulary students will interact with in the *Getting started* section of the unit

Extension: an additional activity for students to do after they've finished a student book activity, as time allows

Option: an alternative way you can have students do a particular activity

FYI: information that you may find useful but that is *not* intended for the students to know

Culture Note: information that will help students understand the cultural context of the language or content

Background Information: factual information about people, places, and events that you may want students to know

Language Note: information for students about how English works, including information about the grammar, functions, pronunciation, and similar topics.

Teaching Tip: a tactic that will help students get the most out of an activity, such as specific conversation management strategies, listening strategies, reading strategies, and so on.

Note: additional information that doesn't fit into any other category

Follow-up: an activity based on what you find when you are circulating and noticing how students are doing on specific tasks

Wrap-up: a whole-class activity that brings closure to a pair or group activity

Cross-references

The unit notes also provide cross-references to the following:

TRB *Teacher's Resource Book*, Reproducible Activities

TRB *Teacher's Resource Book*, Writing models

Workbook practice material for homework*

Workbook self-quizzes

Companion Website, www.longman.com/worldview, supplementary reading material

Video

*Note: If you are not using the *Workbook*, an additional homework assignment is suggested for students to do with the *Student Audio CD*.

At the back of the *Teacher's Edition*, we've included the **Audioscripts** for the *Student Book* (Class Audio Program) and the audio scripts for the *Workbook* (Student Audio CD). The **Answer Key to the *Workbook* exercises** follows the audioscripts.

We would like to thank and officially acknowledge Sharon Goldstein for all her consulting, writing, and editorial work on the pronunciation exercises in the *Student Book*s and *Teacher's Editions*.

We are grateful to the following Pearson Longman editors for their invaluable assistance on this project:

John Barnes	Bill Preston
Nancy Blodgett	Julie Schmidt
Wendy Long	Debbie Sistino
Marc Oliver	Paula Van Ells

UNIT 1

It's the weekend!

Vocabulary Weekend activities
Grammar Simple present and adverbs of frequency
Speaking Talking about how often you do things

Lesson A

Getting started

1 Look at the photos. What are the people doing?

2 Complete the sentences with the verb phrases in the boxes.

| go for a walk | ~~go to the beach~~ | go out for dinner |

1. I love Sundays. I ___*go to the beach*___ on Sunday mornings. In the afternoon, I _____ in the park. Then I sometimes _____ with friends.

| go to the gym | stay home | sleep late | watch TV |

2. Saturday is my favorite day of the week. I _____ on Saturday mornings. I like to exercise, so I _____ in the afternoon. In the evenings, I _____ with my family and we _____ together.

| get takeout | go to the movies | work late |

3. It's Friday—almost the weekend! I _____ on Friday nights because I want to finish my work before the weekend. I don't like to cook, so I _____ on my way home. Then I _____ with friends.

3 *PAIRS.* Talk about the weekend activities in Exercise 2 that you like to do.

I like to sleep late, go to the movies, and go out for dinner.

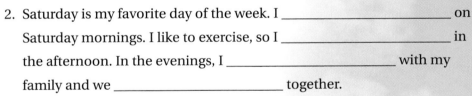

2

It's the weekend!

OBJECTIVES

Students will:

- activate vocabulary related to weekend leisure activities
- do listening, speaking, and writing tasks related to how often activities are done
- focus on using the simple present and adverbs of frequency
- practice rhythm in English sentences, with stress only on the important words

---

WARM-UP: WHAT'S YOUR WEEKEND LIKE?

Groups of 3. Students share ideas for ways to describe weekends.

- Books closed. Tell students that this unit is about weekend leisure activities.
- Write on the board: *What's your weekend like?* Give an example or two about your weekend: *Sometimes my weekend is relaxing. Sometimes my weekend is fun and exciting.*
- Divide the class into groups of 3. Set a time limit of 2 minutes. Each student in the group must say at least one sentence about his or her weekend.
- After 2 minutes, call on a few students to tell the rest of the class about one of their partner's weekends. (For example, *Sometimes Luci's weekend is busy and tiring.*)

Getting started

Exercise ❶

- Tell students to look at the photos.
- Point to each picture and ask students what the people are doing. Elicit as many details as possible.

Answer key

Picture A: They're going to the movies.
Picture B: They're going to/They're at the beach.
Picture C: They're exercising/doing yoga/working out.

OPTION: VOCABULARY PREVIEW

- Tell students to think about activities they do on weekends. Write the phrase *go to the* _____ on the board, and elicit from students words related to weekend activities that can complete the verb phrase. (movies, beach, park, gym)
- Then ask: *What do you do for dinner on Friday nights?* (go out for dinner, cook at home, get takeout)
- Ask about other things they do on the weekend. Ask: *What do you do on weekends if you don't go out?* (sleep late, watch TV, stay home)

Exercise ❷

- Explain the task: Students will complete the sentences with the verb phrases in the boxes. Go over the first sentence and the example.
- Set a time limit of 3 minutes. While students are working, walk around the room, helping as needed.
- Have students work in pairs to compare answers.
- Go over the answers with the class.

Answer key

1. go to the beach; go for a walk; go out for dinner
2. sleep late; go to the gym; stay home; watch TV
3. work late; get takeout; go to the movies

EXTENSION

- Have students create a three-by-three grid for a Bingo board.
- In each of the nine squares, have them write down a verb phrase from Exercise 2 in random order.
- Tell the class they are going to check off each of the activities on the grid as you read them aloud. The first student to check off three squares in a row calls out "Bingo!"

Exercise ❸

LANGUAGE NOTE

You may want to point out the time expressions with *on* in Exercise 2. Explain that when we talk about activities we do regularly, we can use either the plural or the singular form of the day of the week or part of the day with *on* and *in*. For example, we can say *On Saturdays/On Saturday, I go to the movies; I sleep late on Sunday mornings/on Sunday morning; In the afternoons/In the afternoon, we go to the beach.*

- Tell students to think of activities they like to do on weekends. Model the task, using the example in the book or providing your own.
- Pair students and set a time limit of 2 minutes. Remind students to use the verb phrases in Exercise 2 as well as their own ideas.
- Walk around the room, helping as needed.
- After 2 minutes, call on a few students to tell the class what they like to do on weekends.

Listening

Teaching Tip! Listening for different purposes

There are different strategies to use when listening, depending on your purpose. Remind students that Exercise 4 requires them to listen only to get the main, or general, idea of the interviews. Exercise 5, on the other hand, requires them to listen for details.

Exercise ❹

- Explain the task: Students will listen to a radio host talk to two people. As students listen, they will match two of the photos on pages 2 and 3 with the speakers.
- 🎧 Play the audio.
- Go over the answers with the class.

> **Answer key**
>
> Speaker 1 (Yuka): A; Speaker 2 (Marcelo): B

Exercise ❺

> **LANGUAGE NOTE**
>
> There are three different pronunciations of the third person *-s/-es* endings: /s/, /z/, and /əz/. In the verbs in Exercise 5, the ending should be pronounced as an extra syllable /əz/ only in the word *watches*. In the other verbs, the ending should be pronounced as /s/ in *gets*, *cooks*, *meets* or /z/ in *stays*, *goes*.

- Explain the task: Students will underline one of the two choices in bold as they listen to the radio program again.
- Before playing the audio again, have students read the sentences in Exercise 5 and predict the answers. Reading the sentences before listening again will help students focus their listening.
- If necessary, write the first sentence on the board and have a volunteer come up to underline the verb that he or she thinks is correct.
- 🎧 Play the audio again.
- Have students work in pairs to compare their answers.
- Go over the answers with the class.

> **Answer key**
>
> 1. cooks
> 2. meets friends
> 3. goes to the movies
> 4. to the beach
> 5. lunch

EXTENSION

Pair students. Have the pairs discuss whose weekends are similar to theirs, Yuka's or Marcelo's.

◉ Please go to www.longman.com/worldview for additional in-class model conversation practice and supplementary reading practice.

Pronunciation

> **LANGUAGE NOTE**
>
> Every language has its own rhythm, or beat. In English, some syllables are longer and stronger and other syllables are short and weak.

Exercise ❻

- Tell students they are going to listen to some sentences. Ask them to listen to the rhythm.
- 🎧 Play the audio. Highlight the rhythm by tapping out the strong beats.
- 🎧 Play the audio again and have students look at the sentences. Tell students that the words and syllables in red are pronounced longer and stronger, or are stressed.
- Point out, or elicit, that some of the words are pronounced longer than others but that each sentence has the same number of stressed syllables.
- Ask students what kinds of words are stressed in the sentences. (adverbs, verbs, nouns, and *wh-* words)

Teaching Tip! Using visuals as reminders

Many students do not pronounce the vowels in stressed syllables long enough. To encourage them to do so, use visual reminders. For example, stretch a rubber band or write the word on the board and make the stressed vowel extra wide. Also remind students to slow down when they speak.

Exercise ❼

- Tell students they are going to practice saying the sentences with the correct rhythm.
- 🎧 Play the audio, stopping or pausing after each sentence and having students repeat chorally.
- Ask individual students to repeat. Check their pronunciation.
- If students have difficulty, break the sentences down into smaller parts, starting at the end of the sentence and gradually adding parts until the whole sentence is built up again. Model the pronunciation and have students repeat after you. Tap out the beat to reinforce the rhythm. (For example, *on Saturday—work on Saturday—I never work on Saturday.*)

EXTENSION

Pair students. Have them practice the sentences.

HOMEWORK

- 📖 Assign *Workbook* page 12, Vocabulary Exercises 1 and 2; page 14, Listening Exercises 5 and 6; and page 14, Pronunciation Exercises 7 and 8.

Listening

4 🎧 **Listen to the radio program about how people around the world spend their weekend. Find the photo that each speaker describes.**

Speaker 1 (Yuka) _____   Speaker 2 (Marcelo) _____

5 🎧 **Listen again and underline the correct information.**

1. Yuka never **gets takeout / <u>cooks</u>** on Fridays.
2. She often **meets friends / stays home**.
3. She usually **goes to the movies / watches TV** with her friends.
4. Marcelo always goes **to the gym / to the beach** on Sundays.
5. He sometimes goes out for **lunch / dinner**.

Pronunciation

6 🎧 **Listen to the rhythm in the sentences. Notice that the important words are pronounced longer, clearer, and stronger than the other words.**

I **nev**er **work** on **Sat**urday.
I **u**sually **go** to the **gym**.

What do you **do** on **Sun**day?
We **go** for a **walk** on the **beach**.

She **al**ways gets **take**out on **Fri**days.
She **goes** to the **mov**ies with her **friends**.

7 🎧 **Listen again and repeat.**

3

1

Grammar focus

1 Write the adverbs of frequency in the correct place on the scale.

always	never	often	~~sometimes~~	usually

100% _____

_____

_____

_____sometimes_____

0% _____

2 Study the examples with adverbs of frequency.

> I **often work** late on Friday.
> He **always goes** to the beach on the weekend.
> The beach **is usually** crowded.

3 Look at the examples again. Circle the correct words to complete the rules in the chart.

> **Simple present and adverbs of frequency**
>
> The adverb of frequency comes **before / after** the verb *be*.
>
> The adverb of frequency comes **before / after** all other verbs.

Grammar Reference page 143

4 Complete the sentences with a verb and the adverb of frequency in parentheses.

1. A: Her husband _often works_ late on Fridays. Doesn't he? (often)

   B: No, never. He _____ to the movies with friends. (always)

2. A: What do you do on Saturday mornings?

   B: I _____ to the gym. (usually)

3. A: Do you usually go out on Saturday night?

   B: No. I _____ home. (usually)

4. A: How _____ do you _____ takeout for dinner? (often)

   B: I _____ takeout on Saturdays. (sometimes)

5. A: I _____ home on Sunday nights. Do you? (never)

   B: Yes. I _____ a video at home. (sometimes)

5 *PAIRS.* Practice the conversations in Exercise 4.

Grammar focus

LANGUAGE NOTES

- Adverbs of frequency indicate how often something happens. They are often used with the simple present tense to describe routines and habits. For example, *I usually go to the gym on Friday evenings.*

- Adverbs of frequency usually come after the verb *be* and before other verbs. For example, *I'm never hungry in the morning. I always eat lunch at noon.*

- *How often* is a question phrase that is used to ask about frequency. For example, *How often do you go to the gym?*

WARM-UP

Note: Skip this warm-up if you're doing this lesson (Lesson B) during the same class period as Lesson A.

- Books closed. Tell students they are going to listen again to the radio program they heard in the Listening section.

- On the board, write some of the activities that Yuka and Marcelo do: *work late, get takeout, go to the movies; sleep late, go to the beach, go out for lunch.* Tell students to copy the phrases.

- Explain the task: Students will listen for the phrases in the conversation and will write down the words the speakers use to say how often they do the activities.

- 🎧 Play the audio for Lesson A, Listening, Exercise 4. (It models the grammar of the unit.)

- Point to the activities on the board. Tell students to call out the word Yuka and Marcelo used to say how often they do each activity. Write the words on the board. (Answers: *usually, usually, usually; usually, always, sometimes*)

Exercise ❶

- Read the adverbs of frequency aloud and have students repeat after each word.

- Tell students to write each adverb that corresponds to the percentage of time on the scale. If necessary, cue students by asking, *What word means that you do an activity 100 percent of the time?* (*always*)

- Have students compare their answers with a partner's.

- Go over the answers with the class.

Answer key

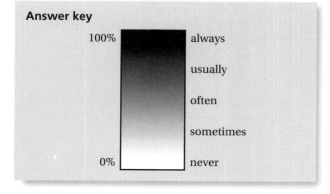

100%	always
	usually
	often
	sometimes
0%	never

Exercise ❷

- Have students look at the examples and study the bold-faced words. Tell them to pay attention to the order of the verbs and frequency adverbs in the sentences. Ask students to call out the verb in each sentence. Make sure they can identify the base form of the verbs. (*work, go, be*)

- Tell students to notice the order of the bold-faced words.

Exercise ❸

- Have students study the examples again.

- Tell them to circle the correct word in each rule.

- Have students compare their answers with a partner's.

- Go over the answers with the class.

- Ask a few questions to elicit the key points about the grammar: *What adverb do we use when we do something every day?* (*always*) *What's the opposite of that adverb?* (*never*) *Do adverbs of frequency come before or after* be? (after) *Do they usually come before or after other verbs?* (before)

Answer key

after (the verb *be*)   before (all other verbs)

Teaching Tip! **Reviewing grammar**

Review the simple present forms of regular and irregular verbs: the verbs used with the third person singular pronouns (*he, she, it*) always end in *–s* or *–es*.

Exercise ❹

- Before beginning Exercise 4, answer any questions students might have. You may also refer the class to the Grammar Reference for Unit 1 on page 143.

- Ask students to look at item 1. Read the example conversation aloud, pointing out the adverb of frequency (*often*) and the verb (*works*).

- Explain the task: Students will write a verb and an adverb to complete each sentence. Remind students to use the context to figure out which verb correctly completes each sentence.

- Have students complete the exercise individually. Set a time limit of 5 minutes. Walk around the room, helping as needed.

- Have students compare their answers with a partner's.

- Go over the answers with the class.

Answer key

1. A: often works
   B: always goes
	4. A: often . . . got
	   B: sometimes get

2. B: usually go	5. A: never stay B: sometimes watch
3. B: usually stay	

Exercise ❺

Students pair up to read the conversations in Exercise 4.

Speaking

> **NOTE**
>
> In activities where students first work individually and then join classmates to work in pairs or groups, it is often helpful to quickly explain the various steps students will be following. Students will be better motivated to concentrate on their individual work if they know they will be working later in pairs or small groups. Then, as students begin each new step, give more detailed guidance to make sure everyone understands what to do next.

Exercise ➏

This exercise provides practice with adverbs of frequency, the simple present, and the vocabulary from the unit. It prepares students to do Exercises 7 and 8.

- Explain the task: Students work individually to write sentences about their weekend activities. Point out the example and read it aloud.
- Set a time limit of 5 minutes for students to write their sentences. Remind them to use all the adverbs of frequency from Exercise 1. Walk around the room, helping as needed.
- Have students share their sentences in pairs.
- Ask a few students to share their sentences with the class.

Exercise ➐

- Divide the class into groups of 3.
- Explain the task: Each of the three students in the group will add one activity to the first column of the survey form. They can use any of the ideas from their sentences in Exercise 6. Set a time limit of 2 minutes.

Exercise ➑

- **Groups of 3.** Have students continue to work with the same group.
- Explain the next part of the task: Students will take turns talking about their weekend activities. In each of their statements, they should use an adverb of frequency to describe how often they do the activity; then they should add a sentence or two with more information. All three group members will put a check mark in the survey under the appropriate adverb of frequency.
- Copy the survey on the board. Ask two volunteers to come up to the front to demonstrate the activity, using the example in the book.
- Encourage students to ask their partners questions to find out more about their activities. If necessary, brainstorm ideas for additional information and write a few examples on the board. (For example, *What's your favorite restaurant? Who do you usually go out with?*)
- Set a time limit of 10 minutes for students to talk about their activities. Walk around the room, helping as needed.

Exercise ➒

- **Groups of 3.** Have students stay in their groups. Tell them to decide who in the group has the busiest weekend and who has the most relaxing weekend. Set a time limit of 2 minutes for the discussion.
- After 2 minutes, call on a few students to tell the class who in their group has the busiest weekend and who has the most relaxing weekend. Encourage them to give some details to support their answers.

TRB For additional interactive grammar practice, have students do the reproducible activity for this unit in the *Teacher's Resource Book*.

Writing

Exercise ➓

- Assign the writing task for class work or homework.
- Explain the task: Students will write a paragraph about a perfect weekend, using adverbs of frequency and vocabulary from the unit.
- Brainstorm ideas for the perfect weekend and write them on the board.
- **TRB** Optionally, give students a copy of the writing model (see the *Teacher's Resource Book*, Writing Models). Ask them to read the model and notice the vocabulary and grammar from the unit.
- If students don't have the model, write the following on the board:

    My weekends are always great! I never work on the weekend, and I only do what I like. On Saturdays, I always get up early.

- Have a student read the sentences aloud. Answer any questions students might have.
- Walk around to make sure everyone understands the task.

For suggestions on how to give feedback on writing, see page xiv of this *Teacher's Edition*.

CONVERSATION TO GO

At the end of class, call on two students to role-play the conversation.

HOMEWORK

- 📖 Assign *Workbook* page 13, Grammar Exercises 3 and 4, and page 14, Pronunciation Exercises 7 and 8.
- 💿 If students do not have the *WorldView Workbook*, assign listening homework from the Student CD. Write on the board:

    Track 2
    Write one thing that Yuka *never does* and one thing that Marcelo and his wife *always do*.

- 🎧 Tell students to listen to the audio and write the answer to the question. Have them bring their answer to the next class.

    (Answers: *Yuka never stays home/cooks. Marcelo and his wife always go for a walk on the beach.*)

Speaking

6 *BEFORE YOU SPEAK.* **Write five sentences about your weekend. Use each of the adverbs of frequency from Exercise 1.**

I never go to the gym on Sundays.

7 *GROUPS OF 3.* **Create a survey together. Each person, add one weekend activity to the survey form.**

How often do you...

Activity	always	usually	often	sometimes	never
go out for dinner?		✓			

8 *GROUPS OF 3.* **Take turns. Tell each other about your weekend activities. Use an adverb of frequency and give additional information. Check (✓) the box in the survey for each answer.**

I usually go out for dinner on the weekend. I usually have Italian food.

9 *GROUPS OF 3.* **Compare your weekends. Who has the most relaxing weekend? Who has the busiest weekend?**

Writing

10 **Imagine that your weekends are always perfect—you do only activities that you love. Write about your perfect weekends. What do you do? What don't you do? Use adverbs of frequency.**

CONVERSATION TO GO

A: How **often** do you work late?
B: **Never!**

5

Excuses, excuses

Vocabulary Parts of the body; illnesses and injuries
Grammar Linking words: *and, but, so*
Speaking Apologizing and making excuses

1. *eye*

2. _____

3. _____

4. _____

5. _____

6. _____

7. _____

8. _____

9. _____

10. _____

11. _____

12. _____

Getting started

1 **Look at the pictures. Label the parts of the body with the words in the box.**

arm	back	ear	~~eye~~	foot	hand
head	leg	mouth	nose	stomach	throat

2 **Listen and check your answers. Then listen and repeat.**

3 **Write the letter of the person in the picture next to the complaint.**

1. "I have a headache." _B_
2. "I have a sore throat." ____
3. "My back is sore." ____
4. "I have a stomachache." ____
5. "I have a fever." ____
6. "I hurt my arm." ____
7. "I have a bad cold." ____
8. "I have a cough." ____

4 *PAIRS.* **Test your partner on the names of illnesses and injuries. Student A, point to a part of your body and act out the problem (for example, touch your throat). Student B, say the problem (for example: *Oh, you have a sore throat!*).**

Excuses, excuses

OBJECTIVES

Students will:

- activate vocabulary related to parts of the body, illnesses, and injuries
- do listening, speaking, and writing tasks related to health problems, apologizing, and making excuses
- focus on using the conjunctions *and, but,* and *so* to talk about minor illnesses and injuries
- practice using intonation to stress the most important words in a sentence

WARM-UP: I MISSED IT!

Groups of 3. Students take turns telling each other about a time they missed something important.

- Tell students that this unit is about health problems and making excuses. Ask the class to give examples of situations where people often make excuses (for example, *coming late to school/work, after an absence from school/work*).
- Explain that the unit title, "Excuses, excuses," is a phrase people use when they think they hear too many excuses about why something is not done.
- Divide the class into groups of 3 and set a time limit of 3 minutes. Explain the task: Each student in the group must say what event or activity he or she missed and why he or she missed it. Clarify the task by giving an example about yourself. (For example, *Last week, I missed a party because I was sick.*)
- After 3 minutes, call on a few students to share with the class some excuses they heard.

Getting started

OPTION: VOCABULARY PREVIEW

Have students work in pairs and explain to each other the meaning of each word in Exercise 1.

Exercise ❶

- Explain the task: Students will use the words in the box to label the parts of the body. Go over the example.
- Set a time limit of 3 minutes. While students are working, walk around the room, helping as needed.
- Tell students they will check their answers in the next activity.

Exercise ❷

- Explain the task: Students will listen to the audio. As they listen, they will check their answers in Exercise 1. Then they will listen again and repeat.
- 🎧 Play the audio. Encourage students to correct any wrong answers.
- 🎧 Play the audio again and have students listen and repeat.

Answer key

1. eye	4. hand	7. mouth	10. throat
2. arm	5. head	8. stomach	11. foot
3. back	6. nose	9. ear	12. leg

EXTENSION

To make sure students have mastered the vocabulary, review the words. Call out the name of a body part and have students point to it. For example, say, *Where's your arm?* Have students touch or point to their arm. Do the same for all twelve body parts learned in Exercise 1.

LANGUAGE NOTES

- There is more than one way to express complaints about most medical problems. For example, *My back hurts, I have a backache, I have a sore back,* and *My back is sore* all have the same meaning.
- Some expressions are used only with certain body parts. For example, only *back, ear, head, stomach,* and *tooth* are combined with *-ache* to create a new noun that names a specific medical problem (*backache, earache, headache, stomachache, toothache*). For other parts of the body, a common structure is *have* + article (*a/an*) + adjective + noun. (For example, *She has a sore arm.*)

Exercise ❸

- Explain the task: Students read each sentence and look at the pictures. Then they decide which of the people is making the complaint. Go over the example.
- Set a time limit of 3 minutes. Walk around the room, helping as needed.
- After 3 minutes, have students work in pairs to compare their answers.
- Go over the answers with the class.

Answer key

1. B	3. A	5. B	7. C
2. C	4. B	6. A	8. C

Exercise ❹

- **Pairs.** Explain the task: Partners will take turns acting out an illness or injury and guessing the problem.
- Model the activity with a volunteer, using the example. Put your hand on your throat and make an expression of pain. Then gesture for the student to say what your problem is (*Oh, you have a sore throat!*).
- Pair students and set a time limit of 10 minutes. Walk around the room, helping as needed.

Listening

Exercise ❺

- Ask students to look at the picture. Point out that they are going to hear a conversation between the two people. Have them make some predictions about the situation by asking questions such as *Who do you think this is? Where is he? Who do you think he's talking to? What do you think he's saying?*

- Explain the task: Students listen to the audio and number Tony's excuses in the order they hear them. Go over the example.

- 🎧 Play the audio.

- Go over the answers with the class. If time allows, play the audio one more time so that students can confirm their answers.

Answer key

2, 4, 1, 3

LANGUAGE NOTE

Point out that the phrase *I'm afraid* in this context doesn't express fear; it is a way to soften the information—usually bad or unwelcome news—that follows it. Give one or two examples where the phrase *I'm afraid* might be used to preface bad news. (For example, *I'm afraid our teacher isn't well.*)

Exercise ❻

- Tell students to look at the apologies and sympathetic responses. Explain that we usually say something reassuring or sympathetic when someone apologizes and makes an excuse. Ask students for other responses to excuses they know. (For example, *It's all right,* or *It doesn't matter.*)

- Explain the task: Students will listen for each of Tony's apologies and Roger's corresponding responses. They will write the letter of the correct response next to each apology.

- 🎧 Play the audio.

- Have students work in pairs to compare their answers.

- Go over the answers in class.

Answer key

1. c   2. a   3. b

Exercise ❼

- Tell students they will practice apologizing and making excuses in this exercise.

- Prepare students for the activity by spending a few minutes brainstorming situations in which people might apologize and make excuses. Write some of the ideas on the board.

- Explain the task: Students will take turns apologizing and making excuses.

- Go over the example. Point out that there are three parts to the sentences: a phrase of apology, an explanation, and an excuse.

- Pair students and set a time limit of 5 minutes. Walk around the room, helping as needed.

- After 5 minutes, call on a few pairs to present one or two of their apologies and excuses to the class.

- 🖳 Please go to www.longman.com/worldview for additional in-class model conversation and supplementary reading practice.

HOMEWORK

- 📖 Assign *Workbook* page 15, Vocabulary Exercises 1 and 2, and page 17, Listening Exercises 5 and 6.

Listening

5 🎧 **Listen to Tony tell his boss, Roger, why he can't come to work. Put his excuses in the correct order.**

____ He has a cough and a sore throat.

____ He hurt his back.

__1__ He has a fever.

____ He has a stomachache.

6 🎧 **What does Tony say to apologize? How does Roger respond? Listen again. Match Tony's apologies with Roger's responses.**

Apology	Sympathetic response
1. ____ I'm really sorry, but . . .	a. That's OK. Hope you get better soon.
2. ____ I'm afraid I can't . . .	b. That's too bad.
3. ____ I'm sorry, but . . .	c. That's OK. Don't worry.

7 *PAIRS.* **Take turns. Student A, use the ideas below and the complaints from Exercise 3 to apologize and make an excuse. Student B, give a sympathetic response.**

A: *I'm sorry, but I can't come to work today. I have a fever.*
B: *That's OK. Hope you get better soon.*

Apology

I'm afraid . . .

I can't play soccer today.
I can't give my report today.
I can't go out for dinner with you.

I'm sorry, but . . .

I can't come to work today.
I can't help you lift that box.
I can't sign my name on the check.

I'm really sorry, but . . .

I can't do my homework.

Grammar focus

1 **Study the examples with the linking words *and*, *but*, and *so*.**

> I have a bad cough, **and** my throat is very sore.
> I can't come in today, **but** I'll probably be there tomorrow.
> I have a fever, **so** I can't come to work today.

2 **Look at the examples again. Complete the rules in the chart with *and*, *but*, or *so*.**

Linking words: *and, but, so*
Use _____ to add a similar idea.
Use _____ to add a different idea.
Use _____ to show the result of something.

Grammar Reference page 143

3 **Combine the sentences with the linking words in parentheses.**

1. She hurt her arm. She can't use the computer. (so)

   She hurt her arm, so she can't use the computer.

2. I have a cough. I don't have a sore throat. (but)

3. My father hurt his back. My brother hurt his leg. (and)

4. I have a stomachache. I'm going to stay home. (so)

5. She doesn't have a fever. She feels sick. (but)

6. He has a headache. I gave him some aspirin. (so)

Pronunciation

4 🎧 **Listen. Notice the way the voice goes up on the most important word in each part of the sentence, and then down.**

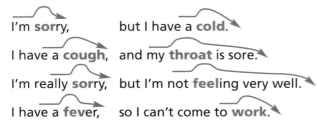

I'm **sorry,**   but I have a **cold.**

I have a **cough,** and my **throat** is sore.

I'm really **sorry,** but I'm not **feel**ing very well.

I have a **fever,**   so I can't come to **work.**

5 🎧 **Listen again and repeat.**

Grammar focus

LANGUAGE NOTES

- The linking words, or the conjunctions, *and, but,* and *so* are often used to join words or complete sentences.
- Each of these three linking words has a different meaning: *and* indicates that what follows is a similar idea; *but* adds a different idea; *so* precedes a result of something.

WARM-UP

Note: Skip this warm-up if you're doing this lesson (Lesson B) during the same class period as Lesson A.

- Books closed. Tell students they are going to listen again to the conversation they heard in the Listening section.
- Write these sentences on the board: *I'm really sorry, _____ I'm not feeling very well. I have a fever, _____ I can't come to work today. I have a bad cough, _____ my throat is very sore.* Tell students to copy the sentences.
- Write *but, and,* and *so* on the board next to the sentences.
- Explain the task: Students will listen for the sentences on the board and complete them with *but, and,* or *so.*
- 🎧 Play the audio for Lesson A, Listening, Exercise 5. (It models the grammar of the unit.)
- Point to the sentences and words on the board. Tell students to call out the linking word they heard in each sentence. Write the words in the blanks.

Exercise ❶

- Have students read the three examples and study the bold-faced words. Point out that each example is actually made up of two sentences joined by linking words. Have students say out loud the two sentences in each example.
- Ask students to think about the type of information added after *but, and,* and *so* in each example.

Exercise ❷

- Have students study the examples again.
- Tell students to write the linking words to complete the rules in the chart.
- Have students compare their answers with a partner.
- Go over the answers with the class.
- Ask these questions to clarify the use of each linking word: *Which linking word adds similar information?* (*and*) *Which linking word shows the result of something?* (*so*) *Which word adds different, or contrasting, information?* (*but*)

Answer key

and	but	so

Exercise ❸

- Before beginning Exercise 3, answer any questions students may have. You may also want to refer the class to the Grammar Reference for Unit 2 on page 143.
- Ask students to look at the example. Ask: *What happened to her?* (She hurt her arm.) *What's the result of that?* (She can't use the computer.) Point out that the linking word *so* in parentheses shows a result of the first.
- Have students complete the exercise individually. Set a time limit of 8 minutes.
- Go over the answers with the class.

Answer key

1. She hurt her arm, so she can't use the computer.
2. I have a cough, but I don't have a sore throat.
3. My father hurt his back, and my brother hurt his leg.
4. I have a stomachache, so I'm going to stay home.
5. She doesn't have a fever, but she feels sick.
6. He has a headache, so I gave him some aspirin.

Pronunciation

Exercise ❹

- Tell students they are going to listen to some sentences. Explain that the word in red (or the word with the syllable in red) is the most important word in that part of the sentence.
- 🎧 Play the audio. Ask students to notice the way the voice goes up on the words in red and then goes down. Point out that the way the voice rises and falls in pitch when speaking is called intonation.
- As you play the audio, move your hand up and down to show how the intonation goes up and then falls. Your hand should drop lower at the end of the sentence than at the end of the first clause.
- 🎧 Play the audio again. Stop the audio after the first clause (*I'm sorry,*). Ask if the sentence sounded finished. Repeat this process with the second clause (*but I have a cold*). Do the same with the second sentence.
- Point out that the voice goes down to a low note at the end of the sentence but doesn't go down to a low note at the end of the first part of the sentence.

Exercise ❺

- Tell students they are going to practice English intonation.
- 🎧 Play the audio.
- Ask students to repeat each item chorally. Have them repeat the first half of each sentence first and then each whole sentence.
- Ask a few individual students to repeat the sentences. Check their intonation. Make sure the voice goes up on the important word and then falls at the end.

Speaking

Exercise ❻

Pairs. This exercise provides practice with apologizing and showing sympathy.

- You may want to start the activity by reviewing the language used in telephone conversations. Ask: *What do people usually say when they answer the phone?* (Hello?) *What does the caller say?* (Hello/Hi. Is [name] there?/ May I speak to [name], please?) If necessary, play the first few lines of the conversation from Lesson A, Listening, Exercise 5.

- Pair students and assign them A and B roles. Tell them that they are going to practice phone conversations in which the caller apologizes and the other person expresses sympathy.

- Tell Student A to turn to page 136 and Student B to page 138. They should not look at each other's page. They will take turns apologizing and expressing sympathy. Give students a minute to go over their information.

- Call on one pair of students to model the example.

- Set a time limit of 10 minutes for students to complete the task. Walk around the room, helping as needed.

- If time allows, ask a few pairs to perform one of their phone conversations for the class.

TRB For additional interactive grammar practice, have students do the reproducible activity for this unit in the *Teacher's Resource Book*.

Writing

> **CULTURE NOTE**
>
> People use email for a variety of reasons. The language used in emails is often less formal than that in other types of written correspondence. As in the examples in Exercise 7, the tone of emails can be informal to the point of being conversational.

Exercise ❼

- Assign the writing task for class work or homework.

- Explain the task: Students will pretend they don't feel well and will write a reply to each of the emails. In their notes, they should apologize, say what they can't do, and give a reason or an excuse.

- Brainstorm ideas for reasons for not being able to do the things suggested in the email messages and write them on the board.

- **TRB** Optionally, give students a copy of the writing model (see the *Teacher's Resource Book*, Writing Models). Ask them to read the model and notice the vocabulary and grammar from the unit.

- If students don't have the model, write the following on the board:

    Hi, Kevin! I'm sorry, but I can't go out for lunch today. I hurt my arm, and I'm going to the doctor. How about next week?

- Have a student read the sentences aloud. Answer any questions students might have.

- Walk around to make sure everyone understands the task.

For suggestions on how to give feedback on writing, see page xiv of this *Teacher's Edition*.

> **WRAP-UP**
>
> Have students write an email inviting a classmate to do something. Tell them to exchange emails and write replies.

CONVERSATION TO GO

At the end of class, call on two students to role-play the conversation.

HOMEWORK

- Assign *Workbook* page 16, Grammar Exercises 3 and 4, and page 17, Pronunciation Exercises 7 and 8.

- If students do not have the *WorldView Workbook*, assign listening homework from the Student CD. Write on the board:

    Track 4.
    How does the story end?

- Tell students to listen to the audio and write the answer to the question. Have them bring their answer to the next class.

    (Answer: *Tony loses his job. Roger fires Tony.*)

Speaking

6 *PAIRS.* **Take turns apologizing and making excuses using the expressions below. Student A, look at page 136. Student B, look at page 138.**

Apologize	**Show sympathy**
I'm (really) sorry, but . . .	That's OK.
I'm afraid . . .	Don't worry.
	That's too bad!

A: *I'm afraid I can't come to work. I have a terrible headache.*
B: *That's too bad!*

Writing

7 **You don't feel well today. Reply to each email message. Give an apology and an excuse.**

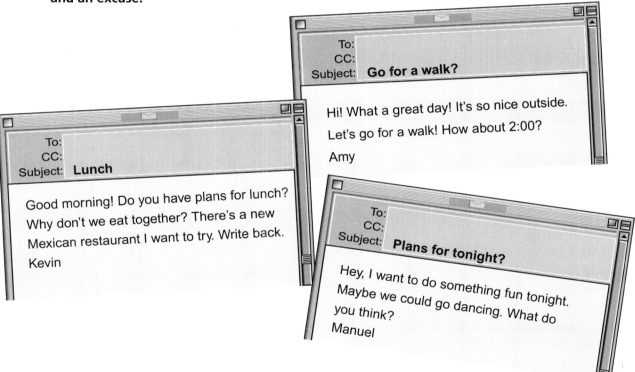

To:
CC:
Subject: **Go for a walk?**

Hi! What a great day! It's so nice outside.

Let's go for a walk! How about 2:00?

Amy

To:
CC:
Subject: **Lunch**

Good morning! Do you have plans for lunch? Why don't we eat together? There's a new Mexican restaurant I want to try. Write back.

Kevin

To:
CC:
Subject: **Plans for tonight?**

Hey, I want to do something fun tonight. Maybe we could go dancing. What do you think?

Manuel

CONVERSATION TO GO

A: **I'm afraid** I can't come to work. I have a sore throat, and I can't talk.
B: **That's too bad!**

9

A life of achievement

Vocabulary Life events
Grammar Simple past: regular and irregular verbs
Speaking Talking about past events

Lesson A

Getting started

1 **Number the life events in the order they usually occur.**

have children ___	find a job ___	graduate from school ___
get married ___	grow up ___	go to school ___
work hard ___	be born _1_	

2 *PAIRS.* **Compare your answers.**

Reading

3 **Look at the pictures of Oprah Winfrey. What do you know about her? Put a check (✓) next to the sentences about her that you think are true.**

She was born in the U.S.
She's an only child.
She's married.
She lives in an apartment in Chicago.
She has a plane.
She doesn't have children.
She gives a lot of money to charity.
She has her own magazine.

4 **Read the article about Oprah Winfrey. Then check your answers in Exercise 3.**

5 *PAIRS.* **Discuss. Did anything in the article surprise you?**

Oprah Winfrey

People in more than 132 countries watch *Oprah*. On this TV talk show, ordinary people talk about their problems and Oprah Winfrey helps them.

Oprah lives in a wonderful apartment in Chicago and has a farm and a house in the mountains. She has great cars and a plane too. But Oprah Winfrey was not always rich and famous.

1 Oprah Winfrey was born.

3 She had her first talk show.

5 She acted in her first movie.

1954

2 She left college.

4 She started *The Oprah Winfrey Show.*

A life of achievement

OBJECTIVES

Students will:

- activate vocabulary related to life events
- do reading, speaking, and writing tasks related to personal life experiences
- focus on using the simple past of regular and irregular verbs to talk about past events
- practice the different pronunciations of the -ed ending

WARM-UP: MY HERO!

Groups of 3. Students take turns telling each other about someone they admire.

- Tell students that this unit is about life events. Give or elicit a definition of the term *life events*. (Life events are things that happen in most people's lives.)
- Point out that in the unit title, "A life of achievement," *achievement* means "success in doing or getting what you have worked for."
- Ask students to think about someone they admire or look up to. Clarify the task by giving a personal example.
- Divide the class into groups of 3 and set a time limit of 5 minutes.
- After 5 minutes, call on a few students to tell the class about the people their partners admire.

Getting started

OPTION: VOCABULARY PREVIEW

Elicit from students some of the major events in a person's life. Write these on the board in random order. Ask questions using the phrases to check that students understand the meaning of each phrase. For example, for the phrase "be born," ask: "*How many of you were born before the year _____?*".

Exercise ❶

- Explain the task: Students will number each life event in order, using number 1 for the event that happens first.
- Go over the example, *be born*. Ask: *What number should be born have?* (1) *Why?* (Because it happens first in every person's life.)

Exercise ❷

- Have students compare their answers in pairs.
- Ask students about any differences in their answers. If any pairs wrote the life events in a different order, ask them to explain their answers.

> **Answer key**
>
> | | | |
> |---|---|---|
> | have children 8 | find a job 5 | graduate from school 4 |
> | get married 7 | grow up 2 | go to school 3 |
> | work hard 6 | be born 1 | |

EXTENSION

Brainstorm additional life events. (For example, fall in love, get a driver's license, leave home, serve in the military, vote in a national election.)

Reading

Teaching Tip! **Using background knowledge**

In pre-reading exercises like Exercise 3, students can either call on their background knowledge or they can make intelligent guesses about what the article will tell them.

Exercise ❸

- Direct students' attention to the photos. Ask: *Who is the woman?* (Oprah Winfrey.) *What does she do?* (She has a TV show.)
- Explain the task: Students will read the sentences and will put a check mark next to the sentences they think are true.
- Go over the example. Ask: *Who thinks Oprah Winfrey was born in the United States?* Have students raise their hands if they think the sentence is true.
- Set a time limit of 2 minutes.
- After 2 minutes, tell students they will find out most of the answers when they read the article.

Exercise ❹

- Explain the task: Students will read the article and will check their guesses in Exercise 3. Tell students there are two sentences with information that are not included in the article.
- Tell students to read the magazine article. Set a time limit of 5 minutes.
- Have students check their answers in Exercise 3. Then pair students to compare answers before going over the answers with the class.

> **Answer key**
>
> All the sentences should be checked except:
>   She's an only child.   She's married.
> (This information is not included in the article.)

Exercise ❺

- Model the activity by asking the class: *Did anything in the article surprise you?* Give a personal example. (For example, *Oprah didn't finish college. That surprised me.*)
- Pair students and set a time limit of 2 minutes.
- After 2 minutes, call on a few students to tell the class what surprised them about Oprah.

Teaching Tip! **Scanning for specific information**

This exercise is designed to give students practice in scanning for specific information. Point out that we scan to find a specific piece of information that answers a question. When scanning, we read only as much as we need to to find the information. In this case, students will be scanning to find the years that correspond to Oprah Winfrey's life events.

Exercise ❻

- Explain the task: Students will reread the article and write the year that corresponds to each of the life events in Oprah Winfrey's timeline.
- Have students read the sentences in the timeline. Explain that this is the information they should focus on when reading the article again.
- Set a time limit of 3 minutes. Walk around the room, helping as needed.
- Have students compare their answers with a partner's.
- Go over the answers with the class.

Answer key

1954	1. Oprah Winfrey was born.
1973	2. She left college.
1977	3. She had her first talk show.
1984	4. She started *The Oprah Winfrey Show*.
1985	5. She acted in her first movie.
1997	6. She started a charity to help other people.
2000	7. She started her own magazine.

EXTENSION

- Tell students to work individually to create five true-or-false statements about the reading.
- Set a time limit of 5 minutes. After 5 minutes, pair students and tell the pairs to take turns reading one of their statements and asking their partner to decide if the statement is true or false. For example, Student A reads a statement. (*Oprah Winfrey was born in 1955.*) Then Student B says if the statement is true or false. If the statement is false, Student B must give the correct information. (*False. She was born in 1954.*)

Please go to www.longman.com/worldview for additional in-class model conversation practice.

HOMEWORK

- Assign *Workbook* page 18, Vocabulary Exercises 1 and 2, and page 20, Listening Exercises 5 and 6.

What kind of life did Oprah have as a child?

Oprah Winfrey was born in 1954 in Mississippi, in the U.S. Her family didn't have a lot of money. Oprah could read and write when she was three, and she loved books. She worked hard and was an excellent student at school, but she left college in 1973 when she was nineteen and didn't finish her education.

How did she start her successful career?

Oprah wanted to be famous, and her dream came true when she found a job in TV. She was the first woman and the first black newscaster on TV in Nashville, Tennessee. In 1977, she had her first TV talk show. In 1984, she moved to Chicago and started *The Oprah Winfrey Show*. It was a great success.

Oprah in *The Color Purple*

What did she do later?

In 1985, Oprah acted in Steven Spielberg's movie *The Color Purple*. After that, she made several other popular films. She didn't have any children, but she used her success to help other people's children. In 1997, she started a charity called Oprah's Angel Network. In the first five years, the charity collected more than $12 million and gave it to people in need. Oprah's Angel Network helps students to go to college, poor families to build their own homes, and communities to become safer. Oprah began her own magazine for women in the spring of 2000. It's simply called *O*. The magazine contains many personal stories and moving articles that reflect her interest in helping people worldwide. Her television program is still very popular, but now it's just called *Oprah*.

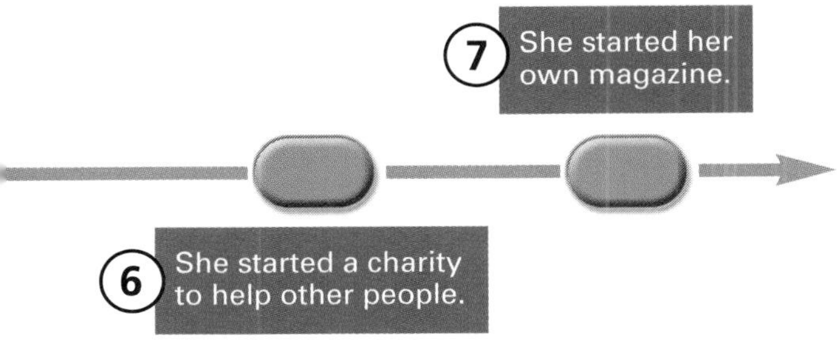

6 Read the article again. Then write the correct years on the timeline.

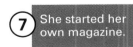
7 She started her own magazine.

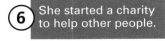
6 She started a charity to help other people.

11

Grammar focus

1 Study the examples of regular and irregular verbs in the simple past.

Regular verbs	Irregular verbs
Examples: *love, work, finish, end, want, move, act, start*	Examples: *be, can, leave, find, do, give, have*
(?) How **did** she **start** her successful career? **(?) Did** she **start** acting right away? **(+)** She **started** *The Oprah Winfrey Show* in 1984. **(–)** She **didn't start** the Angel Network in 1984.	What kind of life **did** she **have** as a child? **Did** she **have** any brothers and sisters? She **had** her first talk show in 1977. Her family **didn't have** a lot of money.

2 Look at the examples again. Is the rule in the chart true (*T*) or false (*F*)?

> **Simple past: regular and irregular verbs**
>
> Use the simple past to talk about completed actions in the past. _____

Grammar Reference page 143

3 Complete the story with the correct simple past form of the verbs in parentheses.

The entrepreneur Anita Roddick ___was___ born in
1. (be)

England in 1942. She _____ the first Body
2. (open)

Shop in 1976 in Brighton. She _____
3. (not have)

experience running a cosmetic shop, but she

_____ a lot of good ideas. She _____
4. (have)   5. (want)

to "make profits with principles." For example, she _____
6. (not allow)

her cosmetics to be tested on animals. She _____ a fair salary to
7. (pay)

all her employees.

By 1993, Anita Roddick _____ one of the five richest women in the
8. (be)

world. But her principles still _____ important to her. In 2000, she
9. (remain)

_____ the world of business and _____ a full-time campaigner
10. (leave)   11. (become)

on social issues.

Grammar focus

LANGUAGE NOTES

- For *Yes/No* questions in the simple past, use this structure: *Did* + subject + base form of the main verb. For example, *Did she start acting right away?*

- To give short answers to a *Yes/No* question, use this structure: *Yes, (subject) did.* Or *No, (subject) didn't.*

- For information (or *wh-*) questions in the simple past, use this structure: Question word + *did* + subject + base form of the main verb. For example, *How did she start her successful career?*

- To make a negative statement in the simple past, use this structure: Subject + *did not (didn't)* + base form of the main verb. For example, *She didn't have any children.*

- Students will probably need to be reminded to use the base form—**not** the past tense form—of the verb in negative statements and questions. For example, *She **didn't have** any children.* NOT *She **didn't had** any children.*

WARM-UP

Note: Skip this warm-up if you're doing this lesson (Lesson B) during the same class period as Lesson A.

- Books closed. Tell students they are going to listen to the article they read in the Reading section.

- Tell students to think about the time period in the article: Is it the past, the present, or the future?

- 🎧 Play the audio for Lesson A, Reading, Exercise 4. (It models the grammar of the unit.)

- Ask students what time period the article uses. (the past)

- Have students call out some of the verbs they remember from the article. Write a few of these on the board.

Exercise ❶

- Tell students to look at the two sets of verbs in the two columns. Ask: *Why are the verbs in the first column called regular verbs?* (Because they form the simple past by adding *-d* or *-ed* to the base form.) *Why are the ones in the second column called irregular verbs?* (Because each of them has a different past form.)

- Have students look at the examples and study the bold-faced words.

- Ask students to focus on the first example in each column. Ask: *What kinds of structures are the first examples in the two columns?* (questions) *What's the verb in each question?* (did start; did have) *What form of the verb is the main verb?* (base form) *What's the word order in questions?* (The subject comes between the auxiliary and the base form of the main verb.)

- Have students look at the other examples in the box. Ask: *What's the difference between the regular past tense verb and the irregular form.* (The regular verb ends in *-ed.*) Point out the use of the base form following *didn't* in the negative statement.

Exercise ❷

- Have students study the examples again.

- Tell students to read the statement in the chart and write *T* for *true* or *F* for *false.*

- Go over the answer with the class.

- Ask a few questions to elicit the key points about the grammar. For example, *What auxiliary do we use in simple past negative statements and questions?* (did) *What form follows the auxiliary in questions and negative statements?* (the base form) *What past tense ending is used with regular verbs?* (*-d* or *-ed*)

Answer key

True

Exercise ❸

- Before beginning Exercise 3, answer any questions students may have. You may also want to refer the class to the Grammar Reference for Unit 3 on page 143.

- Explain the task: Students will complete the story with the simple past tense form of the verbs in parentheses.

- Go over the example. Say: *The verb* was *is one of two simple past forms of the verb* be. *What's the other form?* (were) Call on a few students to give examples of statements and questions using *was* and *were.*

- Have students complete the exercise individually. Set a time limit of 3 minutes. Walk around the room, helping as needed.

- Have students compare their answers with a partner's.

- Go over the answers with the class.

Answer key

1. was	5. wanted	9. remained
2. opened	6. didn't allow	10. left
3. didn't have	7. paid	11. became
4. had	8. was	

EXTENSION

- On the board, write several sentences from the reading in Lesson A. (For example, *Her family didn't have a lot of money. She loved books. She worked hard. She left college when she was nineteen.*)

- Ask students to work individually. Tell them to form questions for each of the sentences. (For example, *Did her family have a lot of money?*) Set a time limit of 2 minutes.

- After 2 minutes, ask volunteers to write the questions on the board.

Pronunciation

> **LANGUAGE NOTE**
>
> The -ed ending is sometimes pronounced as a separate, extra syllable /əd/ and sometimes as just a /t/ or /d/ sound, with no extra syllable.

Exercise ❹

- Tell students they are going to listen for the pronunciation of the -ed ending in simple past verbs.
- 🎧 Play the audio. Stop the audio after the first sentence. Say the verb *lived* aloud. Ask students if they heard an extra syllable. (no) Write the word on the board and draw a slash through the letter *e*. Ask: *How many syllables does* lived *have?* (one)
- Repeat this procedure with the second sentence. Ask: *How many syllables does* wanted *have?* (two) Draw a line between *want-* and *-ed* to show the two syllables.
- Explain the task: Students will listen and will put a check mark next to the verbs in which the -ed ending is pronounced as an extra syllable.
- 🎧 Play the audio. Write the following answer key on the board.

> **Answer key**
>
> lived wanted✓ loved studied decided✓ worked acted✓ finished started✓ watched used collected✓

Exercise ❺

- Tell students they are going to listen to the audio and will repeat each verb.
- 🎧 Play the audio, and have students repeat.
- Call on individual students to read each verb aloud. Check their pronunciation.

Exercise ❻

Have students read the rule and fill in the blanks.

> **Answer key**
>
> /t/ and /d/

Speaking

Exercise ❼

This exercise provides practice with the simple past. It also prepares students for Exercises 8 and 9.

- Explain the task: Students will write in the years of the important events in their lives on a timeline. They should write the date—not the event that took place.
- Model the task by drawing a timeline on the board and writing in a year for an event in your life.
- Tell students to work individually to make their timelines. Encourage them to include the years for at least five events. Set a time limit of 5 minutes.

Exercise ❽

- Pair students. Tell them they are going to guess what happened in each year on their partner's timeline.
- Model the activity, using the timeline that you drew on the board. Encourage them to ask you *Yes/No* questions about the date you wrote on the board. (For example, *Did you get married in _____? Did you start a new job?*)
- Set a time limit of 10 minutes. Walk around the room, helping as needed.

Exercise ❾

Call on students to tell the class something interesting about their partners.

TRB For additional interactive grammar practice, have students do the reproducible activity for this unit in the *Teacher's Resource Book*.

Writing

Exercise ❿

- Assign the writing task for class work or homework.
- Explain the task: Students will write a paragraph about an important time or event in their lives, using the simple past tense and vocabulary from the unit.
- **TRB** Optionally, give students a copy of the writing model (see the *Teacher's Resource Book*, Writing Models). Ask them to read the model and notice the vocabulary and grammar from the unit.
- If students don't have the model, write the following on the board:

  When I was in school, I wasn't a very good student because I didn't like to study. I liked to draw, and I made funny drawings of all my teachers.

- Have a student read the sentences aloud. Answer any questions students might have.
- Walk around to make sure everyone understands the task.

For suggestions on how to give feedback on writing, see page xiv of this *Teacher's Edition*.

CONVERSATION TO GO

At the end of class, call on two students to role-play the conversation.

HOMEWORK

- 📖 Assign *Workbook* page 19, Grammar Exercises 3 and 4, and page 20, Pronunciation Exercises 7 and 8.
- 💿 If students do not have the *WorldView Workbook*, assign listening homework from the Student CD. Write on the board:

  Track 6
  What does Oprah's Angel Network do?

- 🎧 Tell students to listen to the audio and write the answer to the question. Have them bring their answer to the next class.

  (Answer: *It helps students to go to college, poor families to build their own homes, and communities to become safer.*)

Pronunciation

4 🎧 **Listen to the sentences. Notice the pronunciation of the simple past tense verbs. Check (✓) the verbs in which *-ed* is pronounced as an extra syllable.**

lived	wanted ✓	loved	studied	decided	worked
acted	finished	started	watched	used	collected

5 🎧 **Listen to the verbs in Exercise 4. Then listen and repeat.**

6 **Complete the rule.**

The *-ed* ending is pronounced as an extra syllable after the sounds ____ and ____.

Speaking

7 *BEFORE YOU SPEAK.* **Make a timeline of the important dates in your life. Include dates but no other information.**

8 *PAIRS.* **Look at your partner's timeline. Take turns. Ask questions to guess the missing information.**

A: Did you get a new job in 2003?
B: No, I met my fiancé in 2003.

9 **Tell the class something interesting about your partner.**

Sabrina met her fiancé in 2003.

Writing

10 **Oprah Winfrey encourages people to share their life stories on her TV show. What story can you share? Write a paragraph about an important time or event in your life. Use regular and irregular verbs in the simple past.**

CONVERSATION TO GO

A: When **did** you **finish** school?
B: In 2002. Then I **got** a job and **bought** a new car.

13

UNIT 4

Travel with English

Vocabulary Countries and continents; travel
Grammar *be going to* for future
Speaking Talking about plans

Getting started

1 Write the countries under the continents. Then add two more countries under Africa, Europe, Asia, and North America.

| Australia | Canada | India | Ireland | South Africa |

Australia	**Africa**	**Europe**	**Asia**	**North America**
Australia	_____	_____	_____	_____
	_____	_____	_____	_____
	_____	_____	_____	_____

Pronunciation

2 🎧 Listen to the names of some countries and continents. Notice the number of syllables and the stress. Write each name in the correct stress group.

○ ○	○ ○○	○ ○○
England	Italy	Korea

3 🎧 Listen and check your answers. Listen again and repeat.

4 *PAIRS.* Test your partner. Say the name of a country. Your partner says the continent it's in.

A: Australia.
B: Australia.

Reading

5 Match the words to the photos. Write the name of the country.

coast _Australia_   countryside _____   market _____

safari _____   mountains _____

14

Travel with English

OBJECTIVES

Students will:

- activate vocabulary related to countries, continents, and travel
- do reading, speaking, and writing tasks related to personal travel plans
- focus on using *be going to* to talk about future plans
- practice putting stress on the correct syllable in the names of countries and continents

WARM-UP: THE CONTINENTS

Students talk about basic world geography.

- Tell students that this unit is about places in the world and the things tourists do when traveling.
- Explain that the unit title, "Travel with English," refers to places where English is the main language.
- Ask: *How many continents are there?* (seven) *What are their names in English?* (Africa, Europe, Asia, Australia, Antarctica, North America, and South America)
- Give the class a short quiz on the seven continents. Call on volunteers to answer. Possible questions:
  Which is the biggest continent? (Asia)
  Which is the smallest? (Australia)
  In which continent can you find the South Pole? (Antarctica)
  What is the only continent that is its own country? (Australia)

Getting started

OPTION: VOCABULARY PREVIEW

If you think your students will have difficulty with Exercise 1, complete the chart as a whole-class activity.

Exercise ❶

- Explain the task: Students will write the countries under the correct continents. Tell them to add two more countries to each of the last four columns.
- Set a time limit of 3 minutes. While students are working, walk around the room, helping as needed.
- Have students compare their answers with a partner's.

Answer key

Australia: Australia **Asia:** India
Africa: South Africa **North America:** Canada
Europe: Ireland

EXTENSION

- Review the nationalities that correspond to the countries in Exercise 1.
- If time allows, extend the practice by having the class brainstorm additional countries, their nationalities, and the main language spoken in each.

Pronunciation

Exercise ❷

- Have students look at the chart. Explain that the circles represent the number of syllables. The large circles represent the syllables with the main stress.
- Demonstrate the different stress groups in the chart. Count out the syllables of the following names on your fingers: *England, Italy, Korea.*
- Write *England, Italy,* and *Korea* on the board. Mark the correct stress on each word with large and small circles. Then read each word aloud.
- Explain the task: Students will listen to the names of some countries. They will count the number of syllables in each word, listen for the stressed syllable, and write the name in the correct stress group.
- 🎧 Play the audio, stopping or pausing after each item to give students time to write their answer.
- Tell students they will check their answers in the next exercise.

Exercise ❸

- Tell students they are going to check their answers to Exercise 2.
- 🎧 Play the audio, stopping or pausing after each word and asking students to repeat it chorally. Give students enough time to check their answers.

Answer key

● ・		● ・ ・		・ ● ・	
Eng	land	It	a	ly	Ko	re	a
A	sia	Ca	na	da	Aus	tra	lia
Eu	rope	In	di	a		
Ire	land	Af	ri	ca		

Exercise ❹

- **Pairs.** Explain the task: One student in the pair will say the name of a country; the other guesses the continent it is in. Go over the example.

Exercise ❺

- Have students look at the words. Read them aloud.
- Explain the task: Students will look at the pictures and write the names of the countries next to the words. Go over the example.
- Set a time limit of 2 minutes.
- Have students work in pairs to compare their answers.
- Go over the answers with the class.

Answer key

coast: Australia; countryside: Ireland; market: India; safari: South Africa; mountains: Canada

Reading

BACKGROUND INFORMATION

Rajasthan

This sparsely populated state in northwestern India is known for its almost constant fairs and festivals. The tradition of celebration began in medieval times when people came together at festivals to socialize, trade, and be entertained. Today the festivities continue with a variety of religious and secular celebrations held almost every month.

Nunavut

On April 1, 1999, Nunavut became Canada's largest and newest territory. The Inuit, or the people indigenous to the territory, are proud of their 5,000-year-old heritage. The Inuits' existence has been closely tied to the land of the Arctic tundra, and their history is rich in tradition and folklore. Life for the Inuit today spans two worlds. Many people have traded their nomadic traditions for a more sedentary, community-based lifestyle. In the springtime, however, entire communities often return to the wilderness and go hunting and fishing.

St. Patrick's Day

St. Patrick is the patron saint of Ireland. On March 17, St. Patrick's Day, the Irish honor the bishop who dedicated his life to converting the Irish people to Christianity. In Ireland the day remains a religious holiday celebrated with parades, feasts, shows for charity, and religious services. Irish immigrants began celebrating St. Patrick's Day in the United States in 1737. In the United States, the day is usually celebrated by attending parades, wearing green, eating corned beef and cabbage, and drinking green beer.

Teaching Tip! **Using cues to predict content**

Pictures, captions, and paragraph headings enable a reader to predict an article's content. Knowing how to use these cues is a valuable reading skill.

Exercise ❻

- Have students look at the article. Tell them to look at the pictures and to read the title of the article and the headings. Ask: *What's the article about?* (It's about some vacation places.)
- Explain the task: Students will read the article and then complete the chart.
- Ask students to look at the chart. Point out that the headings in the chart indicate the information they should look for when reading the article.
- Have students read the article and complete the chart. Set a time limit of 10 minutes. Walk around the room, helping as needed.
- After 10 minutes, have students compare their charts with a partner's.
- Go over the answers with the class.

Answer key

Country	When to visit	What to see and do
Canada	*November*	see mountains, lakes
Australia	December	*Sightsee in Sydney; rent a car and drive up . . . the coast*
India	January	go to festivals and monuments; visit markets
South Africa	February	see wild animals; find a beach and go swimming
Ireland	March	go to St. Patrick's Day festivities; buy a sweater; see Dublin and the countryside

EXTENSION

- Have students create a timeline of the travel writer's trip similar to the timelines in Unit 3.
- Tell them to write the names of the months (instead of years) on the timeline. If necessary, draw a timeline on the board with five vertical lines. On the first line, write *November*. Then have five volunteers come to the board to complete the timeline.

◉ Please go to www.longman.com/worldview for additional in-class model conversation practice.

HOMEWORK

- 📖 Assign *Workbook* page 21, Vocabulary Exercises 1, 2, and 3, and page 23, Pronunciation Exercises 8 and 9.

6 **Read the article. Then complete the chart.**

Country	When to visit	What to see and do
Canada	November	
Australia		Sightsee in Sydney Rent a car and drive up . . .
India		
South Africa		
Ireland		

THE TRAVEL WRITER'S

Dream **Vacation**

I have five months to travel before I write! I'm going to explore countries where I can practice speaking English. Where am I going to start?

Canada
It's the Rockies for me in November! There are mountains and beautiful lakes everywhere, so the views are great. I'd like to visit Nunavut, the home of the Inuit in the north of Canada, but unfortunately I'm not going to get there . . . there isn't enough time.

Australia
Australia is very hot from November to March. I love hot weather, so I'm going to arrive in Sydney in December. I'm going to sightsee in Sydney—there are so many interesting buildings in the city. Then I'm going to rent a car and drive up the coast.

India
Rajasthan is the perfect introduction to India with its festivals and monuments. There are also exciting markets to visit, with beautiful clothes and jewelry. I'm going to spend the month of January there. They say the weather is really nice then.

South Africa
South Africa offers luxury safaris and the chance to see wild animals. It also has a wonderful coastline, so, after the safari, I'm going to find a beach and go swimming there. I like the sun, so I'm going to go in February.

Ireland
In March I'm going to take part in the St. Patrick's Day festivities in Ireland. I know Ireland can be cold in the spring, but I'm going to buy a beautiful Irish sweater there. Dublin is a great city and the countryside is beautiful, so I think March is going to be a lot of fun.

Grammar focus

1 **Study the examples of *be going to* for the future.**

> (+) I**'m going to spend** a month in India.
> (–) She **isn't going to visit** the Inuit communities in Canada.
> (?) **Are** you **going to arrive** in December?
> (Yes, I **am**. / No, I**'m not**.)

2 **Look at the examples again. Complete the rule in the chart.**

> **be going to for future**
>
> Use a form of the verb _____ + *going to* + the base form of the verb to talk about future plans.

> *Grammar Reference page 143*

3 **Complete the sentences with the correct form of *be going to* and the verbs in parentheses.**

1. She ___isn't going to travel___ (**not travel**) to Australia in July when the weather is cold.

2. She _____ (**see**) beautiful monuments in India.

3. We _____ (**walk**) by the lake in Canada.

4. They _____ (**not stay**) in luxury hotels in India.

5. _____ (**we / swim**) in the ocean in South Africa?

6. I _____ (**visit**) Alice Springs and other famous places in Australia.

7. He _____ (**take part**) in the St. Patrick's Day festivities in Ireland.

8. _____ (**you / climb**) any mountains in Canada?

9. When _____ (**he / leave**) Rio de Janeiro?

4 **Answer these questions about the travel writer in the article on page 15.**

1. What is the woman going to do for five months?
2. Is she going to visit Nunavut in Canada? Why?
3. When is she going to arrive in Sydney? Why?
4. What is she going to do in Rajasthan?
5. Where is she going to go in February? Why?
6. What is she going to buy in Ireland?

Grammar focus

LANGUAGE NOTES

- Both *will* and *be going to* are used for predictions and future plans. *Will* is used only for plans made at the time of speaking. For example,

  A: *We're going to see a movie tonight.*
  B: *Great! I'll come with you.*

- To form the simple future with "be going to," use *am, is,* or *are* + *going to* + the base form of the verb.

- To make a negative statement, use *not* before *going to*.

- Use contractions in speaking and informal writing.

- To form *Yes/No* questions with "be going to," put *am, is,* or *are* before the subject, then add *going to* + the base form of the verb. The short answers are *Yes, I am* or *No, I'm not*.

- To form *wh-* questions, start with the question word and use the correct form of *be* + subject + *going to* + the base form of the verb.

- *Be going to* has two different pronunciations:

  (1) *Going* has a strong pronunciation and *to* has a weak pronunciation: *I'm going to* /gooŋtə/ *spend a month in India.* Note that *to* is pronounced with a clearer vowel sound when it comes before a vowel: *Are you going to* /tu/ *arrive in December?*
  (2) *Going to* is pronounced as /gɔnə/ or /gənə/ (sometimes written informally as "gonna"). Native speakers often use this pronunciation in conversation. Notice that *going to* does not have a /t/ sound when used in conversation.

WARM-UP

Note: Skip this warm-up if you're doing this lesson (Lesson B) during the same class period as Lesson A.

- Tell students they are going to listen again to the article about the trip. Tell students to think about this question: *What tense does the writer use in the article?*

- 🎧 Play the audio for Lesson A, Reading, Exercise 6. (It models the grammar of the unit.)

- Ask students to answer the question above. (the future)

Exercise ❶

- Have students look at the examples and study the bold-faced words.

- Ask: *What's the first verb in each of the sentences?* (*be*) *Is it the present or the past?* (the present)

- Elicit that *going to* is followed by the base form of the main verb. Point out the short answers. Remind students that contractions are not used in affirmative short answers.

Exercise ❷

- Have students study the examples again and fill in the blank in the box.

- Ask a few questions to elicit the key points about the grammar. For example, *What's the negative for "She's going to visit"?* (She isn't going to visit.) *What are the two short answers for "Are you going to arrive in December?"* (Yes, I am. *Or* No, I'm not.)

Answer key

be

Exercise ❸

- Before beginning Exercise 3, answer any questions students might have. You may also want to refer the class to the Grammar Reference for Unit 4 on page 143.

- Explain the task: Students will complete the sentences with the correct form of *be going to* and the verbs in parentheses. Point out that when the sentence is a negative sentence, they will need to use the pronoun that's included with the verb in parentheses. They must add *not* after the verb *be* for negative sentences.

- Go over the example. Point out that because it is a question, students must add *not* as indicated in parentheses.

- Have students complete the exercise individually. Set a time limit of 5 minutes.

- Have students compare their answers with a partner's.

- Go over the answers with the class.

Answer key

1. isn't going to travel
2. is going to see
3. 're going to walk
4. aren't going to stay
5. Are we going to swim
6. 'm going to visit
7. is going to take part
8. Are you going to climb
9. is he going to leave

Exercise ❹

- Explain the task: Students will answer the questions in complete sentences, using the information from the article on page 15. They will write their answers on a piece of paper.

- Remind students to use *be going to* in their sentences.

- Set a time limit of 5 minutes.

- Have students compare their answers with a partner's.

- Go over the answers with the class.

Answer key

1. The woman is going to travel to/explore countries.
2. No, she isn't. Because there isn't enough time.
3. She's going to arrive in Sydney in December. Because she loves hot weather.
4. She's going to see festivals, monuments, and the markets in Rajasthan.
5. She's going to South Africa in February. Because she likes the sun, and it's sunny there in February.
6. She's going to buy a beautiful Irish sweater in Ireland.

Speaking

Teaching Tip! Helping students help each other

Reaching consensus can be difficult, especially when students are also trying to speak in English. To help students during their group discussion, give them the language they can use to ask for opinions and check for agreement, including *What do you think? Do you agree? What is your opinion? What are your ideas?* Encourage students to use these expressions.

Exercise ❺

This exercise provides practice with the *be going to* form and prepares students for Exercises 6 through 8.

- Explain the task: Students will begin planning a vacation. They will choose three English-speaking countries from the Reading in Lesson A and make notes in the chart.

- Have students look at the chart. Point out the three types of information they will note in the chart: *The three countries; When to visit and why;* and *What to see and do.*

- Have students work individually to complete the chart. Set a time limit of 5 minutes.

Exercise ❻

- Students work in groups of 4. Tell the groups they are going to take turns telling one another about their answers to the questions in the chart.

- Set a time limit of 10 minutes. Walk around the room, helping as needed.

Exercise ❼

- **Groups of 4.** Tell students they must decide as a group on a vacation destination. They need to decide on where to go, when they will go, and what they will see and do there.

- Set a time limit of 5 minutes.

Exercise ❽

- Have a representative from each group report on their group's destination and travel plans.

- Ask the class to vote on which trip they should take.

TRB For additional interactive grammar practice, have students do the reproducible activity for this unit in the *Teacher's Resource Book.*

Writing

Exercise ❾

- Assign the writing task for class work or homework.

- Explain the task: Students will write a letter telling a friend about a trip they are going to take.

- Brainstorm ideas for ways to begin a friendly letter (*Dear _____,* or *Hi*) and the type of information that someone would find interesting about a friend's travel plans.

- **TRB** Optionally, give students a copy of the writing model (see the *Teacher's Resource Book,* Writing Models). Ask them to read the model and notice the vocabulary and grammar from the unit.

- If students don't have the model, write the following on the board:

  Dear Kathy,
     I'm going to travel to Greece with Rebecca, my old friend from school. I can't wait!
     We arrive in Athens on July 25th. We're going to stay at a nice hotel . . .

- Have a student read the sentences aloud. Answer any questions students might have.

- Walk around to make sure everyone understands the task.

For suggestions on how to give feedback on writing, see page xii of this *Teacher's Edition.*

CONVERSATION TO GO

At the end of class, call on two students to role-play the conversation.

HOMEWORK

- 📖 Assign *Workbook* page 22, Grammar Exercises 4 and 5, and page 23, Pronunciation Exercises 8 and 9.

- Assign *Workbook* Self-Quiz 1.

- 💿 If students do not have the *WorldView Workbook,* assign listening homework from the Student CD. Write on the board:

  Track 9
  Write a paragraph of five sentences about the trip. Use these words: *First, Then, Next, After that, Finally.*

- 🎧 Tell students to listen to the audio and write the answer for the exercise. Have them bring their paragraph to the next class.

  (Possible answer: *First, she's going to the Rockies in Canada. Then she's going to arrive in Australia. Next, she's going to visit India. After that, she's going to go to South Africa. Finally, she's going to take part in the St. Patrick's Day festivities in Ireland.*)

FOR NEXT CLASS

- Tell students that the next class will be a review class covering Units 1–4.

- Have students review the material in the units to prepare for the activities in Review 1.

TRB Make copies of Quiz 1 in the *Teacher's Resource Book.*

Unit no.	Review Grammar	Listen to Student CD	Study Grammar Reference
1	Review simple present and adverbs of frequency	Track 2	Page 143
2	Linking words: *and, so, but*	Track 4	Page 143
3	Simple past	Track 6	Page 143
4	*be going to*	Track 9	Page 143

Speaking

5 *BEFORE YOU SPEAK.* **You're going to plan a group vacation to three countries where you can use your English. Look again at the article on page 15 and answer these questions. Write notes in the chart.**

1. Which three countries do you want to visit?
2. When do you want to go? Why?
3. What are you going to see and do?

Place	When to visit / Why?	What to see and do
Australia	May—it's cool then	Sightsee in Sydney . . .

6 *GROUPS OF 4.* **Take turns telling each other about your choices. Give reasons.**

I want to go to . . . in . . . because . . .

7 **Discuss your choices. Make a decision together. Where will you go? When will you go? What are you going to see and do there?**

8 **Tell the class your group's decisions. Can you agree on a class vacation?**

Writing

9 **Write a letter to a friend. Tell him or her about a trip you are planning. Where are you going to go? What are you going to do there? Use *be going to*.**

CONVERSATION TO GO

A: What are you going to do next summer?
B: I'm going to fly around the world.

Unit 1 It's the weekend!

1 🎧 Listen to the model conversation.

2 Walk around the room. Find someone who . . .

always goes to the gym on weekends. _____

usually goes out to eat on weekends. _____

sometimes goes to the movies on weekends. _____

never sleeps late on weekends. _____

3 *PAIRS.* Compare your answers. Did you find the same people?

Unit 2 Excuses, excuses

4 🎧 Listen to the model conversation.

5 *TWO PAIRS.* Play the Health Game. Take turns. Toss a coin (one side = move ahead one space, the other side = move ahead two spaces).

When you land on a space, look at the picture. Role-play a conversation between a boss and an employee. Student A, you're the employee. You can't go to work. Give an excuse using the situation in the picture. Student B, you're the boss. Respond to the excuse. The first team to reach FINISH wins.

You may wish to use the video for Units 1–4 at this point.
For video activity worksheets, go to www.longman.com/worldview.

Unit 1: It's the weekend!

OBJECTIVES

- Review the material presented in Unit 1
- Grammar practice: simple present and adverbs of frequency

Exercise ❶

- Books closed. Tell students they will listen to a conversation that models Exercise 2.
- 🎧 Play the audio.
- Ask: *Who always goes to the gym on weekends?* (Jorge) *What does Suki usually do on the weekends?* (goes out to eat)

Exercise ❷

- Explain the task: Students will ask their classmates questions to find someone who does each activity with the specified frequency on the weekends. Explain that when someone answers *yes*, they should write the person's name on the line.
- Have students read the list of activities, drawing their attention to the adverbs of frequency.
- If necessary, briefly review the form that students will use to ask the questions. (*Do + you + verb*)
- 🎧 Play the audio for Review 1, Exercise 1 again while students look at the exercise.
- Remind students that they can use a person's name only once.
- Set a time limit of 5 minutes for the activity. While students are working, walk around the room, helping as needed.

Exercise ❸

- Pair students. Have them compare their answers with a partner's.
- Set a time limit of 1 minute.
- Ask the class which activities they were not able to find a person for.
- Call on individual volunteers to report on a classmate's activities on weekends.

Unit 2: Excuses, excuses

OBJECTIVES

- Review the material presented in Unit 2
- Grammar practice: linking words *and, but, so*

Exercise ❹

- Tell students they will listen to a conversation that models Exercise 5.
- 🎧 Play the audio.
- Ask: *What are the speakers doing?* (playing a board game) *Who are they role-playing?* (an employee and a boss) *In the model conversation, what excuses do the employees give for not coming to work?* (I have a sore throat. *And* I hurt my arm.) *What are the two responses from the boss?* (That's OK. *And* I'm sorry. I hope you feel better.)
- 🎧 If necessary, play the audio again.

Exercise ❺

- **Two pairs**. Ask students to read the directions for Exercise 5.
- Pair students. Have each pair join another pair to form groups of 4.
- Give each group a coin to toss and each pair a different marker. Students can use any objects as markers provided each pair gets a different one.
- Model one round of the game with a student. Walk around the room, helping as needed.

WRAP-UP

Have students report to the class the winner in each group.

Unit 3: A life of achievement

OBJECTIVES

- Review the material presented in Unit 3
- Grammar practice: the simple past of regular and irregular verbs

WARM-UP

- Briefly review how to form the simple past. (For regular verbs, add -d or -ed to the base form of the verb; for irregular verbs, see page 150.)
- Give some examples of your activities in the past such as *I lived in an apartment until I was thirty*. Or *I went to Peru last year*.
- Ask volunteers to say one sentence about something that they did or that happened to them in the past.

Exercise ❻

- Explain the task: Students will listen to a conversation that models how to play the guessing game in Exercise 8. Remind students to listen carefully to the language and the procedures the characters follow for the game.
- 🎧 Play the audio.

Exercise ❼

- Have students write three statements about themselves using the simple past. Tell them to make sure to write both true and false statements about themselves.
- Walk around the room, helping as needed.

Exercise ❽

- Divide the class into groups of 3.
- 🎧 If needed, play the audio again to remind students how to play the game.
- Clarify how to play the game by eliciting the steps from the students. (*The members of the group take turns saying one of the sentences that they wrote in Exercise 7. Then the rest of the group says whether they think each statement is true or not. The member who guesses correctly gets a point.*)
- Walk around the room, helping as needed.

WRAP-UP

Have volunteers report to the class one statement they thought was false but was actually true.

Unit 4: Travel with English

OBJECTIVES

- Review the material presented in Unit 4
- Grammar practice: *be going to* for future

WARM-UP

- Books closed. Tell students to imagine they are going on a trip. Ask them to briefly say where they are going and what they are going to do there.
- Remind students to use the correct forms of *be going to* in their sentences.

Exercise ❾

- Tell students they will listen to a conversation that models Exercise 10.
- 🎧 Play the audio.

Exercise ❿

- **Groups of 3**. Explain the task: Tell students they will work in groups of 3. They will each have a copy of Dario's travel schedule, but each of them will be missing different pieces of information on the schedule. They will ask each other questions to complete their charts.
- 🎧 If needed, play the audio for Exercise 9 again.
- Divide the class into groups of 3. Assign each member A, B, and C roles. Have students read the directions. Tell them to look at their corresponding pages. Answer questions students might have about the activity.
- Model the activity with a student by asking and answering a question to complete one box of the chart.
- Set a time limit of 5 minutes. Walk around the room, helping as needed.

Exercise ⓫

After 5 minutes, have students compare their charts to make sure that they all have the same information about Dario's trip.

Unit 3 A life of achievement

6 🎧 Listen to the model conversation.

7 Write three true statements about your past. Then write three statements that are not true but sound possible.

8 *GROUPS OF 3.* Take turns. Say one statement aloud. The others in the group guess "True" or "False." After everyone guesses, tell the truth! Players receive one point for each correct guess. The person with the most points is the winner.

Points: _____

Unit 4 Travel with English

9 🎧 Listen to the model conversation.

10 *GROUPS OF 3.* Dario is going on a trip. Take turns. Ask questions to fill in his schedule. (Don't look at your partners' schedules.)

Student A, look at page 136.
Student B, look at page 138.
Student C, look at page 142.

11 *GROUPS OF 3.* Compare your schedules. Does everyone have the same information?

World of Music *1*

River Deep, Mountain High
Ike and Tina Turner

Getting Started

1 Complete the sentences with the correct word or words.

deep	faithful	flows	~~followed~~	goes on
let	lost	owned	puppy	robin

1. Tom's little sister always _followed_ him around when they were kids.

2. Ines promised to help Ralph move, but she went dancing instead. She really _____ him down.

3. Yasuhiro is really upset because he _____ his keys.

4. They're excited about their new car. It's the first one they've ever _____.

5. The river _____ into the sea a few miles from here.

6. This isn't the last stop. The train _____ to Washington.

7. The children can't wait to get home from school so they can play with their _____.

8. You know it's spring when you see a _____.

9. A _____ friend is someone who is always there to help you.

10. Don't let the children play near the pool over there. The water is very _____.

The 60s

Tina Turner was a teenager when she began singing with her husband Ike's band in the 60s. She went on to become an international superstar—and a symbol of the independent woman.

Listening

2 🎧 Listen to the song "River Deep, Mountain High." Correct the statements.

1. The singer is singing about a love in the past.

2. The singer thinks that her love is getting weaker.

3. The singer will be as friendly as a puppy.

World of Music *1*

- Introduce the song "River Deep, Mountain High"
- Vocabulary practice: words in context
- Express feelings about a song

BACKGROUND INFORMATION

Tina Turner got her first taste of the entertainment world at age sixteen when her older sister introduced her to the nightlife of St. Louis. On one of the girls' nights out Tina met Ike Turner, who was the leader of a local band, the Kings of Rhythm. Tina joined the band, which soon became known as the Ike and Tina Turner Revue. Two years later Ike and Tina were married. As their careers took off, their relationship deteriorated, with Ike becoming controlling and abusive. The couple was divorced in 1978, the same year that Tina began her solo career. Throughout the 1980s, Tina released several successful albums and gained worldwide popularity. In 1991, Tina Turner was inducted into the Rock and Roll Hall of Fame. She has sold over 50 million albums around the world.

WARM-UP

- Ask students if they have seen any of Tina Turner's concerts on TV. Encourage them to share their impressions of Tina Turner as a performer. Ask: *What do you like best about Tina Turner as a performer?* (Her energy, her dancing, her lively songs, etc.)
- Invite volunteers to name other songs by Tina Turner.
- Ask students if they like Tina Turner and her music. Encourage them to explain why they like her.

The 60s

- Tell students to read the information about the 60s in the *Student Book*. Ask them what they know about the 60s. (Possible answers: *It was a decade of social and political unrest. There were disagreements over the Vietnam War, and the Civil Rights and feminist movements were active.*)
- Explain to the class that it was during this decade of unrest when Tina Turner became a symbol of the independent woman.

Vocabulary

Exercise ❶

- Tell students to read the sentences in Exercise 1. Explain the task: Students will read the sentences and decide which of the words in the box correctly completes each sentence.
- Guide students to use the context of the sentence to get the meaning of a word. For example, the clue to the meaning of "follow around" is "little sister." Younger brothers and sisters like to follow their older siblings around.
- Tell students that this exercise will help them better understand the lyrics of the song they will be listening to.

Answer key

1. followed	6. goes on
2. let	7. puppy
3. lost	8. robin
4. owned	9. faithful
5. flows	10. deep

Listening

Exercise ❷

- Pair students. Tell the pairs they will listen to the song and will correct the information in each sentence.
- Play the song.
- Set a time limit of 1 minute for students to do the exercise.
- Call on volunteer students to share their answers with the class. Encourage them to cite lines from the song to prove their answers.

Answer key

1. The singer is singing about a love <u>in the present</u>.
2. The singer thinks that her love is getting <u>stronger</u>.
3. The singer will be as <u>faithful as</u> a puppy.

NOTES

- In song and in poetry, writers often use sentences and phrases that do not follow the rules of correct grammar. Poets and songwriters often deviate from the rules of grammar for various reasons, such as to draw attention to a word or idea, to make a line rhyme, or to fit the rhythm of the poem or song.

- Point out the reverse noun/adjective order in the title "River Deep, Mountain High" as an example of usage that does not follow the usual order of adjective + noun.

Exercise ❸

- Tell students they will listen to the song again. This time, they will listen to fill in the missing words.

- 🎧 Play the song and have students complete the lyrics. Walk around the room, helping as needed.

- 🎧 If needed, play the song again to give students more time to complete the activity.

- Tell students they will correct their answers in the next exercise.

Exercise ❹

- Pair students and have them compare their answers in Exercise 3.

- Give students time to correct their answers.

> **Answer key**
>
> stronger, deeper, higher
> bigger, sweeter

OPTION

🎧 Play the song again and have students sing along.

Speaking

Exercise ❺

- **Pairs.** Have students work with the same partners.

- Tell them to answer the questions.

- Call on volunteers to share their answers with the class.

> **Answer key**
>
> Possible answers:
> Some words and sentences that the singer uses to talk about her love:
> I love you just the way I loved that rag doll.
> It gets stronger . . .
> It gets deeper . . .
> It gets higher day by day.
> I'm gonna be as faithful as that puppy.
> I love you like the flower loves the spring.
> I love you like a robin loves to sing.
> I love you like a schoolboy loves his pie.

Exercise ❻

- Have students work with the same partners. Have the pairs discuss the questions.

- Set a time limit of 3 minutes.

- After 3 minutes, invite volunteers to share with the class their comments and reactions to the song.

3 🎧 **Listen to the song again. Complete the lyrics with the words you hear.**

River Deep, Mountain High

When I was a little girl I had a rag doll;
The only doll I've ever owned.
Now I love you just the way I loved that rag doll;
But only now my love has grown.
And it gets _____ in every way,
And it gets _____ let me say,
And it gets _____ day by day.

[Chorus]

Do I love you? My, oh, my!
River deep, mountain high
If I lost you, would I cry?
Oh, how I love you, baby, baby, baby, baby.

When you were a young boy did you have a puppy
that always followed you around?
Well, I'm gonna be as faithful as that puppy.
No, I'll never let you down.
'Cause it goes on and on like a river flows.
And it gets _____, baby, and heaven knows,
And it gets _____, baby, as it grows.

[Repeat chorus]

I love you, baby, like a flower loves the spring.
And I love you, baby, like a robin loves to sing.
And I love you, baby, like a schoolboy loves his pie.
And I love you, baby, river deep, mountain high.

[Repeat chorus]

4 *PAIRS.* **Compare your answers.**

Speaking

5 *PAIRS.* **In the song "River Deep, Mountain High," what are some words that the singer uses to talk about her love?**

6 *GROUPS OF 3.* **Discuss the questions.**

Do you like this song?
How does the song make you feel?

Culture shock

Vocabulary Social etiquette
Grammar Modals: *should* and *shouldn't* for advice
Speaking Giving advice

Lesson A

Getting started

1 Match the words and phrases in the box with the pictures. Some pictures have more than one description.

1. give a gift __D__
2. use first names ____
3. take your shoes off ____
4. shake hands ____
5. kiss ____
6. wear a suit ____
7. bow ____
8. arrive on time ____

2 *PAIRS.* **Talk about the pictures.**

Which of these things do you do in your country?

Culture shock

OBJECTIVES

Students will:

- activate vocabulary related to social etiquette
- do listening, speaking, and writing tasks related to social etiquette and giving advice
- focus on using modals *should* and *shouldn't* for advice
- practice weak and strong pronunciations of *should* and *shouldn't*

WARM-UP: CULTURAL DIFFERENCES

Students exchange ideas about the meaning of the word *culture* and talk about how cultures can be different from one another.

- Tell students that this unit is about culture and social etiquette. Explain that the title of the unit, "Culture shock," refers to the strange feelings that we can have when we visit a foreign country or a new place for the first time.

- Elicit ideas for things that might cause "culture shock." (For example, unfamiliar food, different styles of dressing, not being able to communicate.) Ask: *Has anyone in the class experienced culture shock?* If possible, share with the class a personal anecdote.

- Ask students to think about ways in which cultures can be different. Have volunteers share their ideas with the class. If students have no personal experience with other cultures, encourage them to consider situations they have seen in movies or on television, or have read about in books, newspapers, and magazines.

- If necessary, lead the class discussion by asking, *Do people all over the world dress in the same way? Do they eat the same food? What else do people from different cultures do differently?*

Getting started

OPTION: VOCABULARY PREVIEW

Tell students to look at the words and phrases in Exercise 1. Read aloud the first phrase. Ask: *What's another word for* gift? (present) Ask students when gifts or presents are usually given. (Christmas, birthdays, anniversaries) To illustrate the meaning of *give,* call on a student to give you his or her book. Now, illustrate the meaning of the entire phrase *give a gift.* Show a new pencil. Say that the pencil is your gift to a student. Give the pencil to a student. Ask: *What did I give him or her?* (You gave him or her a gift.) Read aloud each of the phrases in the box and call on volunteers to pantomime the actions. If necessary, break the phrases into individual words and elicit the meaning of each before asking students to mime the phrases.

Exercise ❶

- Explain the task: Students will match the pictures to the words and phrases. Point out that some of the pictures illustrate more than one of the actions. Go over the example. If necessary, clarify the meaning of *gift* by pointing to Picture D. Ask: *What does the man have in his hand?* (flowers) *What are the flowers for?* (a gift for the woman) *Why is he giving her flowers?* (Because he's visiting her.)

- Set a time limit of 3 minutes. While students are working, walk around the room, helping as needed.

- Have students compare their answers with a partner's.

- Go over the answers with the class.

Answer key

1. D	3. C	5. D	7. B
2. D	4. A	6. B, A	8. A

Exercise ❷

- Explain the task: Students will look at the pictures and the words and phrases in Exercise 1 and use those ideas to talk about behaviors that are typical in their country. If necessary, model the activity by asking, *Do people here shake hands when they meet for the first time?* Call on one or two volunteers to give their ideas.

- Pair students and set a time limit of 5 minutes. Walk around the room, helping as needed.

- After 5 minutes, call on a few students to give examples of things they do—and don't do—in their country. Encourage them to say when people in their country do the things in the pictures.

EXTENSION

- Write *Always, Sometimes,* and *Never* on the board or on pieces of paper taped to different places in the classroom.

- Have a few students come to the front of the room. Say a sentence using each of the vocabulary items in Exercise 1, and tell the students to move to the word that expresses how often they do each in their culture. For example, students should stand in front of *Always* if they always shake hands when they meet someone new. Possible sentences:

  People arrive on time for parties.
  People arrive on time for business meetings.
  People take off their shoes before entering other people's houses.
  People give gifts when they go to someone's home.
  People kiss to say hello and good-bye.
  People wear suits to business meetings.
  People bow when meeting someone new.
  People use first names with people they work with.

Listening

BACKGROUND INFORMATION

- Behavior in business and social settings is generally more formal in Japan than in the U.S.
- A visitor to a Japanese home should take off his or her shoes before entering the house. Acceptable gifts for the host include pastry or candy.
- Rarely do Japanese businesspeople use first names. Exchanging business cards is usually done very early in a meeting.
- The common form of greeting is a bow—not a handshake.
- Most people in Japan disapprove of lateness for both business and social engagements.

Exercise ❸

- Tell students to read the exercise directions silently. Ask: *What's the meaning of the word "advice"?* (*Advice* is an opinion you give someone about what he or she should do.) Ask students who often gives them advice. (parents, teachers, friends)
- Explain the task: Students will listen and number the topics in the order in which they hear them on the audio.
- Point out the example, explaining that arriving for meetings will be the first topic they will hear about on the audio.
- 🎧 Play the audio.
- Go over the answers with the class.

Answer key

1	5
3	4
2	6

Exercise ❹

- Explain the task: Students will listen again and fill in the blanks with information from the audio.
- Go over the example. Tell students to read the sentences and predict the answers.
- 🎧 Play the audio.
- Have students compare their answers with a partner's.
- Go over the answers with the class.

Answer key

1. on time	5. small gift
2. shake hands	6. take your shoes off
3. business cards	7. a suit
4. last name	

EXTENSION

- Pair students. Tell them to classify the rules of business etiquette in the United States into one of two categories: *Similar to our culture* and *Different from our culture*.
- Write the headings on the board, and have students copy them.
- Tell students to write the sentences from Exercise 4 under the two headings. Set a time limit of 2 minutes.
- After 2 minutes, discuss with the class the similarities and differences they identified.

🔘 Please go to www.longman.com/worldview for additional in-class model conversation practice and supplementary reading practice.

HOMEWORK

- 📖 Assign *Workbook* page 26, Vocabulary Exercises 1 and 2, and page 28, Listening Exercises 5 and 6.

Listening

3 🎧 Listen to a businesswoman give advice to her colleagues on living and working in the U.S. Number the topics in the order she talks about them.

__1__ arriving for meetings

____ shaking hands

____ exchanging business cards

____ visiting someone's home

____ using a person's first or last name

____ deciding what clothing to wear

4 🎧 Listen again and complete the statements about business etiquette in the U.S.

1. For business appointments, always arrive __on time__.

2. The first thing people do at meetings is _____.

3. People usually exchange _____ at some point during a meeting.

4. If it's not clear what you should call a person, use his or her _____.

5. Take flowers or a _____ when you visit someone's home.

6. Don't _____ when you enter someone's home.

7. Wear _____ to formal business meetings.

5

Grammar focus

1 Study the examples of *should* and *shouldn't* for advice.

> You **should arrive** on time.　　You **shouldn't take** your shoes off.
> **Should** we **bow**?　　Yes, you **should**. / No, you **shouldn't**.

2 Look at the examples again. Complete the rules in the chart.

should and *shouldn't* for advice
Use _____ + the base form of the verb to say that something is a good idea.
Use _____ + the base form of the verb to say that something is a bad idea.

Grammar Reference page 144

3 Complete the sentences in the quiz with *should* or *shouldn't*.

Culture Quiz

1 Should you talk about business at a meal in China?
a. Yes, you ___should___. b. No, you shouldn't.

2 Should you wear a suit and tie to meet a new client in Saudi Arabia?
a. Yes, you should. 　 b. No, you _____ .

3 _____ you give a Brazilian purple flowers?
a. Yes, you _____. It's lucky.
b. No, you shouldn't. It's unlucky.

4 When someone gives you a gift in Japan, _____ you open it . . .
a. immediately? 　 b. later?

5 In Mexico, _____ you shake hands with both men and women?
a. Yes, you should. 　 b. No, you _____.

6 _____ you use your right hand or your left hand to accept a gift in Muslim countries?
a. right 　 b. left

7 In the U.S., it is important to arrive on time. When you are invited to a friend's house, you _____ arrive more than 15 minutes late.
a. true 　 b. false

8 You _____ touch a person on the head because it is not polite. This statement is true in which country?
a. Thailand 　 b. Peru

9 You _____ have a meeting in Room 4 because it is unlucky. This statement is true in which country?
a. Mexico 　 b. China

10 In Japan, you _____ use your boss's first name because it is not polite.
a. true 　 b. false

Culture Quiz answers
1.b, 2.a, 3.b, 4.b, 5.a, 6.a, 7.a, 8.a, 9.b, 10.a

4 Take the quiz. Then check your answers.

Grammar focus

LANGUAGE NOTES

- Use *should* and *shouldn't* to give advice or talk about what is right or wrong to do.
- *Should/Shouldn't* + base form refers to the present or future activity. For example, *I should leave now. You should get a haircut soon.*
- *Should/Shouldn't* is followed by the base form of the main verb.
- *Should* goes before the subject in questions.

WARM-UP

Note: Skip this warm-up if you're doing this lesson (Lesson B) during the same class period as Lesson A.

- Books closed. Tell students they are going to listen again to the conversation between the businesswoman and her colleagues that they heard in the Listening section.
- Tell students to listen for the words that the businesswoman uses to say if an action is a good idea or a bad idea.
- 🎧 Play the audio for Lesson A, Listening, Exercise 3. (It models the grammar of the unit.)
- Ask students what word was used to say something is a good idea (*should*), and what word was used to say something is a bad idea (*shouldn't*).
- End the warm-up by asking students what advice they remember. Write some of the answers on the board.

Exercise ❶

Have students read the examples and study the bold-faced words. Tell them to pay attention to the meaning of each sentence. Ask students to notice the form of the verb that follows *should* in each of the examples. (the base form)

Exercise ❷

- Have students study the examples again.
- Tell students to read the rules in the box and to complete them with *should* or *shouldn't*.
- Have students compare their answers with a partner's.
- Go over the answers with the class.
- Ask a few questions to elicit the key points about the grammar: For example, *What form of the verb follows should/shouldn't?* (the base form) *How do you tell someone it's a bad idea to drink too much coffee?* (You shouldn't drink too much coffee.)

Answer key

should	shouldn't

Exercise ❸

- Before beginning Exercise 3, answer any questions students might have. You may also want to refer the class to the Grammar Reference for Unit 5 on page 144.
- Ask students to look at the quiz and ask: *Where might you find a culture quiz like this one?* (in a magazine)
- Explain the task: Students will complete the sentences in the quiz with *should* or *shouldn't*. Point out that they will take the quiz in the next exercise. Encourage them to concentrate on completing the sentences.
- Have students complete the exercise individually. Set a time limit of 5 minutes. Walk around the room, helping as needed.
- Have students compare their answers with a partner's.
- Go over the answers with the class.

Answer key

1. should	6. Should
2. shouldn't	7. shouldn't
3. Should; should	8. shouldn't
4. should	9. shouldn't
5. should; shouldn't	10. shouldn't

Exercise ❹

- Explain the task: Students will answer the quiz. Point out that this is meant to be a fun activity and is not a test of any kind.
- Set a time limit of 2 minutes. Have students check their answers.

EXTENSION

- Pair students. Tell students they will create a quiz about their own culture(s).
- Tell them to write three items for the quiz. Elicit examples and write them on the board.
- After a few minutes, have each pair join another pair and exchange quizzes.
- If time allows, ask a few pairs to read aloud their quiz items.

Pronunciation

> **LANGUAGE NOTE**
>
> *Should* can have either a strong or a weak pronunciation. *Shouldn't* always has a strong pronunciation. The *n* in *shouldn't* is pronounced without adding a vowel before it.

Exercise ❺

- Explain the task: Students will listen to the different pronunciations of *should* and *shouldn't*. Point out the colors representing the weak and strong pronunciations.
- 🎧 Play the audio, stopping after each expression to highlight the weak and strong pronunciations.
- Ask students to notice where the different weak and strong pronunciations are used. (*Should* has its weak pronunciation /ʃəd/ when it is used with a main verb and its strong pronunciation /ʃʊd/ when it is used at the end of a sentence.)

Exercise ❻

- Tell students that they will listen again. This time, they will listen and repeat.
- 🎧 Play the audio again, stopping after each item and having students repeat chorally.
- Ask a few individual students to repeat the sentences.

Exercise ❼

Teaching Tip! **Using pronunciation as listening practice**

Tell students to listen not only for the pronunciation of *should* and *shouldn't* but also for meaning. Exercises like this can help improve students' overall level of comprehension.

- Explain the task: Students will listen for *should* or *shouldn't* in each sentence and underline the word they hear.
- 🎧 Go over the example. Play the audio, and then stop it after the first sentence. Point out the underlined word.
- 🎧 Play the audio. If necessary, stop the audio after each sentence and play it more than once.

> **Answer key**
>
> | | | |
> |---|---|---|
> | 1. shouldn't | 3. Shouldn't | 5. Should |
> | 2. should | 4. should | |

Speaking

Exercise ❽

This exercise provides practice with *should* and *shouldn't* for giving advice. It also prepares students for Exercise 9.

- Explain the task: Students will list things people *should do* and things they *shouldn't do* while visiting their country.
- Go over the categories.
- Set a time limit of 5 minutes for students to write their notes. Walk around the room, helping as needed.

Exercise ❾

- Students work in groups of 4. Explain the task: Students will compare the pieces of advice they listed.
- Tell them to mark on their notes which of their advice is the same as another group member's (+) and which advice is different (–).
- Set a time limit of 8 minutes.
- Call on a few students to share their group's advice.

> **EXTENSION**
>
> - Students stay in the same group. Have each group make a brochure for tourists coming to their country.
> - Tell them to organize their information in two groups: (a) a list of *Do's* and (b) a list of *Don'ts*.

TRB For additional interactive grammar practice, have students do the reproducible activity for this unit in the *Teacher's Resource Book*.

Writing

Exercise ❿

- Assign the writing task for class work or homework.
- Explain the task: Students will write an email to a friend traveling to their country, giving advice about what the friend should or shouldn't do during his or her visit.
- **TRB** Optionally, give students a copy of the writing model (see the *Teacher's Resource Book*, Writing Models). Ask them to read the model and notice the vocabulary and grammar from the unit.
- If students don't have the model, write the following on the board:

  Hi, Ling!
  . . . so here's some useful advice. You should wear formal clothes to business meetings…

- Have a student read the sentences aloud. Answer any questions students might have.
- Walk around to make sure everyone understands the task.

For suggestions on how to give feedback on writing, see page xiv of this *Teacher's Edition*.

CONVERSATION TO GO

At the end of class, call on two students to role-play the conversation.

HOMEWORK

- 📖 Assign *Workbook* page 27, Grammar Exercises 3 and 4, and page 28, Pronunciation Exercises 7 and 8.
- 💿 If students do not have the *WorldView Workbook*, assign listening homework from the Student CD. Write on the board:

  Track 10
  What should a guest take to a dinner party at someone's home in the United States?

- 🎧 Tell students to listen to the audio and write the answer to the question. Have them bring their answer to the next class.

  (Possible answers: *flowers or a small gift*)

Pronunciation

5 🎧 **Listen. Notice the weak and strong pronunciations of *should* and the strong pronunciation of *shouldn't*.**

You should arrive on time.   You shouldn't take your shoes off.
Should I take a gift?   Yes, you should.
Shouldn't I wear a suit?   No, you shouldn't.

6 🎧 **Listen again and repeat.**

7 🎧 **Listen and underline the word you hear.**

1. You **should / <u>shouldn't</u>** arrive early.
2. You **should / shouldn't** ask questions.
3. **Should / Shouldn't** I use first names?
4. You **should / shouldn't** take flowers.
5. **Should / Shouldn't** I shake hands with everyone?

Speaking

8 *BEFORE YOU SPEAK.* **Some friends from another country are going to visit your country. What should they do while visiting? What shouldn't they do? Write your ideas about the topics.**

9 *GROUPS OF 4.* **Compare the advice you're going to give your friends. What advice is the same? What advice is different?**

Greeting/Saying hello
    You should . . .
    You shouldn't . . .
Giving gifts

Eating

Clothes

Other

Writing

10 **Write an email to a friend who is going to visit your country. Give advice about what he or she should and shouldn't do during the trip.**

CONVERSATION TO GO

A: Should I bow when I meet someone?
B: No, you shouldn't. You should shake hands.

Party time!

Vocabulary Planning parties
Grammar Expressions for making suggestions
Speaking Making suggestions

Lesson A

Getting started

1 *PAIRS.* **Look at the photos. In which photo can you see . . .**

1. a birthday party? ___
2. a costume party? ___
3. a going-away party? ___

2 *PAIRS.* **Discuss the questions.**

Do you like parties?

What is your favorite kind of party?

Have you ever been to a going-away party or a costume party?

How do you usually celebrate your birthday?

A

B

C

Party time!

OBJECTIVES

Students will:

- activate vocabulary related to planning and paying for parties
- do listening, speaking, and writing tasks related to planning parties and making suggestions
- focus on using expressions for making suggestions
- practice putting stress on the focus word in sentences

WARM-UP: A GOOD PARTY

Groups of 3. Students talk about what makes a good party.

- Tell students that this unit is about planning parties. Point out that the title of the unit, "Party time!," is an expression often used to start a party.
- Ask students to talk about what makes a good party. Model the activity by asking, *What do you need for a good party?* Elicit a few ideas and write them on the board (for example, *nice people, delicious food, good music*).
- Divide the class into groups of 3. Tell each group to brainstorm as many ideas as possible for what is necessary for a good party. Set a time limit of 3 minutes.
- After 3 minutes, call on a few students to give their ideas. Add them to the list on the board.
- Find out how many ideas each group came up with. Ask: *Who had the most ideas?*

Getting started

CULTURE NOTES

- Going-away parties are given for people who are moving away for a long time or permanently. Sometimes people also throw a party for friends who are going away on a long trip.
- Costume parties are most commonly given on Halloween. On this holiday, celebrated on October 31 in North America and other places, people—especially children—wear costumes, play tricks, and walk from house to house in order to get candy. Adult costume parties are also common as part of New Year's celebrations.
- People of all ages have birthday parties. Guests usually bring a gift for the birthday person. There is usually a cake with birthday candles, and the birthday person makes a wish as he or she blows out the candles.

Exercise ❶

- Explain the task: Students will look at the photos and decide which kind of party is shown in each one.
- Pair students and set a time limit of 1 minute.
- Go over the answers with the class.

Answer key

1. C   2. A   3. B

Exercise ❷

- Explain the task: Students will work with a partner to discuss their answers to the questions. You may want to model the activity, telling the class your answer to one of the questions. (For example, *I love parties. My favorite kinds are birthday parties.*) Then ask a volunteer to give an answer to the same or another question.
- Pair students and set a time limit of 5 minutes. While students are working, walk around the room, helping as needed.
- After 5 minutes, call on a few students to report their answers.

OPTION: VOCABULARY PREVIEW

Ask questions like the ones below to pre-teach the meanings of the verbs. Begin with words that students are likely to know.

- *What do you buy every day?*
- *How much does a cup of coffee at ___ (a place all students know) cost?*
- *How much would you pay for a pair of sneakers?*
- *Do you spend a lot of money on CDs?*
- *Do you buy or rent DVDs/videos?*
- *What's one thing you want, but you can't afford?*

LANGUAGE NOTE

These are prepositions commonly used with some of the verbs:

- *buy* something *for* someone
- *spend* money *on* something
- *pay for* something (*by* credit card / *with* cash)

Exercise ❸

- Tell students to look at the verbs in the *Student Book* and ask: *What are we usually talking about when we use these verbs?* (money)
- Explain the task: Students will fill in the blanks with words from the box. They will use each word twice. Go over the example.
- Have students complete the exercise individually. Set a time limit of 3 minutes.
- Have students compare their answers with a partner's.
- Go over the answers with the class.

Answer key

1. cost	3. afford	5. spend
cost	afford	spend
2. buy	4. pay	6. rent
buy	pay	rent

EXTENSION

- To reinforce the vocabulary and increase fluency, do a speed drill with a beanbag or any soft ball.
- Toss the object to a student and say one of the verbs, such as the verb *afford*, in Exercise 3. The student will respond with a sentence that uses that verb. (For example, *I can't afford to buy a new car right now.*)
- Do the same with all of the verbs, giving as many students as possible a chance to participate.

Exercise ❹

- **Pairs**. Explain the task: Students will use three of the verbs from Exercise 3 to make up sentences about themselves or other people.
- Pair students and set a time limit of 3 minutes.
- Call on a few students to report one sentence their partners said.

Listening

CULTURE NOTES

- In North America, many companies have parties for their employees. Holiday parties are often held near the end of the year—often around Christmas and New Year's. The holiday party may be at the company or at a restaurant or hotel. Employees can usually bring spouses or dates to the party, especially if it is held outside the office.
- Retirement or going-away parties are often given to honor an employee who is leaving the company. Very often the other employees contribute money for a gift.
- Some companies have yearly family outings or picnics that include employees' children as well as their spouses.

Exercise ❺

- Tell students to look at the photo. Have them guess who the people are and what they're doing.
- Have students read the directions. Explain the task: Students will listen and will put a check mark before the things the party planner and the client talk about.
- 🎧 Play the audio.
- Have students compare their answers with a partner's.
- 🎧 Go over the answers with the class. If needed, play the audio again.

Answer key

place, music, food

Exercise ❻

- Tell students to look at the sentences and predict the answers. Answer any questions students may have about vocabulary. If necessary, explain that *DJ* is short for *disk jockey*: someone whose job is to play the music on a radio show or at a party or club.
- Explain the task: Students will listen to the audio again and will underline the correct answers.
- 🎧 Play the audio.
- Have students compare their answers with a partner's.
- Go over the answers with the class.

Answer key

1. the office   2. a DJ   3. dessert

◎ Please go to www.longman.com/worldview for additional in-class model conversation practice and supplementary reading practice.

HOMEWORK

- 📖 Assign *Workbook* page 29, Vocabulary Exercises 1 and 2, and page 31, Listening Exercises 5 and 6.

3 Complete the pairs of sentences with words from the box.

afford	buy	~~cost~~	pay	rent	spend

1. A birthday cake can __cost__ about $25.
   The gifts for Sue and Ron's going-away party __cost__ a lot.

2. I'm going to _____ a new dress for the party.
   I want to _____ a gift for you.

3. Can you _____ that suit? It's very expensive.
   I can't _____ a fancy restaurant. I don't have much money.

4. John is going to _____ for dinner on your birthday.
   He'll _____ by credit card.

5. I usually _____ a lot of money on birthday cards.
   We're going to _____ $300 on the party.

6. I want to _____ a car for the weekend.
   He's going to _____ a ballroom at a hotel for the party.

4 *PAIRS.* Take turns saying three sentences about yourself or people you know. Use the verbs from Exercise 3.

Listening

5 Listen to a professional party planner talking with a client from an advertising company. They are discussing the company's yearly office party. Check (✓) the things they talk about.

Party Planners, Etc.

- ○ date of the party
- ✓ place
- ○ gifts
- ○ number of guests
- ○ music
- ○ food
- ○ parking

6 Listen again and underline the correct information.

1. The party is going to be at **a hotel** / **the office**.
2. They're going to have **a band** / **a DJ**.
3. They're going to serve **dessert** / **dinner**.

6

Grammar focus

1 **Study the examples. Notice the ways to make suggestions.**

> **How about** looking at how much we spent last year?
> **Why don't** we rent the room at the Sheraton again?
> **Let's (not)** have it at the office.
> **Maybe** you **could** get a DJ this time.

2 **Look at the examples again. Complete the rules in the chart.**

Why don't/How about/Let's (not)/Maybe . . . could for suggestions
Use _____ + verb + *-ing*.
Use _____ + subject + *could* + the base form of the verb.
Use _____ + subject + the base form of the verb.
Use _____ + the base form of the verb.

> *Grammar Reference page 144*

3 **Complete the conversation with the expressions in the box.**

Why don't	How about	Let's (not)	Maybe . . . could

A: **(1)** _____Let's_____ have a party next weekend!

B: Good idea. **(2)** _____ getting a band?

A: I don't know. That's expensive. **(3)** _____ we get a DJ instead?

B: But my brother is in a band. **(4)** _____ we _____
   ask them to play for free?

A: OK. Now, what about the food? **(5)** _____ cooking something?

B: Cooking? That's too much work! **(6)** _____ just have
   sandwiches and chips.

A: **(7)** _____ we _____ have cheese and crackers, too.

B: That sounds fine, but **(8)** _____ spend too much money on food.

A: Right. **(9)** _____ you buy the food? **(10)**_____ you
   (11) _____ get everything at SuperSavers. It's cheaper there.

Grammar focus

LANGUAGE NOTES

There are several language patterns used to make suggestions.

- *How about* + verb + *-ing*

    A suggestion using "How about" is phrased as a question. For example, *How about having a party?*

- *Why don't* + subject + the base form of the verb

    A suggestion with "Why don't" is also phrased as a question. *Why don't* is often followed by *I* (for suggestions that include only the speaker); *we* (for suggestions that include the speaker and another person); or *you* (for giving advice to another person). For example, *Why don't we have a party?/Why don't you call your brother?*

- *Let's* + the base form of the verb

    Use "Let's" for suggestions that include the speaker and another person. For example, *Let's have a party.*

- *Maybe* + subject + *could* + the base form of the verb

    For example, *Maybe you could call your brother.*

WARM-UP

Note: Skip this warm-up if you're doing this lesson (Lesson B) during the same class period as Lesson A.

- Books closed. Tell students they are going to listen again to the conversation between the party planner and the client that they heard in the Listening section.
- Tell them to focus on the party planner's role: Is she telling the client what to do or is she offering ideas?
- 🎧 Play the audio for Lesson A, Listening, Exercise 5 again. (It models the grammar of the unit.)
- Ask students about the party planner's role: *Is the party planner telling the client what to do or is she offering ideas?* (She's offering ideas, or making suggestions.)

Exercise ❶

- Have students look at the examples and study the bold-faced words.
- Tell students to focus on the first two examples. Ask: *What kinds of structures are the first two examples?* (questions) *What follows the bold-faced words in each example?* (In the first example, verb + *-ing* follows *How about*; in the second example, a pronoun + base form follows *Why don't*.)
- Ask students to look at the other two examples in the box. Elicit that both *Let's (not)* and *Maybe . . . could* are both followed by the base form of the main verb. Ask: *What kinds of sentences are the last two examples—statements or questions?* (statements)

Exercise ❷

- Have students study the examples again.
- Tell them to read and complete the rules in the chart.
- Have students compare their answers with a partner's.
- Go over the answers with the class.
- Ask a few questions to elicit the key points about the grammar: For example, *What form of the verb do we use after* How about? (verb + *-ing*) *What comes between* Maybe *and* could? (a subject/a pronoun)

Answer key

How about	Maybe	Why don't	Let's (not)

Exercise ❸

- Before beginning Exercise 3, answer any questions students might have. You may also want to refer the class to the Grammar Reference for Unit 6 on page 144.
- Set the context of the conversation by directing students' attention to the picture and asking, *Where do you think the woman and the man are?* (at a party)
- Explain the task: Students will complete the conversation with the expressions in the box. Go over the example.
- Remind students to look at the rules in the chart in Exercise 2 if necessary.
- Have students complete the exercise individually. Set a time limit of 5 minutes. Walk around the room, helping as needed.
- Have students compare their answers with a partner's.
- Go over the answers with the class.

Answer key

A: 1. Let's	B: 6. Let's
B: 2. How about	A: 7. Maybe . . . could
A: 3. Why don't	B: 8. let's not
B: 4. Maybe . . . could	A: 9. Why don't
A: 5. How about	B: 10. Maybe . . . could

EXTENSION

- Pair students. Have them practice the conversation.
- If time allows, have them switch roles.

Pronunciation

> ### LANGUAGE NOTES
>
> - The focus word is the word in a sentence that stands out the most. The voice goes either up or down in pitch to emphasize the focus word. The vowel is also pronounced long and clear, as in other stressed words.
> - The focus word is typically the last content word—the noun, verb, adjective, or adverb—in a sentence. However, unless the information about time is especially important in the sentence, expressions of time are not usually focus words even though they use content words.
> - During a conversation, the focus often moves to a different part of the sentence to highlight new information or to make a contrast. For example,
>
>   A: *Maybe we could order* **pizza**?
>   B: *I don't* **like** *pizza.*
>
>   Notice that words that are repeated are usually not stressed.

Exercise ❹

- Tell students they are going to listen to a conversation. Ask them to notice the way the most important word, or the focus word, in each sentence stands out.

- 🎧 Play the audio.

- Point out the features that make the focus word stand out: (1) The word is stressed, and the vowel is pronounced long and clear, and (2) the voice changes pitch on this word.

- Explain that the focus word gives new information. A word that gives old information (like the repeated word *pizza* in the example above) is not usually stressed.

Exercise ❺

- Explain the task: Students will listen to the audio again and repeat each line chorally. Use gestures to show how the intonation goes up on the focus word and then falls.

- 🎧 Play the audio. Have students listen and repeat each line chorally. Check their intonation.

- Encourage students to use a wide voice range and to start each sentence at a high pitch. Have students exaggerate, if necessary.

Speaking

Exercise ❻

This exercise provides practice with expressions for making suggestions.

- Divide the class into groups of 4. Tell each group they are going to plan a party.

- Explain the task: Students will choose the purpose of their party and then decide how to spend the $500 budget.

- Tell students to look at the costs on page 140 of the *Student Book*.

- Set a time limit of 10 minutes. Walk around the room, helping as needed.

Exercise ❼

Call on a representative from each group to tell the class the type of party they chose and the plans they made for how to spend the money in their budget.

EXTENSION

- Have students remain in their groups. Tell each group to make large-scale versions of a party invitation. The invitation should include time, place, type of party, and other party needs such as music, food, etc. Encourage them to make the party sound fun.

- Have each group draw the invitation on the board or on a large piece of paper that they can tape to the wall.

TRB For additional interactive grammar practice, have students do the reproducible activity for this unit in the *Teacher's Resource Book*.

Writing

Exercise ❽

- Assign the writing task for class work or homework.

- Explain the task: Students will reply to email messages.

- Brainstorm a few ideas for the first writer's problem.

- **TRB** Optionally, give students a copy of the writing model (see the *Teacher's Resource Book*, Writing Models). Ask them to read the model and notice the vocabulary and grammar from the unit.

- If students don't have the model, write the following on the board:

  Why don't you have a costume party? Costume parties are always a lot of fun! Or if you can afford it, hire a band. Live music always makes a party exciting, . . .

- Have a student read the sentences aloud. Answer any questions students might have.

- Walk around to make sure everyone understands the task.

For suggestions on how to give feedback on writing, see page xiv of this *Teacher's Edition*.

CONVERSATION TO GO

At the end of the class, call on two students to role-play the conversation.

HOMEWORK

- 📖 Assign *Workbook* page 30, Grammar Exercises 3 and 4, and page 31, Pronunciation Exercises 7 and 8.

- 🔊 If students do not have the *WorldView Workbook*, assign listening homework from the Student CD. Write on the board:

  Track 13
  Write two differences between last year's party and the party they're planning for this year.

- 🎧 Tell students to listen to the audio and write the answer for the exercise. Have them bring their answer to the next class.

  (Answer: *Last year the party was at a hotel. This year it's going to be in the office. Last year they had a band. This year they're going to have a DJ.*)

Pronunciation

4 🎧 **Listen. Notice the way the focus word (the most important word) in each sentence stands out from the other words.**

A: Let's have a **par**ty next weekend.

B: Good i**dea**. Why don't we get a **band**?

A: We can't af**ford** it. How about getting a **DJ**?

B: **O**K. What about **food**?

A: Maybe we could order **pizza**.

B: I don't **like** pizza. Why don't we just have **snacks**?

5 🎧 **Listen again and repeat.**

Speaking

6 *GROUPS OF 4.* **Your group is going to work together to plan a party. First, choose the purpose of the party.**

- Surprise birthday party for (name)
- End-of-the-year party
- Other: _____

Now think about your budget. You have $500. Look at the costs on page 140. Make suggestions. Decide together how you will spend the money.

A: *Let's have the party at a hotel.*
B: *Why don't we have it at the office? We can save $150.*

7 **Tell the class about your group's party plans.**

Writing

8 **You are a party planner for a company called Parties Unlimited. People write to you for advice on giving parties. Read the email messages on page 136 and write replies to each one. Use** *maybe you could, why don't you,* **and** *how about.*

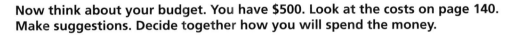

CONVERSATION TO GO

A: It's your birthday. **Let's** have a party!
B: I'd rather get a gift!

UNIT 7

First impressions

Vocabulary Words to describe physical appearance
Grammar *be* and *have* with descriptions
Speaking Describing people

Getting started

1 Write the descriptions in the box next to the correct words in the word webs.

average height	average weight	bald	beard	curly
elderly	heavy	middle-aged	mustache	short
sideburns	slim	straight	tall	~~young~~

young

age

weight

height

hair

2 *PAIRS.* **Look at the photos. Take turns using the words from Exercise 1 to describe someone in the pictures. Your partner guesses which person you are describing.**

A: *Tall and slim.*
B: *Picture A.*
A: *Yes!*

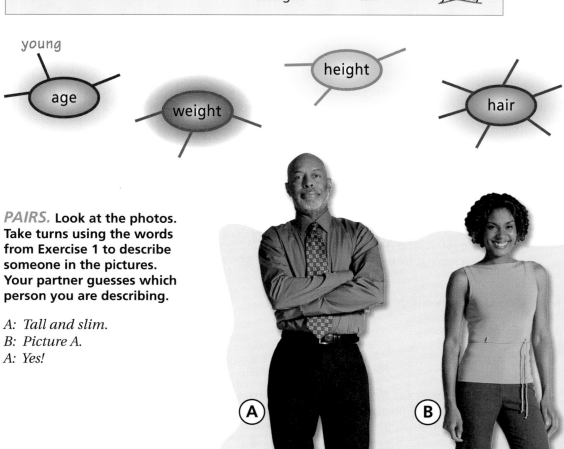

Ⓐ   Ⓑ

First impressions

OBJECTIVES

Students will:

- activate vocabulary related to physical appearance
- do listening, speaking, and writing tasks related to describing people
- focus on using *be* and *have* with descriptions
- practice weak and strong pronunciations of *and* and *or*

WARM-UP: WHO WAS IT?

Groups of 3. Students take turns telling each other about someone who made a good or a bad impression on them.

- Tell students that this unit is about physical appearances. Explain that the title of the unit, "First impressions," refers to our reaction to people, places, or things when we first see them.
- Divide the class into groups of 3. Tell each group to think about someone who made a very good or a very bad first impression on them and the reason.
- Model the activity by giving a personal example. (For example, *My husband made a very good first impression on me because he was polite and friendly.*)
- Set a time limit of 5 minutes. Each person must say at least one sentence about someone who made a good or a bad impression on them.
- Call on a few students to tell the class what one of their group members said.

Getting started

OPTION: VOCABULARY PREVIEW

If needed, write the physical descriptions in Getting started on the board. Form teams of 4. Tell students you are going to call out names or show pictures of local and international celebrities all students know. Each team will write as many physical descriptions as they can. For example, show a picture of Tiger Woods. Give students 2 minutes to write adjectives describing Tiger Woods (*short hair, curly black hair, slim, young*, etc.). Have each team read aloud their descriptions. Give 5 points to the team with more than four descriptions for a celebrity, 3 points to the team that has at least three descriptions, and 1 point to the team with at least two descriptions. The team with the most points wins.

Exercise ❶

- Direct students' attention to the word webs in the *Student Book*. Make sure everyone understands the categories (*age, height, weight, hair*).
- Explain the task: Students will look at the words in the box and will write each word next to the correct category. Go over the example.
- Have students work individually to complete the exercise. Set a time limit of 3 minutes. While students are working, walk around the room, helping as needed.
- Have students compare their answers with a partner's.
- Go over the answers with the class.

Answer key

Age: young, middle-aged, elderly
Height: short, average height, tall
Weight: slim, average weight, heavy
Hair: straight, curly, bald, mustache, beard, sideburns

EXTENSION

Reinforce the vocabulary by having students put the words for age, height, and weight in ascending order. (See the Answer key above.)

Exercise ❷

- Have students look at the photos.
- Explain the task: Students work in pairs to talk about the pictures. One partner describes one of the people in the pictures and the other guesses the person described. They will take turns describing and guessing.
- Go over the example. Remind students to use a variety of words in their descriptions. Tell them they don't need to make complete sentences, although they can if they want to.
- Pair students and set a time limit of 2 minutes. Walk around the room, helping as needed.
- Call on a few students to describe one of the people in the pictures. Have the rest of the class guess who is being described.

Listening

Exercise ❸

- Have students look at the pictures. Elicit words and phrases from Exercise 1 to describe each of the four people.
- Explain the task: Students will listen to a conversation and identify the people the two speakers are describing. They check the box next to the picture that matches each description.
- 🎧 Play the audio.
- Have students compare their answers with a partner's.
- Go over the answers with the class.

Answer key

Maurice: b; Julia: b

Exercise ❹

 **Teaching Tip!** Listening for details

It may be helpful to point out that this task requires students to listen for information that is very different from that in Exercise 3. Having students read the items first helps them focus on the details they need to understand in order to answer the questions.

- Explain the task: Students will listen to the conversation again and will circle the answers that correctly complete the sentences.

- Have students read the sentences before listening again. This will help them focus their listening because they will know what information to listen for.
- 🎧 Play the audio.
- Have students compare their answers with a partner's.
- Go over the answers with the class.

Answer key

1. b   2. b   3. a

🌐 Please go to www.longman.com/worldview for additional in-class model conversation practice and supplementary reading practice.

HOMEWORK

- 📖 Assign *Workbook* page 32, Vocabulary Exercises 1 and 2, and page 34, Listening Exercises 5 and 6.

Listening

3 🎧 **Listen to the conversation between two women. They're talking about two friends, Maurice and Julia. Check (✓) the pictures of Maurice and Julia.**

Maurice

Julia

a. ☐   b. ☐   a. ☐   b. ☐

4 🎧 **Listen again and circle the letter of the correct answer.**

1. Maurice and Amy know each other because they ____.
   a. work in the same office
   b. are in the same English class
   c. met at a party

2. Maurice wants Cristina's phone number because he wants to ____.
   a. study English with her
   b. ask her on a date
   c. have coffee with her

3. Amy ____ give Cristina's phone number to Maurice.
   a. is going to
   b. isn't going to
   c. can't

Grammar focus

1 **Study the examples of *be* and *have* for descriptions.**

He**'s** in his 20s, probably about 28.	She **has** long, straight hair.
She**'s** average height.	He **has** hazel eyes.
He**'s** quite slim.	He **doesn't have** a mustache or beard.

2 **Look at the examples again. Circle the correct verb to complete the rules in the chart.**

be/have with descriptions
Use *be* / *have* to talk about a person's age, height, and weight.
Use *be* / *have* to talk about a person's hair and eyes.
Note the following exception: *He is bald*.

Grammar Reference page 144

3 **Complete the descriptions with the correct forms of *be* or *have*. You can use contractions.**

My friend Judy and I (1) _____are_____ both 21 years old,

but she and I look completely different. I (2) _____

short, and she (3) _____ tall. I (4) _____ a little

heavy, and she (5) _____ average weight.

I (6) _____ long, curly blond hair, and she

(7) _____ long, straight black hair.

My friends Tony and Tom are identical twins. They look

exactly alike. They (8) _____ about 30. They

(9) _____ black hair and brown eyes. They

(10) _____ tall, and they (11) _____ slim.

 The only way I can tell them apart is this:

Tony (12) _____ a mustache, and Tom

(13) _____(not) one.

Grammar focus

LANGUAGE NOTES

- *Be* and *have* are the most common verbs used in descriptions, but they are not used interchangeably.
- Use *be* to talk about age, weight, and height. Use *have* to describe hair and eyes.
- In descriptions, a common pattern is *be* + adjective. For example, *He's handsome, and she's very pretty. They're both young.*
- For descriptions with *have* as the verb, the pattern is often *have* + noun phrase, which may include an adjective. For example, *He has brown hair and hazel eyes.*

WARM-UP

Note: Skip this warm-up if you're doing this lesson (Lesson B) during the same class period as Lesson A.

- Books closed. Tell students that they are going to listen to the conversation between the two friends that they heard in the Listening section.
- Refer to the Tapescript on page T158. On the board, write a few of the key words and phrases from the descriptions in the conversation such as *tall, blond hair, hazel eyes.* Tell students to copy the words and phrases.
- Explain the task: Students will listen to the audio. Next to the words and phrases from the conversation, they will write either *is* or *has*—depending on what they hear.
- 🎧 Play the audio for Lesson A, Listening, Exercise 3. (It models the grammar of the unit.)
- Point to the words and phrases on the board. Tell students to call out the verb they heard for each of the descriptions.

Exercise ❶

- Have students look at the examples and study the bold-faced forms of *be* and *have*.
- Ask students to focus on the sentences in the left-hand column. Elicit from students that the *'s* is the contracted form of the third person singular form of the verb *be*.
- Tell students to look closely at the examples in the right-hand column. Elicit what each description refers to. If necessary, remind students of the categories in Exercise 1 in Lesson A.

Exercise ❷

- Have students study the examples again.
- Tell students to circle the correct verbs to complete the rules in the chart.
- Have students compare their answers with a partner.
- Go over the answers with the class.
- Ask a few questions to elicit the key points about the grammar: For example, *Which verb do we use to talk about age—be or have?* (be) *Which verb do we use to talk about hair?* (have) *How do we describe a man with no hair?* (He's bald.)

Answer key

be   have

Exercise ❸

- Before beginning Exercise 3, answer any questions students might have. You may also want to refer the class to the Grammar Reference for Unit 7 on page 144.
- Explain the task: Students will complete the descriptions with the correct forms of the verbs *be* or *have*. Go over the example.
- Have students complete the exercise individually. Set a time limit of 3 minutes. Walk around the room, helping as needed.
- Have students compare their answers with a partner's.
- Go over the answers with the class.

Answer key

1. are	6. have	11. are / 're
2. am / 'm	7. has	12. has
3. is / 's	8. are / 're	13. doesn't have
4. am / 'm	9. have	
5. is / 's	10. are / 're	

EXTENSION

- Pair students. Have each pair write sentences comparing themselves.
- Tell them to use the descriptions in Exercise 3 as a model. Set a time limit of 2 to 3 minutes.
- After 2 or 3 minutes, call on a few students to read their descriptions aloud.

Pronunciation

> ### LANGUAGE NOTES
> - The words *and* and *or* are usually unstressed and pronounced with their weak forms.
> - After a /t/ or /d/ sound, the weak form of *and* can also be pronounced as a syllabic consonant /n/, with no vowel sound at all. For example, *He has a beard and* (/n/) *mustache.*

Exercise ❹
- Tell students that they will listen to sentences using *and* and *or*.
- 🎧 Play the audio. Ask students to notice the short, weak pronunciation of the words *and* and *or*.
- Contrast the strong and weak pronunciations of *and* and *or* by saying the words first by themselves and then in phrases (for example, *tall and slim; not tall or slim*). Point out the silent *d* in *and*.

Exercise ❺
- Tell students they will listen again to the audio. This time, they will listen and repeat.
- 🎧 Play the audio, stopping after each item to allow students to repeat chorally. Encourage students to link *and* and *or* to the words around them.
- If students have difficulty with the longer sentences, break the sentences down into more manageable parts, gradually adding parts until the sentence is built up again. For example, *brown eyes—long black hair—long black hair and brown eyes—She has long black hair and brown eyes.*
- Call on a few individual students to repeat the sentences. Check their pronunciation.

Speaking

Exercise ❻
Pairs. Both Exercises 6 and 7 provide practice with using *be* and *have* for descriptions.

- Explain the task: One of the students in each pair will imagine that they are going to the airport to meet people they don't know. They must listen to the descriptions their partner gives and find the people in the picture.
- Tell Student A to turn to page 137 and Student B to look at the picture in the book. They should not look at each other's pages. Student A will follow the directions on page 137; Student B will identify the people in the picture. As each person is described, B should show Student A the picture of the person to confirm that his or her answer is correct.
- Pair students. Designate one Student A and the other Student B. Set a time limit of 5 minutes. Walk around the room, helping as needed.
- After 5 minutes, lead a class discussion about the activity. Ask: *Were Student A's descriptions clear and accurate? Was Student B able to identify the people?*

Exercise ❼
- Have the partners switch roles. Tell Student B to turn to page 139 and Student A to look at the picture in the book. Student B will follow the directions on page 139; Student A will identify the people in the picture.
- Set a time limit of 5 minutes.
- Ask the class which three people were described.

EXTENSION
- Divide the class in small groups. Have students think of a famous person.
- Have the members of the group take turns describing someone and guessing who the person is.

TRB For additional interactive grammar practice, have students do the reproducible activity for this unit in the *Teacher's Resource Book.*

Writing

Exercise ❽
- Assign the writing task for class work or homework.
- Explain the task: Students will write a paragraph describing someone.
- Brainstorm ideas that students might use for their descriptions.
- **TRB** Optionally, give students a copy of the writing model (see the *Teacher's Resource Book,* Writing Models). Ask them to read the model and notice the vocabulary and grammar from the unit.
- If students don't have the model, write the following on the board:

  My friend Jeremy is in his early 20s. He wants to be an actor, but he's not tall or slim like many actors are.

- Have a student read the sentences aloud. Answer any questions students might have.
- Walk around to make sure everyone understands the task.

For suggestions on how to give feedback on writing, see page xiv of this *Teacher's Edition.*

CONVERSATION TO GO
At the end of class, call on two students to role-play the conversation.

HOMEWORK
- 📖 Assign *Workbook* page 33, Grammar Exercises 3 and 4, and page 34, Pronunciation Exercises 7 and 8.
- 💿 If students do not have the *WorldView Workbook,* assign listening homework from the Student CD. Write on the board:

  Track 15
  Write a description of Maurice.

- 🎧 Tell students to listen to the audio and write the answer for the exercise. Have them bring their answer to the next class.

  (Answer: *He's tall, and he has curly brown hair and brown eyes. He's quite slim and very athletic-looking. He's in his late twenties.*)

Pronunciation

4 🎧 **Listen. Notice the weak pronunciations of *and* and *or*.**

She's tall and slim.

He's average height and has black hair.

He has curly brown hair and hazel eyes.

She has long black hair and brown eyes.

I'm not tall or slim.

He isn't short or heavy.

He doesn't have a beard or mustache.

She doesn't have blond hair or blue eyes.

5 🎧 **Listen again and repeat.**

Speaking

6 *PAIRS.* **You're going to the airport to meet your partner's visitors. Take turns describing the people and finding them in the picture.**

Student A, look at page 137. Student B, look at the picture on the left. Find each person that your partner describes. Did you find the right person? Check with your partner.

A: My colleague, Sandra Vazquez, is going to arrive on Saturday. Can you meet her at the airport?

B: Sure. What does she look like?

A: She . . .

7 **Now switch roles. Student B, look at page 139.**

Writing

8 Write a paragraph describing someone's physical appearance. Write about a family member, a friend, or a famous person. Use *be* and *have*.

CONVERSATION TO GO

A: What does she look like?

B: She's tall and slim. She has curly brown hair and brown eyes.

At the movies

Vocabulary Words related to the movies
Grammar *say* and *tell*
Speaking Talking about movies

Lesson A

Getting started

1 **Match the quotes with the photos.**

1. ____ "The best romantic movie in the history of film. A classic black-and-white movie."

2. ____ "Another fast and exciting action movie."

3. ____ "Best science fiction film ever."

4. ____ "It makes everyone laugh. A comedy for the entire family."

2 **In which photo(s) can you see . . .**

1. an actor?   _____

2. an actress?   _____

3. special effects?   _____

4. costumes?   _____

3 *PAIRS.* **Discuss the questions.**

What kinds of movies do you like?
Who is your favorite actor or actress?
What movies are playing now in movie theaters?
Which ones do you want to see? Why?

At the movies

OBJECTIVES

Students will:

- activate vocabulary related to movies
- do reading, speaking, and writing tasks related to movies
- focus on using *say* and *tell*
- practice pronouncing consonant sounds

WARM-UP: HANGMAN

- Think of a well-known movie in English that all the students will know. Play "Hangman" on the board with the title of the film (for example, *Charlie's Angels*). Write short lines on the board to represent each letter of the movie's title. (For example, you need to write fourteen short lines to represent the fourteen letters in the title *Charlie's Angels*.)
- Ask students to guess a letter that appears in the title. If a student guesses correctly, write the letter in. For example: C _ _ r _ _ _ ' _   _ n _ _ l s.
- If a student chooses a letter that doesn't appear in the name, write the letter on the board and draw one part of the "hangman." If the students make twelve incorrect guesses, the "hangman" is completed and you win. For example, *x t y o j z v f d u b m*.

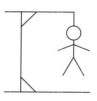

Getting started

BACKGROUND INFORMATION

Picture A: In *The Nutty Professor* (1996) and *The Nutty Professor II* (2000), Eddie Murphy starred as a shy Professor Klump, who invented a fat gene formula. Every time he drinks the formula he is transformed into an overconfident Casanova, Buddy Love.

Picture B: In 1962, Sean Connery starred as the first James Bond in the movie *Dr. No* and became identified with the fictional British agent for many years.

Picture C: *Casablanca* (1942), starring Ingrid Bergman and Humphrey Bogart, is the classic black-and-white romantic story of two men fighting for the same woman's love. *Casablanca* is set in Morocco during World War II.

Picture D: *Star Wars* (1977) is one of the most popular science fiction films ever. It was famous for its advanced use of special effects and won six Academy Awards.

OPTION: VOCABULARY PREVIEW

Have students brainstorm titles of movies that are currently popular. Write the titles on the board. Make sure students give titles for each of the four types of movies. Then for each title, ask what kind of movie it is.

Exercise ❶

- Point to each picture and ask: *What movie do you think does this picture comes from? How many have seen or are familiar with (title of movie)?*
- Explain the task: Students will match the quotes with the photos by writing the letter of the picture.
- Have students work individually to complete the exercise. Set a time limit of 1 minute.
- Go over the answers with the class.

Answer key			
1. C	2. B	3. D	4. A

Exercise ❷

- Explain the task: Students will choose the photos that answer the questions. Point out that more than one photo may answer a question.
- If necessary, demonstrate the task by asking students, *In which photo or photos can you see an actor?* Have students call out the answers and write them on the board.
- Set a time limit of 2 minutes.
- Go over the answers with the class.

Answer key			
1. A, B, C, D	2. C	3. B, D	4. B, D

Exercise ❸

- Pair students. Tell them to take turns asking and answering the questions. Encourage them to use the vocabulary from Exercises 1 and 2.
- Set a time limit of 3 minutes. While students are working, walk around the room, helping as needed.
- Call on a few students to report to the class their answers to the questions.

EXTENSION

- Divide the class into small groups.
- Write on the board the names of several movies that are now playing in theaters.
- Tell them to choose the movie they will go to as a group and to give reasons for their choice. Set a time limit of 2 minutes for the discussion.
- After 2 minutes, call on a representative from each group to report on the group's decision.

Reading

Exercise 4

- Set the context by asking, *What type of reading is this?* (It's a magazine article.) *What is it about?* (It's about movies.)
- Explain the task: Students will read the article and will circle the correct answers. Encourage students to read the entire article before answering the questions.
- Set a time limit of 5 minutes. Walk around the room, helping as needed.
- Have students compare answers with a partner's.
- Go over the answers with the class.

Answer key

1. a	3. b	5. b
2. b	4. b	6. a

FYI

Adjectives that end in *-ing* and *-ed* are called participial adjectives because they are derived from the present and past participles of verbs. Adjectives ending in *-ing* often describe a quality, whereas those ending in *-ed* often describe an emotion.

Exercise 5

- Explain the task: Students will reread the article and will check the adjectives the "readers" used to describe things about the three movies. Give an example if necessary.

- Have students read the list of adjectives so they know what to look for when reading the article again.
- Set a time limit of 5 minutes. Walk around the room, helping as needed.
- Have students compare their answers with a partner's.
- Go over the answers with the class.

Answer key

Star Wars: amazing, fantastic, interesting
Dr. No: excellent, slow
Casablanca: good, romantic

EXTENSION

- Tell students to think of bad movies they have seen.
- Elicit examples of negative adjectives that could be used to describe movies (for example, *bad, terrible, awful, boring, dumb, unoriginal, confusing*) and write them on the board.
- Divide the class into small groups. Tell the members of each group to take turns saying at least one sentence about a bad movie they have seen. If necessary, model the activity by giving a personal example (*I saw the new* Terminator *movie last week. I thought it was terrible!*).

Please go to www.longman.com/worldview for additional in-class model conversation practice.

HOMEWORK

- Assign *Workbook* page 35, Vocabulary Exercises 1 and 2, and page 37, Listening Exercises 5 and 6.

Reading

4 Read the article about memorable moments in film history. Then circle the letter of the correct answer.

1. Which movie does Tomás like?
   a. *Star Wars*　　　b. *Casablanca*
2. Why does he like it?
   a. the actors　　　b. the special effects
3. Which movie does Reiko like?
   a. *Star Wars*　　　b. *Dr. No*
4. Why does she like it?
   a. the scenery　　　b. the actor
5. Which movie does Mariana like?
   a. *Dr. No*　　　b. *Casablanca*
6. Why does she like it?
   a. the story　　　b. the director

"In your opinion, what are the most memorable movies in the history of film?"
That's the question we asked our readers.

"I think the first *Star Wars* movie is the best science fiction film. I didn't like the new ones very much, but the original *Star Wars* is a fantastic movie. The special effects are amazing, and the story is interesting. I can't remember the names of the actors, but I love the scene where Luke fights Darth Vader." **Tomás, Mexico**

"I love James Bond movies, and my favorite is *Dr. No*. It was the first 007 movie, and although the beginning is slow, the ending is excellent. Sean Connery was the best actor who played James Bond, and he always will be." **Reiko, Japan**

"One of my favorite movies is *Casablanca*—I love old, romantic films. I think the story and the music are really good. Black-and-white films are my favorites." **Mariana, Brazil**

5 Read the article again and check (✓) the adjective(s) used to describe things about each movie.

	Star Wars	Dr. No	Casablanca
amazing			
excellent			
fantastic	✓		
good			
interesting			
romantic			
slow			

Grammar focus

1 **Study the examples with *say* and *tell*. Underline the object.**

> Tomás **said** (that) he **really** liked *Star Wars*.
> He **told us** (that) he **loved** the special effects.
> Mariana **told me** (that) she **loved** *Casablanca*.
> She **said** (that) black-and-white films **were** her favorites.

2 **Look at the examples again. Circle the correct word to complete the rules in the chart.**

say and *tell*
There is no object after **say / tell**.
There is always an object after **say / tell**.
Use the **present / past** after *said* and *told*.
NOTE: You can leave out the word **that** after **say** and **tell**.

Grammar Reference page 144

3 **Circle *said* or *told* in each sentence.**

1. She **said** / **told** she liked comedies.
2. He **said** / **told** me he went to the movies every weekend.
3. I **said** / **told** that I didn't go to the movies very often.
4. Tara **said** / **told** Elizabeth that she loved science fiction films.
5. Elizabeth **said** / **told** that she hated action movies.
6. I **said** / **told** Carlos that I was taking a filmmaking course.
7. Carlos **said** / **told** me he didn't want to take the course.
8. Pete **said** / **told** he was late for the movies.
9. Rachel **said** / **told** that he had to hurry.
10. He **said** / **told** me his favorite actress was Halle Berry.

4 **Complete the sentences. Use the correct form of *say* or *tell* and the correct form of the verb in parentheses.**

1. Tomás ____told____ John that the special effects in *Star Wars* ____were____ **(be)** amazing.
2. Reiko _____ that she _____ **(love)** James Bond films.
3. She _____ me that Sean Connery _____ **(be)** a good actor.
4. She _____ that *Dr. No* _____ **(be)** her favorite Bond movie.
5. Mariana _____ her favorite film _____ **(be)** *Casablanca*.
6. She _____ us that she _____ **(like)** old films.
7. She _____ me that she _____ **(love)** the music in *Casablanca*.

Grammar focus

LANGUAGE NOTES

- *Tell* is almost always followed by an indirect object. For example, *Please tell <u>me</u> the truth.*
- *Say* is never used with an indirect object. For example, *I said I loved movies.*
- The present tense in direct speech changes to the past tense in indirect, or reported, speech.

WARM-UP

Note: Skip this warm-up if you're doing this lesson (Lesson B) during the same class period as Lesson A.

- Books closed. Tell students they are going to listen to the article they read in the Reading section.
- Write these headings on the board: *What Tomas said, What Reiko said, What Mariana said.* Have students copy the headings.
- Tell students they will listen to the audio and will take notes, using each of the headings. For example, under *What Tomas said* they might write *The special effects are amazing and the story is interesting.*
- 🎧 Play the audio for Lesson A, Reading, Exercise 4. (It models the grammar of the unit.)
- Call on a few students to read aloud some of their notes for each heading.

Exercise ❶

- Tell students to read the examples and study the bold-faced words.
- Ask them to focus on the second and third examples. Ask: *What follows the verb* told *in each sentence?* (an object or an object pronoun)
- Tell students to look at the first and fourth examples in the box. Ask: *Is there an object after* said? (no)
- Make sure students notice the use of the past tense after *said* and *told.*

Exercise ❷

- Have students study the examples again.
- Tell students to read the statements in the chart and circle the correct word to complete each rule.
- Go over the answers with the class.
- Ask a few questions to elicit the key points about the grammar: For example, *What's the main difference between* said *and* told? (There's always an object after *told.*) *Do we ever use the present tense after* said *and* told? (no) *Why is the word* that *in parentheses?* (Because it's optional: You can use it or not use it.)

Exercise ❸

- Before beginning Exercise 3, answer any questions students might have. You may also want to refer the class to the Grammar Reference for Unit 8 on page 144.
- Go over the example. Ask students why *said* is correct for item 1. (Because there's no object that comes after it.)
- Have students complete the exercise individually. Set a time limit of 5 minutes.
- Have students compare their answers with a partner.
- Go over the answers with the class.

Answer key

1. said	4. told	7. told	10. told
2. told	5. said	8. said	
3. said	6. told	9. said	

Exercise ❹

- Explain the task: Students will complete the sentences using the correct form of either *say* or *tell* and the correct form of the verb in parentheses. Go over the example.
- Remind students that the past tense is used after *said* and *told.*
- Set a time limit of 3 minutes.
- Have students compare their answers with a partner's.
- Go over the answers with the class.

Answer key

1. told; were	4. said; was	7. told; loved
2. said; loved	5. said; was	
3. told; was	6. told; liked	

Pronunciation

> **LANGUAGE NOTE**
> Consonant clusters are common in English. An example of a consonant cluster is *cl* in the word *classic*.

Exercise ❺

- Tell students they will listen to the sounds of consonant clusters, shown in bold in the *Student Book*.
- 🎧 Play the audio.
- Explain that the number of consonant sounds and the number of consonant letters is not always the same. For example, the single letter *x* in *exciting* represents two sounds (/ks/), while the two letters *th* in *that* and *sh* in *she* each stand for a single sound.
- Point out syllables in a word, such as *interesting*—a vowel is not pronounced resulting in a consonant cluster.

Exercise ❻

- Tell students they will listen to the audio again. This time they will listen and repeat.
- 🎧 Play the audio, stopping or pausing after each item to allow students to repeat chorally. Encourage students to link the consonant at the end of the first word to the vowel at the beginning of the next word. For example, "tol-dus" for *told us*.
- Remind students not to leave out the /k/ sound of the letter *x* in *exciting* and *excellent*.
- Also remind students not to leave out the /t/ or /d/ sound at the end of *liked* and *loved*.

Speaking

Exercise ❼

This exercise provides practice with the unit vocabulary. It prepares students to do Exercises 8 and 9.

- Tell students to look at the outline on the notepad.
- Explain the task: Students will make notes about their favorite movie. Point out that students will use these notes later to talk about their favorite movies.
- Copy the heads for the notes on the board.

Exercise ❽

- Pair students. Tell students they will take turns asking each other about their favorite movie.
- Model the activity. Tell the class about your favorite movie.
- Set a time limit of 5 minutes.

Exercise ❾

- Go over the example.
- Have each student report to the rest of the class what their partner said/told them about their favorite movie.

TRB For additional interactive grammar practice, have students do the reproducible activity for this unit in the *Teacher's Resource Book*.

Writing

Exercise ❿

- Assign the writing task for class work or homework.
- Explain the task: Students will write a review of a movie.
- Brainstorm ideas for possible movies and for adjectives.
- **TRB** Optionally, give students a copy of the writing model (see the *Teacher's Resource Book*, Writing Models). Ask them to read the model and notice the vocabulary and grammar from the unit.
- If students don't have the model, write the following on the board:

    The Pirates of the Caribbean *is the best comic adventure ever! It is full of action, suspense, and fun.*

For suggestions on how to give feedback on writing, see page xiv of this *Teacher's Edition*.

CONVERSATION TO GO

At the end of class, call on two students to role-play the conversation.

HOMEWORK

- 📖 Assign *Workbook* page 36, Grammar Exercises 3 and 4, and page 37, Pronunciation Exercise 7.
- Assign *Workbook* Self-Quiz 2.
- 💿 If students do not have the *WorldView Workbook*, assign listening homework from the Student CD. Write on the board.

    Track 17
    Complete these sentences.
    Tomas said he didn't like _____.
    Reiko said the beginning of *Dr. No* was _____.
    Mariana told the magazine she loved _____.

- 🎧 Tell students to listen to the audio and complete the sentences. Have them bring their answers to the next class.

    (Answers: the new Star Wars; *slow; old, romantic films*)

FOR NEXT CLASS

- Tell students that the next class will be a review class covering Units 5–8.
- Have students review the material in the units to prepare for the activities in Review 2.
- **TRB** Make copies of Quiz 2 in the *Teacher's Resource Book*.

Unit no.	Review Grammar	Listen to Student CD	Study Grammar Reference
5	*Should/shouldn't*	Track 10	Page 144
6	Expressions for making suggestions	Track 13	Page 144
7	*be* and *have* with descriptions	Track 15	Page 144
8	*say* and *tell*	Track 17	Page 144

Pronunciation

5 🎧 **Listen. Notice the groups of consonant sounds in the words.**

a **cl**assic **bl**ack-and-white fi**lm**

an int**é**re**st**ing **st**ory

e**xc**iting **sp**ecial effe**cts**

He said that he li**kéd** *Star Wars*.

the be**st** sci**ence** fi**cti**on movie

a **sl**ow **st**art

an e**xc**ellen**t** a**ctr**ess

She to**ld** us she lo**véd** o**ld** fi**lms**.

6 🎧 **Listen again and repeat.**

Speaking

7 *BEFORE YOU SPEAK.* **Make notes about your favorite movie.**

8 *PAIRS.* **Take turns asking each other questions and telling about your favorite movie. Use your notes.**

A: *My favorite movie is a classic—E.T. It's a science fiction movie. I loved the story.*

B: *Who are the actors?*

9 **Tell the class what you learned about your partner's favorite movie.**

Elena's favorite movie is E.T. She said that she loved the story.

Name of film:

Actor(s)/Actress(es):

Director:

Story:

Special effects:

Music:

Scenery:

Costumes:

Writing

10 **Write a short review of a good movie you recently saw. Include information about the actors, director, story, special effects, music, scenery, and costumes.**

CONVERSATION TO GO

A: Steve **said** he **liked** Bond movies because of the special effects.
B: Really? He **told me** he **liked** Bond movies because of the beautiful actresses!

Unit 5 Culture shock

1 🎧 Look at the list of situations. Then listen to the model conversation.

- meet a friend's parents for the first time
- pick someone up at the airport
- go to class on the first day
- go to dinner with your boss
- start a new job
- go to a job interview
- go to a friend's home for dinner
- go to a surprise birthday party

2 Choose a situation from the list in Exercise 1, but don't say it aloud. Think about the things you should and shouldn't do in that situation.

3 *GROUPS OF 4.* Play the guessing game. Take turns. Say what you should and shouldn't do in the situation you chose. Your partner will guess the situation.

Unit 6 Party time!

4 *GROUPS OF 3.* You planned a party together. Now the party is over. Look at the picture. This is the scene before the people arrived. Describe the scene.

5 🎧 Imagine that it is now last week and you are just starting to plan the party. Listen to the model conversation.

6 Role-play. Pretend that you're planning the party. You want the party to look like the picture. Take turns. Make suggestions for planning the party.

You may wish to use the video for Units 5–8 at this point.
For video activity worksheets, go to www.longman.com/worldview.

Unit 5: Culture shock

OBJECTIVES

- Review the material presented in Unit 5
- Grammar practice: *should* and *shouldn't* for giving advice

WARM-UP

Books closed. Invite students to say one thing that is not allowed in their culture. Remind them to use *shouldn't*. Have them compare the practice with another culture. For example, *In our culture, a girl shouldn't invite a boy out. In American culture, it's OK for a girl to invite a boy out.*

Exercise ❶

- Have students read the situations. Tell them you will read aloud each situation. Ask students to raise their hands if they have experienced the situation they hear.
- Explain the task: Students will listen to an exchange that models Exercise 3. Tell them that, in the audio, a person gives several clues. The other person guesses the situation.
- 🎧 Play the audio.

Exercise ❷

- Explain the task: Each student will choose a situation from Exercise 1. Tell students not to choose the situation "go to a friend's home for dinner." It's the example that they will be listening to. Remind them to keep their selection to themselves.
- On a piece of paper, have each student write three clues for the situation they have chosen. Remind them to use *should* and *shouldn't* in their clues.

Exercise ❸

- Divide students into groups of 4.
- 🎧 If needed, play the audio for Exercise 1 again.
- Have the members of each group take turns giving clues and guessing which situation is being described.
- While students are working, walk around the room, helping as needed.

WRAP-UP

Invite volunteers to give clues for the entire class to guess.

Unit 6: Party time!

OBJECTIVES

- Review the material presented in Unit 6
- Grammar practice: expressions for making suggestions

WARM-UP

- Books closed. Ask students to say some expressions that they can use for making suggestions. (For example, *why don't we . . . , let's . . . , maybe . . . could, how about . . .*) List these on the board.
- Check if students remember the sentence structure for making suggestions with the expressions on the board. Ask: *When you use* why don't *to make a suggestion, what parts of the sentence follow it?* (Why don't + subject + base form of the verb) Ask a similar question for the other expressions.

Exercise ❹

- Divide students into groups of 3.
- Have them look at the picture and describe what's going to happen at the party. For example, *A band is going to play.*

Exercise ❺

- Explain the task: Students will listen to a conversation among three people who are planning a party. Tell students to pay attention to the suggestions given.
- 🎧 Play the audio.
- After listening to the audio, ask this question: *What suggestions are given for the party?* (have the party outside, have a band, get balloons, serve hamburgers, have a barbecue)

Exercise ❻

- Explain the task: Students will pretend they are planning a party. They will make suggestions so that the party turns out like the party in the picture.
- Divide the class into groups of 3 and set a time limit of 10 minutes for the role play.
- After 10 minutes, ask volunteer students to share with the class their suggestions for the party.

WRAP-UP

- Ask the class: *Whose party seems to be the most fun? Whose party seems to be the most expensive?*
- Invite the class to make other suggestions to make the party in the picture even better.

Unit 7: First impressions

- Review the material presented in Unit 7
- Grammar practice: *be* and *have* with descriptions

WARM-UP

Books closed. Ask students to name some physical characteristics used to describe people such as height, weight, length and type of hair, and age.

Exercise 7

- Tell students they will listen to people describe pictures of two women. Have them listen to identify what the women have in common. (They are both middle-aged.)
- 🎧 Play the audio.

Exercise 8

- Explain the task: Students will work in pairs. They will each look at four photographs of people and will take turns describing each person. For each photo, the pairs will then decide whether they are looking at the same person or two different people.
- Pair students. Assign them roles A and B.
- Explain the activity: Student A says one physical feature of the person in the first photo. Student B responds by saying whether the person in his or her photo also has that characteristic. Then it's Student B's turn to say a physical feature of the person in his or her photo. Student A responds whether the person in his or her photo also has that characteristic. Have students repeat the process with the other three photos.
- 🎧 If needed, play the audio again for Exercise 7.
- Set a time limit of 2 minutes for the pairs to compare their photos. Walk around the room, helping as needed.

WRAP-UP

- Have the pairs place their photos side by side.
- Tell them to point out the differences between the people in photographs B and C.

Unit 8: At the movies

OBJECTIVES

- Review the material presented in Unit 8
- Grammar practice: *say* and *tell*

WARM-UP

- Ask students if they know the meaning of the word *survey.*
- Invite students to name kinds of surveys they have taken or are familiar with. Ask: *Do you like participating in surveys? Why or why not?*

Exercise 9

- Tell students they are going to listen to a conversation among people conducting a survey. Tell them to listen for the kinds of information asked for in the survey on movies. (favorite kind of movie, favorite movie, why a particular movie is a favorite)
- 🎧 Play the audio.

Exercise 10

- Draw students' attention to the chart. Explain the task. Students will use the chart to record the results of the survey.
- Before starting the survey, brainstorm kinds of movies, such as science fiction, drama, comedy, action, thriller, or animation. Write the types of movies on the board.
- 🎧 If needed, play the audio for Exercise 9 again to model how students should conduct the survey.
- Set a time limit of 6 minutes. To encourage greater interaction, tell students to look for five people who like different kinds of movies. Walk around the room, helping as needed.

Exercise 11

Have students report their findings to the class.

Unit 7 First impressions

7 🎧 Listen to the model conversation.

8 *PAIRS.* Student A, go to page 137. Student B, go to page 139. Look at the pictures. Take turns describing the person in each one. How many people are the same?

Unit 8 At the movies

9 🎧 Listen to the model conversation.

10 Interview five people. Find out what kind of movies they like. Take notes in the chart.

Name	Favorite kind of movie	Favorite movie	Why?

11 Report back to the class about your classmates' favorite movies.

What would you like?

Vocabulary Words related to eating at a restaurant
Grammar *would like / like, would prefer / prefer*
Speaking Ordering food and drinks in a restaurant

Lesson A

Getting started

1 *GROUPS OF 3.* **Look at the words in the box. Find them in the photos.**

customer	fork	glass	knife	menu
napkin	pepper	salt	spoon	waiter

What would you like?

OBJECTIVES

Students will:

- activate vocabulary related to eating at a restaurant
- do listening, speaking, and writing tasks related to ordering in a restaurant
- focus on using *would like/like, would prefer/prefer* to talk about food
- practice weak and strong pronunciations of *would*

WARM-UP: LOCAL RESTAURANTS

Students will participate in a whole-class discussion about local restaurants.

- Tell students that this unit is about going to restaurants. Elicit or explain that the title of the unit, "What would you like?," refers to a typical question asked of a restaurant customer.
- Ask students about local restaurants they know. Write the names of these restaurants on the board.
- Encourage students to comment on each restaurant's location, the type of food it serves, the prices, the quality, and any other details they want to discuss.

Getting started

Teaching Tip! Reviewing useful language

The words in the box in Exercise 1 are all nouns. Students may want to describe the photos using *There is* or *There are* followed by singular or plural forms of these words. Before beginning the exercise, you may want to review count and non-count nouns, including the plural forms of the nouns in the box. If necessary, point out that the irregular plural form of *knife* is *knives*.

OPTION: VOCABULARY PREVIEW

The restaurant-related vocabulary in Exercise 1 will be familiar to many students at this level. The challenge in this exercise will be using the terms appropriately and in grammatically correct sentences. Encourage students to help one another express themselves by making suggestions for phrasing their descriptions of the photos.

Exercise 1

- Ask questions about the pictures such as *Where are these people?* (They're in a restaurant.) *What are they doing?* (They're ordering food.)
- Explain the task: Students will talk about the photos, using the words in the box.
- Model the activity by pointing to the larger photo and saying, *There are two customers at the table.* Elicit another example from the class. (For example, *A waiter is standing next to the woman.*)
- Divide the class into groups of 3. Tell them to take turns saying one thing about each picture. Tell them to describe as many details as they can. Set a time limit of 2 minutes.
- Call on a few students to describe each of the photos.

EXTENSION

- Tell students this is a speed drill to reinforce the vocabulary.
- Demonstrate the activity. Call on a student and say one of the words. Have him or her tell you where it is in the pictures. For example, you say *waiter*, and the student responds, *This is the waiter,* and points to the waiter in the picture.

Exercise ❷

- Explain the task: Students will look at the menu and will complete the sentences with the words in the box. Tell students they will use each word only once.
- Go over the example. Ask students to identify the other appetizers on the menu (shrimp cocktail, garden salad).
- Have students complete the exercise individually. Set a time limit of 1 minute.
- Have students compare their answers with a partner's.
- Go over the answers with the class.

Answer key

1. appetizer 3. side dish 5. tea
2. entrée 4. dessert

Exercise ❸

- **Pairs.** Explain the task: Students will talk with a partner about restaurants.
- Have students read the questions.
- Model the activity by giving answers about yourself. (For example, *I go to restaurants once or twice a month. My favorite restaurant is* Chez Pierre. *The food is delicious, and it's not very expensive.*)
- Pair students and set a time limit of 3 minutes.
- After 3 minutes, call on several students to tell the class their partners' answers to the questions.

EXTENSION

- Tell each pair of students to join another pair. Explain that this activity will help them practice the grammar they learned in Unit 8.
- Quickly review the difference between *say* and *tell*. (*Tell* is followed by an indirect object. For example, *He told me.*)
- Tell students they will take turns telling the other pair about their partner's answers. (For example, *Julian told me his favorite restaurant was* Mario's *because he liked the pasta there. He said he and his family go to restaurants to celebrate birthdays and other special occasions.*)

Listening

CULTURE NOTES

- Dinner in the United States is normally served between 6:00 and 8:00 P.M.
- Cold beverages are always served with ice.
- Soup or salad (or another appetizer) is served first, then the entrée, and lastly, dessert.
- Food is served to everyone at the table at the same time.
- Good service generally includes fast service. People do not tend to linger over drinks, coffee, or dessert.
- The customer does not need to ask for the check. The waiter or waitress automatically brings the check to the table when he or she thinks you are finished or nearly finished. Sometimes the check is presented before you finish eating.
- Tipping is expected. A standard tip is 15 percent of the bill, although it is appropriate to leave 20 percent for excellent service.

Exercise ❹

- Explain the task: Students will listen to a man and a woman ordering a meal at the Shrimp Boat. As they listen, students will put an *M* next to the foods the man orders and a *W* next to the food the woman orders.
- 🎧 Play the audio.
- Go over the answers with the class.

Answer key

M: Shrimp Plaza, rice W: Shrimp Ritz, pasta

Exercise ❺

- Explain the task: Students will listen to the audio a second time and will match the name of each dish with its description.
- To help students listen for subtle differences in phrasing, have them read the descriptions and note which phrases distinguish one dish from another. (For example, *black olive sauce, tomato sauce, herb sauce.*)
- 🎧 Play the audio.
- Have students compare their answers with a partner.
- Go over the answers with the class.

Answer key

1. c 2. a 3. b

🌐 Please go to www.longman.com/worldview for additional in-class model conversation practice and supplementary reading practice.

HOMEWORK

- 📖 Assign *Workbook* page 40, Vocabulary Exercises 1 and 2, and page 42, Listening Exercises 5 and 6.

The Shrimp Boat

APPETIZERS

Shrimp Cocktail
Soup of the Day
Garden Salad

* * *

ENTRÉES

Shrimp Savoy
Shrimp Plaza
Shrimp Ritz

served with rice or pasta
and mixed vegetables

* * *

DESSERTS

Cheesecake
Chocolate Ice Cream
Raspberry Sorbet
Coffee   Tea
Cappuccino   Espresso

2 Look at the menu. Complete the sentences with the words in the box.

appetizer	dessert	entrée
side dish	tea	

1. The soup is an __appetizer__ .
2. The Shrimp Savoy is an _____.
3. The pasta is a _____.
4. The ice cream is a _____.
5. After your meal, you can have coffee or _____.

3 *PAIRS.* Discuss the questions.

How often do you go to restaurants?
What is your favorite restaurant?
Why do you like it?

Listening

4 🎧 Look at the menu. Listen to two people ordering a meal at The Shrimp Boat. On the menu, put an *M* next to the food the man orders and a *W* next to the food the woman orders.

5 🎧 Listen again. Match the name of the dish with the description.

1. Shrimp Savoy ____   a. shrimp in black olive sauce with tomatoes and herbs

2. Shrimp Plaza ____   b. shrimp in tomato sauce with herbs and olives

3. Shrimp Ritz ____   c. shrimp in herb sauce with tomatoes and olives

Grammar focus

1 **Look at the examples. Write *a* or *b* in each blank.**

> Key: a = what you like in general
>   b = what you want now or in the future

1. **Do** you **prefer** chocolate ice cream or vanilla ice cream?
   I **prefer** chocolate. __a__

2. **Do** you **like** seafood?
   Yes, I **do**. I **like** all kinds of seafood. _____

3. **Would** you **prefer** rice or pasta?
   I'**d prefer** the rice. _____

4. What **would** you **like**?
   I'**d like** the Shrimp Savoy. _____

2 **Look at the examples again. Circle *a* or *b* to complete the rules in the chart.**

would like/like, would prefer/prefer
Use _____ to talk about things you like in general.
a. *I like* or *I prefer*   b. *I'd like* or *I'd prefer*
Use _____ to ask for something you want.
a. *I like* or *I prefer*   b. *I'd like* or *I'd prefer*
NOTE: *I'd prefer = I would prefer; I'd like = I would like*

Grammar Reference page 145

3 **Circle the correct answers.**

1. A: Would you like a table near the window?
   B: Yes, I like to sit near the window. / Yes, thank you.
2. A: Do you prefer black or green olives?
   B: I'd prefer black. / I prefer black.
3. A: Would you like to see the menu?
   B: Yes, we would, thanks. / We like the menu.
4. A: Would you prefer soup or salad?
   B: I prefer soup. / I'd prefer soup.

Grammar focus

LANGUAGE NOTES

- *Would like* is a polite way of saying *want*.
- In this unit, the focus is on the difference in meaning between *would like* and *like* and *would prefer* and *prefer*.
- Use *would + prefer/like* to ask for something.
- Use *prefer* or *like*—conjugated and without the modal *would*—to talk about things you like in general.

WARM-UP

Note: Skip this warm-up if you're doing this lesson (Lesson B) during the same class period as Lesson A.

- Books closed. Tell students they are going to listen again to the restaurant conversation that they heard in the Listening section.
- Tell them to listen to the questions that the waiter asks the man and the woman. Write these sentences on the board: _____ *to sit here by the window or outside on the patio?* _____ *olives?* _____ *rice or pasta?* Have students copy the sentences.
- Explain the task: Students will listen and will fill in what they hear on the audio.
- 🎧 Play the audio for Lesson A, Listening, Exercise 4. (It models the grammar of the unit.) You may need to play the audio a second time.
- Go over the answers with the class. (*Would you like/Do you like/Would you prefer*)

Exercise ❶

- Have students read the four conversations and study the bold-faced words.
- Tell the class to look at each question and response and decide whether each is talking about something the speaker usually likes or about something the speaker wants now or in the future. Go over the example.
- Have students work individually to write *a* or *b* next to each sentence. Set a time limit of 1 minute.
- Have students compare their answers with a partner's.
- Go over the answers with the class.

Answer key

1. a   2. a   3. b   4. b

Exercise ❷

- Have students study the examples again.
- Tell students to circle *a* or *b* to complete the rules in the chart.
- Have students compare their answers with a partner.
- Go over the answers with the class.
- Ask a few questions to elicit the key points about the grammar: For example, *What's the affirmative short answer to the question, "Would you like some soup?"* (Yes, I would.) *Which expression do we use to say we like something—would prefer or prefer?* (prefer) *Which expression do we use to say we want something now?* (would prefer)

Answer key

1. a   2. b

Exercise ❸

- Before beginning Exercise 3, answer any questions students might have. You may want to refer the class to the Grammar Reference for Unit 9 on page 145.
- Explain the task: Students will read each question and circle the correct response. If necessary, model the activity by reading the first question aloud and asking a volunteer to give the answer.
- Have students complete the exercise individually. Set a time limit of 2 minutes.
- Have students compare their answers with a partner's.
- Go over the answers with the class.

Answer key

1. B: Yes, thank you.
2. B: I'd prefer black.
3. B: Yes, we would, thanks.
4. B: I'd prefer soup.

Pronunciation

> **LANGUAGE NOTES**
> - *Would* is usually contracted to *'d* after a pronoun: *I'd*
> - When *would* comes before *you* in questions, the two words are often blended together and pronounced "wouldja" in informal conversation.
> - When *would* ends a sentence, it has a strong pronunciation: *Yes, I would* /wʊd/.

Exercise ❹

- Explain the task: Students will listen to a conversation. Tell them to notice the pronunciations of *would*.
- 🎧 Play the audio.
- Point out the different ways that *would* is pronounced on the audio: as the single sound /d/ in *I'd*, part of the blended form "wouldja," and the strong form /wʊd/.
- Point out the pronunciation of *would you* ("wouldja").
- Point out that the strong pronunciation of *would* /wʊd/ is usually used only at the end of a sentence.

Exercise ❺

- Tell students they are going to practice the conversation in Exercise 4.
- 🎧 Play the audio again, stopping or pausing after each sentence to allow students to repeat chorally.
- Note that in the alternative question *Would you prefer rice or pasta*, the voice goes up on the first choice (*rice*) and down on the last choice (*pasta*).
- Call on pairs of students to role-play the conversation.

Speaking

Exercise ❻

- Explain the task: Students will use the cues to create a conversation between a waiter and a customer.
- Go over the example.
- Pair students and set a time limit of 5 minutes. Walk around the room, helping as needed.
- Have each pair join another pair to compare their conversations.
- Go over the answers with the class.

Answer key

Waiter:	Would you like to order?
Customer:	Yes, I'd like the shrimp.
Waiter:	Would you like an appetizer?
Customer:	No, thank you.
Waiter:	What would you like to drink?
Customer:	I'd like some iced tea.
Waiter:	Would you like dessert?
Customer:	Yes, I would.
Waiter:	Would you prefer cake or ice cream?
Customer:	I'd prefer cake.
Waiter:	Would you like anything else?
Customer:	I'd like the check, please.

Exercise ❼

- Explain the task: Students will role-play in groups of 3. One student acts as the server and the other two as customers.
- Divide the class into groups of 3. Assign the members A, B, and C roles. Tell Student A to look at page 43 of the *Student Book*. Tell Students B and C to turn to page 142. Set a time limit of 5 minutes.
- Walk around the room, helping as needed.
- Have students switch roles.

TRB For additional interactive grammar practice, have students do the reproducible activity for this unit in the *Teacher's Resource Book*.

Writing

Exercise ❽

- Assign the writing task for class work or homework.
- Explain the task: Students will pretend they are famous chefs opening a new restaurant. They write a memo to the person who is developing the menu.
- Brainstorm types of American foods for these categories: appetizers, entrées, side dishes, desserts, drinks.
- **TRB** Optionally, give students a copy of the writing model (see the *Teacher's Resource Book*, Writing Models). Ask them to read the model and notice the vocabulary and grammar from the unit.
- If students don't have the model, write the following on the board:

  I need a new menu for the restaurant I'm going to open next month. Can you design one for me? I prefer bright colors, . . .

- Have a student read the sentences aloud. Answer any questions students might have.
- Walk around to make sure everyone understands the task.

For suggestions on how to give feedback on writing, see page xiv of this *Teacher's Edition*.

CONVERSATION TO GO

At the end of class, call on two students to role-play the conversation.

HOMEWORK

- 📖 Assign *Workbook* page 41, Grammar Exercises 3 and 4, and page 42, Pronunciation Exercises 7 and 8.
- 🔘 If students do not have the *WorldView Workbook*, assign listening homework from the Student CD. Write on the board:

  Track 19
  What word does the waiter use three times to describe the food at the Shrimp Boat?

- 🎧 Tell students to listen to the audio and write the answer to the question. Have them bring their answer to the next class.

  (Answer: *delicious*)

Pronunciation

4 🎧 **Listen to the weak and strong pronunciations of *would*. Notice the /d/ sound in *I'd like* and *I'd prefer* and the linking in *would you*.**

What would you like?   I**'d** like the shrimp.

Would you like salad?   Yes, thanks. I **would**.

Would you prefer rice or pasta?   I**'d** prefer pasta.

5 🎧 **Listen again and repeat.**

Speaking

6 *PAIRS.* **Use the cues to complete the conversation between a waiter and a customer.**

Waiter: *Order?* Would you like to order?	**Waiter:** *Dessert?*
Customer: *The shrimp.*	**Customer:** *Yes.*
Waiter: *An appetizer?*	**Waiter:** *Cake or ice cream?*
Customer: *No.*	**Customer:** *Cake.*
Waiter: *Drink?*	**Waiter:** *Anything else?*
Customer: *Iced tea.*	**Customer:** *Check, please.*

7 *GROUPS OF 3.* **Student A, you are a waiter/waitress at Rosie's Restaurant. Students B and C, you are customers. Student A, look at this page. Students B and C, look at page 142. Student A, take the customers' order. Write it on the guest check.**

Guest Check

TABLE	SERVER	SECTION	CHECK NUMBER
			044052

TAX

TOTAL

Writing

8 **You're a famous chef. You're going to open a new American restaurant in your city. What would you like to have on the menu? Write a memo to the person who will design the menu. Include information about appetizers, entrées, side dishes, desserts, and drinks.**

CONVERSATION TO GO

A: **Would** you **like** the check?
B: No, thank you!

43

Big issues

Vocabulary Global issues
Grammar *will* for predicting
Speaking Making predictions

Lesson A

Getting started

1 **Match the words on the left with the examples on the right.**

1. economy _b_
2. transportation ____
3. space ____
4. politics ____
5. population ____
6. communication ____
7. climate ____

a. United States: 288 million people
b. money, bank
c. rainy, hot
d. car, airplane, bus
e. the moon, Mars, a space station
f. phone, fax, email
g. government, president, the White House

Pronunciation

2 🎧 **Listen. Notice the stressed (strong) syllable in each word. Mark the stress.**

• climate	prediction
transportation	politics
population	communication
economy	government

3 🎧 **Listen again and repeat. Check your answers.**

4 *PAIRS.* **Look at the photos. Tell which photo matches each topic in Exercise 1.**

I think Photo A matches politics.

Big issues

OBJECTIVES

Students will:

- activate vocabulary related to global issues
- do reading, speaking, and writing activities related to making predictions
- focus on using *will* for predicting
- practice putting the strongest stress on the appropriate syllable

WARM-UP: TIMES CHANGE

Groups of 3. Students talk about changes that have taken place in the world.

- Tell students that this unit is about global issues. Explain that the title of the unit, "Big issues," refers to topics that affect people all over the world.
- Write *1997* and *Now* on the board. Elicit today's date and write it next to *Now*.
- Ask students to give an example of a change that occurred between 1997 and now that affects them as individuals. (For example, *I got married.*)
- Tell students to think of one thing that has changed in that period that affects a larger group of people, for example, the election of a new president. Write the examples under the correct heading.
- Divide the class into groups of 3. Have each group think of two more differences on an individual or national/global level.
- Set a time limit of 3 minutes.
- Call on a few students to share their examples.

Getting started

OPTION: VOCABULARY PREVIEW

Call out an example for each word and have students say what global issue it is. For example, call out your country's currency. The class should answer, "economy." Do the review as quickly and snappy as you can. To make the review fun, you may turn it into a competition.

Exercise ❶

- Have students look at the photo montage and identify each picture. If necessary, help students identify the White House in picture A.
- Explain the task: Students will match the topics on the left with specific examples of these topics on the right.
- Go over the example.

Answer key

1. b	3. e	5. a	7. c
2. d	4. g	6. f	

Pronunciation

LANGUAGE NOTE

Some words have two types of stressed syllables: a syllable with a stronger stress (primary stress) and a syllable with weaker stress (secondary stress).

Exercise ❷

Option: You can have students work either individually or in pairs to complete this exercise.

- Explain that words with two or more syllables have one strong, or stressed, syllable. Tell students that the vowel in a stressed syllable is given emphasis.
- Write *airplane* and *prediction* on the board. Say the words with the main stress on different syllables and ask students to identify the correct one: For example, *air-PLANE*, *AIR-plane* (correct); *PRE-dic-tion*, *pre-DIC-tion* (correct), *pre-dic-TION*. Draw a large circle over the stressed syllable in each word.
- Tell students they are going to listen to some words. Explain the task: Students will listen for the stress and draw a circle over the stressed syllable—the syllable that has the strongest sound. Point out the example.
- ⌒ Play the audio.
- Tell students they will check their answers in the next exercise.

Exercise ❸

- ⌒ Play the audio again, and tell students to check their answers in Exercise 2. Encourage them to correct any words they may have marked incorrectly.
- Ask students to look at the words that end with *-ion*: *prediction, transportation, population, communication.* Ask: *Where is the stress in words that end with* -ion? (Words that end with *-ion* have stress on the syllable just before the *-ion* ending.)
- ⌒ Play the audio again, and ask students to repeat each word chorally.
- Ask a few individual students to repeat the words. Check their pronunciation.

Exercise ❹

- Explain the task: Students will work in pairs to match the words from Exercise 1 with the photos.
- Pair students and set a time limit of 3 minutes.

Answer key

Photo A = *politics*	Photo E = *climate*
Photo B = *space*	Photo F = *economy*
Photo C = *communication*	Photo G = *transportation*
Photo D = *population*	

Reading

BACKGROUND INFORMATION

Arthur C. Clarke is a British scientist and science fiction writer whose fictional ideas have closely mirrored real life, particularly in the development of space and satellite communications. Born in the United Kingdom and now living in Sri Lanka, Clarke is best known for his writing and collaboration on Stanley Kubrick's classic science fiction film *2001: A Space Odyssey.*

Exercise 5

• Have students read the information about Arthur C. Clarke. Check comprehension by asking questions such as *Who is Arthur C. Clarke? What does he do?*

• Ask students if they know the name of his most famous book/movie. Give this hint: It includes a specific year in the title. (*2001: A Space Odyssey*)

• Explain the task: Students will read Clarke's predictions for the future.

• Set a time limit of 8 minutes.

Exercise 6

• **Pairs.** Explain the task: Students will scan Clarke's predictions and put a check mark next to the ones that are true for most people today.

• Set a time limit of 3 minutes. Walk around the room, helping as needed.

• Go over the answers with the class. Ask: *Does everyone agree on the predictions that have already come true?*

Exercise 7

• Ask students to read the words in the box. Suggest that they scan for these words in the reading in order to complete the sentences.

• Go over the example. Ask students to find the answer in the reading and to tell you where it is. (It's in the first prediction.)

• Have students work individually to complete the exercise. Set a time limit of 5 minutes.

• Have students compare their answers with a partner's.

• Go over the answers with the class.

Answer key

1. programs	4. cities	7. Cars
2. the news	5. population	8. food
3. messages	6. offices	9. space

Please go to www.longman.com/worldview for additional in-class model conversation practice.

HOMEWORK

• Assign *Workbook* page 43, Vocabulary Exercises 1 and 2, and page 45, Listening Exercises 5 and 6.

Reading

5 Arthur C. Clarke is a scientist. He has also written many science fiction novels, including *2001: A Space Odyssey*. Read his predictions.

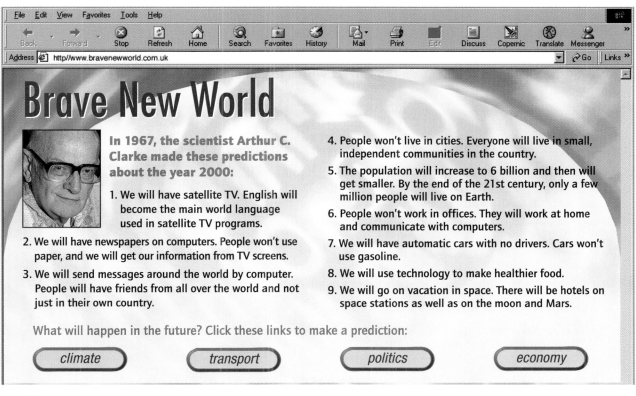

> **Brave New World**
>
> Address: http//www.bravenewworld.com.uk
>
> In 1967, the scientist Arthur C. Clarke made these predictions about the year 2000:
>
> 1. We will have satellite TV. English will become the main world language used in satellite TV programs.
>
> 2. We will have newspapers on computers. People won't use paper, and we will get our information from TV screens.
>
> 3. We will send messages around the world by computer. People will have friends from all over the world and not just in their own country.
>
> 4. People won't live in cities. Everyone will live in small, independent communities in the country.
>
> 5. The population will increase to 6 billion and then will get smaller. By the end of the 21st century, only a few million people will live on Earth.
>
> 6. People won't work in offices. They will work at home and communicate with computers.
>
> 7. We will have automatic cars with no drivers. Cars won't use gasoline.
>
> 8. We will use technology to make healthier food.
>
> 9. We will go on vacation in space. There will be hotels on space stations as well as on the moon and Mars.
>
> What will happen in the future? Click these links to make a prediction:
>
> (climate) (transport) (politics) (economy)

6 *PAIRS.* Which of Arthur C. Clarke's predictions have come true? Put a check (✓) next to the predictions that are true for most people today.

7 Complete the predictions from the reading with the words in the box.

cars	space	~~programs~~	messages	offices
cities	food	the news	population	

1. We will have satellite TV _programs_.

2. We will read _____ on the computer.

3. People around the world will send _____ to each other by computer.

4. No one will live in _____.

5. The _____ of the world will get smaller.

6. No one will work in _____.

7. _____ won't need drivers or gasoline.

8. The _____ we eat will be healthier.

9. There will be hotels in _____.

Grammar focus

1 **Study the examples of *will* for predicting.**

We **will go** on vacation in space.	I think we**'ll go** on vacation in space.
People **won't live** in cities.	I don't think people **will live** in cities.
What **will happen** in the future?	What do you think **will happen**?

2 **Look at the examples again. Circle the correct words to complete the rules in the chart.**

> **will for predicting**
>
> After *will* or *won't,* use **the base form of the verb / verb + -ing**.
>
> Use *I think* + **subject** + **won't** / *I don't think* + **subject** + *will* to predict what will not happen.

Grammar Reference page 145

3 **Use the words to make sentences about the year 2100.**

1. The population of the world / not increase.
   The population of the world won't increase.
2. Where / people / go on vacation?

3. I / not think / people / go on vacation in space.

4. Everyone / have / a computer?

5. I think / everyone / speak one language.

6. The world's weather / not get warmer.

7. You think / technology / cost less?

8. I think / transportation / be cheaper.

9. The world economy / be stronger.

10. There be / flying cars.

11. I / not think / we find life on another planet.

Grammar focus

LANGUAGE NOTES

Although there are several ways to talk about the future tense in English, the focus in this unit is on *will*.

- *Will* is used for general facts about the future, to make predictions, to make a promise or give assurance, to ask for or offer something, and to make decisions at the time of speaking. Using *will* to make predictions is the focus in this unit.

- *Won't* is the contraction of *will* + *not*. It has two meanings: to indicate the negative future (*She won't be in class today.*) and to refuse (*I won't clean up my room.*).

- To predict what will not happen, the pattern is *not think* + subject + *will*. For example, *I don't think there will be flying cars*. Note: The pattern *think* + subject + *will not*, is not considered grammatically correct. (For example, the sentence *I think there won't be flying cars* is not correct.)

- After a pronoun, contractions are generally used.

- Note that when *will* is contracted to *'ll* after a pronoun, the vowel in the pronoun is often reduced (weakened or relaxed). For example, *we'll* can sound like *will* instead of having the same vowel sound as in *we*.

WARM-UP

Note: Skip this warm-up if you're doing this lesson (Lesson B) during the same class period as Lesson A.

- Books closed. Tell students they are going to listen to the article they read in the Reading section.

- Tell them to think about the time period that Clarke is talking about: Is it the past, the present, or the future?

- 🎧 Play the audio for Lesson A, Reading, Exercise 5. (It models the grammar of the unit.)

- Ask students to answer the question about the time period in the reading. (the future)

- Ask them what verb forms they remember from the reading. Write a few of these on the board.

Exercise ➊

- Have students read the example and study the bold-faced words. Write *will* on the board. Ask: *What's the contraction, or short form, of* will? (*'ll*) *What two words is* won't *a contraction of?* (*will* and *not*)

- Tell students to notice the negative form of *think* and the affirmative form of *will*. Explain that the expression *don't think* + subject + *will* expresses the opinion that something will not happen.

Exercise ➋

- Have students study the examples again.

- Tell students to read the statements in the chart and circle the correct information to complete the rules.

- Go over the answers with the class.

- Ask a few questions to elicit the key points about the grammar: For example, *What form of the main verb follows* will/won't? (the base form) *What's the contracted form of* will + not? (*won't*) *What expression is used to predict what will not happen?* (*I don't think* + subject + *will*)

Answer key

the base form of the verb
I don't think + subject + *will*

Exercise ➌

- Before beginning Exercise 3, answer any questions students might have. You may also refer the class to the Grammar Reference for Unit 10 on page 145.

- Explain the task: Students will use the words in each item to create sentences expressing predictions about the year 2100. Remind students to use *will* and *won't* in their sentences. Explain that they will also be making affirmative and negative statements as well as questions.

- Go over the example.

- Have students complete the exercise individually. Set a time limit of 3 minutes. Walk around the room, helping as needed.

- Have students compare their sentences with a partner's.

- Go over the answers with the class.

Answer key

1. The population of the world won't increase.
2. Where will people go on vacation?
3. I don't think people will go on vacation in space.
4. Will everyone have a computer?
5. I think everyone will speak one language.
6. The world's weather won't get warmer.
7. Do you think technology will cost less?
8. I think transportation will be cheaper.
9. The world economy will be stronger.
10. There will be flying cars.
11. I don't think we will/we'll find life on another planet.

Speaking

Teaching Tip! **Expressing agreement or disagreement**

Students may agree or disagree with the predictions of others in Exercise 3. Go over expressions of agreement (*I agree, I think so too, You're right*) and disagreement (*I don't agree, I disagree, I don't think so*). Model this with a volunteer by asking the student to make a prediction and using one of the expressions to agree or disagree.

Exercise **4**

Groups of 3. This exercise provides practice with making predictions with *will*. It prepares students for Exercise 5.

• Tell students to look at the web page buttons, and ask: *What types of buttons are they?* Or *What topics are represented by the buttons?* (They represent "big issues.")

• Explain the task: In groups of 3, students will use *will/won't* to make predictions about each of the topics. Go over the example.

• Divide the class into groups of 3 and set a time limit of 10 minutes. Walk around the room, helping as needed.

• If students are having difficulty, refer them to the Reading on page 45.

Exercise **5**

• Have students form new groups of 3. Tell them to talk about their predictions with their new group members to find out which predictions are the same and which are different.

• Set a time limit of 10 minutes.

• Have a few students report on the predictions that their groups agreed upon. Is there anything that everyone agreed on?

EXTENSION

• Write *Agree* on one side of the board and *Disagree* on the other.

• Call on a few students to come to the front of the room.

• Read sentences predicting the future, and tell students to move to stand in front of the word that indicates their opinion. Ask them to explain their opinions.

• After a few sentences, repeat with another group of students.

(Possible sentences: *By the year 2100, the climate will be much warmer. Cars won't need drivers. All governments will be democratic. There will be one system of currency. There will be fewer nations, and they will be larger.*)

TRB For additional interactive grammar practice, have students do the reproducible activity for this unit in the *Teacher's Resource Book.*

Writing

Exercise **6**

• Assign the writing task for class work or homework.

• Explain the task: Students will look at the web page and use Arthur C. Clarke's predictions as a model. They will then write their own web page with predictions about five big issues for the year 2100.

• Brainstorm issues that might be significant in the year 2100.

• **TRB** Optionally, give students a copy of the writing model (see the *Teacher's Resource Book,* Writing Models). Ask them to read the model and notice the vocabulary and grammar from the unit.

• If students don't have the model, write the following on the board:

> 1. *New treatments for diseases and illnesses will be discovered as scientists and doctors get a better understanding of the human body.*

• Have a student read the sentences aloud. Answer any questions students might have.

• Walk around to make sure everyone understands the task.

For suggestions on how to give feedback on writing, see page xiv of this *Teacher's Edition.*

CONVERSATION TO GO

At the end of class, call on two students to role-play the conversation.

HOMEWORK

• 📖 Assign *Workbook* page 44, Grammar Exercises 3 and 4, and page 45, Pronunciation Exercises 7 and 8.

• 💿 If students do not have the *WorldView Workbook,* assign listening homework from the Student CD. Write on the board:

> Track 22
> What three things Clarke predicted would disappear by the year 2000?

• 🎧 Tell students to listen to the audio and write the answer to the question. Have them bring their answer to the next class.

> (Possible answers: *Paper, cities, offices, drivers, gasoline*)

Speaking

4 *GROUPS OF 3.* **You are visiting a website called Y2K100. It asks you to send your predictions for the year 2100. Discuss your predictions for the topics below.**

In 2100, people will work ten hours a week.

politics	transportation
clothing	food
work	economy
communication	climate
vacations	

5 **Change groups and discuss your predictions. Are there any predictions that everyone agrees on?**

Writing

6 Look again at the web page on page 45. Use Arthur C. Clarke's predictions as a model. Write your own web page with predictions about five big issues for the year 2050. Use *will*.

CONVERSATION TO GO

A: In 2050, math **will** still **be** an important subject in school.
B: I hope not!

UNIT 11

Hard work

Vocabulary Activities related to work
Grammar *have to/don't have to*
Speaking Describing jobs

Getting started

1 Complete the job descriptions with the words in the boxes.

| type letters and contracts | ~~arrange meetings~~ | make decisions |

Administrative Assistant

"I work for a lawyer. My boss tells me what he needs, and I call clients to **(1)** _arrange meetings_. I also use a computer to **(2)** _____. Sometimes I don't like my job because I can't **(3)** _____. Mostly I do what my boss tells me to do."

| meet with clients | travel | communicate | give presentations |

Sales Manager

"I sell computer software for a large company. I have clients all over the country, and I **(1)** _____ to different cities all the time. I like to **(2)** _____ because I enjoy talking to people in person. When I'm traveling, I use a laptop to **(3)** _____ about my company's products. I use my cell phone and email to **(4)** _____ with my clients and boss when I'm on the road."

| work as a team | make much money | wait on customers | work long hours |

Salesperson

"I work in a large department store. I **(1)** _____ and help them find what they are looking for. I **(2)** _____ with other salespeople in my department. We all **(3)** _____; for example, I work from 11:00 A.M. to 9:00 P.M., Tuesday through Sunday. We don't **(4)** _____, but we get employee discounts on the things we buy."

2 *GROUPS OF 3.* **Talk about activities you do in your job now or want to do in a future job.**

Hard work

OBJECTIVES

Students will:

- activate vocabulary related to job descriptions
- do reading, speaking, and writing tasks related to describing jobs
- focus on using *have to/don't have to* to talk about job requirements
- practice the reduced pronunciation of *have to* and *has to*

WARM-UP: JOBS

Students discuss places people work and the different jobs they do at work.

- Tell students that this unit is about work and jobs. Make sure everyone understands that *hard* in the unit title, "Hard work," means "difficult."
- With the class, brainstorm a list of jobs that are done in different places. For example, write *School* on the board and ask students to name some jobs that might be found in a school. (For example, *teacher, secretary, nurse.*) Write students' ideas on the board.
- Do the same with a few more places such as hospital, restaurant, factory, and other workplaces.

Getting started

OPTION: VOCABULARY PREVIEW

Tell students to look at the phrases in the boxes. Ask them what the phrases refer to. (They're job descriptions.) Tell them you will read aloud each job description in the boxes. Tell them to raise their hands if any of the job descriptions fit theirs at work. Answer any questions students might have.

Exercise ❶

- Explain the task: Students will read the descriptions and use the words and phrases in the boxes to complete the sentences about three people's jobs.
- Have students read the three phrases in the first box. Answer any questions about the task. If necessary, go over the first item by reading the first two sentences. (*I work for a lawyer. My boss tells me what he needs, and I call clients to _____.*) Pause before the word *to*, and ask: *What does she call clients to do?* Elicit *arrange meetings.*
- Have students work individually to complete the sentences. Set a time limit of 3 minutes. While students are working, walk around the room, helping as needed.
- Have students compare their answers with a partner.
- Go over the answers with the class.

EXTENSION

Pair students. Reinforce the vocabulary by having the pairs use the words and phrases in Exercise 1 to briefly discuss which of the three jobs they would like the best and why. (For example, *I would like the administrative assistant job the best because I like to type.*)

Answer key

1. arrange meetings; type letters and contracts; make decisions
2. travel; meet with clients; give presentations; communicate
3. wait on customers; work as a team; work long hours; make much money

Exercise ❷

- **Groups of 3.** Explain the task: Students will take turns telling their partners about activities they do in their jobs now. If students are not working, have them talk about activities they want to do in a future job.
- Model the task by describing the activities that you do in your job. (For example, *I work as a team, and I work long hours.*)
- Divide the class in groups of 3 and set a time limit of 5 minutes. Tell students to listen to their partners carefully.
- Call on a few students to tell the class about one of their partners' activities. (For example, *Luci waits on customers and works long hours.*)

Reading

> **CULTURE NOTE**
>
> In the United States, it is considered good etiquette to tip 15 percent for pizza (or other food) delivery. A general rule is that $2.00 is the minimum amount to tip, even if 15 percent of your bill is less than $2.00. It is appropriate to tip more for excellent service, during bad weather, or if your location is quite a distance from the store.

Exercise ❸

- Tell students to look at the photo and the article. Ask: *What's the man's job?* (He's a pizza delivery person.)
- Explain the task: Students will predict and write down two activities from Exercise 1 that they think the pizza delivery person does in his job.
- Set a time limit of 1 minute.
- Have students compare their answers with a partner's.
- Elicit ideas from students and write them on the board.

Teaching Tip! **Making inferences**

The ability to make inferences is an important reading skill. Tell students that sometimes information in the reading is stated directly (for example, *I don't earn much per hour*), and sometimes it is implied. When the information is implied, the reader has to "read between the lines," or make inferences, about what is being said. For example, when Marcus says "I have to be polite, even when I'm tired," the reader can make the inference that it is sometimes difficult to be polite.

Exercise ❹

- Tell students they will confirm their answers in Exercise 3 by reading the article.
- Set a time limit of 5 minutes. Walk around the room, helping as needed.
- Ask students which activities were mentioned in the article.

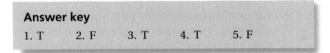

Answer key

works long hours, waits on customers

Exercise ❺

- Explain the task: Students will reread the article and decide if each statement is true or false.
- Tell students to look at the statements before they reread the article so they know what information to look for.
- Set a time limit of 3 minutes.
- Have students compare their answers with a partner's.
- Go over the answers with the class.

Answer key

1. T   2. F   3. T   4. T   5. F

HOMEWORK

- 📖 Assign *Workbook* page 46, Vocabulary Exercises 1 and 2, and page 48, Listening Exercises 5 and 6.

Reading

3 Look at the photo of the pizza delivery person. Which two activities in Exercise 1 do you think he does in his job?

_____   _____

4 Read the article "Nine to Five." Then check your guesses in Exercise 3.

PIZZA To Go

Name: Marcus Willis

Job: Pizza delivery person

Wages: $5.50/hour

Nine to Five

So you think my job is easy? You pick up the pizza, drive around town, go back to the shop, and then do it all again. It isn't that easy.

First, I don't earn much per hour, so I have to work long hours—sometimes I start at 3:00 P.M. and finish at 2:00 A.M. I also have to drive a lot. I drive about 80 miles every day, and I have to use my own car because the company doesn't give me one. That's a real problem. Another problem is the tips. Customers don't have to give me tips, but without the extra money, I don't earn much. Finally, I'm always busy. When I finish driving, I have to wait on customers in the shop and, of course, I have to be polite, even when I'm tired! Then my boss answers the phone, and I have to leave again and deliver another pizza.

The next time a delivery person brings you a pizza, remember: Does he have to work hard? Yes, he does! So be nice to him, and give him a big tip!

5 How does Marcus feel about his job? Read the article again and write _T_ (true) or _F_ (false) after each statement.

Marcus feels that . . .

1. delivering pizza is a difficult job.

2. his job pays well.

3. the pizza company should give him a car.

4. getting tips is important.

5. he isn't always busy at work.

Grammar focus

1 **Study the examples with *have to*.**

> I **have to** work long hours.
> He **has to** pick up the pizza.
> **Does** he **have to** work hard? Yes, he **does**. / No, he **doesn't**.
> Customers **don't have to** give him tips.

2 **Look at the examples again. Complete the rules in the chart with *is* or *isn't*.**

have to/don't have to
Use *have to/has to* + the base form of the verb when something _____ necessary.
Use *don't have to/doesn't have to* + the base form of the verb when something _____ necessary.

> Grammar Reference page 145

3 **Write conversations. Use the words given and the correct form of *have to*.**

1. A: What / do / in your job? *What do you have to do in your job?*
   B: We / meet clients. *We have to meet clients.*
2. A: What / your boss / do?
   B: He / give presentations.
3. A: You / travel?
   B: Yes / do.
4. A: You / work as a team?
   B: No / not.
5. A: She / use a computer?
   B: Yes / she / answer email from customers.

Pronunciation

4 🎧 **Listen. Notice the pronunciation of *have to* ("hafta") and *has to* ("hasta").**

have to   have to work   I have to work long hours.
Does he have to work hard?

has to   has to drive   He has to drive a lot.
He has to pick up the pizza.

5 🎧 **Listen again and repeat.**

6 *PAIRS.* **Practice the conversations in Exercise 3.**

Grammar focus

LANGUAGE NOTES

- Use *have to/has to* to talk about necessity.
- Use *don't have to/doesn't have to* to say that something is not necessary (you have a choice).

WARM-UP

Note: Skip this warm-up if you're doing this lesson (Lesson B) during the same class period as Lesson A.

- Books closed. Tell students they are going to listen to the article about the pizza delivery person they read in the Reading section.
- Write *necessary* on the board. Ask: *What are some things that are necessary in this class?* (bring our books, do our homework, listen to the teacher)
- Ask students to listen for the words that tell that an activity is necessary at Marcus's job.
- 🎧 Play the audio for Lesson A, Reading, Exercise 4. (It models the grammar of the unit.)
- Elicit from students what words indicate that an activity is necessary. (*have to* and *has to*)

Exercise ❶

- Tell students to read the examples and study the bold-faced words. Ask: *What are the two present tense forms of* have*?* (*have* and *has*) *What form of* have *is used in questions and negative statements?* (the base form)
- Encourage students to think about the meaning of each sentence in the examples: *What does* have to *mean?* (Something is necessary.) *What does* don't have to *mean?* (Something is not necessary. There is a choice.)

Exercise ❷

- Have students study the examples again.
- Tell students to complete each rule in the chart with either *is* or *isn't*.
- Go over the answers with the class.
- Ask a few questions to elicit the key points about the grammar: For example, *What's another way to say, "It's necessary for you to wear a suit to work"?* (You have to wear a suit to work.) *What's another way to ask, "Is it necessary for everyone to speak English in class?"* (Does everyone have to speak English in class?)

Answer key

is   isn't

Exercise ❸

- Before students begin Exercise 3, answer any questions they might have. You may also want to refer the class to the Grammar Reference for Unit 11 on page 145.
- Explain the task: Students will use the words given and the correct form of *have to* to write conversations.

- Go over the example. Point out that the auxiliary *do*, a subject pronoun (*you*), and *have to* were added to the words to make the question.
- Have students complete the exercise individually. Set a time limit of 5 minutes. Walk around the room, helping as needed.
- Have students compare their answers with a partner's.
- Go over the answers with the class.

Answer key

1. A: What do you have to do in your job?
   B: We have to meet clients.
2. A: What does your boss have to do?
   B: He has to give presentations.
3. A: Do you have to travel?
   B: Yes, I/we do.
4. A: Do you have to work as a team?
   B: No, we/I don't.
5. A: Does she have to use a computer?
   B: Yes, she does. She has to answer email from customers.

Pronunciation

LANGUAGE NOTES

- The main verb *have* is normally pronounced /hæv/ as in the question, *Do you have* /hæv/ *a job?* But when it is part of the expression *have to*, the two words are blended together and pronounced as "hafta." The voiced /v/ sound in *have* changes to the voiceless /f/ and *to* is pronounced with its weak form /t/.
- The verb *has* on its own is normally pronounced /hæz/. When it is blended together with *to* in *has to*, the voiced /z/ sound changes to voiceless /s/ and the two words are pronounced together as "hasta."

Exercise ❹

- Tell students they are going to listen to the audio. Ask them to notice the way the words are blended together in *have to* and *has to*.
- 🎧 Play the audio. Point out the weak pronunciation of *to* /tə/.
- Say the words *have* and *to* and *has* and *to* separately and then in the blended forms "hafta" and "hasta" to emphasize the difference in their pronunciation.

Exercise ❺

- Tell students they are going to listen again. This time, they will listen and repeat.
- 🎧 Play the audio again, stopping after each item to allow students to repeat chorally.

Exercise ❻

- Explain the task: Students will practice the conversations they wrote for Exercise 3.
- Pair students and set a time limit of 3 minutes.

Speaking

Exercise 7

This exercise provides practice with *have to/don't have to* to talk about things people in different jobs have to and don't have to do. It prepares students to do Exercises 8 and 9.

- Tell students to look at the list of jobs in the chart. Make sure everyone understands the meanings of the names of the jobs given in the chart.

- Ask students to think of one more job and add it to the list at the bottom. If necessary, brainstorm some examples with the class.

- Explain the task: Students will complete the middle column with activities the person *has to do* in that job and the last column with activities the person *doesn't have to do* in the job.

- Have students complete the activity individually. Point out that they will work in groups later. Set a time limit of 10 minutes. Walk around the room, helping as needed.

- After 10 minutes, elicit some examples of activities students listed in the chart.

- Tell students to rank the six jobs in their order of preference (1 = the best, 6 = the worst).

Exercise 8

- **Groups of 3.** Explain the task: Students will take turns telling each other their opinions about the best and worst jobs in the chart in Exercise 7.

- Go over the example. Remind students to use *have to/has to* and *don't have to/doesn't have to* when explaining their reasons for their opinions.

- Divide the class into groups of 3 and set a time limit of 8 minutes. Walk around the room, helping as needed.

Exercise 9

- Call on a student from each group to report to the class their group's opinions and their reasons.

- Lead a class discussion by asking questions such as *Who thinks that administrative assistants have the worst job? Why? Who thinks that flight attendants have the best job? Why?*

- Have the class vote on the best and the worst jobs.

- Tell students to think about the job they have now or one they had in the past. Ask them to explain how they would rank that job.

EXTENSION

- Divide the class into teams of 4. Tell the teams they will have a competition.

- Ask them to write a list of job responsibilities that include vocabulary from the unit or other ideas. Give a few examples: *has to order food, has to clean bathrooms.* Tell them to write as many as they can.

- Next, tell them to think of jobs that might include those responsibilities (for example, *restaurant owner, housekeeper*).

- After the brainstorming, have each team take turns calling out a responsibility. The other team will name the job that has that responsibility. The team gets a point with each correct answer. The team with the most points wins.

TRB For additional interactive grammar practice, have students do the reproducible activity for this unit in the *Teacher's Resource Book*.

Writing

Exercise 10

- Assign the writing task for class work or homework.

- Explain the task: Students will pretend they are working in their ideal job. They will write an article describing a typical day at work.

- Brainstorm activities that they have to do and don't have to do in their jobs every day.

- **TRB** Optionally, give students a copy of the writing model (see the *Teacher's Resource Book*, Writing Models). Ask them to read the model and notice the vocabulary and grammar from the unit.

- If students don't have the model, write the following on the board:

  I like my job because I enjoy traveling and helping people. My salary is OK, and I get an allowance for each flight I work. Do you want to know what I do?

- Have a student read the sentences aloud. Answer any questions students might have.

- Walk around to make sure everyone understands the task.

For suggestions on how to give feedback on writing, see page xiv of this *Teacher's Edition*.

CONVERSATION TO GO

At the end of class, call on two students to role-play the conversation.

HOMEWORK

- Assign *Workbook* page 47, Grammar Exercises 3 and 4, and page 48, Pronunciation Exercises 7 and 8.

- If students do not have the *WorldView Workbook*, assign listening homework from the Student CD. Write on the board:

  Track 23
  What do you think are the worst things about Marcus's job? Why?

- Tell students to listen to the audio and write the answer to the questions. Have them bring their answers to the next class.

  (Possible answers: *The job doesn't pay much money. / He has to work long hours. / He has to drive a lot, and he has to use his own car. / People don't always give him a tip. / He's always busy. / He has to be polite, even when he's tired.*)

Speaking

7 **BEFORE YOU SPEAK.** Look at the list of jobs. Add one more job to the list. Complete the chart with activities people *have to* do and *don't have to* do in these jobs. Then rank the jobs in your order of preference (1 = the best and 6 = the worst).

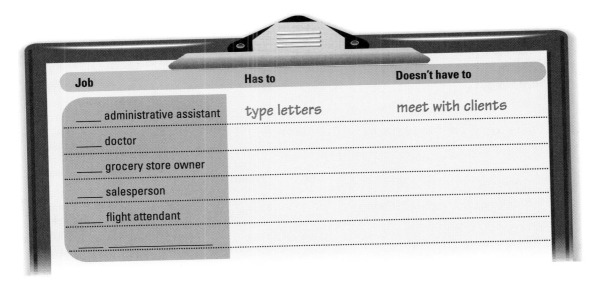

Job	Has to	Doesn't have to
_____ administrative assistant	type letters	meet with clients
_____ doctor		
_____ grocery store owner		
_____ salesperson		
_____ flight attendant		
_____		

8 **GROUPS OF 3.** Which jobs do you think are best and worst. Discuss your opinions and give reasons.

A: *I think doctors have the worst job. They have to help very sick people. They have to work long hours.*
B: *I don't think they have the worst job. They don't have to . . .*

9 Compare your group's answers with the rest of the class. Which job did most people think was the best? The worst?

Writing

10 Imagine that you are working in your ideal job. Write an article like the one on page 49 describing a typical day at work. Describe the activities that you *have to* do and *don't have to* do every day.

CONVERSATION TO GO

A: **Do** you **have to make** decisions in your job?
B: Yes, I **do**. Umm . . . no, I **don't**. Well, yes . . .

Island life

Lesson A

Vocabulary Practical activities
Grammar Present perfect for indefinite past: *ever, never*
Speaking Talking about practical experience

Getting started

1 *PAIRS.* **Look at the photo of Mulkinney Island. Would you like to live there? Why?**

2 **Read the advertisement for a new television show, *Adventure Island*. Complete the sentences with the verbs in the box.**

build	catch	grow	have	make
spend	take care of	~~travel~~	work	

Adventure Island

A new reality TV show

Do you like to (1) __travel__ to new places and (2) _____ time outdoors? Are you ready to (3) _____ an adventure?

Mulkinney Island is in the north Atlantic. No one lives there. There are no houses, no stores, and no hospitals. We are looking for sixteen adventurous people from around the world to live on the island for a year.

We need people who can (4) _____ houses, (5) _____ clothes, and (6) _____ food.

We also need people who know how to (7) _____ fish, (8) _____ on a farm, and (9) _____ animals.

Send your application today. Explain why we should pick you to join us on Adventure Island!

3 *PAIRS.* **Compare your answers in Exercise 2.**

OBJECTIVES

Students will:

- activate vocabulary related to practical activities
- do reading, speaking, and writing tasks related to practical experience
- focus on using the present perfect to describe personal experience
- practice linking a vowel sound at the end of a word to a vowel at the beginning of the next word

---

WARM-UP: WHAT'S ON TV?

Groups of 3. Students talk about their favorite TV programs and why they like them.

- Tell students that this unit is organized around practical activities. Explain that the unit title, "Island life," refers to a reality TV program called *Adventure Island.*
- Divide students in groups of 3 and set a time limit of 5 minutes. Tell them to take turns telling each other about their favorite TV programs and giving a reason.
- Call on a few students to name their favorite TV program and say why they enjoy it.

Getting started

CULTURE NOTE

Reality shows are not new to the United States. The first American reality show debuted in 1948. The show *Candid Camera* created strange and embarrassing situations and recorded people's reactions to them. A few other reality shows enjoyed popularity over the next 50 years, but the recent popular trend started in 2000 with the success of the program *Survivor.*

Reality television has become wildly popular in the United States. There is now a reality show for practically every interest, including relationships, wilderness survival, and interior design.

OPTION: VOCABULARY PREVIEW

Write the verbs from Exercise 2 on the board. Elicit from students nouns that can follow each verb. Give the verb *build* as an example. Ask: *What things can you build?* (a house, a bridge) Alternatively, you can write the verbs in one column, the nouns in another, and have students match each verb with a noun.

Exercise ❶

- Tell students to look at the photo. Ask: *What's in the picture? How would you describe this place? What are they advertising?*
- Brainstorm some television programs that are similar to the one in the advertisement.

- Have students look at the picture. Explain the task: Students will discuss whether or not they would like to live on the island and give a reason.
- You may want to clarify the task by giving an example about yourself. (For example, *I wouldn't want to live on Mulkinney Island because nobody lives there. I like to be around a lot of people.*)
- Set a time limit of 2 minutes. While students are working, walk around the room, helping as needed.
- Call on a few students to report on their discussion.

Exercise ❷

- Tell students that they are going to read the ad.
- Explain the task: Students will choose the verbs in the box to complete the sentences. Go over the example.
- Check comprehension by asking questions such as *Where is Mulkinney Island? Who lives there? How many people are they looking for? How long will the people live there?*
- Give the students 3 minutes to complete the sentences. Walk around the room, helping as needed.
- Tell students they will check their answers in the next activity.

Exercise ❸

- Pair students and tell them to compare their answers in Exercise 2.
- Go over the answers with the class.

Answer key

1. travel	4. build	7. catch
2. spend	5. make	8. work
3. have	6. grow	9. take care of

EXTENSION

Reinforce the collocations in Exercise 2 by calling out sentences without verbs and asking volunteers to add the missing verbs. You may use these sentences or you may create your own.

1. We _____ tomatoes in our backyard. (grow)
2. Who _____ Mary's children while she's at work? They can't stay home alone. (takes care of)
3. I like to _____ time with my brother. We always have a lot of fun. (spend)
4. Would you like to _____ an adventure? Let's join a tour! (have)
5. Mike's father has a construction company. He _____ houses. (builds)
6. Sarah _____ all her own clothes. (makes)
7. We always see people fishing in the lake. Does anyone ever _____ anything? (catch)

Exercise ❹

- **Pairs.** Tell students to look at the list in the chart.
- Explain the task: Students will check *Yes* (if the ability is useful) or *No* (if the ability is not useful) and write a reason for the answer under *Why?*
- Go over the example.
- Pair students and set a time limit of 5 minutes. Walk around the room, helping as needed.

Exercise ❺

- Have students compare their answers with a partner's.
- Call on a few volunteers to share their answers with the class.

EXTENSION

Have students rank each of the skills in order of their usefulness on the island, with *1* being the most useful and *5* the least useful.

Answer key

Answers will vary. Students will probably say that using a computer, starting a business, and writing newspaper articles are less useful than cooking for a group.

Reading

Exercise ❻

- Explain the task: Students will read Andrew Ho's application form and check *Yes* or *No* to each question about his experience.
- Clarify the activity by reading aloud Andrew's answer to the first question and then asking the question, *Has Andrew ever spent time outdoors?* Elicit the answer *yes*, and have students check that box.
- Set a time limit of 3 minutes. Walk around the room, helping as needed.
- Have students compare their answers with a partner's.
- Go over the answers with the class.

Answer key

1. Yes   2. No   3. No   4. Yes

EXTENSION

- Ask students to create two sentences about the reading, leaving a blank for information from the ad. (For example, *Andrew is a(n) _____ person.*)
- Pair students and have them take turns completing each other's sentences.

Exercise ❼

- Explain the task: Students will discuss whether or not Andrew Ho is a good choice for *Adventure Island* and explain why.
- Give the students a minute to look over the reading and decide how they will answer the questions.
- Call on several students to tell you if Andrew is a good choice or not and to give you a reason for selecting him (for example, *He can cook for a large group.*) or a reason against choosing him (for example, *He hasn't lived overseas.*).

◉ Please go to www.longman.com/worldview for additional in-class model conversation practice.

HOMEWORK

- 📖 Assign *Workbook* page 49, Vocabulary Exercises 1 and 2, and page 51, Listening Exercises 5 and 6.

4 What other abilities will be useful on the island? Check *Yes* or *No* and write why.

Does *Adventure Island* need people who can . . .	Yes	No	Why?
use a computer?			
start a business?			
cook for a large group?			
write newspaper articles?			
teach a class?			

5 *PAIRS.* **Compare your answers.**

I don't think Adventure Island needs people who can use a computer. There are no computers on the island!

Reading

6 **Andrew Ho wants to be on *Adventure Island*. Read his application form. Then check (✓) *Yes* or *No* to each question about his experience.**

Name: Andrew Ho

Age: 25

ADVENTURE ISLAND
REALITY ADVENTURE TELEVISION

1. Have you ever spent time outdoors?   YES ☐ NO ☐

I've gone camping many times, and I like hiking and mountain climbing. I've also gone fishing in the ocean, and I've caught a lot of fish! I love the outdoors.

2. Have you ever worked on a farm?   YES ☐ NO ☐

I haven't worked on a farm, but my family has had several pets, and I think I'm good at taking care of animals. I've had a vegetable garden, and I've grown carrots, tomatoes, and lettuce in my backyard.

3. Have you ever lived overseas?   YES ☐ NO ☐

I've never lived overseas, but I've traveled abroad and around the United States. I like to travel and meet new people. I'm an adventurous person.

4. Have you ever cooked for large groups?   YES ☐ NO ☐

I'm a cook in a hospital. I think this experience will be useful because I cook for large groups all the time.

7 **Discuss. Is Andrew Ho a good choice for *Adventure Island*? Why? What can he do?**

Grammar focus

1 **Look again at the application form on page 53 and answer the questions.**

Is Andrew growing vegetables now?
Do we know exactly when he grew vegetables?

2 **Study the examples of the present perfect for the indefinite past.**

> I**'ve grown** vegetables in my backyard.
> My family **has had** a lot of pets.
> **Have** you **ever spent** time outdoors? Yes, I **have.** / No, I **haven't.**
> I **haven't worked** on a farm.
> I**'ve never lived** overseas.

3 **Look at the examples again. Circle the correct words to complete the rules in the chart.**

Present perfect: indefinite past; *ever, never*
Use the present perfect when the exact time of an action **is / is not** important.
Use *have* or *has* + the **present / past** participle to form the present perfect.
Use **never / ever** + present perfect to ask a question.
Use *not* or **never / ever** + present perfect to make a negative statement.
NOTE: The past participle of regular verbs is the base form of the verb + -*ed*.   See page 150 for a list of irregular past participles.

Grammar Reference page 146

4 **Complete the conversations with the correct present perfect form of the verbs in parentheses.**

1. A: __Have__ they ever __used__ (**use**) a computer?

   B: Yes, they __have__.

2. A: _____ you ever _____ (**build**) a fire?

   B: Yes, I _____. I _____ (**go**) camping several times.

3. A: _____ she ever _____ (**take care of**) farm animals?

   B: No, she _____, but she _____ (**have**) a few pets.

4. A: _____ they ever _____ (**live**) overseas?

   B: They _____ (**not live**) overseas, but they _____ (**travel**) abroad.

5. A: _____ you ever _____ (**go**) fishing?

   B: Yes, I _____. I _____ (**go**) hiking, too.

6. A: _____ he ever _____ (**cook**) for large groups?

   B: Yes, he _____. He's a cook in a hospital.

Grammar focus

- The present perfect is used to talk about things that started in the past, continue up to the present, and may continue into the future. It is also used to talk about things that have happened in a period of time that is not finished.

- The focus in this unit is on the present perfect used to talk about things that happened at an unspecified or indefinite time in the past. If the specific time such as last year, yesterday, etc., is indicated, use the simple past.

- The present perfect is used with the adverbs *ever, never, yet, already,* and with expressions of time beginning with *since* and *for.*

- The auxiliary verb *have* usually has a short, weak pronunciation before another verb: *My family has* /həz/ *had a lot of pets.*

- It has a strong pronunciation at the end of a sentence: *Yes, I have* /hæv/.

- Note the contracted forms *'s, 've, hasn't,* and *haven't.* Students sometimes confuse the contraction *'s* for *has* with the contraction of the verb *be.*

WARM-UP

Note: Skip this warm-up if you're doing this lesson (Lesson B) during the same class period as Lesson A.

- Tell students they are going to listen to the interview with Andrew Ho from the Reading section.

- Ask them to pay attention to the period of time: When did the actions happen?

- 🎧 Play the audio from Lesson A, Reading, Exercise 6. (This models the grammar of the unit.)

- Ask: *Do we know when exactly Andrew did some of the activities?*

- Elicit a few verb forms students remember. Write them on the board.

Exercise ❶

- Have students answer the two questions. You may need to play the audio a second time.

- Go over the answers with the class.

Answer key

a. No   b. No

Exercise ❷

- Have students look at the examples and study the bold-faced words.

- Tell them to focus on the first and last two examples. Ask: *What's the form of the main verb in these sentences?* (the past participle) *What auxiliary verb is used with the present perfect tense?* (*have*)

- Call attention to the use of *never* in the last sentence. Explain that *never* is used with the affirmative form of the verb.

- Tell students to look at the third example—a question with short answers. Point out the position of the word *ever* in the question. It comes before the main verb (the present participle form) in present perfect questions.

Exercise ❸

- Have students study the examples again.

- Tell students to read the statements in the chart and circle the word that correctly completes each one.

- Have students compare answers with a partner's.

- Go over the answers with the class.

- Ask a few questions to elicit the key points about the grammar: For example, *What auxiliary is used in present perfect statements and questions?* (*have*) *What form is used for the main verb in present perfect statements and questions?* (the past participle) *What ending is used with regular verbs to form the past participle?* (*-ed*) *What words are used with the present perfect to ask questions?* (*ever* and *never*)

Answer key

is not   past   *ever*   *never*

Exercise ❹

- Before beginning Exercise 4, answer any questions students might have. You may also want to refer the class to the Grammar Reference for Unit 12 on page 146.

- Go over the example. Ask why *have* is the correct auxiliary in the sentence. (The subject, *they,* is plural.) Ask: *What form is the main verb?* (past participle)

- Have students complete the exercise individually. Set a time limit of 3 minutes.

- Have students compare answers with a partner's.

- Go over the answers with the class.

Answer key

1. A: Have . . . used
   B: have
2. A: Have . . . built
   B: have; have gone/'ve gone
3. A: Has . . . taken care of
   B: hasn't; has had/'s had
4. A: Have . . . lived
   B: haven't lived; have traveled/'ve traveled
5. A: Have . . . gone
   B: have; have gone/'ve gone
6. A: Has . . . cooked
   B: has

Pronunciation

> **LANGUAGE NOTE**
> English speakers link words together, without a break, when they speak. Recognizing words that are linked will help them understand spoken English.

Exercise **5**

- Tell students they will listen to words that are linked together.
- 🎧 Play the audio. Point out that the sounds joined by the linking lines are vowel sounds.
- Explain that English speakers often add a very short /w/ or /y/ sound to link two vowel sounds. The choice of adding either /w/ or /y/ depends on the first vowel sound: /w/ is added after /u/ (as in *you*) and /y/ is added after /i/ (as in *he*) and /ey/ (as in *they*).

Exercise **6**

- Tell students they will listen to the audio again. This time, they will listen and repeat.
- 🎧 Play the audio again, stopping after each item to allow students to repeat chorally.
- Encourage students to link the words smoothly where shown, without stopping their voice between the words.

Speaking

Exercise **7**

This exercise provides practice with the vocabulary from the unit. It prepares students for Exercises 8 and 9.

- Explain the task: Students will put a check mark next to each activity that they have done. They will put the check marks under the column *You*.
- Model the activity.
- Tell students to write two more activities in the chart. After writing in their own ideas, tell students to put a check mark if they have also done these activities.

Exercise **8**

- Explain the task: Students will take turns interviewing one another. They must create questions about each of the activities in the chart.
- Have the students in each group take turns asking questions about the activities and follow-up questions. They should check the activities that each of the other members of their group has done.
- Divide the class in groups of 3. Set a time limit of 5 minutes. Walk around the room, helping as needed.

Exercise **9**

- Elicit suggestions from different groups about which students seem to have the most skills that would be useful on *Adventure Island*.

TRB For additional interactive grammar practice, have students do the reproducible activity for this unit in the *Teacher's Resource Book*.

Writing

Exercise **10**

- Assign the writing task for class work or homework.
- Explain the task: Students will apply to go on *Adventure Island*.
- Brainstorm things that people may have done or not done that will help them on the island.
- **TRB** Optionally, give students a copy of the writing model (see the *Teacher's Resource Book*, Writing Models). Ask them to read the model and notice the vocabulary and grammar from the unit.
- If students don't have the model, write the following on the board:

    I think you should choose me because I've spent a lot of time outdoors.

For suggestions on how to give feedback on writing, see page xiv of this *Teacher's Edition*.

CONVERSATION TO GO

At the end of the class, call on two students to role-play the conversation.

HOMEWORK

- 📖 Assign *Workbook* page 50, Grammar Exercises 3 and 4, and page 51, Pronunciation Exercises 7, 8, and 9.
- Assign *Workbook* Self-Quiz 3.
- 💿 If students do not have the *WorldView Workbook*, assign listening homework from the Student CD. Write on the board:

    Track 25
    Answer the question.
    What is Andrew's occupation?

- 🎧 Tell students to listen to the audio and choose the correct word for each sentence. Have them bring their answers to the next class.

    (Answers: *He is a cook in a hospital.*)

FOR NEXT CLASS

- Tell students that the next class will be a review class covering Units 9–12.
- Have students review the material in the units to prepare for the activities in Review 3.
- **TRB** Make copies of Quiz 3 in the *Teacher's Resource Book*.

Unit no.	Review Grammar	Listen to Student CD	Study Grammar Reference
9	*would like/like, would prefer/prefer*	Track 19	Page 145
10	*will* for predicting	Track 22	Page 145
11	*have to/don't have to*	Track 23	Page 145
12	*ever/never;* present perfect	Track 25	Page 146

Pronunciation

5 🎧 Listen. Notice how a vowel sound at the end of a word links to a vowel sound at the beginning of the next word.

Have you ᵂever   Have you ever lived overseas?

Has he ʸever   Has he ever grown vegetables?

Have you ᵂever   Have you ever spent time outdoors?

Have they ʸever   Have they ever used a computer?

6 🎧 Listen and repeat.

Speaking

7 *BEFORE YOU SPEAK.* **Look at the chart and check (✓) the activities that you have done. Then add two more activities to the chart.**

Activities	You	Classmate 1	Classmate 2
grow vegetables			
take care of animals			
go camping			
make clothes			
catch a fish			
travel overseas			

8 *GROUPS OF 3.* **Interview each other. Ask follow-up questions to get more information. Record the answers in the chart.**

A: *Have you ever grown vegetables?*
B: *Yes, I have.*
A: *Really? What kind of vegetables?*
B: *I've grown tomatoes.*

9 **Which person in your group should be on the TV show *Adventure Island*?**

Writing

10 **The TV show *Adventure Island* has invited you to apply for their next adventure. Are you ready to go? Write a letter explaining why you should go. Describe the things you have done that will help you on the island. Use the present perfect.**

CONVERSATION TO GO

A: Have you ever made your own clothes?
B: Yes, I have.

Unit 9 What would you like?

1 🎧 Listen to the model conversation.

2 *PAIRS.* Make the menu for your own American restaurant. Think of a name for the restaurant. Then think of two interesting appetizers, two entrées, two side dishes, and two desserts. Write the names of the dishes in the menu. (Be sure you can describe each dish.)

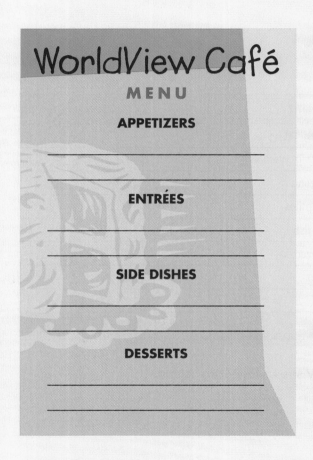

WorldView Café

M E N U

APPETIZERS

_____

_____

ENTRÉES

_____

_____

SIDE DISHES

_____

_____

DESSERTS

_____

_____

3 *PAIRS.* Find a new partner. Student A, you're the waiter; Student B, you're the customer. The waiter gives the menu to the customer and explains the dishes on it. The customer orders. Then switch roles.

4 Discuss. Which restaurant has the best or the most interesting menu?

Unit 10 Big issues

5 🎧 Listen to the model conversation.

6 Make three predictions about the future. Predict something that will happen in 20 years, in 50 years, and in 100 years. Write your predictions on the timeline.

20 years ⟶ 50 years ⟶ 100 years ⟶

Today

7 Walk around the room. Tell one of your predictions to a classmate, and ask if he or she agrees with it. If your classmate agrees, you get one point. Continue telling classmates your predictions. The person with the most points at the end of the game is the winner.

8 Share your results with the class. Which predictions did the most people agree with? Which did they disagree with?

You may wish to use the video for Units 9–12 at this point. For video activity worksheets, go to www.longman.com/worldview.

Unit 9: What would you like?

OBJECTIVES

- Review the material presented in Unit 9
- Grammar practice: *would like/like, would prefer/prefer*

> **WARM-UP**
>
> Books closed. Tell students to imagine that they own a restaurant. Ask them to decide what their restaurant's specialty is. (A specialty is a dish a restaurant is known for. It doesn't have to be difficult or fancy.)

Exercise ❶

- Tell students they will listen to a conversation between a server and a customer at a restaurant. Tell them to find out what the customer orders. (the soup)
- 🎧 Play the audio.

Exercise ❷

- Explain the task: Students will work in pairs to write a menu for a restaurant that serves American food. Remind them to make sure they can explain or describe each dish on their menu.
- Pair students and set a time limit of 5 minutes. Tell them they will have to answer customers' questions about each item on their menu in Exercise 3.

Exercise ❸

- 🎧 If needed, play the audio again for Exercise 1. Tell students that the conversation is a model for their role-play.
- Pair students with different partners from Exercise 2. Assign roles A and B.
- Have Student A role-play the part of a waiter/waitress. Have Student B role-play the customer who will be asking questions and ordering from the menu.
- Set a time limit of 3 minutes for the role-play. Walk around the room, helping as needed. Encourage customers to ask about the menu items.
- After 3 minutes, have partners switch roles.

Exercise ❹

- Pair students with new partners. Assign roles A (waiter/waitress) and B (customer).
- Set a time limit of 3 minutes. Walk around the room, helping as needed.

Unit 10: Big issues

OBJECTIVES

- Review material presented in Unit 10
- Grammar practice: *will* for predicting

> **WARM-UP**
>
> - Books closed. Ask students what verb forms are used to talk about future events. (*will, be going to*)
> - Write these phrases on the board: *people/live on Mars/twenty years, mass transportation/be more common/fifty years,* and *world population/increase/ 100 years*.
> - Give this example of a prediction using *will* or *won't: People won't live on Mars in twenty years.* Have volunteers make predictions with *will* or *won't*.

Exercise ❺

- Tell students they will listen to a conversation that models Exercise 7.
- Have them listen and answer these questions: *What does [the woman] think will happen in twenty years?* (She thinks cars won't need gasoline in twenty years.) *Does the man agree?* (He agrees but thinks that it won't happen for 100 years.)
- 🎧 Play the audio.

Exercise ❻

- Explain the task: Students will write sentences about three predictions that they think will happen in twenty, fifty, and 100 years. Then they will compare their predictions with a partner.
- Set a time limit of 5 minutes. Walk around the room, helping as needed.

Exercise ❼

- Explain the task: Students will compare their predictions with a partner.
- Pair students and set a time limit of 3 minutes.
- 🎧 If needed, play the audio for Exercise 5 again to remind students how to do the activity.
- Have students compare their predictions with their partner's. Remind them to keep track of their points.

Exercise ❽

- Ask volunteers to tell the class who had the most points.
- Have volunteers read aloud some of their predictions. Invite the rest of the class to agree or disagree with the predictions and to explain why.

Unit 11: Hard work

- Review the material presented in Unit 11
- Grammar practice: *have to/don't have to*

WARM-UP

- Books closed. Call out a job, for example, flight attendant. Ask students to say some of the tasks that a flight attendant has to do. As a follow-up question, ask them what a flight attendant doesn't have to do.
- Play a quick guessing game similar to "Twenty Questions." Tell students that you are thinking of a job. Tell them to ask you *Yes/No* questions about the job that you are thinking of. They can ask up to seven questions to guess the job. Remind them to use *has to/have to* and *doesn't/don't have to* in their questions.
- Keep track of how many questions students ask to guess the correct answer.

Exercise ❾

- Tell students they will listen to a model of the guessing game in Exercise 10. Tell them to listen for at least one thing that the person has to do and doesn't have to do at his job. (*The person has to work inside and outside, work with people, work with food, and drive a car. He or she doesn't have to use a computer.*)
- 🎧 Play the audio.

Exercise ❿

- **Groups of 3.** Explain the task: Students will play the guessing game.
- Divide the class into groups of 3.
- 🎧 If needed, play the audio for Exercise 9 again to remind students how to play the game. Walk around the room, helping as needed.
- Remind students to keep score.

WRAP-UP

Encourage students to compare their scores with members of other groups. Ask which job was the most difficult to guess.

Unit 12: Island life

- Review the material presented in Unit 12
- Grammar practice: *ever/never* with the present perfect

WARM-UP

- Books closed. Conduct an informal survey of the class. Ask a few questions with the present perfect, such as *Who has read a novel in English? Who has met triplets?*
- Have students raise their hands if they have done any of the activities they hear.

Exercise ⓫

- Tell students that they will listen to people take a survey. Ask them to listen and find out who has taken care of animals. (the woman)
- 🎧 Play the audio.

Exercise ⓬

- Tell students to look at the pictures in the chart. Tell them to pretend that they have done six of the activities in the pictures. Have them choose and put a check mark next to the six activities in the chart that they have done.
- Explain the task: Students will take a survey to find out which activities their classmates have done, based on the pictures they checked in the chart.
- Briefly review the question form that students will use: *Have you ever* + past participle of verb.
- 🎧 If needed, play the audio for Exercise 11 again to remind students how to do the survey.

Exercise ⓭

- Tell students to go around and conduct the survey.
- Set a time limit of 4 minutes. Walk around the room, helping as needed.

WRAP-UP

Have students share their results with the rest of the class.

Unit 11 Hard work

9 🎧 Listen to the model conversation.

10 *GROUPS OF 3.* Student A, think of a job. Students B and C, ask *Yes/No* questions about the job. When you have enough information, guess what job it is. Keep track of the number of questions you ask. Take turns until everyone thinks of a job and everyone asks and answers questions. The person whose job requires the most questions wins.

Unit 12 Island life

11 🎧 Listen to the model conversation.

12 Check (✔) at least six activities that you have done. (You can use your imagination.)

13 Take turns asking *Yes/No* questions to find out what experience your classmates have. When you find someone who answers yes, write the student's name in the appropriate box. The person with the most names filled in at the end of the game is the winner.

World of Music 2

Wonderful Tonight

Eric Clapton

Vocabulary

1 **PAIRS.** Match each verb with the correct word or phrase.

1. ask __c__
2. brush ____
3. feel ____
4. give ____
5. go ____
6. help ____
7. put on ____
8. say ____
9. turn off ____
10. walk around ____

a. "yes"
b. her a present
c. him a question
d. me sit down
e. the lights
f. to a party
g. with me
h. wonderful
i. your hair
j. your makeup

The 70s

*The "British invasion" of rock 'n' roll was in full swing in the 70s. **Eric Clapton**, a guitar virtuoso, became—and remains— one of rock music's most admired stars.*

Listening

2 🎧 Listen to the song. Put the pictures in order.

1. ____   2. ____   3. ____

World of Music 2

- Introduce Eric Clapton's song "Wonderful Tonight"
- Vocabulary practice: verbs
- Express personal reaction to a song

BACKGROUND INFORMATION

The song "Wonderful Tonight" by Eric Clapton is about Patti Harrison. Clapton fell in love with Patti Harrison in the early 1970s. Patti was married to George Harrison at the time. Eric and Patti met when Eric collaborated on an album with George. In 1977, Patti and George Harrison were divorced, and Eric and Patti were married shortly thereafter. Eric Clapton and George Harrison remained good friends. Harrison even played at Eric and Patti's wedding.

WARM-UP

- Books closed. Ask students what they know about Eric Clapton. (He is known for his guitar playing. His most popular song is "Tears from Heaven," a song he wrote to express his grief over the death of his son, Connor, who fell forty-nine stories from his New York apartment.)
- Ask students what other Eric Clapton songs they know. ("Wonderful Tonight," "Layla," and "Change the World" to name a few.)
- Tell students they are going to listen to one of Clapton's most requested songs, "Wonderful Tonight."
- Tell them to think about some signs that show that a man and a woman are in love.

The 70s

- Tell students to read the information about the 70s in the *Student Book.* Ask: *What does the term "British invasion" refer to?* It refers to the influx of British rock-'n'-rollers on the American music scene, which began with the appearance of the Beatles in 1964.
- Tell them to name British singers and bands that became popular in the United States and all over the world in the 70s. (Eric Clapton, The Beatles, The Rolling Stones)
- Ask them to give examples of some 70s songs. Encourage them to sing a few lines from these songs.

Vocabulary

Exercise 1

- Tell students to look at the words and phrases in the two columns. Point out that the first column contains verbs, and the second column contains words and phrases that can follow each verb.
- Tell students to decide which phrase or word in the second column can follow a verb in the first column. Write the letter of the word or phrase next to each verb.
- Set a time limit of 3 minutes. Walk around the room, helping as needed.
- Have students compare their answers with a partner's.
- Check the answers as a class.

Answer key			
1. c	4. b	7. j	10. g
2. i	5. f	8. a	
3. h	6. d	9. e	

Listening

Exercise 2

- Have students look at photos A, B, and C. Ask them to say what's happening in each photo. (A = The woman is brushing her hair. B = The man has a headache. C = A man and a woman are dancing at a party.)
- Explain the task: Students will listen to the song and will put the pictures in the order they happen in the song.
- Prepare students to listen by helping them identify key words to listen for such as *brush hair, headache, party.*
- 🎧 Play the song.
- Have students check their answers as a class.

Answer key		
1. A	2. C	3. B

Exercise ❸

- Explain the task: Students will listen to the song again. This time they will read the lyrics as they listen and fill in the missing words.
- Have students read through the lyrics once. Clarify any unfamiliar vocabulary.
- 🎧 Play the song again. You may want to play the song a third time to give students more time to fill in all of the missing words.
- Tell students they will check their answers in the next exercise.

Exercise ❹

- Have students compare their answers from Exercise 3 with a partner's.
- Then ask students to check their answers as a class. Read the lines aloud and call on volunteers to fill in each missing word by calling it out. Write the words on the board as they are given.
- Answer any questions students might have.

Answer key		
Line 3: *puts on*	Line 8: *turns*	Line 17: *give*
Line 4: *brushes*	Line 10: *walking*	Line 18: *helps*
Line 5: *asks*	Line 11: *asks*	Line 19: *tell*
Line 6: *say*	Line 12: *feel*	Line 20: *turn off*
Line 7: *go*	Line 15: *go*	

OPTION
🎧 Play the audio again for students to sing along.

Speaking

Exercise ❺

- Divide the class into groups of 3. Tell each group to discuss the questions and their reactions to the song.
- 🎧 If needed, play the song again.
- Have volunteers share their answers to the questions as well as their reactions to the song.

3 🎧 **Listen to the song again. Complete the lyrics.**

Wonderful Tonight

It's late in the evening.
She's wondering what clothes to wear.
She _____ her makeup
and _____ her long blonde hair.
And then she _____ me, "Do I look all right?"
and I _____, "Yes, you look wonderful tonight."

We _____ to a party
and everyone _____ to see
this beautiful lady,
who's _____ around with me.
And then she _____ me, "Do you feel all right?"
and I say, "Yes, I _____ wonderful tonight."

I feel wonderful because I see the love light in your eyes,
and the wonder of it all, is that you just don't realize how much I love you.

It's time to _____ home now
and I've got an aching head.
So I _____ her the car keys
and she _____ me to bed.

And then I _____ her,
as I _____ the light,
I say, "My darling, you were wonderful tonight."
"Oh, My darling, you were wonderful tonight."

4 *PAIRS.* **Compare your answers in Exercise 3.**

Speaking ◀▬▬▬▬▬

5 *GROUPS OF 3.* **Discuss the questions.**

What is the song about? Tell the story.
What do you like about the song (for example, the words, the music, the singer's voice)?
Is there something you don't like?

Keepsakes

Vocabulary Possessions; phrasal verbs related to possessions
Grammar Review: possessive *'s*; possessive
adjectives/pronouns; *belong to*
Speaking Talking about special possessions

Getting started

1 **Look at the photos of the keepsakes.
What do you think *keepsakes* are?**

2 **Match the words in the box with the photos.**

1. ballet shoes _I_	2. baseball glove ___	3. camera ___	4. doll ___
5. jewelry box ___	6. photo album ___	7. pin ___	8. shawl ___
9. toy truck ___	10. watch ___		

3 🎧 **Listen and check your answers. Then listen and repeat.**

4 *PAIRS.* **Discuss. What things do you keep as keepsakes?**

Keepsakes

OBJECTIVES

Students will:

- activate vocabulary related to possessions
- do listening, speaking, and writing tasks related to special possessions
- focus on using the possessive -s, possessive adjectives/pronouns, and *belong to*
- practice stress and linking in phrasal verbs

WARM-UP: WHAT'S THE STORY?

Groups of 3. Students take turns telling each other about one of their possessions.

- Tell students that this unit is about possessions, or things we own. Explain that the unit title, "Keepsakes," refers to a special kind of possession.
- Ask students to think of something they have with them that they could say something interesting about.
- Clarify the task. Take a few personal items from your pocket or bag (for example, your keys, a book, a pen, a photograph). Tell a story about one of the items. (For example, *This is a picture of my sister. She's a few years younger than me. We weren't friends as children, but now we're very close.*)
- Divide the class into groups of 3 and set a time limit of 5 minutes. Each partner should choose a possession and say at least two sentences about it. Tell students to listen to one another closely.
- After 5 minutes, call on a few students to tell the class what they found out about one of their partners' possessions.

Getting started

Exercise ❶

- Tell students to look at the photos. Read the question aloud, and ask students to think about what the things in the pictures have in common. Ask questions such as *Are these things new or old?* (They're old.) *Why do people save things like these?* (Because they were a gift from someone special or because they are reminders of a special time or event.)
- After a brief class discussion, elicit a definition of the word *keepsake*. (A keepsake is an object that reminds us of someone or something special.)

OPTION: VOCABULARY PREVIEW

Encourage students to match the familiar words first and then to make intelligent guesses about the remaining items. Give an example by choosing one of the lower-frequency items (for example, *pin* or *shawl*) and using it to model the activity.

Exercise ❷

- Explain the task: Students will match the words with the photos by writing the letter of each photo next to the correct word or phrase in the box.
- Have students work individually to complete the exercise. Set a time limit of 3 minutes. While students are working, walk around the room, helping as needed.
- Have students compare their answers with a partner. Tell them they will listen to the correct answers in Exercise 3.

Exercise ❸

- Explain the task: Students will listen to the audio. As they listen, they will check their answers in Exercise 2. Then they will listen again and repeat the words.
- 🎧 Play the audio. Encourage students to correct any wrong answers.
- 🎧 Play the audio again and have students listen and repeat.

Answer key				
1. I	3. A	5. F	7. B	9. G
2. E	4. H	6. C	8. J	10. D

EXTENSION

- Reinforce the new vocabulary by calling out an item from Exercise 2 and having students say the letter of the corresponding photo.
- To make the activity more challenging, call out the letter of the photo and have students say the corresponding keepsake item.

Exercise ❹

- Tell students to read the question and to think about how they will answer. Model the activity by giving an example about one or two things you keep as keepsakes. (For example, *I have a collection of small glass animals. They belonged to my godmother. She gave them to me before she died.*)
- Pair students and set a time limit of 3 minutes. Walk around the room, helping as needed.
- After 3 minutes, call on a few students to tell the class about one of their keepsakes.

EXTENSION

- Divide the class into groups of 3.
- Have students each write a brief description of a keepsake without saying what the object is. They will take turns reading their descriptions and guessing the keepsakes.
- Model the activity by describing a keepsake you have. (For example, *This is something I had when I was a child. I used to catch balls with it. It's made of leather.* Answer: *a baseball glove.*)

FYI

A phrasal verb is a two-part verb, consisting of a verb + particle. A particle looks like a preposition, but it is part of the verb phrase and often changes the meaning of the verb. Phrasal verbs can be transitive or intransitive.

Exercise ❺

- Tell students to look at the list of verbs in the left column. Point out that these are phrasal verbs. Explain what a phrasal verb is using the information in the FYI above.
- Explain the task: Students will match the phrasal verbs on the left with their meanings on the right. Go over the example.
- Have students complete the exercise individually. Set a time limit of 3 minutes.
- Have students compare their answers with a partner's.
- Go over the answers with the class.

Answer key

1. g	3. b	5. f	7. c
2. e	4. h	6. a	8. d

EXTENSION

- Have students create sentences using one of the phrasal verbs from Exercise 5 and one of the vocabulary items from Exercise 2.
- Model the activity by giving an example, *I put my ballet shoes away when I stopped dancing.*
- Pair students and set a time limit of 5 minutes.

Listening

Exercise ❻

- Have the students read the two questions first, so they know what information they will be listening for. Ask students to predict the answers to the questions.
- 🎧 Play the audio.
- Have students compare their answers with a partner's.
- Go over the answers with the class.

Answer key

1. a	2. a

Exercise ❼

- Explain the task: Students will listen to the conversation again and will match the things in the trunk to the person it belongs or belonged to. Go over the example.
- 🎧 Play the audio again.
- Go over the answers with the class.

Answer key

1. c	2. d	3. b	4. a

🌐 Please go to www.longman.com/worldview for supplementary reading practice.

Pronunciation

LANGUAGE NOTES

- When a phrasal verb has no object (for example, *It's falling apart.*) or has a pronoun as the object (for example, *Take it out.*), the main stress usually falls on the particle.
- Phrasal verbs are pronounced as a single unit. A consonant sound at the end of the first word is linked smoothly to a vowel sound at the beginning of the next word: *Take it out.* If the first word ends with a vowel and the next word begins with a vowel, a short /w/ or /y/ sound is often added to link the sounds smoothly: *Let's throw /w/ it away. I'll try /y/ it on.*
- In American English, the *t* in *it* sounds like a quick English /d/ sound when it is linked to a following vowel (as in *take it out* or *give it away*).

Exercise ❽

- Tell students that they will listen to the pronunciation of some phrasal verbs. Remind them to pay attention to the linking of the words.
- 🎧 Play the audio. Ask students to notice which word is stressed, or sounds the strongest—the verb or the particle.
- Point out that the main stress in these phrasal verbs is on the particle. If there is a pronoun, the particle is not stressed.

Exercise ❾

- Tell students they will listen again. This time, they will listen and repeat.
- 🎧 Play the audio, stopping after each item and asking students to repeat chorally.
- Encourage students to link the words smoothly. Write some phrases on the board with the words run together to illustrate: for example, *takeitout, throwitaway.* Point out that each phrase is pronounced as though each were a single word.

Exercise ❿

- Tell students to discuss the answers to the questions.
- To help students get started, tell them some of your own answers to the questions.
- Pair students and set a time limit of 5 minutes.
- Encourage students to ask each other follow-up questions. For example, *What kinds of things do you throw away?*
- After 3 minutes, call on a few students to tell the class their partner's answers.

HOMEWORK

- 📖 Assign *Workbook* page 54, Vocabulary Exercises 1 and 2, and page 56, Listening Exercises 6 and 7.

Listening

5 Match the phrasal verbs with their meanings.

1. give away _g_
2. put away ____
3. try on ____
4. pass on ____
5. take out ____
6. fall apart ____
7. throw away ____
8. fall out ____

a. separate into small pieces
b. wear a piece of clothing for a short time to see if it fits
c. put something in the garbage
d. drop out of the place where it belongs
e. put something in the place where it is usually kept
f. remove something from a place
g. give something to someone instead of selling it
h. give something to someone else

6 Mr. Freeman and his young daughter, Lisa, are talking. Listen to their conversation. Circle the letter of the correct answer.

1. What are Mr. Freeman and Lisa doing?
   a. taking things out of a trunk
   b. putting things away in a trunk
2. Are the things old or new?
   a. old
   b. new

7 Listen again. Match each keepsake in the trunk with the person it belongs (or belonged) to.

1. jewelry box
2. watch
3. photo album
4. baseball glove

a. Lisa's mother
b. Lisa's father
c. Lisa's grandmother
d. Lisa's grandfather

Pronunciation

8 Listen. Notice the stress and linking in these phrasal verbs.

Take it **out**.
It's falling a**part**.
Let's throw it a**way**.

Don't give it a**way**.
I'll try it **on**.
Wait! Something is falling **out**.

9 Listen again and repeat.

10 *PAIRS.* Discuss the questions.

When you don't need something anymore (clothing, books, furniture), what do you do? Do you put it away and keep it, throw it away, or give it away to someone? Why?

Grammar focus

1 Study the examples. Notice the ways to express possession. Notice the use of the apostrophe (').

Possessive 's	Possessive adjective	Possessive pronoun	*belong to* + object pronoun
	It's **my** baseball glove.	It's **mine**.	It **belongs to me**.
These are **Grandma's** dolls.	They're **her** dolls.	They're **hers**.	They **belong to her**.
This is **George's** watch.	It's **his** watch.	It's **his**.	It **belongs to him**.
That's the **neighbors'** car.	It's **their** car.	It's **theirs**.	It **belongs to them**.

2 Look at the examples again. Circle the correct words to complete the rules in the chart.

> **Possessive 's; possessive adjectives/pronouns; *belong to***
>
> To show possession:
>
> Use a possessive adjective (*my, your, his, her, our, their*) **before / after** a noun.
>
> Use a possessive pronoun (*mine, yours, his, hers, ours, theirs*) **alone / before a noun**.
>
> Add *'s* to a **singular / plural** noun.
>
> Add *'* to a **singular / plural** noun that ends in *s*.
>
> Use **an object pronoun / a possessive pronoun** after *belong to*.

> *Grammar Reference page 146*

3 Circle the correct words to complete the sentences.

1. That's not her doll. It's **our /(ours.)**
2. This isn't **me / my** sweater. Is it **your / yours**?
3. These are my **parent's / parents'** books.
4. This photo album belongs to **her / she**.
5. My sisters don't like to clean **their / her** room.
6. Is this **her / hers** book? Or is it **him / his**?
7. These old clothes **belong / belongs** to **they / them**.

4 Rewrite the sentences using the words in parentheses.

1. This doll belonged to your grandmother. (your grandmother)
   This was your grandmother's doll.
2. That's my photo album. (belong to)
3. This is your mother's dress. (hers)
4. Their car is very old. (my grandparents)
5. Where is Jason's house? (his)
6. These are our CDs. (belong to)
7. I like to look at her pictures. (Lucia)

Grammar focus

LANGUAGE NOTES

- Possessive nouns (for example, *Lisa's*) and possessive adjectives (for example, *her*) show possession.

- Add an apostrophe (') + –s to a singular noun or an irregular plural noun. (For example, *Yoko's room, the men's room*)

- Add only an apostrophe to a plural noun ending in -s to show possession. (For example, *boys'*)

- Possessive adjectives replace possessive nouns. Possessive adjectives agree with the possessive noun they replace. (For example, *Victor's sisters = his sisters*)

- A noun always follows a possessive noun or a possessive adjective.

- A possessive pronoun replaces a possessive adjective + noun (for example, *my book = mine*) or possessive noun + noun (for example, *This is Yoko's book. = This is hers.*).

- The phrasal verb *belong to* is also used to indicate possession. (For example, *This book belongs to Ann. = It's Ann's book.*) *Belong to* is followed by an object noun or an object pronoun.

WARM-UP

Note: Skip this warm-up if you're doing this lesson (Lesson B) during the same class period as Lesson A.

- Books closed. Tell students they are going to listen again to the conversation between Mr. Freeman and Lisa that they heard in the Listening section.

- Write on the board a few possessive phrases from the Listening: For example, *your _____ jewelry box; her _____ jewelry; _____ watch; That belongs to _____ .*

- Tell students to copy the phrases. Tell them to listen to the audio and complete the phrases.

- 🎧 Play the audio for Lesson A, Listening, Exercise 6. (It models the grammar of the unit.)

- Go over the answers and write them on the board (grandmother's; mother's; Grandpa's; your mother). Elicit other possessive forms students recognize.

Exercise ❶

- Have students read the examples and study the bold-faced words. Elicit or point out that there are four ways to express possession.

- Ask students to compare the possessive forms *'s* and *s'* as well as possessive adjectives and possessive pronouns.

- Tell them to look closely at the form following *belong to*.

Exercise ❷

- Have students study the examples again.

- Tell students to circle the correct words to complete the sentences in the chart.

- Have students compare their answers with a partner.

- Go over the answers with the class.

- Ask a few questions to elicit the key points about the grammar: For example, *Are possessive pronouns used with nouns?* (No. Possessive pronouns are used alone.) *When do we use 's?* (with a singular noun) *When do we use only the apostrophe to show possession?* (before a plural noun that ends in –s)

Exercise ❸

Answer key

before	plural
alone	an object pronoun
singular	

- Have students complete the exercise individually. Set a time limit of 3 minutes. Walk around the room, helping as needed.

- Have students compare their answers with a partner's.

- Go over the answers with the class.

Answer key

1. ours	5. their
2. my; yours	6. her; his
3. parents'	7. belong; them
4. her	

Exercise ❹

- Explain the task: Students will rewrite the sentences using the words in parentheses. Point out that the new sentences will have the same meaning but will be expressed in a different way.

- Go over the example. Point out that both sentences use simple past verbs.

- Tell students to complete the exercise individually. Set a time limit of 5 minutes. Walk around the room, helping as needed.

- Have students compare their sentences.

- Go over the sentences with the class.

Answer key

1. This was your grandmother's doll.
2. That photo album belongs to me.
3. This is hers.
4. My grandparents' car is very old.
5. Where is his house?
6. These CDs belong to us.
7. I like to look at Lucia's pictures.

Speaking

Exercise ❺

This exercise provides practice with various ways to talk about possessions. It prepares students for Exercises 6 and 7.

- Explain the task: Students will imagine that they are filling a trunk with keepsakes. Each keepsake will be a reminder of one person in the class. Give each student the name of a classmate and tell them to choose one thing that reminds them of that person.

- Model the exercise by choosing someone in the class all students know. Brainstorm possible keepsakes for that person. Prompt by asking, *Does _____ wear something a lot? Is there something _____ always has?*

- Tell students to work individually to write down their classmate's name and the person's possession they choose as a keepsake. Set a time limit of 2 minutes.

Exercise ❻

- Divide the class into groups of 4. Tell them they are going to talk about the keepsakes they have chosen. Have them agree on one keepsake for each of the four group members.

- Go over the example. Tell students to complete their lists. Encourage them to give reasons for their choices.

- Set a time limit of 5 minutes. Walk around the room, helping as needed.

Exercise ❼

- Explain the task: A representative from each group will come to the board and write the list of the keepsakes they have chosen. Remind them not to write the names of the students with the keepsakes. The rest of the class will try to guess who is represented by each keepsake.

- Call on one student from each group to write the keepsakes on the board (or have them read the keepsakes aloud).

- Tell the groups to work together to guess the names that go with the keepsakes. Go over the example. Ask students to identify the possessives with *'s*, the possessive adjectives, and the possessive pronouns in the example.

- Go over a few of the keepsakes with the entire class. Ask questions such as *Who do you think this keepsake is for? Why? Did anyone think of someone else?*

TRB For additional interactive grammar practice, have students do the reproducible activity for this unit in the *Teacher's Resource Book.*

Writing

Exercise ❽

- Assign the writing task for class work or homework.

- Explain the task: Students will write a paragraph about a personal keepsake using possessive forms and vocabulary from the unit.

- Brainstorm ideas about keepsakes and the people, things, or events that the keepsakes remind students of.

- **TRB** Optionally, give students a copy of the writing model (see the *Teacher's Resource Book*, Writing Models). Ask them to read the model and notice the vocabulary and grammar from the unit.

- If students don't have the model, write the following on the board:

  I have a few keepsakes. My favorite is a beautiful ring that belonged to my grandmother. It reminds me of her because she wore it all the time.

- Have a student read the sentences aloud. Answer any questions students might have.

- Walk around to make sure everyone understands the task.

For suggestions on how to give feedback on writing, see page xiv of this *Teacher's Edition.*

CONVERSATION TO GO

At the end of class, call on two students to role-play the conversation.

HOMEWORK

- 📖 Assign *Workbook* page 55, Grammar Exercises 3, 4, and 5, and page 56, Pronunciation Exercises 8, 9, and 10.

- ⊙ If students do not have the *WorldView Workbook*, assign listening homework from the Student CD. Write on the board:

  Track 27
  Write one detail about each of the things in the trunk.

  The jewelry box:
  The watch:
  The photo album:
  The baseball glove:

- 🎧 Tell students to listen to the audio and write the answers to the cues. Have them bring their answers to the next class.

  (Possible answers: *The jewelry box:* It's pretty. / It's empty.; *The watch:* Grandpa wore it all the time. / It still works.; *The photo album:* It has pictures from when Lisa's father was in school. / It's falling apart. / The pages are falling out.; *The baseball glove:* It belongs to Lisa's mother. / It fits Lisa.)

Speaking

5 *BEFORE YOU SPEAK.* **Imagine you are filling a trunk with keepsakes of the people in your class. Your teacher will give you the name of a classmate. Choose one thing that reminds you of that person, such as a piece of clothing that the person wears a lot or something that the person always has.**

6 *GROUPS OF 4.* **Talk about the keepsakes that you chose. As a group, agree on one thing to put in the trunk to remember each person by.**

A: I think we should put Julia's blue sweater in the trunk. She wears it a lot.
B: No, I think we should put in her cell phone. She loves to talk on the phone after class.

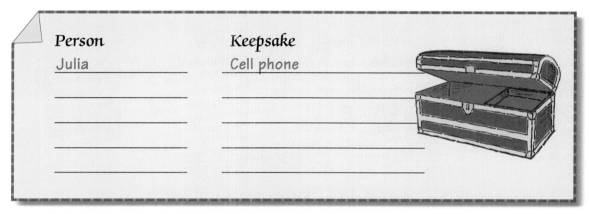

Person	Keepsake
Julia	Cell phone
_____	_____
_____	_____
_____	_____
_____	_____

7 **Each group writes the list of keepsakes (with no names!) on the board or reads it to the class. Others in the class guess the people who go with each keepsake. Give reasons.**

Anna: The first thing on our list is a cell phone.
José: I think it's yours. You like talking on the phone.
Anna: No, it's not mine.
María: I think it's Julia's. She uses her phone more than anyone!
Anna: You're right. The cell phone belongs to Julia.

Writing

8 **Think of a keepsake that belongs to you or to a member of your family. Write a paragraph describing the keepsake and the person, thing, or event it reminds you of. Use possessive forms.**

CONVERSATION TO GO

A: Is this **your** phone?
B: No, it's **Susan's**. **Mine** is at home.

Tales of Nasreddin Hodja

Vocabulary Adjectives describing feelings and behavior
Grammar Adverbs of manner; comparative adverbs
Speaking Describing actions

Getting started

1 **Choose the correct synonym for each adjective.**

1. upset _a_   a. unhappy   b. happy

2. embarrassed ____   a. comfortable   b. ashamed

3. calm ____   a. relaxed   b. nervous

4. suspicious ____   a. trusting   b. not trusting

5. proud ____   a. shy   b. pleased with yourself

6. polite ____   a. kind   b. rude

7. absent-minded ____   a. forgetful   b. interested

8. rude ____   a. nice   b. bad-mannered

9. loud ____   a. quiet   b. noisy

A

2 🎧 **Listen and check your answers. Then listen and repeat.**

3 *PAIRS.* **Nasreddin Hodja is a character from Turkish folktales. Look at the pictures. Use adjectives from Exercise 1 to describe how Hodja and the other men look.**

In Picture A, Hodja looks calm, and the men look suspicious.

B

D

C

Tales of Nasreddin Hodja

OBJECTIVES

Students will:

- activate vocabulary related to feelings and behavior
- do reading, speaking, and writing tasks to describe actions
- focus on using adverbs of manner and comparative adverbs to describe people's actions and behavior
- practice putting stress on the appropriate syllables in adverbs

BACKGROUND INFORMATION

Nasreddin Hodja was born in 1208, in what is today central Turkey. He became known for his wit and wisdom. Through his words and actions he revealed and ridiculed human flaws and follies. His stories target human cruelty and injustice. Hodja's thought-provoking words earned him the love and respect of the Turkish people. The legend of Hodja is deeply embedded in Turkish tradition. He is often quoted in daily life. Today, he remains a popular character in literature, music, and art.

WARM-UP: BEDTIME STORIES

Groups of 3. Students take turns telling each other a story they heard when they were children.

- Tell students that this unit is about different ways people act or behave. Explain that in the unit title, "Tales of Nasreddin Hodja," Nasreddin Hodja is the name of a character that appears in many very old stories that originated in Turkey. Point him out in the pictures on the page.
- Ask students to think about a story they have known since they were children. It can be a folktale, a fairy tale, or any other story they enjoyed. Tell them that they will summarize the story during a group sharing. Demonstrate the task by telling a story you remember.
- Divide the class in groups of 3 and set a time limit of 5 minutes. Each student in the groups must give a short summary of a favorite childhood story.
- After 5 minutes, call on a few students to tell the class their stories.

Getting started

OPTION: VOCABULARY PREVIEW

Tell students to look up the meanings of the words in Exercise 1. Then ask students questions to elicit each adjective. For example, for the adjective *upset*, ask: *How do you feel when you fail an exam?* (upset) For *absent-minded*, ask: *What do you call someone who always forgets things?* (absent-minded)

Exercise ❶

- Explain the task: Students will write the letter of the synonym next to each adjective. Go over the example.
- Have students complete the exercise individually. Set a time limit of 3 minutes. While students are working, walk around the room, helping as needed.
- Have students compare their answers with a partner's. Tell them they will hear the correct answers in Exercise 2.

Exercise ❷

- Explain the task: Students will listen to the audio and check their answers in Exercise 1. Then they will listen again and repeat the words.
- 🎧 Play the audio. Tell students to correct any wrong answers.
- 🎧 Play the audio again and have students listen and repeat.

Answer key

1. a	3. a	5. b	7. a	9. b
2. b	4. b	6. a	8. b	

Exercise ❸

- **Pairs.** Tell students to look at the pictures again.
- Explain the task: In pairs, students will take turns describing how Hodja and the other men look. Point out that the adjectives are not physical descriptions, rather they describe how the person in the picture is acting or feeling. Remind students to use the words in Exercise 1.
- Go over the example.
- Pair students and set a time limit of 5 minutes. Walk around the room, helping as needed.
- Point to each picture and call on a few students to describe how the person looks.

Answer key

(*Possible answers*)

Picture A: Hodja looks calm. The men look suspicious.
Picture B: Hodja looks absent-minded. The men look angry.
Picture C: Hodja is rude. The men look upset.
Picture D: Hodja looks calm. The other man looks embarrassed/upset.

Reading

CULTURE NOTE

One of the most famous characters of American folklore is Paul Bunyan, the giant lumberjack. According to tradition, the legend of Paul Bunyan was started by workers at logging camps in the north woods (in the states of Michigan, Wisconsin, and Minnesota). The men supposedly told stories of Paul's adventures to pass the long, cold winter nights.

Paul Bunyan, together with Babe, his giant blue ox, embodied incredible strength, speed, and skill. He is credited with creating the Great Lakes, Puget Sound, and the Grand Canyon, among other parts of the American landscape. The stories of Paul Bunyan are appreciated for their humor and exaggeration.

Exercise ❹

- Lead a short class discussion to elicit or write examples of folktales on the board.

- Tell students to think about the folktales they are familiar with. Ask: *What's the purpose of folktales?* (Folktales teach lessons. They communicate values. They explain things about people and the world.)

Exercise ❺

- Explain the task: Students will read the stories and will match each picture to the section of the story that it illustrates.

- Have students read the first paragraph of "Hodja, the King." Go over the example.

- Have students work individually to complete the exercise. Set a time limit of 8 minutes.

- Have students compare their answers with a partner's.

- Go over the answers with the class.

Answer key			
B	D	A	C

Exercise ❻

 **Teaching Tip!** **Identifying the main idea**

Recognizing the main idea in a reading is an important skill. Often students focus on finding specific information to answer questions. In Exercise 6, students need to identify the main idea; in this case, the main idea is the lesson the story teaches. Tell students that they can get the main idea by skimming, or reading the whole story quickly to get an overview.

- Explain the task: Students will choose the lesson each story teaches and circle *a, b,* or *c*. Encourage students to look back at the stories if they need to.

- Set a time limit of 2 minutes.

- Have students compare their answers with a partner's.

- Go over the answers with the class.

Answer key	
1. b	2. c

◉ Please go to www.longman.com/worldview for additional in-class model conversation practice.

PHOMEWORK

- 📖 Assign *Workbook* page 57, Vocabulary Exercises 1 and 2, and page 59, Listening Exercises 5, 6, 7, and 8.

Reading ●━━━━━━

4 Think about folktales you know. What's their purpose?

5 Read the stories. Then match the paragraphs with the pictures.

Hodja, the King

One day, Nasreddin Hodja was walking down the road. He was looking at the sky absent-mindedly and not watching where he was going. Suddenly, he bumped into a man. _B_

"Do you know who I am?" the man shouted angrily. "I am the King's advisor!"

"That's very nice," said Hodja calmly. "As for me, I am a king." _____

"A king?" asked the man suspiciously. "What country do you rule?"

"I rule over myself," said Hodja proudly. "I am king of my emotions. I never get angry as you did just now."

The man apologized and walked away quickly, feeling very embarrassed.

Eat, My Coat, Eat

A friend invited Nasreddin Hodja to a banquet. He went to the banquet wearing his everyday clothes. _____

Everyone, including his friend, was very rude to him, so Hodja left quickly. He went back home, put on his best coat, and returned to the banquet. Now everyone greeted him more politely than before and invited him to sit down and eat.

When the soup was served, Hodja put the sleeve of his coat in the bowl. He said loudly, "Eat, my coat, eat!" _____

His friend angrily asked Hodja to stop.

"When I came here in my other clothes," said Hodja calmly, "you treated me badly. But when I returned wearing this fine coat, you gave me the best of everything. So I thought that you wanted my coat, not me, to eat at your banquet!"

6 What lessons do these stories teach? Choose the best answer for each story.

1. "Hodja, the King"
   a. Some people are more important than others.
   b. It is important to control your anger.
   c. Everyone gets angry at times.

2. "Eat, My Coat, Eat"
   a. True friends are not rude to each other.
   b. Wear clothes that are right for the occasion.
   c. Look at the person, not at his or her clothes.

Grammar focus

1 **Study the examples of adverbs of manner.**

> Hodja walked **absent-mindedly** down the road.
> The man walked away **quickly**.
> Everyone greeted him **more politely than** before.
> The man shouted **angrily**.

2 **Look at the examples again. Circle the correct words to complete the chart.**

Adverbs of manner
Use adverbs of manner to describe **how / why** something is done.
Use *more* + adverb + *than* to compare two **actions / things**.
Many adverbs are formed by adding *-ly* to **a verb / an adjective**.
For adjectives ending in *-y,* change the *y* to **a / i** before adding *-ly*.
NOTE: Some adverbs such as *fast*, *hard*, and *early,* have the same form as adjectives.

Grammar Reference page 146

3 **Complete the sentences with adverbs of manner. Form the adverbs from the adjectives in parentheses.**

1. Nathan walked __happily__ down the street. (happy)

2. The man sat _____ in front of the house. (quiet)

3. "Where did you go?" the little girl asked the little boy _____. (suspicious)

4. "I designed that building," the architect said _____. (proud)

5. The man shouted _____ at his neighbor. (angry)

4 **Complete the sentences. Use the comparative form of the adverbs in the box. Include *than* when necessary.**

calmly	comfortably	~~loudly~~	politely	quickly

1. John is quiet. Janet is loud. Janet speaks __more loudly than__ John.

2. Eduardo never rushes. Roberto is always in a hurry. Roberto does everything _____ Eduardo.

3. The salesperson wasn't rude, but the customer was. The salesperson behaved _____ the customer.

4. Sam was angry when he heard the news. Jennifer wasn't upset about the news. Jennifer reacted _____ Sam.

5. Just after his operation my friend was in a lot of pain, but now he's resting _____.

Grammar focus

WARM-UP

Note: Skip this warm-up if you're doing this lesson (Lesson B) during the same class period as Lesson A.

- Books closed. Tell students they are going to listen to the stories they read in the Reading section.
- On one side of the board, write the following verbs from the first story: *looking at, shouted, said, asked, walked away.* On the other side, write these adverbs: *angrily, proudly, absent-mindedly, calmly, quickly, suspiciously.*
- Explain the task: Students will listen for the verbs and adverbs written on the board. Tell them they will match each verb with the adverb that describes it.
- 🎧 Play the audio for Lesson A, Reading, Exercise 5. (It models the grammar of the unit.)
- Point to each verb on the board. Ask students to call out the adverb that was used with that verb. Draw lines matching the adverbs and the verbs.

Exercise ❶

- Have students read the examples and study the bold-faced words. Ask what the bold-faced words have in common. If necessary, call attention to the *–ly* endings.
- Ask students what kind of information the adverbs add to the sentence. (They tell how the action is done.)

Exercise ❷

- Have students study the examples again.
- Tell students to circle the correct information to complete the rules in the chart.
- Have students compare their answers with a partner's.
- Go over the answers with the class.
- Ask a few questions to elicit the key points about the grammar: For example, *How are most adjectives turned into adverbs?* (by adding *-ly*) *What's the adverb form of* hungry? *Spell it.* (hungrily) *Do adverbs of manner usually go before or after the verb?* (after) *Name three adverbs with the same form as adjectives.* (fast, hard, late)

Answer key

how	an adjective
actions	*y* to *i*

Exercise ❸

- Before beginning Exercise 3, answer any questions students might have. You may also want to refer the class to the Grammar Reference for Unit 14 on page 146.
- Explain the task: Students will form adverbs from the adjectives in parentheses and will add the adverbs to the sentences.
- Have students read the example. Ask: *How was the adjective* happy *changed into an adverb?* (It was changed to *happily* by changing the *y* to *i* before adding *-ly*.)
- Tell students to complete the exercise individually. Set a time limit of 3 minutes. Walk around the room, helping as needed.
- Have students compare their answers with a partner's.
- Go over the answers with the class.

Answer key

1. happily	3. suspiciously	5. angrily
2. quietly	4. proudly	

Exercise ❹

- Explain the task: Students will use the comparative form of the adverbs in the box to complete the sentences.
- Point out that the comparative form includes *than* when it is unclear what two things are being compared or when followed by an object. (For example, *I walk more quickly <u>than</u> John.*) It is not necessary when it is clear what is being compared. (For example, *I used to be a slow walker; now I walk more quickly.*)
- Set a time limit of 3 minutes. Walk around the room, helping as needed.
- Have students compare their answers with a partner's.
- Go over the answers with the class.

Answer key

1. more loudly than
2. more quickly than
3. more politely than
4. more calmly than
5. more comfortably

Pronunciation

> **LANGUAGE NOTE**
>
> The vowels in unstressed syllables are shorter and weaker. Sometimes an unstressed vowel such as the vowel in **happy**, has a clear sound, but very often the vowel is reduced to a very short, unclear /ə/, sound (as in suspic<u>iou</u>s).

Exercise ❺

- Tell students they are going to listen to some adverbs.
- 🎧 Play the audio. Ask students to look at the adverbs and notice the stressed, or strong, syllable in each—the part of the word marked with a black circle.
- Remind students that the vowel in a stressed syllable is pronounced long and clear.

Exercise ❻

- Tell students they are going to listen to the same words again. Ask them this time to notice the sound of the vowels in light blue.
- 🎧 Play the audio. Ask students if the vowels shown in light blue sound different from each other. (They don't.)
- Elicit or point out the different ways this sound is spelled here: ang<u>ri</u>ly, suspici<u>ou</u>sly, qui<u>e</u>tly, comfort<u>a</u>bly. Highlight the fact that the vowels sound the same regardless of the differences in spelling. Tell students that this sound is called *schwa*.
- 🎧 Play the audio again and ask students to repeat each word chorally.
- Point out the pronunciation of *comfortably* /kʌmftəbli/, which is usually pronounced as three syllables (the *-or* is silent).

Exercise ❼

- Explain the task: Students will listen to the words, draw a circle over the stressed syllable, and underline any vowels pronounced as the unstressed vowel /ə/.
- Use one of the words from Exercise 5 as an example.
- 🎧 Play the audio.

> **Answer key**
>
> hápp<u>i</u>ly   pol<u>i</u>tely   nérv<u>ou</u>sly   húng<u>ri</u>ly

Exercise ❽

- 🎧 Play the audio, asking students to repeat each word chorally.
- Go over the answers with the class.

Speaking

Exercise ❾

- Explain the task: Students will work in groups to tell a folktale that teaches a lesson. They will choose the story and then divide the tasks so that each group member tells part of the folktale.

- Direct students' attention to the categories on the page. Make sure they understand what each category means.
- Tell students to take notes on each aspect of the folktale.
- Divide students in groups of 4 and set a time limit of 15 minutes. Walk around the room, helping as needed.

Exercise ❿

- Have the groups take turns coming to the front of the room and telling or acting out their folktale.
- After each folktale, ask the class: *What lesson does the folktale teach?*

TRB For additional interactive grammar practice, have students do the reproducible activity for this unit in the *Teacher's Resource Book*.

Writing

Exercise ⓫

- Assign the writing task for class work or homework.
- Explain the task: Students will write a folktale.
- **TRB** Optionally, give students a copy of the writing model (see the *Teacher's Resource Book*, Writing Models). Ask them to read the model and notice the vocabulary and grammar from the unit.
- If students don't have the model, write the following on the board:

   Once there was an old man. When his wife died, he became very lonely. He had three sons, . . .

- Have a student read the sentences aloud. Answer any questions students might have.
- Walk around to make sure everyone understands the task.

For suggestions on how to give feedback on writing, see page xiv of this *Teacher's Edition*.

CONVERSATION TO GO

At the end of class, call on two students to role-play the conversation.

HOMEWORK

- 📖 Assign *Workbook* page 58, Grammar Exercises 3 and 4, and page 59, Pronunciation Exercises 9, and 10.
- 💿 If students do not have the *WorldView Workbook*, assign listening homework from the Student CD. Write on the board:

   Track 29
   Answer the questions.

   Hodja, the King
   How did Hodja react to the King's advisor?

   Eat, my Coat, Eat
   How did the guests treat Hodja at first?

- 🎧 Tell students to listen to the audio and answer the questions. Have them bring their answers to the next class.

   (Answers: *calmly; rudely*)

Pronunciation

5 🎧 **Listen. Notice the stressed (strong) syllable in each word.**

<u>an</u>grily   su<u>spi</u>ciously   <u>qui</u>etly   <u>com</u>fortably

6 🎧 **Listen again. This time, notice the pronunciation of the vowels shown in blue. They all have the short, unclear sound /ə/. Then listen again and repeat.**

7 🎧 **Now listen to these words. Draw a circle over the stressed syllables and underline the vowels that have the short, unclear sound /ə/.**

happily   politely   nervously   hungrily

8 🎧 **Listen again and repeat. Check your answers.**

Speaking

9 *GROUPS OF 4.* **Work together to tell a folktale that teaches something. Decide which folktale you'd like to tell, and take notes. Take turns telling different parts. Add or change parts of the folktale to make it as funny or dramatic as you like.**

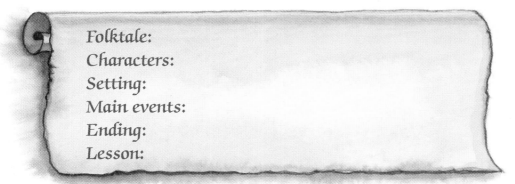

Folktale:
Characters:
Setting:
Main events:
Ending:
Lesson:

10 **Share your folktale with the class. What does each folktale teach?**

Writing

11 **Write a short story or folktale you know. Use adverbs of manner.**

CONVERSATION TO GO

A: You speak **quickly**!
B: No, I don't. You just listen **more slowly** than I speak!

Popular sports

Vocabulary Sports
Grammar Verbs for likes/dislikes + noun/verb + *-ing*
Speaking Talking about sports you like doing

Getting started

1 **Match the words with the pictures.**

1. aerobics __A__
2. basketball ____
3. biking ____
4. jogging ____
5. karate ____
6. swimming ____

2 **Write the sports in the box next to the correct verbs in the word webs.**

aerobics	basketball	~~biking~~	golf	hockey	jogging
karate	skiing	soccer	swimming	tennis	volleyball

biking

go

play

do

3 🎧 **Listen and check your answers. Then listen and repeat.**

4 *PAIRS.* **Discuss the questions.**

Which sports do you like to play?
Which sports do you like to watch?

Popular sports

OBJECTIVES

Students will:

- activate vocabulary related to sports
- do listening, speaking, and writing tasks related to sports
- focus on using adverbs of degree with verbs for likes and dislikes followed by nouns or verbs + -ing
- practice using stress to contrast or compare ideas

WARM-UP: WHY PEOPLE EXERCISE

Students talk about reasons people exercise or do sports.

- Elicit a definition for the word *popular* in the unit title, "Popular sports." (For example, many people like them.)
- Lead a brief class discussion about why people exercise or do sports. If necessary, give an example. (For example, *I exercise because it gives me more energy.*)

Getting started

OPTION: VOCABULARY PREVIEW

Tell students to read the words in Exercise 2. Ask them what the words are. (They're forms of exercise and sports activities.) Call on volunteer students to explain the meaning of each word. Write the words in one column on the board. Tell them that you will take a class survey to find out how many in the class participate in these activities. Start with *aerobics*. Call out the word and have those who do aerobics raise their hands. Count the number of raised hands and write the number next to the word. Continue with the rest of the words on the board. Have students look at the numbers on the board and ask: *Are most students in the class athletic or not?* After the survey, call on a few volunteer students and ask them if they like the activities they do and why.

Exercise ❶

- Explain the task: Students will write the letter of the picture next to the correct sport.
- Go over the example. Tell students not to worry about the pronunciation of the words because they will hear them on the audio in Exercise 3.
- Have students work individually to complete the exercise. Set a time limit of 2 minutes. While students are working, walk around the room, helping as needed.
- Have students compare their answers with a partner's.
- Go over the answers with the class.

Answer key

| 1. A | 2. C | 3. F | 4. B | 5. D | 6. E |

Exercise ❷

- Tell students to look at the word webs on page 68 of the *Student Book*.
- Explain the task: Students will write the sports in the box next to the correct verb.
- Go over the example. Clarify the task by asking, *Do we say "I love going biking," "I love playing biking," or "I love doing biking"?*
- Have students complete the exercise individually. Set a time limit of 3 minutes. Walk around the room, helping as needed.
- Tell students they will hear the correct answers in the next activity.

Exercise ❸

- Explain the task: As students listen to the audio, they will check their answers in Exercise 2. Then they will listen again and repeat the words.
- 🎧 Play the audio. Encourage students to correct any wrong answers.
- 🎧 Play the audio again and have students listen and repeat.

Answer key

go: biking, jogging, skiing, swimming
play: basketball, golf, hockey, soccer, tennis, volleyball
do: aerobics, karate

Exercise ❹

- Explain the task: Students will talk about the sports they like to play and watch.
- Model the activity by giving a personal example. (For example, *I like to go jogging, and I like to watch soccer.*)
- Pair students and set a time limit of 3 minutes. Walk around the room, helping as needed.
- Call on a few students to tell the class what sports they like to play and watch.

EXTENSION

- Have students rank the sports in Exercise 2 according to how much they like to play them and then according to how much they like to watch them. (*1* is their favorite, *12* is their least favorite.)
- Have them compare their rankings with a partner's.
- Lead a brief class discussion about the results. (For example, ask: *How many people ranked golf as the number 1 sport they like to play?*)

Listening

Exercise ➎

- Explain the task: Students will listen to part of a TV report about sports in Canada. The TV report will tell what percentages of the population like a variety of sports. Students will listen for the name of the sport and the corresponding percentage.
- Have students look at the bar graph. Ask what percentage of people like golf. (8 percent)
- 🎧 Play the audio.
- Have students compare their answers with a partner's.
- Go over the answers with the class.

> **Answer key**
>
> golf 8%, hockey 7%, baseball 6%, swimming 5%, volleyball 3%, basketball 3%

EXTENSION

Ask comprehension questions about the graph: For example, *Which sport is the most popular?* (golf) *Which sports are the least popular?* (volleyball, basketball) *Which sports are more popular than volleyball?* (golf, hockey, baseball, swimming)

Exercise ➏

- Explain the task: Students will continue listening to the TV interview. As they listen, they will check the group that like to play each of several sports: mostly women, mostly men, or equal numbers of men and women.
- Before playing the audio for Exercise 6, have students make predictions about who likes to play each sport. Tell them to put a light check mark next to each box to indicate their predictions.

- 🎧 Play the audio.
- Have students compare their answers with a partner's.
- Go over the answers with the class. Find out if students' predictions were accurate. Ask: *How many did you predict correctly? Which ones were they? Was there any survey finding that surprised you?*

> **Answer key**
>
> *golf:* mostly men
> *hockey:* mostly men
> *volleyball:* equal men and women
> *swimming:* mostly women
> *baseball:* mostly men
> *basketball:* mostly men

Exercise ➐

- **Pairs.** Explain the task: Students will discuss the questions about gender differences in sports preference in their country.
- Have students compare the results for Canada in Exercise 6 with what they think is the situation in their own country. Tell them to look at each of the six sports mentioned in the Listening section.
- Pair students and set a time limit of 3 minutes. Walk around the room, helping as needed.
- Call on a few students to share their opinions with the rest of the class.

🌐 Please go to www.longman.com/worldview for additional in-class model conversation practice and supplementary reading practice.

HOMEWORK

- 📖 Assign *Workbook* page 60, Vocabulary Exercises 1 and 2, and page 62, Listening Exercises 5 and 6.

Listening

5 🎧 Listen to the TV report about sports in Canada. How popular are the sports in the box? Write each sport in the correct place in the graph.

| baseball | basketball | ~~golf~~ | hockey | swimming | volleyball |

Popular sports in Canada

Sports	0%	2%	4%	6%	8%	10%
golf						

6 🎧 Listen to the rest of the interview and check (✓) who like playing each sport.

	Mostly women	Mostly men	Equal men and women
golf	☐	✓	☐
hockey	☐	☐	☐
volleyball	☐	☐	☐
swimming	☐	☐	☐
baseball	☐	☐	☐
basketball	☐	☐	☐

7 *PAIRS.* Discuss these questions. In your country who likes team sports more, men or women? Who likes individual sports more?

Grammar focus

1 Put the verbs in the correct order.

love	hate	like	~~don't like~~

_____   *don't like*   _____   _____

☹   ☹   ☺   ☺

2 Study the examples of adverbs of degree.

Some men like playing golf **a lot**.   She **really** loves volleyball.
Some men **really** like playing golf.   He doesn't like swimming **very much**.
Some women **really** hate hockey.   He doesn't **really** like swimming.

3 Look at the examples again. Complete the rules in the chart.

Adverbs of degree
Use *a lot* with _____ to add emphasis.
Use _____ with *like, love,* and *hate* to add emphasis.
Use _____ and _____ with *not like* to reduce the negative meaning of a sentence.

Grammar Reference page 147

4 Complete the conversations with the correct form of the words in parentheses.

1. A: What sports do you ___*like doing*___ (like/do)?

   B: I _*don't really like sports*_ (really not like/sports),
   but I _*love swimming*_ (love/swim).

2. A: Do your parents do any exercise?

   B: My father _____ (love/play basketball),
   and my mother _____ (like a lot/play golf).

3. A: Do you like jogging?

   B: No, I _____ (hate/jog). I think it's boring.

4. A: Do your brothers _____ (like/play) any sports?

   B: Well, they _____ (not like very much/play soccer).
   They're not very good at it!

5. A: Do you _____ (like/do aerobics)?

   B: Yes, I do. I go to a class before work.

6. A: Does your boyfriend _____ (like/ski)?

   B: Yes, he _____ (really love/it). He goes every weekend.

Grammar focus

LANGUAGE NOTES

- The verbs used to express likes and dislikes (*like, love, don't like, don't love*) can be followed by nouns or by gerunds. Gerunds are formed by adding *-ing* to the base form of a verb.

- These verbs can also be followed by infinitives (*to* + base form of the verb), but this unit focuses only on their use with nouns and gerunds.

- Adverbs of degree are commonly used to add emphasis or to reduce the negative meaning of a sentence. Some combinations are *like + a lot, really + like/love/hate*, and *not like + very much*.

WARM-UP

Note: Skip this warm-up if you're doing this lesson (Lesson B) during the same class period as Lesson A.

- Books closed. Tell students they are going to listen to the TV report that they heard in the Listening section.

- Ask students to pay attention to the verbs that are used to talk about how people feel about some sports. Tell them to listen for the adverbs of degree that are sometimes used with verbs.

- 🎧 Play the audio for Lesson A, Listening, Exercise 5. (It models the grammar of the unit.)

- Elicit examples of the verbs used to describe people's feelings about some sports (for example, *like, don't like, love, hate*).

- Ask students to identify any adverbs of degree used in the news report.

Exercise ❶

- Have students look at the verbs. Tell them to put them in order from the most negative feeling (on the left) to the most positive feeling (on the right). Go over the example.

- Go over the answers with the class.

Answer key

hate, don't like, like, love

Exercise ❷

- Tell students to read the six examples and to study the bold-faced words. Point out or elicit that the adverbs are in different positions in the sentences. Sometimes they go after the verb, and sometimes they go before the verb.

- Ask students what type of information is added with each of the adverbs. (The adverbs *a lot* and *really* add emphasis; *very much* and *really*, when used with a negative verb reduces the negative meaning of the sentence.)

Exercise ❸

- Have students look at the examples again.

- Tell students to complete the rules in the chart with the adverbs of degree from the example box above.

- Have students compare their answers with a partner's.

- Go over the answers with the class.

- Ask a few questions to elicit the key points about the grammar: For example, *Which adverbs of degree add emphasis?* (*a lot, really*) *Which adverbs do we use with* not like *to reduce the negative meaning of a sentence?* (*very much, really*) *Does* really *come before the verb or after?* (before)

Answer key

| *like* | *really* | *very much; really* |

Exercise ❹

- Before beginning Exercise 4, answer any questions students might have. You may also want to refer the class to the Grammar Reference for Unit 15 on page 147.

- Explain the task: Students will complete the conversations with the correct form of the words in parentheses. Go over the example.

- Have students work individually to complete the exercise. Set a time limit of 5 minutes. Walk around the room, helping as needed.

- Have students compare their answers with a partner.

- Go over the answers with the class.

Answer key

1. A: like doing
   B: don't really like sports; love swimming
2. B: loves playing basketball; likes playing golf a lot
3. B: hate jogging
4. A: like playing
   B: don't like playing soccer very much
5. A: like doing aerobics
6. A: like skiing?
   B: really loves it

Pronunciation

> **LANGUAGE NOTES**
> * At the beginning of a conversation, the focus word is typically the last content word (noun, verb, adjective, or adverb) in the sentence: *Do you like **skiing**?*
> * But as a conversation continues, the focus often moves to a different part of the sentence to highlight new information or to make a contrast: *Do you like ski*ing? *Yes, I **love** skiing.*
> * Repeated words are usually not stressed.

Exercise ❺

* Tell students that they will listen to the audio. Remind them to notice the words that stand out.
* 🎧 Play the audio.
* Point out that the prominent words make a contrast: For example, *love* vs. *like* in the first pair of sentences or *women* vs. *men* in the third sentence.
* Ask students what happens to words that are repeated.

Exercise ❻

* Tell students that they will listen again to the audio. This time, they will listen and repeat.
* 🎧 Play the audio. Students repeat each line chorally.
* Encourage students to make the focus words stand out by pronouncing the vowel longer and clearer and making the voice go up on the stressed syllable.

Exercise ❼

* **Pairs.** Explain the task: Students will practice saying the conversations they completed in Exercise 4.
* Pair students. Assign A and B roles to each pair. Set a time limit of 3 minutes. Then have the pairs switch roles.
* Ask students to decide which words in their lines should be prominent, especially in B's responses.

Speaking

Exercise ❽

This exercise prepares students to do Exercises 9 and 10.

* Explain the task: Students will write the names of five sports in the first column.
* Set a time limit of 1 minute.

Exercise ❾

* Write two headings on the board: *Sport* and *Student/ Points*.
* Explain the task: Students will take a survey of six other students in the class about their favorite sports. They will use the sports they wrote in Exercise 8.
* Go over the example. Write the names of five sports under the heading *Sport* and call six volunteers to the front of the class. For each of the sports on your list, ask the students, *Do you like* (name of sport)*?* For each student that replies, *Yes, I like it*, write that student's name and *1* under the heading *Student/Points*. For each

student that replies, *Yes, I love it*, write that student's name and *2* under *Student/Points*. Do not give any points to other responses. After asking all six students the question, add up the points for each sport.

* Have students do the activity. Set a time limit of 10 minutes.

Exercise ❿

Go over the results with the class. Ask: *Which sport scored the most points? What sports do men like? What sports do women like?*

TRB For additional interactive grammar practice, have students do the reproducible activity for this unit in the *Teacher's Resource Book.*

Writing

Exercise ⓫

* Assign the writing task for class work or homework.
* Explain the task: Students will write a paragraph expressing their feelings about a favorite or least favorite sport, using verbs for likes and dislikes, and adverbs of degree.
* **TRB** Optionally, give students a copy of the model (see the *Teacher's Resource Book*, Writing Models). Ask them to read the model and notice the vocabulary and grammar from the unit.
* If students don't have the model, write the following on the board:

  I don't really like sports, but I sometimes play some types of sports because my friends are into them.

* Have a student read the sentences aloud. Answer any questions students might have.
* Walk around to make sure everyone understands the task.

For suggestions on how to give feedback on writing, see page xiv of this *Teacher's Edition.*

CONVERSATION TO GO

At the end of class, call on two students to role-play the conversation.

HOMEWORK

* 📖 Assign *Workbook* page 61, Grammar Exercises 3 and 4, and page 62, Pronunciation Exercises 7 and 8.
* 💿 If students do not have the *WorldView Workbook*, assign listening homework from the Student CD. Write on the board:

  Track 32
  Complete these sentences with *more* or *less*.

  1. In Canada, hockey is _____ popular than golf.
  2. Most women in Canada like swimming _____ than playing golf.
  3. Most men in Canada like team sports _____ than individual sports.

* 🎧 Tell students to listen to the audio and write their answers to the exercise. Have them bring their answers to the next class.

  (Answers: *1. less; 2. more; 3. more*)

Pronunciation

5 🎧 **Listen. Notice the way stress is used to contrast or compare ideas.**

Do you like **ski**ing?   Yes, I **love** skiing.
Do you like playing **golf**?   No, I **hate** playing golf.
Women liked **swim**ming, and men liked **bas**ketball.
My **sis**ter likes doing ae**ro**bics, and my **broth**er likes playing **soc**cer.

6 🎧 **Listen again and repeat.**

7 *PAIRS.* **Practice the conversations in Exercise 4.**

Speaking

8 *BEFORE YOU SPEAK.* **Write five more sports on the chart.**

9 **Take a survey.**

Ask six students in the class how they like
each sport. Give one point for each person
who likes the sport, and two points for
each person who loves the sport.

A: *Do you like swimming?*
B: *Yes, I love it.* (2 points)

10 **Discuss the questions.**

What is the most popular sport in your class?
Do men and women like different sports?

Sport	A	B	C	D	E	F
swimming		2				

Student/Points

Writing

11 **Write a paragraph. Choose a sport that you love or hate. Explain how you feel about the sport and why. Use verbs for likes/dislikes and adverbs of degree.**

CONVERSATION TO GO

A: Do you like jogging?
B: No, I hate jogging, but I love watching TV!

UNIT 16

Food for thought

Vocabulary Food
Grammar Quantifiers + count/non-count nouns
Speaking Talking about what you eat

Lesson A

Getting started

1 Match the words with the photos.

1. bread _B_
2. chocolate ____
3. cookies ____
4. fruit ____
5. juice ____
6. lettuce ____
7. onions ____
8. oranges ____
9. salt ____
10. strawberries ____
11. vegetables ____
12. water ____
13. yogurt ____

2 🎧 Listen and check your answers. Then listen and repeat.

3 *PAIRS.* Discuss. Which foods in Exercise 1 do you like? Which do you dislike? Why?

Pronunciation

4 🎧 Listen to the words. Notice the pronunciation of the vowel. Write each word in the correct sound group.

Soup /u/	Sugar /ʊ/

5 🎧 Listen and check your answers. Then listen again and repeat.

6 *PAIRS.* Take turns asking these questions.

Which foods are good for you?
Is fruit good for you?

Are cookies good for you?
Is juice good for you?

WVUE Radio
....

6.00 P.M. FOOD FOR THOUGHT!
Listen to the latest information on health and nutrition, and find out what we should and shouldn't eat!

72

Food for thought

OBJECTIVES

Students will:

- activate vocabulary related to food
- do listening, speaking, and writing tasks related to talking about what they eat
- focus on using quantifiers + count/non-count nouns
- practice pronouncing specific vowel sounds

WARM-UP: MY FAVORITE MEAL

Groups of 3. Students take turns telling each other what their favorite meal of the day is and why.

- Tell students that this unit is about food. Explain that the title of the unit, "Food for thought," is an expression that refers to an interesting idea or "something to think about."
- Have students name the meals they eat each day. Write *breakfast, lunch, dinner* on the board.
- Ask students to think about their favorite meal of the day and give reasons why they enjoy it the most.
- Divide the class in groups of 3 and set a time limit of 2 minutes.
- After 2 minutes, call on a few students to tell the rest of the class about their favorite meal of the day.

Getting started

OPTION: VOCABULARY PREVIEW

Read aloud the words in Exercise 1 and have students repeat after you. Call on volunteer students to give the equivalent term for each word in their language.

Exercise ❶

- Tell students to look at the pictures and to think about how many of the items they can identify.
- Explain the task: Students will match the pictures with the words on the list by writing the letter of each picture next to the correct word. Go over the example.
- Have students complete the activity individually. Set a time limit of 3 minutes.
- Tell students they will check their answers in the next activity.

Exercise ❷

- Explain the task: Students will listen to the audio and will check their answers.
- 🎧 Play the audio. Encourage students to correct any answers they got wrong.
- 🎧 Play the audio again and have students listen and repeat.

Answer key

1. B	4. E	7. A	10. I	12. F
2. M	5. G	8. J	11. C	13. H
3. D	6. L	9. K		

Exercise ❸

- **Pairs.** Explain the task: Students will talk about foods they like and dislike and their reasons for liking and disliking them.
- Pair students and set a time limit of 3 minutes. Walk around the room, helping as needed.
- Call on a few students to tell the class about a food they like or dislike and why.

Pronunciation

LANGUAGE NOTES

- To produce the sound /u/, the lips are pushed forward and rounded into a tight circle. The tongue is pulled back and raised high.
- To produce the sound /ʊ/, the lips are pushed forward a little, but not rounded. The tongue is pulled back and up, but not as much as for /u/.

Exercise ❹

- Tell students that they will listen to some words and will write each word under the correct sound group. Remind them to pay attention to the difference in the vowel sounds /u/ and /ʊ/.
- 🎧 Play the audio. Stop after the word *sugar*. Ask: *Which word has the long /u/ sound? Which one has the short /ʊ/ sound?*
- Explain the task: Students will listen for the vowel sound /u/ or /ʊ/ in each word. Then they will write the word in the correct sound group. Tell students they will check their answers in Exercise 5.
- 🎧 Play the rest of the audio.

Exercise ❺

- 🎧 Have students listen to the audio again to check their answers in Exercise 4.
- Pause after each item to allow students to check their answers and change any that were incorrect.
- 🎧 Play the audio again and have students repeat each word chorally.
- Point out the difference in lip position: For /ʊ/, the lips are relaxed and not pushed forward into a tight circle.

Exercise ❻

- **Pairs.** Explain the task: Students will take turns asking and answering the questions.
- Pair students and set a time limit of 2 minutes.

Listening

BACKGROUND NOTES

Most of us would immediately say that all the foods in the chart in Exercise 7 "are bad for us"—with the exception of fruit. As students will hear on the audio, this is not necessarily true.

- Chocolate contains compounds called flavonoids that can help maintain a healthy heart and good circulation. These compounds reduce blood clotting, which can cause heart attacks and stroke.

- A diet without salt can be dangerous.

- The advice against eating apples between meals is based on the discovery that the acids contained in apples and citrus fruits can cause erosion of the teeth's enamel.

- It can be argued that if carbohydrates caused weight gain, obesity rates in China and Japan would be very high. But obesity rates in these countries are a fraction of those in the West.

Exercise ❼

- Tell students to look at the ad on page 72 of the *Student Book*. Ask questions such as *What's* Food for Thought? (It's a radio program.) *What's the program about?* (It's about health and nutrition.) *What time is it on?* (It's on at 6:00 P.M.)

- Explain the task: Students will write *good* or *bad* under "Your opinion" to express their opinions about the foods in the first column. Under "Why?", students will write the reason for their opinions.

- Tell students to look at the chart and go over the example.

- Have students work individually to complete the activity. Set a time limit of 3 minutes. Walk around the room, helping as needed.

Exercise ❽

- Explain the task: Students will work in pairs to compare their answers in Exercise 7.

- Pair students and set a time limit of 3 minutes.

- Encourage students to defend their opinions. Remind them of the language used to express agreement and disagreement. (For example, *You're right. I don't think that's true.*)

- Call on a few students to tell the class what they think about some of the foods.

Exercise ❾

- Tell students that they are going to listen to the radio program *Food for Thought!* that they read about earlier.

- Explain the task: Students will listen to the opinions of the host of the radio program. If the host thinks a food is good, they will write *good* in the fourth column; if he thinks the food is bad, they should write *bad*.

- Go over the example.

- 🎧 Play the audio.

- Have students compare their answers with a partner's.

- Go over the answers with the class.

Answer key

Good: chocolate, salt, bread, potatoes, coffee, tea
Bad: fruit

Exercise ❿

- Explain the task: Students will listen to the radio program again. This time, they will write the reason the host gives for his opinions.

- Go over the example. Encourage students to write their answers in the note form used in the model.

- 🎧 Play the audio.

- Have students compare their answers with a partner's.

- Go over the answers with the class.

Answer key

chocolate: live longer; *salt:* live longer; *bread and potatoes:* lose weight, get thinner; *fruit:* bad for your teeth; *coffee:* an antidepressant, can make you happy; *tea:* can help you think

EXTENSION

- Pair students. Have the pairs compare the host's opinions with their own.

- Write these questions on the board: *Which of the host's opinions did you agree/disagree with? What surprised you the most about the host's opinions?*

- Lead a class discussion and have students share ideas.

◉ Please go to www.longman.com/worldview for additional in-class model conversation practice and supplementary reading practice.

HOMEWORK

- 📖 Assign *Workbook* page 63, Vocabulary Exercises 1 and 2, and page 65, Listening Exercises 5 and 6.

Listening

7 Look at the chart. Are the foods in the first column good for you or bad for you? In the second column, write *good* or *bad*. In the third column, write your reasons.

	Your opinion	Why?	Host's opinion	Why?
chocolate	bad	makes you fat	good	live longer
salt				
bread				
potatoes				
fruit				
coffee				
tea				

8 *PAIRS.* Compare your answers.

9 Listen to the radio show *Food for Thought!* Does the host think the foods listed in Exercise 7 are good for you or bad for you? In the fourth column of the chart, write *good* or *bad*.

10 Listen again. In the last column, write the reasons for the host's opinions.

Grammar focus

1 **Study the examples of the quantifiers with count and non-count nouns.**

much/many, a little/a few, a lot of	
(+) I eat	**a little** bread. **a few** potatoes. **a lot of** fruit/vegetables.
(–) I don't eat	**much** bread. **many** cookies.
(?) How **much** bread How **many** potatoes	do you eat?

some/any
(+) I have **some** bread/potatoes every day. (–) They don't have **any** tea/cookies in their house. (?) Do you have **any** chocolate/cookies?

2 **Look at the examples again. Fill in the blanks with *some, any, a little, a few,*** ***a lot of, much,*** **and *many*.**

Quantifiers + count/non-count nouns
Use _____ in questions and negative statements. Use _____ to talk about a large quantity. Use _____, _____, and _____ with count nouns (e.g., potatoes, oranges). Use _____, _____, and _____ with non-count nouns (e.g., bread, salt).

Grammar Reference page 147

3 **Underline the correct words in the conversations.**

1. A: How **much / many** strawberries did you eat last week?
   B: I ate **much / <u>a lot of</u>** strawberries. I didn't leave **some / any** for you!
2. A: Do you buy **any / many** fruit?
   B: Yes. I like to have **a lot of / many** fruit in the house.
3. A: How **much / many** tomatoes do you usually put in a salad?
   B: Not **much / many**. I use just **a little / a few**.
4. A: How **much / many** bread do you buy each week?
   B: I don't eat **a little / much** bread. I'm on a diet.
5. A: Do you drink **much / many** tea?
   B: No, and I don't drink **some / any** coffee either.
6. A: Do you eat **much / many** potatoes?
   B: Yes, I eat **much / a lot of** potatoes.

4 *PAIRS.* **Take turns asking and answering the questions in Exercise 3.**
Give true answers.

Grammar focus

WARM-UP

Note: Skip this warm-up if you're doing this lesson (Lesson B) during the same class period as Lesson A.

- Books closed. Tell students they are going to listen again to the radio program that they heard in the Listening section.
- Tell students to listen for statements or questions containing the quantifiers *some, any, much, many, a little, a few, a lot of.* Write the words on the board.
- 🎧 Play the audio for Lesson A, Listening, Exercise 9. (It models the grammar of the unit.)
- Call on students to say any statements or questions they remember from the audio that included the quantifiers on the board.

Exercise ❶

- Have students read the examples and study the bold-faced words. Tell students to look at the first group of examples. Ask: *What's the difference between* bread *and* potatoes*? (Potatoes* is a plural count noun, and *bread* is a non-count noun.)
- Point out or elicit that in the second group of examples, *some* is used in the affirmative statement, while *any* is used in the negative statement and the question.

Exercise ❷

- Ask students to study the examples again. Tell them to fill in the blanks with the correct answer for each rule.
- Have students compare their answers with a partner's.
- Go over the answers with the class.

- Ask a few questions to elicit the key points about the grammar. For example, *Which do we use in negative statements and questions—*any *or* some? (any) *Which do we use with non-count nouns:* a few *or* a little? (a little) *What three quantifiers are used to talk about a large quantity? (*much, many, a lot of*) Which quantifier can be used with both count and non-count nouns? (*a lot of*)*

Answer key

any	*a few/many/a lot of*
much/many/a lot of	*a little/much/a lot of*

Exercise ❸

- Before beginning Exercise 3, answer any questions students might have. You may also want to refer the class to the Grammar Reference for Unit 16 on page 147.
- Explain the task: Students will underline the correct words or phrases in bold to complete the conversations.
- Tell students to look at the first item and ask which word is correct. (*many*)
- Elicit an explanation for why the quantifier *many*—and not *much*—is correct. (*Strawberries* is a plural count noun.)
- Have the students work individually to complete the exercise. Set a time limit of 3 minutes. Walk around the room, helping as needed.
- Have students compare their answers with a partner's.
- Go over the answers with the class.

Answer key

1. A: many
   B: a lot of; any
	4. A: much
	   B: much

2. A: any
   B: a lot of
	5. A: much
	   B: any

3. A: many
   B: many; a few
	6. A: many
	   B: a lot of

Exercise ❹

- Explain the task: In pairs, students will take turns asking and answering the questions in Exercise 3. Point out that one partner will ask A's questions, and the other partner will give true answers about him/herself rather than reading B's lines in the conversations.
- Model the exercise with a volunteer. Have the student ask you the question in item 1: *Do you eat many potatoes?* Answer truthfully. (For example, *Yes, I do. I eat a lot of potatoes.*) Ask the student question 2, and elicit a true answer.
- Pair students and set a time limit of 5 minutes. Walk around helping as needed.
- Call on a few students to describe their eating habits. (For example, *I eat a lot of bread each week.*)

Speaking

Exercise ❺

This exercise provides practice with quantifiers + count and non-count nouns. It also prepares students for Exercises 6 and 7.

- Have students look at the chart. Write the headings on the board. Elicit the meaning of *snacks*, and brainstorm examples of popular snack foods.
- Explain the task: Students will write one of the quantifiers in each column to describe how much they eat of each type of food at each meal.
- Model the activity. Complete the first row on the board by saying aloud how much meat you eat at each meal.
- Set a time limit of 5 minutes. Walk around the room, helping as needed.

Exercise ❻

- **Groups of 3.** Explain the task: Students will take turns talking about what they usually eat and what is good and bad about their food choices. Remind them to use the words for quantities that they wrote in their charts.
- Go over the example and check comprehension. Ask: *When does this person eat bread? Does this person eat much meat? What does he or she eat a lot of? Does the person think his or her diet is healthy?*
- Divide the class in groups of 3 and set a time limit of 10 minutes. Walk around the room, helping as needed.

Exercise ❼

- Call on a member of each group to tell about the similarities and differences in their group's diets.
- Ask students what makes a healthy diet. Write their ideas on the board.
- Ask the class who has a healthy diet according to the ideas on the board.

EXTENSION

- Have students work with the same groups of 3. Tell the groups to create a poster about healthy eating.
- Tell them to include drawings of their ideas of what healthy eating is, a list of healthy foods, and a list of foods to avoid. Set a time limit of 15 minutes.
- Have the class vote on the best poster.

TRB For additional interactive grammar practice, have students do the reproducible activity for this unit in the *Teacher's Resource Book*.

Writing

Exercise ❽

- Assign the writing task for class work or homework.
- Explain the task: Students will write a paragraph giving advice for healthy eating.
- **TRB** Optionally, give students a copy of the model (see the *Teacher's Resource Book*, Writing Models). Ask them to read the model and notice the vocabulary and grammar from the unit.

- If students don't have the model, write the following on the board:

  Eating a balanced diet is important. We should eat a lot of fruit and vegetables every day. We should also have some carbohydrates such as bread, cereal . . .

For suggestions on how to give feedback on writing, see page xiv of this *Teacher's Edition*.

CONVERSATION TO GO

At the end of class, call on two students to role-play the conversation.

HOMEWORK

- 📖 Assign *Workbook* page 64, Grammar Exercises 3 and 4, and page 65, Pronunciation Exercises 7 and 8.
- Assign *Workbook* Self-Quiz 4.
- 💿 If students do not have the *WorldView Workbook*, assign listening homework from the Student CD. Write on the board:

  Track 36
  What advice does the radio host give? Circle the correct words to complete these sentences.

  1. **Don't eat much / Eat a lot of** chocolate.
  2. **Eat a lot of / a little** bread.
  3. **Don't eat many / Eat a lot of** apples.
  4. Drink **a lot of / a little** tea.

- 🎧 Tell students to listen to the audio and write the answers to the exercise. Have them bring their answers to the next class.

  (Answers: *1. Don't eat much; 2. Eat a lot of; 3. Don't eat many; 4. a little*)

FOR NEXT CLASS

- Tell students that the next class will be a review class covering Units 13–16.
- Have students review the material in the units to prepare for the activities in Review 4.

TRB Make copies of Quiz 4 in the *Teacher's Resource Book*.

Unit no.	Review Grammar	Listen to Student CD	Study Grammar Reference
13	Possessive *'s*, possessive adjectives and pronouns, *belong to*	Track 27	Page 146
14	Adverbs of manner	Track 29	Page 146
15	Verbs for likes and dislikes + noun or verb + *-ing*	Track 32	Page 147
16	Quantifiers with countable and non-count nouns	Track 36	Page 147

Speaking

5 *BEFORE YOU SPEAK.* **Look at the foods in the first column in the chart. How much of each do you eat for each meal? Write** *some, a little, a lot of, not many,* **or** *not much* **for each one.**

	Breakfast	Lunch	Dinner	Snack
Meat				
Poultry (chicken, turkey)				
Fish and seafood				
Bread, pasta, and rice				
Dairy (milk, cheese)				
Beans				
Vegetables				
Fruit				
Sweets (cake, candy)				

6 *GROUPS OF 3.* **Take turns talking about what you usually eat. Discuss what's good and bad about the foods you eat.**

I have bread for breakfast and lunch. I guess I eat a lot of bread every day! I don't think it's bad for me. Sometimes I put a little butter or a little cheese on it. I don't eat much meat, and I don't eat many cooked vegetables. But I eat a lot of fruit and salad. That's healthy, isn't it?

7 **How similar or different are everyone's diets? Who has the healthiest diet?**

Writing

8 **Write a paragraph. What is your advice for healthy eating? Which foods should people eat a lot of? Which foods should people try not to eat? Which foods are good and bad to eat? Why? Use the quantifiers** *some, any, much, many, a little, a few, a lot of.*

CONVERSATION TO GO

A: Do you eat much fruit?
B: Yes, I eat a lot of fruit, but I don't eat many vegetables.

Unit 13 Keepsakes

1 🎧 Listen to the model conversation.

2 Think of a keepsake that you or your family has. Where is it from? What does it look like? Why is it important to you?

3 *PAIRS.* Student A, talk for two minutes. Tell Student B about your keepsake. Explain as many details as you can. Student B, don't ask questions, just listen. Then switch. Student B, talk for two minutes about your keepsake.

4 Change partners. This time you each have only one minute. Talk about the keepsake.

5 Change partners again. This time you each have only thirty seconds. Talk about the keepsake.

Unit 14 Tales of Nasreddin Hodja

6 🎧 Listen to the model conversation.

7 Write each adverb below on a small piece of paper. Fold all the pieces of paper in half, put them in a box, and mix them up.

happily	quickly	calmly	proudly
sadly	angrily	nervously	shyly
slowly	thoughtfully	respectfully	rudely
politely	absent-mindedly	suspiciously	hungrily

8 *GROUPS OF 4.* Make up a group story. Take turns picking a piece of paper. Add two sentences to the story using the adverb on your paper. Continue until all the papers are gone. The person who uses the last adverb finishes the story.

9 Share your stories with the class. Which group has the most unique story?

📼 You may wish to use the video for Units 13–16 at this point.
For video activity worksheets, go to www.longman.com/worldview.

Unit 13: Keepsakes

OBJECTIVES

- Review the material presented in Unit 13
- Grammar practice: possessive *'s*, possessive adjectives and pronouns, *belong to*

WARM-UP

Books closed. Review the meaning of *keepsake*. Ask students to give examples of the kinds of things that some people have as keepsakes.

Exercise ❶

- Tell students they are going to listen to a person describe a keepsake that is special to him.
- 🎧 Play the audio.
- Ask comprehension questions about the audio.

Exercise ❷

- Ask students to think of a keepsake that is important to them or to their family.
- Write these guiding questions on the board: *Where is it from? Whose was it? How old is it? What does it look like? Why is it special?*

Exercise ❸

- Explain the task: Students will work in pairs to talk about their keepsakes. Student A will talk for 2 minutes about his or her keepsake. Student B will only listen.
- Tell the pairs they will switch roles afterward.
- 🎧 If needed, play the audio for Exercise 1.
- Pair students. Assign roles A and B. Set a time limit of 2 minutes.

Exercise ❹

- Pair students with different partners. Assign roles A and B.
- Have the new partners talk about their keepsakes as they did in Exercise 3. Set a time limit of 1 minute.

Exercise ❺

- Pair students with different partners. Assign roles A and B.
- Have the new partners talk about their keepsakes again. Set a time limit of 30 seconds.

WRAP-UP

Invite students to talk about what they just did. Ask them at what point it was easier to talk about the keepsake and if they gave the same information about their keepsakes to all their partners.

Unit 14: Tales of Nasreddin Hodja

OBJECTIVES

- Review the material presented in Unit 14
- Grammar practice: adverbs of manner

WARM-UP

List a few adverbs of manner on the board. Act out each adverb and call on a student to guess the adverb.

Exercise ❻

- Tell students they will listen to people use adverbs to tell a story.
- Have them listen for the four adverbs the people use (*happily, absent-mindedly, calmly, quickly*).
- 🎧 Play the audio.

Exercise ❼

- Have each group member pick a row of adverbs from the chart and have each member write these adverbs on small pieces of paper. Have them fold the pieces of paper, making sure the writing cannot be seen.
- Give each group a small box to put the folded pieces of paper in. Tell them to mix up the folded pieces of paper.

Exercise ❽

- **Groups of 4.** Explain the task: Students will work in groups to tell a story. Each member will contribute two sentences, using adverbs they will pick, to make a story.
- 🎧 If needed, play the audio for Exercise 6 again to remind students how to do the activity.
- Divide the class into groups of 4 and set a time limit of 5 minutes.
- Tell the members of the group to take turns picking a piece of paper with an adverb on it. Each member will read aloud the adverb he or she picks and will make two related sentences. They must use the adverb in one of their two sentences. Encourage students to be creative in their stories.
- Walk around the room, helping as needed.

Exercise ❾

- After 5 minutes, call on each group to tell their stories.
- Have the class vote on the most unique story.

Unit 15: Popular sports

OBJECTIVES

- Review the material presented in Unit 15
- Grammar practice: verbs for likes and dislikes + noun or verb + *-ing*

WARM-UP

Ask students what they do during their vacation. Ask them what factors they consider when they decide on a vacation place.

Exercise ❿

- Tell students they will listen to a conversation of three people deciding which resort to visit. Tell them to listen for sports people say they love doing. (*skiing, aerobics, doing karate, playing golf*)
- 🎧 Play the audio as students look at the ads.

Exercise ⓫

- **Groups of 3.** Explain the task: Students will read the ads and will discuss their likes and dislikes in terms of sports. Then they will decide as a group which resort to go to.
- Divide students into groups of 3. Assign students roles A, B, and C. Tell them to read the directions in the *Student Book*.
- 🎧 If needed, play the audio again for Exercise 10. Answer any questions about the activity students might have.
- Set a time limit of 5 minutes for the groups to decide which resort they will visit.

WRAP-UP

Have a member from each group report his or her group's decision to the class. Remind the reporters to give some of the reasons for their choices.

Unit 16: Food for thought

OBJECTIVES

- Review the material presented in Unit 16
- Grammar practice: quantifiers with countable and non-count nouns

WARM-UP

Ask students what kinds of food they usually eat and how much of each they eat and buy.

Exercise ⓬

- Tell students they are going to listen to a conversation about food shopping between two roommates. Tell them to listen for the amounts of food mentioned. (*They have a lot of oranges, a few strawberries, some lettuce and tomatoes, a lot of onions. They don't have any apples or bananas.*)
- 🎧 Play the audio.

Exercise ⓭

- **Pairs.** Explain the task: Tell students they are going to role-play two roommates talking on the phone. One is at a supermarket, the other is at home telling the other what foods to buy.
- 🎧 If needed, play the audio for Exercise 12 again.
- Pair students and set a time limit of 5 minutes. Have Student B begin by answering the telephone.

Exercise ⓮

After students complete the conversation, have them switch roles. Student A begins the role-play by answering the telephone.

WRAP-UP

Have partners check their answers by comparing their food lists with the foods in the pictures.

Paradise Island Resort

Enjoy: **swimming, playing volleyball, jogging on the beach and playing tennis**

Come to the
BLUE MOUNTAIN CLUB

SUMMER SPORTS
biking
hiking

WINTER SPORTS
skiing

Sports Plus Club

Relax and get in shape with:
• doing aerobics • playing basketball
•golf or soccer • doing karate

Unit 15 Popular sports

10 🎧 Listen to the model conversation. Look at the ads.

11 *GROUPS OF 3.* Your group has just won a free weekend to a resort.

Student A, you really love the outdoors, and you like doing sports outside in any weather. You like hiking, and skiing, but you hate aerobics. You don't like playing volleyball or golf.

Student B, you really like the sun, and you hate doing exercise inside. You love jogging, but you don't like hiking. You don't like doing aerobics or karate.

Student C, you really love doing aerobics. You don't like doing sports in very hot or very cold weather. You like doing karate a lot. You hate volleyball and hiking.

Look at the ads. Discuss which sports you love, like, don't like, or hate doing. Then as a group, decide which resort to go to.

Unit 16 Food for thought

12 🎧 Listen to the model conversation.

13 *PAIRS.* Imagine that you and your partner are roommates.

Student A, you're at the supermarket. Call Student B to ask what you should buy. Write a shopping list on a piece of paper.

Student B, look at page 142. Tell Student A what food you have at home and what Student A needs to buy at the supermarket.

14 Switch roles. Student B, call Student A to ask what you should buy. Write a shopping list. Student A, look at page 140.

A nice place to work

Vocabulary Office practices
Grammar Modals: *have to/had to* for present and past necessity
Speaking Talking about obligations

Getting started

1 **Look at the photo. Where do you think the people are?**

2 *PAIRS.* **Look again at the photo. Describe the clothes the people are wearing.**

3 **Complete the sentences with the words in the box.**

break	casual
commute	downsize
flextime	formal
~~full-time~~	part-time
supervisor	telecommute

1. I have a ___full-time___ job. I work forty hours a week.

2. When I get tired, I take a _____ from work and get some coffee.

3. I wear jeans to work. My office has a _____ dress code.

4. My _____ manages about twenty employees.

5. Janet has a _____ schedule. She works different hours every day.

6. My neighbors _____ to work by train—two hours each way.

7. Marco's office is somewhat _____, so he wears a suit and tie to work.

8. Raymond works only 20 hours a week, but he's happy having only a _____ job.

9. I work from home; in other words, I _____. I stay in touch with the office by email, telephone, and fax.

10. My company is going to _____, so many of us are going to lose our jobs.

4 *PAIRS.* **Compare your answers in Exercise 3. What kind of dress code does the office in the photo have?**

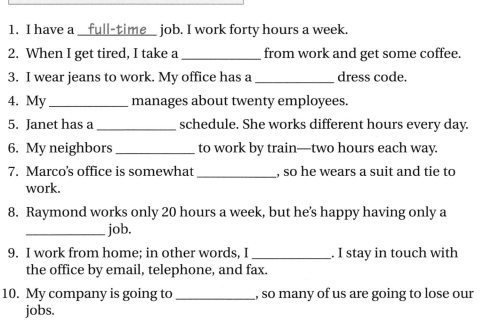

A nice place to work

OBJECTIVES

Students will:

- activate vocabulary related to office practices
- do listening, speaking, and writing tasks related to necessity and obligations
- focus on using *have to*/*had to* for present and past necessity and obligation
- practice weak and strong pronunciations of *to*

WARM-UP: WHAT SHOULD I WEAR?

Students participate in a class discussion about clothing.

- Tell students that this unit is about office practices. Point out that one of the topics is dress codes, or the clothes people should wear to work.
- Write headings on the board for places where people might wear different types of clothes: *at work, at school, at a party, at a soccer game, at home.*
- Brainstorm the types of clothes people generally wear. Write students' ideas on the board. (For example, *At work*: suit, tie, jacket, dress; *At school*: jeans, T-shirt or a uniform.)

Getting started

Exercise ❶

- Tell students to look at the picture.
- Ask: *Where do you think the people are?* Call on volunteers to give their ideas.

Answer key

They are at work/in an office/in a conference room.

Exercise ❷

- Explain the task: In pairs, students will look at the picture and describe the clothes the people are wearing. Tell them to take turns pointing to one person in the picture and saying one sentence about what that person is wearing.
- Pair students and set a time limit of 3 minutes. While students are working, walk around the room, helping as needed.
- Call on a few students to describe the clothing one of the people is wearing.

Answer key

Possible answers (starting from the left): She's wearing a dress.; He's wearing a shirt, a tie, and pants.; He's wearing a denim shirt and pants.; She's wearing a sweater and a skirt.; He's wearing jeans.; She's wearing a blouse and pants.; She's wearing a dress.

CULTURE NOTES

- In the United States, a job is usually considered "full time" if it is 35 to 40 hours a week. Anything less than 35 hours a week is usually considered part time.
- Some employers allow "flextime." With flextime, the employee is often free to work a schedule that is convenient—as long as he or she puts in the required number of hours per week.

OPTION: VOCABULARY PREVIEW

Tell students to look at the words in Exercise 3. Ask: *In what situations do you usually use these words?* (in work situations) Ask questions to clarify their meanings. For example, ask students what times their breaks are at work. Or ask them how many have flextimes, how they commute to and from work, how many telecommute, and how many have experienced downsizing in their companies.

Exercise ❸

- Explain the task: Students will complete the sentences using the words in the box. Go over the example.
- Have students work individually to complete the exercise. Set a time limit of 5 minutes.
- Tell students they will check their answers in the next exercise.

CULTURE NOTE

Many businesses favor "business attire": suits and ties for men, and suits or dresses for women. Some businesses have a "business-casual" dress code, which is less formal than business attire but does not usually allow jeans and T-shirts. "Business casual" allows pants and collared shirts.

Exercise ❹

- **Pairs.** Explain the task: Students will compare their answers to Exercise 3 in pairs. They will then talk about the dress code in the picture.
- Pair students and set a time limit of 3 minutes.
- Go over the answers to Exercise 3 with the class.
- Call on a few students to describe the office dress code in the photo.

Answer key

1. full-time	5. flextime	9. telecommute
2. break	6. commute	10. downsize
3. casual	7. formal	
4. supervisor	8. part-time	

This office has a casual or business-casual dress code.

Listening

Exercise ❺

- **Pairs.** Have students read the directions silently. Answer any questions they may have about vocabulary.
- Explain the task: Students will discuss office practices in their country.
- Pair students and set a time limit of 3 minutes. Walk around the room, helping as needed.
- Call on a few students to give their answers to each question.

Exercise ❻

- Explain the task: Students will listen to an interview with a businessman and will check the topics that the interviewer asks him about.
- 🎧 Play the audio.
- Have students compare their answers with a partner's.
- Go over the answers with the class.

> **Answer key**
>
> clothing, work relationships, work schedule

EXTENSION

- Tell students that this activity will help them develop the skill of listening for specific words.
- Prepare enough slips of paper, so everybody in the class will get one. Write the following words and phrases on the slips of paper: *twenty years, ten years, computer firm, computer field, suit, business-casual, sneakers, comfortable, formal, work schedule, flexible, flextime, telecommute, good employees.* Since there may be more students than words, some students will get the same words.
- Tell students that you will play the audio. Remind them to listen carefully. When they hear the word or phrase from their slip of paper, they should stand up.
- 🎧 Play the audio.
- All students should be standing by the end of the interview.

Exercise ❼

- Have students read the statements silently. Explain the task: Students will listen to the interview again and will write *T* after the true statements and *F* after the false statements. Go over the example.
- 🎧 Play the audio.
- Have students compare their answers with a partner's.
- Go over the answers with the class.

> **Answer key**
>
> | | | | |
> |---|---|---|---|
> | 1. T | 3. F | 5. T | 7. T |
> | 2. F | 4. T | 6. T | 8. F |

EXTENSION

- Have students rewrite the false statements to make them true. (For example, *2. He works in a large computer firm.*)
- Have them compare their sentences with a partner's.
- Go over the answers with the class.

  (Answers: *2. He works in a large computer firm. 3. He wears a suit to work every day except Fridays. / He doesn't wear a suit on Fridays. 8. The office practices at his company are different from twenty years ago.*)

🌐 Please go to www.longman.com/worldview for additional in-class model conversation practice and supplementary reading practice.

HOMEWORK

- 📖 Assign *Workbook* page 68, Vocabulary Exercises 1 and 2, and page 70, Listening Exercises 5 and 6.

Listening

5 *PAIRS.* **Discuss the questions.**

How do people dress in offices in your country?

Do people call their co-workers by their first names or by their titles and last names (for example, *Ms. Marino*)?

How often do people take breaks? When?

6 🎧 **Listen to an interview with a businessman. Check (✓) the topics that the interviewer asks him about.**

❑ clothing   ❑ work schedule
❑ amount of work   ❑ vacation time
❑ work relationships

7 🎧 **Listen again and write *T* (true) or *F* (false) after each statement.**

1. Tom Banks works in New York. T
2. He works in a bank.
3. He wears a suit to work every day.
4. He likes casual Fridays.
5. He calls his supervisors by their first names.
6. He can work at different times of the day.
7. He doesn't always work in the office.
8. The office practices at his company are the same as twenty years ago.

Grammar focus

1 **Study the examples with *have to* and *had to*.**

Present	Past
(+) Today, I **have to work** longer hours.	Twenty years ago, I **had to wear** a suit every day.
(–) We **don't have to wear** suits and ties.	We **didn't have to work** long hours.
(?) **Does** he **have to go** to the office every day?	**Did** you **have to spend** money on expensive suits?
Yes, he **does.** / No, he **doesn't.**	Yes, I **did.** / No, I **didn't.**

2 **Look at the examples again. Complete the rules in the chart.**

Modals: *have to/had to* for present and past necessity
Use _____ when something is required in the present.
Use _____ when something was required in the past.

Grammar Reference page 147

3 **Write sentences using the correct form of *have to* or *had to*.**

1. call the managers Mr. and Ms. (required?)

   (she) _Does she have to call the managers Mr. and Ms._____?

2. work from 9 A.M. to 5 P.M. (not required)

   You _____.

3. wear business clothes before 1996 (required?)

   (they) _____?

4. carry a cell phone at all times (required)

   He _____.

5. wear business clothes (not required)

   She _____.

6. speak many languages (required?)

   (you) _____?

7. go to the office every day last year (not required)

   We _____.

8. arrive early yesterday morning (required)

   They _____.

9. have a computer at home (required?)

   (I) _____?

Grammar focus

LANGUAGE NOTE

In Unit 11, students learned the use of *have to*—to express necessity. In this unit, the focus is on the contrast between *have to* to express necessity in the present and *had to* for necessity in the past.

WARM-UP

Note: Skip this warm-up if you're doing this lesson (Lesson B) during the same class period as lesson A.

- Tell students they will listen again to the interview with Tom Banks from the Listening section.
- Point out that Tom talks about things that are necessary in his office now and things that were necessary in the office in the past. Ask students to pay attention to the words that express necessity in the present and in the past.
- 🎧 Play the audio from Lesson A, Listening, Exercise 6. (It models the grammar of the unit.)
- Ask students what words were used to express necessity. (*have to/had to*)

Exercise ❶

- Have students read the two sets of examples and study the bold-faced words. Point out or elicit that the first set is labeled *Present* and the second *Past*.
- Ask: *What are the differences between the present and the past forms?* (The present tense *have to* becomes *had to* in the past tense; the present form *don't* becomes *didn't* in the past; and the present form *does* becomes *did* in the past.)

Exercise ❷

- Have students look again at the examples in Exercise 1 and complete each of the rules in the chart.
- Have students compare their answers with a partner's.
- Go over the answers with the class.
- Ask a few questions to elicit the key points about the grammar. For example, *What auxiliary verb do we use to express past necessity in negative statements and questions?* (*did*) *What form do we use to say something is required in the present?* (*have to*) *How do we express that something was required in the past?* (*had to*)

Answer key

have to
had to

Exercise ❸

- Before students begin Exercise 3, answer any questions they might have. You may also want to refer the class to the Grammar Reference for Unit 17 on page 147.
- Explain the task: Students will use the correct form of *have to* or *had to* to write sentences. Point out that the information in parentheses indicates what kinds of sentences they should write: (*required*) means they should write affirmative sentences; (*not required*) means they should write negative ones, and (*?*) means they should write a question.
- Go over the example.
- Set a time limit of 10 minutes. Walk around the room, helping as needed.
- Have students compare their answers with a partner's.
- Go over the answers with the class.

Answer key

1. Does she have to call the managers Mr. and Ms.?
2. You don't have to work from 9:00 A.M. to 5:00 P.M.
3. Did they have to wear formal clothes before 1996?
4. He has to carry a cell phone at all times.
5. She doesn't have to wear business clothes.
6. Do you have to speak many languages?
7. We didn't have to go to the office every day last year.
8. They had to arrive early yesterday morning.
9. Do I have to have a computer at home?

EXTENSION

- Pair students. Tell them that they will create mini-conversations around each item in Exercise 3.
- Model the activity with a student. Tell the student to ask you the first question (*Does she have to call the managers Mr. and Ms.?*). Make sure you demonstrate not only how to answer the question, but also how to add further information, especially to a *Yes/No* question. (For example, *No, she doesn't. She calls them by their first names.*)
- Set a time limit of 5 minutes. Have volunteers perform one of their conversations for the class.

Pronunciation

> **LANGUAGE NOTES**
> - The word *to,* either as part of an infinitive or as a preposition, is usually pronounced as the weak form /tə/, especially before a word beginning with a consonant sound: *I had to /tə/ wear a suit to /tə/ the office.*
> - *To* usually has its strong pronunciation /tu/ at the end of a sentence: For example, *I can work from 11 to 7 if I want to /tu/.*
> - The expression *have to* is usually pronounced as the blended form "hafta": *I don't have to /hæftə/ wear a suit.* When *to* is used at the end of a sentence, it has a stronger pronunciation: *But now I don't have to /hæftu/.*

Exercise 4

- Tell students that they will listen to the audio. Remind them to notice the weak pronunciation of *to,* shown in light blue, and its stronger pronunciation, shown in red.
- 🎧 Play the audio. Ask students to notice the contrast between the strong and weak pronunciations of *to* by saying the word first by itself and then in a phrase. For example, *to /tu/; to /tə/ the office.*
- Remind students about the pronunciation of *have to* /hæftə/. Write "hafta" on the board to illustrate the pronunciation.

Exercise 5

- Tell students that they will listen again. This time, they will listen and repeat.
- 🎧 Play the audio again, stopping after each item to allow students to repeat chorally.
- Some of the sentences are quite long and may be difficult for students to say. You may want to break the sentences down into smaller parts to make them more manageable: For example, *to the office—a suit to the office—wear a suit to the office—I had to wear a suit to the office.*
- Ask a few individual students to repeat the sentences to check their pronunciation.
- If necessary, remind students to give *to* a short and weak pronunciation and to pronounce the words *have to* as if they were the single word "hafta."

TRB For additional interactive grammar practice, have students do the reproducible activity for this unit in the *Teacher's Resource Book.*

Speaking

Exercise 6

This exercise provides practice with *have to* and *had to* for present and past necessity.

- Explain the task: Students will think about what is required or not required at their school or at work and will compare what is true now with what was true in the past. They will take notes, using the ideas in the *Student Book.* Then they will discuss their ideas with a partner.

- Have students read the list of ideas. Go over the example.

Exercise 7

- Pair students and set a time limit of 10 minutes. Have each pair discuss their ideas.
- Walk around the room, helping as needed.
- After 10 minutes, call on a few students to share their ideas about one of the topics.

Writing

Exercise 8

- Assign the writing task for class work or homework.
- Explain the task: Students will write to an American friend who is coming to work in an office in their country. In the letter, they will write about work practices in their country.
- Brainstorm ideas about work practices related to clothes, schedules, meals, breaks, and work relationships.
- **TRB** Optionally, give students a copy of the model (see the *Teacher's Resource Book,* Writing Models). Ask them to read the model and notice the vocabulary and grammar from the unit.
- If students don't have the model, write the following on the board:

  Hi, Michael!
  I'm so glad you're coming to work in my country! Where exactly are you going to work?

  Do you want to know about office practices in my country? Well, the work environment is a bit formal here. Most men have to wear a suit and tie to work. Several years ago, some companies here introduced casual Fridays, which means that workers don't have to wear a suit and tie on Fridays.

- Have a student read the sentences aloud. Answer any questions students might have.
- Walk around to make sure everyone understands the task.

For suggestions on how to give feedback on writing, see page xii of this *Teacher's Edition.*

CONVERSATION TO GO

At the end of class, call on two students to role-play the conversation.

HOMEWORK

- 📖 Assign *Workbook* page 69, Grammar Exercises 3 and 4, and page 70, Pronunciation Exercises 7 and 8.
- 💿 If students do not have the *WorldView Workbook,* assign listening homework from the Student CD. Write on the board:

  Track 37
  Why did Tom's company have to change its office practices?

- 🎧 Tell students to listen to the audio and write the answer to the question. Have them bring their answer to the next class.

  (Answer: *It had to change to keep its good employees.*)

Pronunciation

4 🎧 **Listen. Notice the short, weak pronunciation of the word *to* when it comes before another word and the stronger pronunciation when it comes at the end of a sentence.**

I had to wear a suit to the office.   I had to work from 9 to 5.
But now I don't have **to**.
I don't have to wear a suit to work.   I don't have to go to the office every day.
I can work from 11 to 7 if I want **to**.   But I have to work longer hours!

5 🎧 **Listen again and repeat.**

Speaking

6 *BEFORE YOU SPEAK.* **Think about work or school. Write two things you have to do and two things you don't have to do. Look at the list for ideas. Put an asterisk (*) next to the things that are different from 50 years ago.**

- the clothes you/others wear
- what you call your clients/ co-workers/teachers
- the times you work or study
- the place(s) you work or study
- the way you work or study

Things you have to do:

Things you don't have to do:

7 *PAIRS.* **Ask questions about the things on your list.**

A: (clothes) *What do people wear to work at your company?*
B: *Now most people wear casual clothes. They don't have to wear suits.*

Writing

8 **Write to an American friend who is coming to work in an office in your country. Tell him or her about work practice. Write about clothes, schedules, breaks, and work relationships. Use *have to/had to* to describe necessity.**

CONVERSATION TO GO

A: **Do you have to wear** a suit to work?
B: No, I **don't**. But in my last job, I **had to wear** one every day.

Lesson A

Hollywood mystery

Vocabulary Words related to police investigations
Grammar Simple past and past continuous
Speaking Describing activities in the past

Getting started

1 **Match the words to the pictures.**

| intruder | police officer | suspect | thief | victim | witness |

2 *PAIRS.* **Compare your answers.**

3 **Match each verb with its meaning.**

1. get arrested __e__   a. tell the police about a crime

2. confess ____   b. try to find out the truth about a crime

3. investigate ____   c. ask someone questions about a crime

4. question ____   d. admit that you have done something wrong

5. report ____   e. be taken away by the police because they believe
                                 the person is guilty of a crime

4 **Read the newspaper article. Answer the questions.**

1. Who are the victims?
2. Who is investigating the crime?
3. Were there witnesses to the crime?
   Did anyone question the witnesses?
4. Who is the thief?
5. Did someone get arrested for the crime?

5 *PAIRS.* **Compare your answers.**

Stolen Necklace!

HOLLYWOOD An intruder stole a valuable diamond necklace from the house of movie director Richard Price. The necklace belonged to Mr. Price's wife. Police think that the Prices' security system wasn't working when the thief entered the house. Several people saw a man running away from the house after the theft. Police want to question this man.

Hollywood mystery

OBJECTIVES

Students will:

- activate vocabulary related to police investigations
- do reading, speaking, and writing tasks related to describing activities in the past
- focus on using the simple past and past continuous
- practice the weak pronunciation of *was* and *were*

WARM-UP: FAVORITE MYSTERIES

Groups of 3. Students will talk about their favorite mystery book or movie.

- Point to the title, "Hollywood mystery." Ask: *Where is Hollywood?* (Hollywood is a city in California.) *What is it associated with?* (It is associated with movies and movie stars.)
- Elicit or explain that a mystery is a story in which events are not explained until the end.
- Explain the task: Students will work in groups of 3 to take turns telling one another about their favorite mystery book or movie.
- Divide the class in groups of 3 and set a time limit of 3 minutes.
- Call on a few students to tell the class about their favorite mystery.

Getting started

OPTION: VOCABULARY PREVIEW

Tell students that they may use their dictionaries to do the activity. Write these groups of words on the board. Tell students to circle the words that don't belong:

1. intruder   burglar   victim
2. suspect   police officer   detective
3. police officer suspect   accused
4. thief   witness   robber
5. observer   detective   witness

(*1. victim; 2. suspect; 3. witness; 4. witness; 5. detective*)
Clarify any difficulties students might have.

Exercise ❶

- Explain the task: Students will match the words to the different people shown in the pictures. Point out that more than one word can be matched to a picture.
- Set a time limit of 2 minutes.
- Tell students they will check their answers in the next exercise.

Exercise ❷

- Pair students and have them compare their answers in Exercise 1.
- Go over the answers with the class.

Answer key

intruder: A; police officer: C; suspect: C; victim: B; witness: B

Exercise ❸

- Explain the task: Students will write the letter of each meaning next to the verb it defines.
- Set a time limit of 2 minutes. Walk around the room, helping as needed.
- Have students compare their answers with a partner's.
- Go over the answers with the class.

Answer key

1. e   2. d   3. b   4. c   5. a

Exercise ❹

Teaching Tip! **Highlighting key information**

In this unit, students are asked to pay attention to certain kinds of information. Underlining or highlighting key information in a text such as names, times, and other facts is an important academic skill.

Before each task, help students identify the information they should be looking for.

- Tell students to look at the article and to read the headline. Remind them that the unit title is "Hollywood mystery." Ask them to predict what the story is about.
- Tell students to take a quick look at the questions in Exercise 4. Ask: *What word do three questions begin with?* (*who*) Ask students what kind of information they think they should pay attention to in the article. (They should focus on references to people and their names.)
- Pair students and have them answer the questions.
- Set a time limit of 3 minutes. Walk around the room, helping as needed.

Exercise ❺

- **Pairs.** Have students compare their answers with a partner's.
- Discuss the answers with the class.

Answer key

1. Richard Price and his wife are the victims.
2. The police are investigating the crime.
3. Yes, there were several witnesses. The police questioned them.
4. The suspected thief is the man who was running away.
5. No, nobody was/got arrested. The police are looking for the suspect.

Reading

Exercise 6

- Explain the task: Students will read statements that witnesses gave the police. Then they will write the information to complete the chart.
- Have students read the questions in the chart and the people's names. Remind them to underline or highlight this information as they read.
- Set a time limit of 10 minutes. Walk around the room, helping as needed.
- Have students compare their charts with a partner's.
- Go over the answers with the class.

Answer key

When the necklace was stolen . . .	Where was . . .	What was he or she doing?
Richard Price	in the living room	watching TV
Camille Price	in the bedroom	reading a book
Brad Price	in Brad's room upstairs	playing video games
Martha McGuire	in the kitchen	cleaning up

EXTENSION

- Have students close their books. Tell them you are going to test their memory.
- Read individual sentences from the statements made by the people in the Price house in random order. Have students identify who said the statement.
- Alternatively, pair students and have them take turns reading statements to each other. The student listening to the statement should try to identify the speaker without looking at the reading.

Exercise 7

- Explain the task: Students will reread the statements by the four witnesses and choose the picture of the man they described.
- Set a time limit of 3 minutes.
- Have students compare their answers with a partner.
- Go over the answer with the class.

Answer key

Picture B

ⓖ Please go to www.longman.com/worldview for additional in-class model conversation practice and supplementary reading practice.

HOMEWORK

- 📖 Assign *Workbook* page 71, Vocabulary Exercises 1 and 2, and page 73, Listening Exercises 5 and 6.

Reading

6 The police questioned the people at the Prices' house the night of the robbery. Read the people's statements. Where was each person? What were they doing when the necklace was stolen?

Richard Price (husband)

I was watching TV in the living room when I heard a loud noise from my study. I saw that the safe door was open and the necklace wasn't there! I ran outside and saw a man. He was running away from the house. He was wearing a blue jacket.

Camille Price (wife)

I was reading a book in the bedroom when I heard the sound. Then I looked out the window, and someone was running away. He was wearing a baseball cap. Then I went down to the study and saw Richard, and he told me my necklace was gone!

Brad Price (son)

I was in my room upstairs with my sister Jill. We were playing video games. I heard a loud noise and looked out the window. It was dark, but we saw a man outside. He was wearing white sneakers, and he was running away from the house. My sister stayed upstairs. When I went downstairs, my dad was calling the police and my mom was looking in the safe.

Martha McGuire (cook/housekeeper)

I was cleaning up after dinner when I heard a sound. I thought it was a car. When I looked out the kitchen window, a man was running into the trees. He was holding something in his hand. The necklace, I guess. I'm just glad the kids were upstairs!

When the necklace was stolen...	Richard Price	Camille Price	Brad Price	Martha McGuire
Where was . . . ?				
What was he or she doing?				

7 Look at the pictures and read again the four witnesses' descriptions of the man running away. Circle the picture of the man that the witnesses described.

(A)

(B)

(C)

Grammar focus

1 **Look at the examples. Underline the past continuous verbs.**

> We **were playing** video games upstairs when we **heard** a loud noise.
> I **saw** a man outside. He **was running** away from the house.
> When I **went** downstairs, my dad **was calling** the police.

2 **Look at the examples again. Circle the correct words to complete the explanations in the chart.**

Simple past and past continuous
The action in the simple past started **before / after** the action in the past continuous.
The action that started first **was / wasn't** finished before the second action started.

> *Grammar Reference page 147*

3 **Complete the stories with the correct form of the verb in parentheses. Use the simple past or the past continuous.**

1. I ___was taking out___ (**take out**) the trash
   when I _____ (**hear**) a dog barking.
   There _____ (**be**) a man in someone's
   backyard. When I _____ (**see**) him, he
   _____ (**run**) into the trees. He
   _____ (**wear**) a dark jacket and a
   baseball cap.

2. I _____ (**get**) something from my
   car in the driveway. My neighbor and I _____ (**talk**). We
   _____ (**not/look**) at the Prices' house, so we _____
   (**not/see**) anything.

3. I _____ (**drive**) home when I _____ (**pass**) the Prices' house.
   A few police officers _____ (**stand**) in front of the house, and two officers
   _____ (**talk**) to Richard. The police cars _____ (**block**) the street,
   so I _____ (**drive**) home another way.

Grammar focus

LANGUAGE NOTES

- The past continuous is used to show that an action was in progress at a specific time in the past.
- To form the past continuous, use the past form of *be* + verb + *-ing*. Add *not* after *was* or *were* to form the negative.
- Use the past continuous and the simple past in a sentence to show that one event (the simple past event) interrupted another (the past continuous) event.
- *When* is often used with the simple past (*When I went downstairs*) and *while* with the past continuous (*While I was cleaning up*).

WARM-UP

Note: Skip this warm-up if you're doing this lesson (Lesson B) during the same class period as Lesson A.

- Tell students they will listen to the statements that they read in the Reading section.
- Ask students to write down what the witnesses were doing when they saw the man.
- 🎧 Play the audio from Lesson A, Reading, Exercise 6. (It models the grammar of the unit.)
- Call on a few students to tell what each of the witnesses was doing. (Answers: *watching TV; reading a book; playing video games; cleaning up*)

Exercise ❶

- Have students look at the examples and study the bold-faced words.
- Tell students to underline the past continuous verbs.
- Go over the answers with the class.
- Ask: *What's the verb tense of the other verb in each sentence?* (the simple past) Tell students to focus on the order of the two actions described in each of the examples. Ask: *Which action happened first in each example: the simple past verb or the past continuous verb?* (the past continuous verb)

Answer key

were playing	was running	was calling

Exercise ❷

- Tell students to study the examples again.
- Ask them to read the statements in the chart and to circle the information that correctly completes the explanations.
- Have students compare their answers with a partner's.
- Go over the answers with the class.
- Ask a few questions to elicit the key points about the grammar: *How do we form the past continuous?* (*was/were* + verb + *-ing*) *In a sentence with both a simple past and a past continuous verb, which action started first?* (the action in the past continuous)

Answer key

after	wasn't

Exercise ❸

- Before students begin Exercise 3, answer any questions they might have. You may also want to refer the class to the Grammar Reference for Unit 18 on page 147.
- Explain the task: Students will complete the stories with the correct form of the verb in parentheses—simple past or past continuous. Point out that *when* often introduces a verb in the simple past.
- Go over the example.
- Have students complete the exercise individually. Set a time limit of 5 minutes. Walk around the room, helping as needed.
- Have students compare their answers with a partner's.
- Go over the answers with the class.

Answer key

1. was taking out; heard
   was; saw; was running; was wearing
2. was getting; were talking; weren't looking; didn't see
3. was driving; passed; were standing; were talking; were blocking; drove

EXTENSION

- Tell students to watch your actions and those of others carefully.
- Drop your book loudly on the floor. Ask students to write three sentences about what was going on when you dropped the book.
- Have them compare their sentences with a partner's. Call on a few students to read their sentences to the class.

Pronunciation

> **LANGUAGE NOTES**
> - In English, only the important words in a sentence are stressed, while unimportant words have short and weak pronunciations. In past continuous forms, the main verb is stressed, and the affirmative auxiliary verb *was* or *were* is usually unstressed and has a weak pronunciation.
> - The unstressed sound /wəz/ is a very short sound. To make this sound, the mouth is open just a little and the tongue is relaxed in the center of the mouth, without being pushed forward or pulled back.
> - To make the sound /wɚ/, the tongue is pulled back a little and bunched up. The tip of the tongue turns up, but does not touch the roof of the mouth.

Exercise ❹

- Tell students they will listen to the audio. Remind them to notice the pronunciation of *was* and *were*.
- 🎧 Play the audio.
- Ask: *Why do* was *and* were *have weak pronunciations?* (Because they are auxiliary verbs.) If necessary, remind them about important words being pronounced longer and clearer (or stressed) and unimportant words being pronounced shorter and weaker (or unstressed).
- Call attention to the past continuous forms by writing one or more of them on the board.
- 🎧 Play the audio again and ask students to notice which words are stressed in the past continuous.

Exercise ❺

- Tell students they will listen to the audio again. This time they will listen and repeat.
- 🎧 Play the audio, stopping or pausing after each sentence and asking students to repeat it chorally.
- Ask a few individual students to repeat. Check their pronunciation.

Speaking

This exercise provides an opportunity for students to practice the past continuous. It also prepares them for Exercise 7.

Exercise ❻

- Explain the task: Students will imagine that they are witnesses to a jewelry store robbery. They will look at the picture and try to remember what everyone was wearing and doing when the robbery took place.
- Set a time limit of 3 minutes for students to study the picture.

Exercise ❼

- **Pairs.** Have students turn to page 140.
- Explain the task: In pairs, they will try to answer the questions on this page. They cannot look back at the picture.

- Pair students and set a time limit of 8 minutes.
- Call on a few students to answer the questions.
- Have students look at the picture and check their answers.

EXTENSION

- Ask students how many questions they answered correctly. Ask: *Did anyone answer all of the questions correctly?*
- Ask those who were able to answer all the questions correctly what helped them to be good witnesses.
- Brainstorm ideas for improving memory in these situations. Write the ideas on the board.

TRB For additional interactive grammar practice, have students do the reproducible activity for this unit in the *Teacher's Resource Book.*

Writing

Exercise ❽

- Assign the writing task for class work or homework.
- Explain the task: Students will write a paragraph about an event that was important to them. They will use both simple past and past continuous.
- Brainstorm ideas about memorable events.
- **TRB** Optionally, give students a copy of the model (see the *Teacher's Resource Book,* Writing Models). Ask them to read the model and notice the vocabulary and grammar from the unit.
- If students don't have the model, write the following on the board:

   I was lying on my bed, reading my favorite book, All About Dogs. *Mom was preparing dinner in the kitchen. My little brother and sister were playing in their bedroom.*

- Have a student read the sentences aloud. Answer any questions students might have.
- Walk around to make sure everyone understands the task.

For suggestions on how to give feedback on writing, see page xiv of this *Teacher's Edition.*

CONVERSATION TO GO

At the end of class, call on two students to role-play the conversation.

HOMEWORK

- 📖 Assign *Workbook* page 72, Grammar Exercises 3 and 4, and page 73, Pronunciation Exercises 7 and 8.
- If students do not have the *WorldView Workbook,* assign listening homework from the Student CD. Write on the board:

   Track 39
   How did the people in the Prices' house first know there was a problem?

- 🎧 Tell students to listen to the audio and write the answer to the question. Have them bring their answer to the next class.

   (Answer: *They heard a loud noise/a sound.*)

Pronunciation

4 🎧 **Listen. Notice the weak pronunciation of *was* and *were*.**

We were playing video games.

Our housekeeper was working in the kitchen.

My parents were standing in the study.

A man was running away.

They were waiting for the police.

He was wearing sneakers.

5 🎧 **Listen again and repeat.**

Speaking

6 *BEFORE YOU SPEAK.* **Are you a good witness? Someone robbed a jewelry store. Look at the picture for a few minutes. Notice what everyone in the picture is doing and what each is wearing.**

7 *PAIRS.* **Turn to page 140. Try to answer the questions together. Don't look back at the picture! When you finish the questions, look at the picture again and check your answers.**

Writing

8 **Think of a memorable event in your life. Write a paragraph about the event, describing what you and others were doing at the time.**

CONVERSATION TO GO

A: What **were** the police **doing** at your house yesterday?
B: They **were asking** questions about a robbery.

Bargain hunters

Vocabulary Stores and purchases
Grammar *because, for,* and infinitives of purpose
Speaking Giving reasons

Lesson A

A __1__

B ___

C ___

Getting started

1 **Match the place names with the photos.**

1. a convenience store __C__   5. a restaurant ___

2. a newsstand ___   6. a hair salon ___

3. a drugstore ___   7. a clothing store ___

4. a coffee house ___

2 *PAIRS.* **Which of the places in Exercise 1 do you go to most often?**

A: *I go to a coffee house most often. I go there every day!*
B: *Not me. I go to a newsstand every day.*

3 **Where can you get these things? Write the place next to each item. (You can get some things at more than one place.)**

1. a cup of coffee *a convenience store*   6. sandwiches
2. a haircut   7. socks
3. a candy bar   8. a blouse
4. a bottle of aspirin   9. a magazine
5. perfume   10. a shampoo and blow-dry

4 *PAIRS.* **Compare your answers in Exercise 3.**

BARGAIN HUNTERS

Three shoppers . . . One shopping list
Who can find the best bargains?

A TV game show that COUNTS!

BARGAIN HUNTERS   Weekdays at 2:00 P.M.
on Channel 6

Bargain hunters

OBJECTIVES

Students will:

- activate vocabulary related to stores and purchases
- do listening, speaking, and writing tasks related to shopping and giving reasons
- focus on using *because, for,* and infinitives of purpose
- practice putting stress on one syllable in a compound word

WARM-UP: GAME SHOWS

Groups of 3. Students take turns telling each other about their favorite game show and why they like it.

- Tell students that this unit is about shopping. Explain that the title of the unit, "Bargain hunters," refers to shoppers who look for low prices. It is also the name of a game show about shopping.
- Have students think about different game shows on television. Tell them they will take turns telling their partners about their favorite game show and explaining why it's their favorite.
- Divide the class in groups of 3 and set a time limit of 3 minutes. While students are working, walk around the room, helping as needed.
- After 3 minutes, call on a few students to tell the class about their favorite game show.

Getting started

OPTION: VOCABULARY PREVIEW

Have students look at the place names in Exercise 1. Pair students. Have each pair name a favorite place for each and why it's their favorite. Give a personal example. (*My favorite convenience store is Sam's Store, the one across from my house. It's my favorite store because it has everything I need. My favorite newsstand is . . .*) Call on a few volunteers to share with the class their favorite places.

Exercise 1

- Tell students to look at the photos.
- Explain the task: Students will write the letter of the photo next to the correct place name. Go over the example.
- Have students work individually to complete the exercise. Set a time limit of 2 minutes.
- After 2 minutes, have students compare their answers with a partner's.
- Go over the answers with the class.

Answer key

1. C	2. A	3. F	4. D	5. B	6. E	7. G

EXTENSION

To reinforce the vocabulary, tell students you are going to call out a letter identifying a picture. Tell students to say the name of the place.

Exercise 2

- **Pairs.** Explain the task: Students will talk about which places in Exercise 1 they go to most often.
- Go over the example. Point out that *Not me* is a way to disagree, similar in content to saying *I don't.* Tell students that if they have the same experience as their partner, they can say *Me too.* Write these expressions on the board and encourage students to use them.
- Pair students and set a time limit of 2 minutes. Walk around the room, helping as needed.
- Call on a few students to tell the class about the places they go to most often.

Exercise 3

- Explain the task: Students will write next to each item the place or places where one can get that item.
- Point to the example. Ask: *Where can you get a cup of coffee?* (*a convenience store, a coffeehouse, a restaurant*) Encourage students to come up with as many answers as possible.
- Have students work individually to complete the exercise. Set a time limit of 5 minutes. Walk around the room, helping as needed.
- Tell students they will check their answers in the next exercise.

Exercise 4

- Pair students. Tell them to compare their answers in Exercise 3.
- Go over the answers with the class.

Answer key
Possible answers
a cup of coffee: a convenience store, a coffeehouse, a restaurant
sandwiches: a convenience store, a coffeehouse, a restaurant
a haircut: a hair salon
socks: a convenience store, a clothing store
a candy bar: a convenience store, a newsstand, a drugstore
a blouse: a clothing store
a bottle of aspirin: a drugstore, a newsstand, a convenience store
a magazine: a newsstand, a drugstore, a convenience store
perfume: a drugstore, a clothing store
a shampoo and blow-dry: a hair salon

Pronunciation

LANGUAGE NOTES

- In Exercises 5 to 8, students will practice stress in compound nouns. A compound noun is a combination of two words that functions as a single noun with its own meaning.
- A compound noun is pronounced as if it were a single word, with one main stress. The main stress is typically on the first word, or the stressed syllable of that word, if there is more than one syllable.

Exercise 5

- Tell students they are going to listen to compound nouns from Exercise 1. Explain what a compound noun is.
- Direct students' attention to the question about stress. Ask them to think about the answer as they listen.
- 🎧 Play the audio.

Exercise 6

- Tell students that they will listen to the audio again. This time, they will listen and repeat.
- 🎧 Play the audio. Ask students to repeat the words chorally. Then ask a few individual students to repeat the words. Check their pronunciation.

Exercise 7

- **Pairs.** Explain the task: Students will mark the stress in each compound noun by drawing a large circle over the stressed syllable.
- Model the activity by doing the first item with the class. Write *drugstore* on the board. Say the word, putting the stress on different syllables. Ask: *Which is the correct pronunciation?* (**drug**store) Have a volunteer go to the board to mark the stress on the word.
- Pair students and set a time limit of 2 minutes.

Exercise 8

- Tell students that they will listen to the audio again to check their answers.
- 🎧 Play the audio. Ask students to repeat the words, first chorally and then individually.
- Go over the answers with the class. Make sure students understand the rule about stress in compound nouns.
- Students may need help with the pronunciation of *convenience:* /kənvinyəns/. Note that in the compound *convenience store,* the main stress is on the second syllable of *convenience.*

Listening

Exercise 9

- **Groups of 3.** Tell students to look at the ad on page 86. Ask: *Where would you find this kind of advertisement?* (the TV guide section of newspapers and magazines)
- Explain the task: Students will discuss the questions.

- Clarify the task by giving a personal example for the second question. (For example, *I wouldn't like to be a contestant on this TV show because I get nervous in front of a lot of people.*)
- Divide students in groups of 3 and set a time limit of 5 minutes. Walk around the room, helping as needed.
- Call on a few students to report on their group's discussion.

Exercise 10

- Have students read the directions. Then ask a few questions to make sure students understand the situation. (For example, *Who is Courtney? What is she going to talk about?*) Elicit the meaning of the term *contestant.* (someone who competes in a contest or a game)
- Explain the task: Students will number the places in the photos in the order Courtney visited them.
- 🎧 Play the audio.
- Go over the answers with the class.

Answer key

1. newsstand (A); 2. drugstore (F); 3. hair salon (E); 4. coffeehouse (D); 5. clothing store (G); 6. convenience store (C); 7. restaurant (B)

Teaching Tip! Pronouncing numbers and prices

Some students may have difficulty distinguishing between numbers ending in *–teen* and numbers ending in *–ty.* Remind them that numbers 13 to 19 usually have a more strongly stressed second syllable, whereas the main stress on the multiples of 10 (30, 40, etc.) is on the first syllable. Review the way we say prices. Write several prices on the board and ask the class to read them aloud.

Exercise 11

- Tell students to look at Courtney's shopping list.
- Explain the task: Students will listen again and will write the amount of money Courtney spent next to each thing on the shopping list. Go over the example.
- 🎧 Play the audio.
- Go over the answers with the class.

Answer key

magazine: $3.95; aspirin: $4.99; haircut: $35.00; coffee: $2.50; blouse: $24.99; candy bar: 65¢; Chinese food: $7.50

ⓒ Please go to www.longman.com/worldview for additional in-class model conversation practice and supplementary reading practice.

HOMEWORK

- 📖 Assign *Workbook* page 74, Vocabulary Exercises 1 and 2, and page 76, Listening Exercises 5 and 6.

Pronunciation

5 🎧 **Listen. Notice the stress in these compound nouns. When two words come together to make a compound noun, which part has the main stress?**

newsstand   coffeehouse   hair salon

6 🎧 **Listen again and repeat.**

7 *PAIRS.* **Mark the main stress in these compound nouns.**

drugstore   clothing store   haircut

candy bar   convenience store

8 🎧 **Listen and check your answers. Then listen and repeat.**

Listening

9 *GROUPS OF 3.* **Look at the advertisement for the new TV game show *Bargain Hunters* on page 86. Discuss these questions. What is a bargain hunter? Would you like to be a contestant on this TV show? Why?**

10 🎧 **Courtney was a contestant on *Bargain Hunters*. Listen to Courtney describe her shopping trip. Number the places in the photos in Excercise 1 in the order she visited them.**

11 🎧 **Listen again. Look at Courtney's shopping list. Write the amount she spent next to each item.**

BARGAIN HUNTERS

SHOPPING LIST

Contestant: Courtney

magazine	$3.95
aspirin	_____
haircut	_____
coffee	_____
blouse	_____
candy bar	_____
Chinese food	_____

Grammar focus

1 **Study the examples. Notice the ways to express reasons.**

Action	Reason
I went to the coffeehouse	**because** I wanted a cup of coffee. **for** a cup of coffee. **to get** a cup of coffee. **to relax**.

2 **Look at the examples again. Complete the rules in the chart with *because*, *for*, or the infinitive of purpose (*to* + verb).**

Giving reasons: *because*, *for*, infinitives of purpose
_____ is always followed by a noun.
_____ is usually followed by a clause.
_____ is sometimes followed by a noun.

Grammar Reference page 147

3 **Use the information in parentheses to rewrite the sentences.**

1. She went on vacation because she wanted a rest. (for)
   She went on vacation for a rest.
2. He joined the club because he wanted to make new friends. (infinitive)
3. They bought some chicken because they wanted it for dinner. (for)
4. I stopped at the gas station to buy some gas. (because)
5. I bought some stamps to put in my stamp collection. (for)
6. She came into the living room to get a chair. (because)
7. They went to the gym because they wanted to play basketball. (infinitive)

4 **Complete the sentences with *to*, *for*, or *because*.**

1. She went to a restaurant ____to____ have lunch.
2. He bought his grandmother a gift _____ it was her birthday.
3. We are going to the park _____ a walk.
4. She went to the store _____ buy some milk.
5. I bought this dress _____ it was on sale.
6. We went to the post office _____ get some stamps.
7. She called the doctor's office _____ an appointment.

Grammar focus

LANGUAGE NOTES

- *Because, for*, and infinitives of purpose all answer the question "Why?" They tell us the reason for an action, but they are followed by different structures.
- *Because* is usually followed by a clause. For example, *I bought a new dress because I'm going to a party tonight.*
- *For* is followed by a noun. For example, *I bought a new dress for the party tonight.*
- Infinitives can be followed by a noun. For example, *I went to Macy's to buy a new dress for the party tonight.*
- Infinitives of intransitive verbs are used without a noun. For example, *I went to Macy's to shop.*

WARM-UP

Note: Skip this warm-up if you're doing this lesson (Lesson B) during the same class period as Lesson A.

- Books closed. Tell students they will listen again to Courtney from the Listening section.
- Write these questions on the board: *Why does Courtney go to the hair salon? Why does she go to the coffee shop? Why does Courtney go to a clothing store?* Ask students to write down the reasons Courtney gives for going to each place.
- 🎧 Play the audio from Lesson A, Listening, Exercise 10. (It models the grammar of the unit.)
- Call on a few students to answer the questions. (*Answers:* to get a shampoo, haircut, and blow-dry; for a cup of coffee; because a blouse was next on the list.)

Exercise ❶

- Tell students to look at the examples. Point out that there are patterns commonly used to express reasons, or to answer the question "Why?"
- Elicit or explain that the reasons in the examples all answer the question "Why did you go to the coffeehouse?"

Exercise ❷

- Tell students to look again at the examples and complete the rules, using *because, for*, or *infinitives of purpose*.
- Have students compare their answers with a partner's.
- Go over the answers with the class.
- Ask a few questions to elicit the key points about the grammar. For example, *Which of the ways to express reasons is followed by a clause?* (because) *Which is sometimes followed by a noun?* (infinitives of purpose) *Which is always followed by a noun?* (for)

Answer key

For
Because
An infinitive of purpose

Exercise ❸

- Before students begin Exercise 3, answer any questions they might have. You may also want to refer the class to the Grammar Reference for Unit 19 on page 147.
- Explain the task: Students will rewrite the sentences, using the information in parentheses.
- Go over the example. Point out that students may have to make changes to the rest of the sentence when substituting the new structure.
- Have students work individually to complete the exercise using their own paper. Set a time limit of 8 minutes. Walk around the room, helping as needed.
- Have students compare their answers with a partner's.
- Go over the answers with the class.

Answer key

1. She went on vacation for a rest.
2. He joined the club to make new friends.
3. They bought some chicken for dinner.
4. I stopped at the gas station because I wanted/needed (to buy) some gas.
5. I bought some stamps for my stamp collection.
6. She came into the living room because she wanted to get a chair.
7. They went to the gym to play basketball.

Exercise ❹

- Explain the task: Students will complete the sentences using *to, for*, or *because*. Point out to students that they are <u>not</u> going to write the complete infinitive of purpose; they will write in the blanks only the word *to*.
- Go over the example. Ask why *to* is the correct answer. (A main verb, *have*, follows.)
- Set a time limit of 3 minutes. Walk around the room helping as needed.
- Have students compare their answers with a partner's.
- Go over the answers with the class.

Answer key

1. to	3. for	5. because	7. for
2. because	4. to	6. to	

EXTENSION

- **Groups of 4.** Tell students that they will each write the beginning part of a sentence that ends with *to, for*, or *because* on a strip of paper. Write this example on the board: *I went to the post office to . . .*
- Elicit possible endings to the sentence: *mail a letter, buy some stamps.*
- Divide the class into groups of 4. Tell each group to write the beginnings of sentences. Make sure students provide the correct form.
- Have two groups exchange papers and complete each other's sentences.

T88

Speaking

Exercise ❺

This exercise provides practice with giving reasons using *because, for,* and infinitives of purpose. It also prepares students for Exercises 6 and 7.

- Explain the task: Students will write a list of five places. Next to each place, they will write three or four reasons why they go there. You may want to suggest that students use each of the different ways to express reasons (*for, because,* infinitives of purpose) at least once.
- Remind the students not to discuss or show their list to their classmates.
- Set a time limit of 5 minutes. Walk around the room, helping as needed.

Exercise ❻

- **Pairs.** Explain the task: Students will play a guessing game. Student A will begin by saying one reason to go to a certain place—without saying the name of the place. Student B will try to guess the place. Student A should keep a tally of Student B's guesses.
- Copy the scorecard on the board.
- Model the activity by going over the example with a student. You read A's lines in the example, and have the student read B's.
- Make a tally mark for each guess. Write 3 on the scorecard. Make sure students understand that the person with the lowest number of points wins.
- Pair students, and tell students to play the game. Set a time limit of 10 minutes. Walk around the room, helping as needed.

Exercise ❼

- Ask students to raise their hands when both partners finish guessing five places (or a total of ten places per pair).
- Ask who the winner in each pair is. Ask for the winning scores. Who had the lowest score of all?

TRB For additional interactive grammar practice, have students do the reproducible activity for this unit in the *Teacher's Resource Book.*

Writing

Exercise ❽

- Assign the writing task for class work or homework.
- Explain the task: Students will write an article about five of their favorite stores or eating places and give reasons why they go there.
- Brainstorm ideas about popular places and the reasons people go there.
- **TRB** Optionally, give students a copy of the model (see the *Teacher's Resource Book,* Writing Models). Ask them to read the model and notice the vocabulary and grammar from the unit.
- If students don't have the model, write the following on the board:

    My favorite place to shop for clothes and other household items is Brands, a big department store near my house. I usually go to Brands to shop for clothes because they have great sales!

    My favorite restaurant is Tacos, a Mexican restaurant downtown. I go to Tacos because I love spicy food, and the service there is great.

- Have a student read the sentences aloud. Answer any questions students might have.
- Walk around to make sure everyone understands the task.

For suggestions on how to give feedback on writing, see page xii of this *Teacher's Edition.*

CONVERSATION TO GO

At the end class, call on two students to role-play the conversation.

HOMEWORK

- 📖 Assign *Workbook* page 75, Grammar Exercises 3 and 4, and page 76, Pronunciation Exercises 7 and 8.
- 🎧 If students do not have the *WorldView Workbook,* assign listening homework from the Student CD. Write on the board:

    Track 43
    What was Courtney's most expensive stop? What was the least expensive?

- 🎧 Tell students to listen to the audio and write the answers to the questions. Have them bring their answers to the next class.

    (Answers: *Her most expensive stop was the hair salon. The least expensive was the convenience store.*)

Speaking

5 *BEFORE YOU SPEAK.* **Where do you go in a typical week? Write a list of five places. Write the reasons you go to each place.**

Place	Reasons to go there
1. convenience store	because I'm hungry; to get something sweet; for a newspaper
2.	
3.	
4.	
5.	

6 *PAIRS.* **You're going to play a guessing game. Take turns. Choose one place on your list. Say one reason you go there. Your partner will guess the place. If your partner doesn't guess correctly, give one more reason. Play three times. The person with the lowest total score wins.**
(one guess = one point)

A: *I go there because I'm hungry.*
B: *A restaurant?*
A: *No. I go there to get something sweet.*
B: *A bakery?*
A: *No. I go there for a newspaper.*
B: *A convenience store!*
A: *That's right! You have three points.*

7 **Who in the class has the lowest total score?**

Scorecard

YOU	YOUR PARTNER
1. ____	1. ____
2. ____	2. ____
3. ____	3. ____
TOTAL ____	TOTAL ____

Writing

8 **Write an article about five of your favorite stores or restaurants. Give reasons why you go there. Use *because*, *for*, and infinitives of purpose.**

CONVERSATION TO GO

A: Why did you go to the hair salon?
B: For a haircut—and to see the hairstylist!

A long run

Vocabulary Words related to the theater
Grammar *a/an, the*
Speaking Talking about the theater

Lesson A

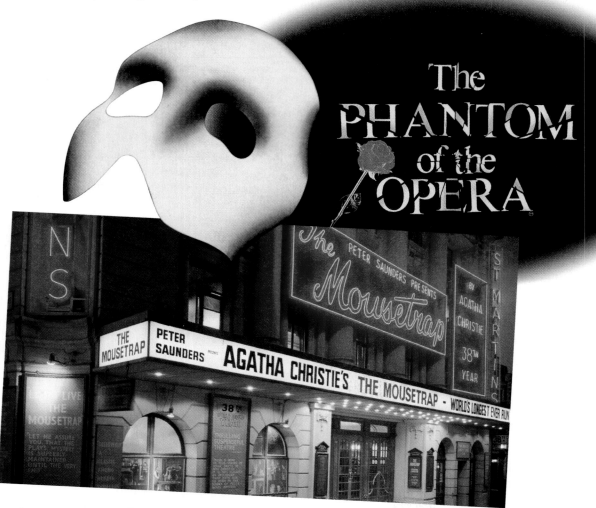

Getting started

1 **Underline the correct words to complete the sentences.**

1. The Globe is the name of a **theater** / **playwright** in London.
2. Actors perform in **plays** / **games**.
3. In **an opera** / **a musical**, the performers sing all the words.
4. The **spectators applaud** / **audience applauds** at the end of the play.
5. The **playwright** / **composer** writes the music.
6. The most expensive **seats** / **chairs** are at the front of the theater.

2 *PAIRS.* **Discuss the questions.**

Do you prefer seeing a play or a movie? Why?
Can you name any famous English-language musicals or plays?
Do you know any famous playwrights?

A long run

OBJECTIVES

Students will:

- activate vocabulary related to the theater
- do reading, speaking, and writing tasks related to talking about the theater
- focus on using the articles *a/an* and *the*
- practice different pronunciations of *a/an* and *the*

WARM-UP: AN IDEAL DATE

Groups of 3. Students share ideas about a perfect date.

- Tell students that this unit is about the theater. Explain that the title of the unit, "A long run," refers to a long period of time that a play, movie, or TV show is shown or performed regularly.
- Tell students to imagine that they are going out on an ideal date. Have them think about what they would like to do and why. Give a personal example. (For example, *I'd like to go out for a candle-lit dinner because it's romantic.*)
- Divide the class in groups of 3 and set a time limit of 3 minutes. Each student in the group must say what he or she would like to do on his or her ideal date and give a reason for his or her choice.
- Call on a few students to tell the class about one of their partner's ideas.

Getting started

BACKGROUND INFORMATION

The Phantom of the Opera was originally a novel written by Gaston Leroux in 1911. Andrew Lloyd Webber adapted the novel for the theater, and the musical premiered in 1986. Webber has written many other musicals including *Evita, Cats, Jesus Christ Superstar,* and *Joseph and the Amazing Technicolor Dreamcoat.*

Agatha Christie wrote 66 mystery novels. Her first book was published in 1920. More than 30 of her mysteries featured Hercule Poirot. Several of her novels were made into movies including *Murder on the Orient Express.* Christie was made a Dame of the British Empire in 1971.

OPTION: VOCABULARY PREVIEW

Write the bold-faced words in Exercise 1 in one column on the board. Skip number 4. For each word, ask the students to give one example. For example, for *theater,* give the name of a local playhouse; for *playwright,* mention Shakespeare. You might need to give some clues to help students with some of the words.

LANGUAGE NOTES

Some of the pairs of words in Exercise 1 are very similar in meaning but differ in the context in which they are used.

- *Seats* and *chairs* are similar, but we use *seats* to refer to where people sit in a restaurant, play, or movie. *Seats* can refer to chairs or benches and are sometimes connected in rows. *Chairs* usually have four legs and a back.
- *Spectators* watch an event or a game; an *audience* watches or listens to a play, movie, or concert.
- *An opera* is a play in which all the words are sung. A *musical* is a play or movie in which the story may be told through music or song, but some of the words are usually spoken.

Exercise ❶

- Explain the task: Students will underline the correct words to complete the sentences. Go over the example.
- Set a time limit of 2 minutes. While students are working, walk around the room, helping as needed.
- Have students compare their answers with a partner's.
- Go over the answers with the class.

Answer key

1. theater	4. audience applauds
2. plays	5. composer
3. an opera	6. seats

EXTENSION

- Reinforce the new vocabulary. Pair students.
- Tell each pair to create sentences using the words that were not chosen as the answers in Exercise 1.
- Call on volunteers to read their sentences aloud.

Exercise ❷

- **Pairs.** Have students read the questions.
- Explain the task: Students will discuss the questions with a partner.
- Pair students and set a time limit of 3 minutes. Walk around the room, helping as needed.
- Call on a few students to share their ideas. (Examples of English-language musicals: *My Fair Lady, Miss Saigon* Plays: *Hamlet, Death of a Salesman* Playwrights: Shakespeare, George Bernard Shaw.)

Reading

Teaching Tip! **Using visuals to predict content**

Exercise 3 focuses on the important skill of using visuals to predict the content of a text. Tell students not to look at the body of the articles at all while they discuss the pictures. Encourage them to use the photos and the headings to gather information. For example, the picture for *The Phantom of the Opera* provides a number of clues on the content. Ask students what they see in the picture. (*a rose and a mask*) The photo of *The Mousetrap* marquee also provides a lot of information: length of run (*38 years*), producer (*Peter Saunders*), playwright (*Agatha Christie*).

Exercise ❸

- Tell students to look at the photos and read the directions.
- **Pairs.** Explain the task: In pairs, students will discuss what they know about the plays. They will tell or guess which of the two is a musical; which one is a mystery.
- Pair students and set a time limit of 2 minutes.
- Call on a few students to share what they know about the two plays.

Exercise ❹

- Explain the task: Students will read the articles and complete the chart.
- Have students look at the chart. Elicit the type of information they need to gather about each show.
- Remind students that they can underline or highlight information as they read.
- Set a time limit of 10 minutes. Walk around the room, helping as needed.
- Have students compare their answers with a partner's.
- Go over the answers with the class.

Answer key

The Phantom of the Opera	The Mousetrap
1986	1952
A musical	A play
The Phantom helps Christine and Raoul to be together.	The murderer asks the audience not to reveal the secret.
Audiences love the costumes, the scenery, the story, and the music.	It has a surprise ending.

⊚ Please go to www.longman.com/worldview for additional in-class model conversation practice and supplementary reading practice.

HOMEWORK

- 📖 Assign *Workbook* page 77, Vocabulary Exercises 1 and 2, and page 79, Listening Exercises 5 and 6.

Reading

3 *PAIRS.* **Look at the pictures on page 90. Which do you think is a musical? Which do you think is a mystery?**

4 **Read the web article "Long Theater Runs" and complete the chart.**

	The Phantom of the Opera	*The Mousetrap*
date of first performance	1986	1952
type of show		
how it ends		
reasons for popularity		

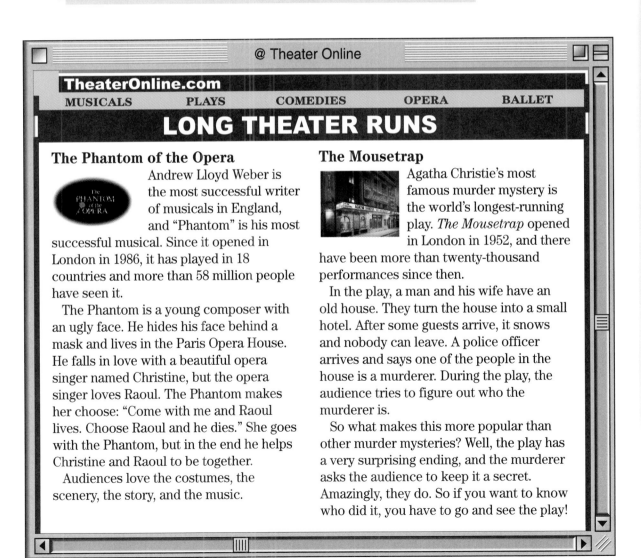

@ Theater Online

TheaterOnline.com

MUSICALS   PLAYS   COMEDIES   OPERA   BALLET

LONG THEATER RUNS

The Phantom of the Opera

Andrew Lloyd Weber is the most successful writer of musicals in England, and "Phantom" is his most successful musical. Since it opened in London in 1986, it has played in 18 countries and more than 58 million people have seen it.

The Phantom is a young composer with an ugly face. He hides his face behind a mask and lives in the Paris Opera House. He falls in love with a beautiful opera singer named Christine, but the opera singer loves Raoul. The Phantom makes her choose: "Come with me and Raoul lives. Choose Raoul and he dies." She goes with the Phantom, but in the end he helps Christine and Raoul to be together.

Audiences love the costumes, the scenery, the story, and the music.

The Mousetrap

Agatha Christie's most famous murder mystery is the world's longest-running play. *The Mousetrap* opened in London in 1952, and there have been more than twenty-thousand performances since then.

In the play, a man and his wife have an old house. They turn the house into a small hotel. After some guests arrive, it snows and nobody can leave. A police officer arrives and says one of the people in the house is a murderer. During the play, the audience tries to figure out who the murderer is.

So what makes this more popular than other murder mysteries? Well, the play has a very surprising ending, and the murderer asks the audience to keep it a secret. Amazingly, they do. So if you want to know who did it, you have to go and see the play!

Grammar focus

1 **Study the examples with *a*, *an*, and *the*.**

> *The Mousetrap* is **the** longest-running play.
> **A** couple has **an** old house.
> They turn **the** house into **a** hotel.
> You have to see **the** play.
> **The** ending is very surprising.

2 **Look at the examples again. Complete the rules in the chart with *a*, *an*, or *the*.**

a/an, the
Use _____ the first time you talk about something.
Use _____ to talk about the same thing again.
Use _____ when there is only one.
Use _____ with superlative adjectives.

3 **Complete the article with *a*, *an*, or *the*.**

Romeo and Juliet
(A Summary)

Romeo and Juliet is **(1)** __the__ most popular of Shakespeare's plays. **(2)** _____ story is about **(3)** _____ young woman and **(4)** _____ young man who fall in love. **(5)** _____ young man is named Romeo, and **(6)** _____ young woman is named Juliet.

Their families are enemies, so they get married in secret. Romeo gets into **(7)** _____ fight and kills **(8)** _____ young man. **(9)** _____ young man is Juliet's cousin. Romeo has to leave **(10)** _____ city. Juliet sends him **(11)** _____ message. **(12)** _____ message is very important because it explains how they can stay together. But Romeo never gets **(13)** _____ message. Because of this, Romeo and Juliet both kill themselves at **(14)** _____ end of **(15)** _____ play.

Grammar focus

LANGUAGE NOTES

- *A* and *an* are indefinite articles. They are used to talk about singular count nouns. *A* is used before a consonant sound and *an* before a vowel sound.
- Use the definite article *the* before singular count nouns, plural count nouns, and non-count nouns.
- Use *a/an* when something is mentioned for the first time; afterward, use *the*. *The* is also used when something is unique, that is, it's the only one. For example, *A new play opened last night. The star of the play is a famous movie star.*
- Use *the* with superlatives. For example, *She is the most famous Broadway star.*

WARM-UP

Note: Skip this warm-up if you're doing this lesson (Lesson B) during the same class period as Lesson A.

- Books closed. Tell students they will listen to the articles from the Reading section.
- Write these sentences on the board and have students copy them:
  _____ *Phantom is* _____ *young composer with* _____ *ugly face.*
  Agatha Christie's most famous murder mystery is _____ *world's longest-running play. In* _____ *play,* _____ *man and his wife have* _____ *old house.*
- Tell students to write in the missing articles as they listen.
- 🎧 Play the audio from Lesson A, Reading, Exercise 4. (It models the grammar of the unit.)
- Call on students to come to the board to fill in the missing articles. (*the, a, an*; *the, the, a, an*)

Exercise ❶

- Have students read the five examples and study the bold-faced words. Point out or elicit that the word *longest* in the first sentence is a superlative form.
- Tell students to think about the different uses of *a, an,* and *the.*

Exercise ❷

- Have students look at the examples again. Tell them to complete the rules in the chart with *a/an* or *the*.
- Have students compare their answers with a partner's.
- Go over the answers with the class.

- Ask a few questions to elicit the key points about the grammar. For example, *Which article do we use to talk about something for the first time and when the word following the article starts with a vowel sound?* (*an*) *Which article is called the definite article?* (*the*) *Why do you think it is called such?* (Because it refers to specific things that both the speaker and the listener know about.)

Answer key

a/an	the	the	the

Exercise ❸

- Before students begin Exercise 3, answer any questions they might have. You may also want to refer the class to the Grammar Reference for Unit 20 on page 148.
- Explain the task: Students will complete the article by writing *a, an,* or *the* in the blanks. Go over the example.
- Have students complete the exercise individually. Set a time limit of 5 minutes. Walk around the room, helping as needed.
- Have students compare their answers with a partner's.
- Go over the answers with the class.

Answer key

1. the	5. The	9. The	13. the
2. The	6. the	10. the	14. the
3. a	7. a	11. a	15. the
4. a	8. a	12. The	

EXTENSION

- Ask students to classify the nine noun phrases beginning with *the* in the paragraph into three groups: (1) talk about the same thing again (for example, <u>The young man</u> is named Romeo.), (2) there is only one (for example, *The story*), and (3) with superlatives (for example, *the most popular*).
- Have them check their answers with a partner. *Answers:* Talk about the same thing (5 *the young man,* 6 *the young woman,* 9 *The young man,* 12 *The message,* 15 *the play*); There is only one (2 *The story,* 10 *the city,* 13 *the end, the play*); With superlatives (1 *the most*).

Pronunciation

> **LANGUAGE NOTES**
> - The words *a, an,* and *the* normally have weak pronunciations in connected speech.
> - The word *the* has two different weak pronunciations. The pronunciation /ðə/ is used before a consonant sound: *You have to see the* /ðə/ *play*. The pronunciation /ði/ is used before a vowel sound: *The* /ði/ *ending is very surprising*.

Exercise 4

- Tell students to look at the examples in Lesson B, Grammar focus, Exercise 1. Tell them they are going to listen to these examples. Ask them to notice the short, weak pronunciation of the words *a, an,* and *the*.
- 🎧 Play the audio.

Exercise 5

- Tell students that they will listen to the audio again. This time, they will listen and repeat.
- 🎧 Play the audio, stopping after each sentence to allow students to repeat chorally.
- Encourage students to link the words smoothly in *an old house*.
- Encourage students to add a short /y/ sound to link the vowel sounds in the phrase *the ending*.

Speaking

Exercise 6

This exercise provides practice with the unit grammar and vocabulary. It also prepares students for Exercise 7.

- Explain the task: Students will make notes to answer questions about a play or a movie that they saw.
- Tell students to work individually to write notes for each of the questions. Point out that they will use their notes later when they share the information with classmates.
- Set a time limit of 5 minutes. Walk around the room, helping as needed.

Exercise 7

- **Groups of 3.** Explain the task: Students will take turns describing their play or movie and having their group members guess what it is. Remind them not to mention the title in their descriptions.
- Model the activity by telling the class about a play or movie you liked. Ask students to guess the name of the play or movie.
- Divide the class in groups of 3 and set a time limit of 15 minutes. Walk around the room, helping as needed.
- Call on a few students to describe a play or movie they have seen and have the class guess the title.

TRB For additional interactive grammar practice, have students do the reproducible activity for this unit in the *Teacher's Resource Book.*

Writing

Exercise 8

- Assign the writing task for class work or homework.
- Explain the task: Students will use the cues to write the story of the musical *West Side Story*.
- **TRB** Optionally, give students a copy of the model (see the *Teacher's Resource Book,* Writing Models). Ask them to read the model and notice the vocabulary and grammar from the unit.
- If students don't have the model, write the following on the board:

    West Side Story *is a modern-day* Romeo and Juliet *set in New York. The story is about a young man . . .*

For suggestions on how to give feedback on writing, see page xiv of this *Teacher's Edition.*

CONVERSATION TO GO

At the end of class, call on two students to role-play the conversation.

HOMEWORK

- 📖 Assign *Workbook* page 78, Grammar Exercises 3 and 4, and page 79, Pronunciation Exercises 7 and 8.
- Assign *Workbook* Self-Quiz 5.
- 💿 If students do not have the *WorldView Workbook,* assign listening homework from the Student CD. Write on the board:

    Track 44
    Which of these details go with which play? Write *M* for *The Mousetrap* and *P* for *The Phantom of the Opera.*

    1. a singer *P*   4. the police *M*
    2. a theater *P*   5. bad weather *M*
    3. a hotel *M*   6. a mask *P*

- 🎧 Tell students to listen to the audio and write the answers to the exercise. Have them bring their answers to the next class.

FOR NEXT CLASS

- Tell students that the next class will be a review class covering Units 17–20.
- Have students review the material in the units to prepare for the activities in Review 5.
- **TRB** Make copies of Quiz 5 in the *Teacher's Resource Book.*

Unit no.	Review Grammar	Listen to Student CD	Study Grammar Reference
17	Verbs for likes/dislikes + noun/verb + *-ing*	Track 37	Page 147
18	Simple past and past continuous	Track 39	Page 147
19	*Because, for,* and infinitives	Track 43	Page 147
20	*A/an, the*	Track 47	Page 148

Pronunciation

4 🎧 **Listen to the examples in Exercise 1. Notice the pronunciations of** *a*, *an*, **and** *the*.

5 🎧 **Listen again and repeat.**

Speaking

6 *BEFORE YOU SPEAK.* **Think of an interesting play or movie that you have seen. Think about the answers to these questions.**

Was it a play or a movie?
Who were the actors in it?
What was it about?
Why did you like it?

7 *GROUPS OF 3.* **Take turns. Describe the play or movie to your group, but don't say its name. Your partners will try to guess the name.**

A: *It's about a teenage Indian girl.*

B: *Monsoon Wedding!*

A: *No. She meets a young British woman. The woman plays . . . .*

Writing

8 **Write the story of the musical *West Side Story*. Use the cues.**

- modern-day *Romeo and Juliet*, set in New York
- young man (Tony) / fall in love / young woman (Maria)
- Tony / in a street gang (the Jets)
- Maria's brother / in another street gang (the Sharks)
- Jets / Sharks / enemies
- Jets / Sharks / fight
- a Jet / kill / Maria's brother
- then a Shark / kill / Tony

CONVERSATION TO GO

A: I saw a play last night.
B: How was it?
A: The story was interesting, but the acting was awful.

Unit 17 A nice place to work

1 🎧 Listen to the model conversation and look at the job ads.

2 *PAIRS.* Look at the job advertisements. Decide on a job to talk about.

3 *PAIRS.* Role-play a job interview. Student A, you're the job applicant. Student B, you're the interviewer. Student A, explain what you had to do in your last job. Student B, explain what Student A has to do in this job.

4 Switch roles and choose another job from the ads. Do another role-play.

CAREERS

Building Manager
• supervise ten employees
• order repairs
• meet with new tenants

Bookstore Salesperson
• wait on customers
• put books on the shelves
• work weekends

Chef
• create new menus
• cook food
• supervise wait staff

Teacher
• teach English to children ages 6-12
• have a college degree
• start work at 7:00 A.M.

Designer
• design clothing for women
• travel to fashion shows
• have experience in the fashion industry

Computer Technician
• go to clients' offices
• install computer systems
• fix broken computers

Unit 18 Hollywood mystery

5 🎧 Listen to the model conversation.

6 *GROUPS OF 4.* Students A and B, you are police officers trying to solve a robbery. You have five minutes to prepare to talk to the suspects. Make a list of questions to ask the suspects about what they were doing on the night of the robbery.

Students C and D, you are suspects in the robbery. You say that you were together when it happened, so you can show that you are innocent. You have five minutes to prepare for the police officers' questions. Decide exactly what you were doing on the night of the robbery.

7 Student A, interview Student C. Student B, interview Student D. Conduct the interviews on opposite sides of the room so the suspects can't hear each other's answers! Students A and B, take notes.

8 Compare interviews. Students A and B, talk about your notes. Do you believe Students C and D were together during the robbery? Students C and D, talk about the police officers' questions. Did you give the same answers?

📼 You may wish to use the video for Units 17–20 at this point.
For video activity worksheets, go to www.longman.com/worldview.

Unit 17: A nice place to work

OBJECTIVES

- Review the material presented in Unit 17
- Grammar practice: verbs for likes/dislikes + noun/verb + -ing

WARM-UP

Books closed. Ask students to think of some questions that an interviewer might ask a job applicant.

Exercise ❶

- Tell students they will listen to a conversation between an interviewer and a job applicant. Tell them to listen for the information the interviewer asked the job applicant. (*He/She wanted to know about the applicant's job experience.*)
- 🎧 Play the audio as students look at the ads.

Exercise ❷

- **Pairs.** Tell students to look at the job ads.
- Pair students. Have them choose which job they will talk about in Exercise 3.

Exercise ❸

- Explain the task: Students will role-play an interview for one of the jobs in the ads.
- Assign roles A and B to the pairs.
- 🎧 If needed, play the audio for Exercise 1 again.
- Set a time limit of 5 minutes for the role-play.
- Remind students that it is important that employees like their jobs. Tell them to ask and tell each other their likes and dislikes in a job.

Exercise ❹

- Have partners switch roles and choose another job to talk about.
- Set a time limit of 5 minutes for the role-play.

WRAP-UP

Invite students to say why they would hire their partner. Encourage them to report particularly good answers that their partners gave.

Unit 18: Hollywood mystery

OBJECTIVES

- Review the material presented in Unit 18
- Grammar practice: simple past and past continuous

WARM-UP

- Explain the term *alibi*. (An *alibi* is proof that a person was not where a crime happened and is therefore not guilty of the crime.)
- Ask students to think of some good alibis.

Exercise ❺

- Tell students they are going to listen to a conversation. Tell them to listen to the alibis given. (*I was at the video store with my friend. We were looking for a movie to watch.*)
- 🎧 Play the audio.

Exercise ❻

- Divide the class into groups of four. Assign roles A, B, C, and D to the members of each group.
- Explain the task: Students A and B are police officers trying to find out who committed a robbery. They have five minutes to plan the questions they will ask suspects. Students C and D are suspects in the robbery. They have five minutes to discuss the details of their alibi.
- Set a time limit of 5 minutes.

Exercise ❼

- Tell Students A and C in each group to pair up and move to one side of the room. Have Students B and D in each group to pair up and move to the other side of the room.
- Explain the task: Students A and B will ask Students C and D what they did on the night of the robbery. A and B will take notes about C and D's answers. Students C and D will try to remember all the details they discussed. If Student A or B asks a question that they don't know the answer to, Students C and D should make up an answer.
- 🎧 If needed, play the audio for Exercise 5 again to model the interview.

Exercise ❽

- Have students A and B pair up again. Tell them to compare their notes and decide whether or not they believe C and D's alibi.
- Have students C and D pair up again. Tell them to compare their interviews.
- Tell each group to briefly talk about the interviews. Ask: *Which questions did Students C and D answer the same way? Which did they answer differently?*

Unit 19: Bargain hunters

OBJECTIVES

- Review the material presented in Unit 19
- Grammar practice: *because, for,* and infinitives of purpose

WARM-UP

Books closed. Have students brainstorm reasons for going to each of the following places: a newsstand, a convenience store, a drugstore, a coffeehouse, a restaurant, a hair salon, a clothing store, and a department store.

Exercise 9

- Tell students they will listen to a conversation that models the game in Exercise 10. Have them listen to get the answers to the following questions: *Who is going to . . .*

    —*the newsstand?* (Ari) *What is he going to do there?* (buy a magazine)

    —*the convenience store?* (Jenny) *What is she going to buy there?* (some gum)

    —*the drugstore?* (Roberto) *Why is he going there?* (because he needs aspirin)

    —*the hair salon?* (I) *Why are you going there?* (to get a haircut)

- 🎧 Play the audio.
- Have students answer the questions.

Exercise 10

- Divide students into groups of 4. Assign roles A, B, C, and D to the members of each group.
- Explain the task: Each group will play a memory game.
- 🎧 If needed, play the audio for Exercise 9 again.
- Choose one person in each group to begin the game.
- Explain that when a player makes a mistake, he or she has to start again at the beginning of the list.

WRAP-UP

Ask which groups were able to remember all the people, the places, and the reasons perfectly.

Unit 20: A long run

OBJECTIVES

- Review the material presented in Unit 20
- Grammar practice: *a, an, the*

WARM-UP

Have students look at the pictures in Exercise 11. Ask them what they think might be happening in each one.

Exercise 11

- Tell students they will listen to a conversation that models Exercise 12. Tell students to listen and find out which picture the speakers talked about. (*picture 5*)
- 🎧 Play the audio.

Exercise 12

- Divide the class into groups of 3. Explain the task: Students will work with their groups to make up stories about the pictures. Remind them to use the vocabulary from Unit 20 in their story. They can use the pictures in any order. Encourage them to be creative in their stories!
- Set a time limit of 7 minutes. Walk around the room, helping as needed.

WRAP-UP

Have each group retell their stories to the entire class. Ask the class to vote on the most original story and the one they liked best.

Unit 19 Bargain hunters

9 🎧 Listen to the model conversation and look at the picture.

10 *GROUPS OF 4.* Student A, say one place in the picture. Give a reason for going there. Student B, repeat Student A's information. Then say a new place and give a new reason. Students C and D continue. Go around the group two times. You can't repeat a place.

Unit 20 A long run

11 🎧 Listen to the model conversation and look at the pictures.

12 *GROUPS OF 3.* Make up a group story about the pictures. Take turns adding two sentences to the story. Give names to the characters and describe what is happening in the pictures. You can talk about the pictures in any order.

World of Music 3

Matter of Time
Los Lobos

Vocabulary

1 Complete the sentences with the words in the box.

be	believe	feel like
make	~~send~~	worry

1. I'm not going to take you with me now. I'll
   ___send___ for you when I get there.

2. You don't need anyone's help. _____ in
   yourself.

3. Don't _____ about me. I'll be fine.

4. This is a great party. I don't _____ going
   home.

5. I wish you could come with me, but we'll
   _____ together soon.

6. Be quiet. Don't _____ a sound.

Listening

2 🎧 **Listen to the song. Circle *a* or *b* to complete
the sentences.**

1. The song is a conversation between ___.
   a. two friends
   b. a husband and wife

2. The singer is going to ___ home soon.
   a. leave
   b. come

3. He thinks the future will be ___ than the present.
   a. better
   b. worse

The 80s

*Many American musicians began exploring
music of other cultures in the 80s, and some
celebrated their own roots.* **Los Lobos** *(Spanish
for The Wolves) are a Los Angeles-born group
with their own distinct Tex-Mex style.*

World of Music 3

- Introduce the song "Matter of Time" by Los Lobos
- Vocabulary practice: verbs
- Express opinions

BACKGROUND INFORMATION

Los Lobos was formed in the 1970s by four friends who grew up in the Mexican-American neighborhoods of East Los Angeles. Their music is influenced by rock and roll, blues, and traditional Mexican music. In 1984, Los Lobos won a Grammy award for Best Mexican-American Performance. In the fall of 2003, they appeared in Martin Scorsese's film *From Mali to Mississippi,* a movie about the multicultural influences on blues music.

WARM-UP

- Books closed. Tell students to look at the picture. Ask: *What do you think is the man's nationality?* (He's Hispanic./He's Mexican.) *What do you think is he a member of?* (a member of a Mexican band)
- Have students look at the name of the band that plays the song "Matter of Time." Ask: *What does "Los Lobos" mean?* (It means "the wolves.") Tell the class that the band's full name is Los Lobos del Este de Los Angeles. The group is from East Los Angeles, thus the name.
- Ask students if they know of any Los Lobos songs. Have them mention a few. ("Come on Let's Go," "Don't Worry Baby," "A Matter of Time," "Will the Wolf Survive")
- Tell students they are going to listen to a Los Lobos song, "A Matter of Time."

The 80s

- Tell students to read the information about the 80s on page 96 in the *Student Book*. Ask: *Why were the 80s an important period for Latin musicians and other foreign musicians who were living in the United States at the time?* (Because the music industry in the United States started to recognize and appreciate music and musicians from other cultures, making it possible for artists such as Los Lobos to make it in a tough market, the U.S. market.)
- Ask students to give other examples of foreign musicians who have made it big in the United States.

- Explain that the members of Los Lobos were born in Los Angeles, California, but their parents are of Mexican origin. They grew up in a Hispanic neighborhood in Los Angeles.

Vocabulary

Exercise ❶

- Have students look at Exercise 1. Answer any questions students might have about vocabulary.
- Tell them to complete the sentences with the words in the box.
- Have students correct their answers as a class.

Answer key	
1. send	4. feel like
2. Believe	5. be
3. worry	6. make

Listening

Exercise ❷

- Explain the task: Students will listen to the song "Matter of Time" by Los Lobos and will circle the letter of the correct answer.
- Have students read and answer the exercise.
- 🎧 Play the audio.
- Have students check their answers as a class.
- You may want to replay the song, pausing to point out lyrics that answer each question.

Answer key		
1. b	2. a	3. a

Exercise ❸

- Explain the task: Students will listen to the song again while they read the lyrics. They will circle the correct words that complete the lyrics.
- Have students read through the lyrics once. Explain the meanings of any unfamiliar vocabulary.
- 🎧 Play the song as students complete the exercise. Walk around the room, helping as needed.

Exercise ❹

- Pair students.
- Have the pairs compare their answers.

> **Answer key**
>
> Don't, have to, there's, will be, I'll send
> know, have to, there's, Will
> I hope, There's
> Don't, you're doing, can't, We'll be, we'll be
> we'll
> We'll

Speaking

OPTION

🎧 Play the song again and have students sing along.

Exercise ❺

- Divide the class into groups of 3. Have them discuss the questions.
- Encourage them to imagine the situation in the song. Have them describe the picture they imagine.
- Call on volunteers to answer the questions.
- Ask: *Do you like the song? What did you like about the song? What didn't you like about it?* Encourage students to give their opinions.

> **Answer key**
>
> *Possible answers*
> 1. The man has to leave his family to find work. The song doesn't mention a specific place, but he's going to a place where he thinks he can find work.
> 2. The song is hopeful. The man tells his wife there is a better world out there and they will all be together "in a matter of time."
> 3. a. We have to be patient and wait for a while.

3   **Listen again. Circle the correct words or phrases to complete the song.**

Matter of Time

Speak softly.
(**I won't** / **Don't**) wake the baby.
Come and hold me once more,
Before I (**have to** / **can**) leave.
Hear (**there isn't** / **there's**) a lot of
work out there.
Everything (**is** / **will be**) fine.
And (**I sent** / **I'll send**) for you, baby.
Just a matter of time.

Our life,
The only thing we (**know** / **knew**).
Come and tell me once more,
Before you (**need to** / **have to**) go.
But (**there's** / **there'll be**) a better
world out there,
Though it don't feel right.
(**Will** / **Does**) it feel like our home?
Just a matter of time.
And (**I'm hoping** / **I hope**) this song
we sing's,
Not another empty dream.
(**There was** / **There's**) a time for you
and me,
In a place living happily.

[repeat]

Walk quietly.
(**I didn't** / **Don't**) make a sound.
Believe in what (**you've done** /
you're doing),
I know we (**won't** / **can't**) be wrong.
Don't worry about a thing,
(**We'll be** / **We're**) all right.
And (**we're** / **we'll be**) there with you,
Just a matter of time.

And (**we'll** / **we can**) all be together,
Just a matter of time.
Matter of time
Matter of time

(**We can** / **We'll**) be together,
In a matter of time.
You and me,
In a matter of time.
Feel like a home,
Matter of time.

4 *PAIRS.* **Compare your answers in Exercise 3.**

Speaking

5 *GROUPS OF 3.* **Discuss the questions.**

1. Why do you think the man has to leave? Where is he going?
2. What is the feeling of the song: sad, happy, hopeful, angry? Explain.
3. What does the expression "just a matter of time" mean in the song?

   a. We have to be patient and wait for a while.
   b. We don't have to wait because things will happen quickly.

Long life

Vocabulary **Time expressions**
Grammar **Present perfect: *how long/for/since***
Speaking **Talking about how long you have done something**

Getting started

1 *PAIRS.* **Look at the photos in the article. How old are the women in the pictures? Guess.**

2 **Match the expressions on the left with the similar expressions on the right.**

1. over ten years ___*e*___   a. two days ago

2. the day before yesterday _____   b. two months

3. ages _____   c. December 31

4. a couple of months _____   d. 12:00 P.M.

5. noon _____   e. more than ten years

6. New Year's Eve _____   f. a long time

Pronunciation

3 🎧 **Listen. Notice the pronunciation of the voiceless *th* sound /θ/ in the words in the first row and the voiced *th* sound /ð/ in the words in the second row.**

thirty-first   three   month

there   more than   the day

4 🎧 **Listen again and repeat.**

5 🎧 **Listen to the question and answers. Then listen and repeat.**

When did you start work there? { In 2002.
When I was twenty-three.
The beginning of the month.
More than three months ago.
On Thursday, the 30th.

OBJECTIVES

Students will:

- activate vocabulary related to time expressions
- do reading, speaking, and writing tasks related to talking about how long people have done something
- focus on using the present perfect and expressions with *how long/for/since*
- practice voiceless and voiced pronunciations of *th*

WARM-UP: HOW LONG?

Students will guess how long you have done a number of activities.

- Tell students that this unit is about time. Explain that the title of the unit, "Long life," refers to people who live for a long time and who remain active during their old age.
- Think of how long you have done some activities: For example, been a teacher, lived in your house, studied a language. Choose activities that vary in range of time such as twenty years, two months, a week. Write the activities and the periods of time on the board.
- Have students guess which activity goes with each period of time.

Getting started

Exercise ❶

- Have students look at the photos and discuss the question.
- Pair students and set a time limit of 1 minute.
- Call on a student to answer the question.

OPTION: VOCABULARY PREVIEW

Have students look closely at each of the time phrases in Exercise 2 and think of another way of expressing the same concept. Ask a few questions to get them started. For example, *What time is "noon"?* (12:00 P.M.) *What does a* couple *of mean?* (two) Alternatively, have students work in pairs to help each other complete the exercise.

Exercise ❷

- Have students take a quick look at the expressions and ask what the expressions have in common. (They all relate to time.)
- Explain the task: Students will match the expressions on the left with their synonyms on the right. Go over the example.
- Set a time limit of 2 minutes.
- Have students compare their answers with a partner's.
- Go over the answers with the class.

Answer key

1. e	2. a	3. f	4. b	5. d	6. c

Pronunciation

LANGUAGE NOTE

To make the voiced and voiceless sounds of *th*, place the tongue between the upper and lower teeth. The tip of the tongue very lightly touches the upper teeth. In the voiced *th*, the vocal cords vibrate; while in the voiceless *th*, the vocal cords do not vibrate.

Exercise ❸

- Tell students that they will listen to the voiced and voiceless sounds of *th*. Tell them to notice the pronunciation of the words with *th*.
- 🎧 Play the audio. Model the pronunciation of the sounds /θ/ and /ð/. Demonstrate the position of the tongue: the tip lightly touches the top teeth.
- Point out the difference between the voiceless sound /θ/, used in the words in the first row, and the voiced sound /ð/, used in the words in the second row. Demonstrate the difference between voiced and voiceless sounds by asking students to place a thumb and index finger on either side of the throat. Model the /s/ sound then the /z/ sound and have students repeat these after you. Ask students which sound makes their throat vibrate. Repeat the procedure with the /θ/ and /ð/ sounds.

Exercise ❹

- Tell students they will listen to the audio again. This time, they will listen and repeat.
- 🎧 Play the audio. Have students repeat the words chorally as well as individually.
- Point out the difference in the position of the tongue. To say /ð/ or /z/, the tongue needs to come forward a little, until it is between the upper and lower front teeth, lightly touching the upper teeth.
- If students substitute a /t/ or /d/ sound for /θ/, demonstrate the way the sound /θ/ or /ð/ can be prolonged—/θθθ/, /ððð/, while /t/ or /d/ cannot. Also point out the difference in the position of the tongue. To say /θ/ or /ð/, the tongue needs to come forward a little and touch the upper teeth very lightly—enough to let the air continue to flow out.

Exercise ❺

- Tells students that they will listen to a question and the various ways to answer the question.
- 🎧 Play the audio. Tell students to listen carefully.
- 🎧 Play the audio again and ask students to repeat chorally as well as individually.

Reading

Exercise 6

- Have students read the list of jobs and predict which woman has or had which job. Ask: *Who do you think is a singer? A model? A tennis player?*
- Tell students to read the article and match the names with the jobs.
- Set a time limit of 5 minutes.
- Have students compare their answers with a partner's.
- Go over the answers with the class.

Answer key

Dodo Cheney: tennis player
Carmen Dell'Orefice: model
Omara Portuondo: singer

Exercise 7

- Explain the task: Students will reread the article and complete the sentences with the correct information about the three women.
- Have students read the sentences so they know what information to look for.
- Remind students to scan, or read quickly, to find the specific information they need.
- Set a time limit of 3 minutes. Walk around the room, helping as needed.
- Have students compare their answers with a partner's.
- Go over the answers with the class.

Answer key

1. 73	4. 86	7. 71
2. 50	5. 70	8. 58
3. jazz	6. 320	9. photographer

Exercise 8

- **Pairs.** Tell students that they will talk about their reactions to the stories about the three women. If necessary, prompt the students with these questions: *Were you surprised by the stories? Why? Which of the three women do you think is the most interesting? Why? Give a personal example.* (For example, *I think Dodo Cheney is the most interesting because it is so hard to remain in good shape as you get older.*)
- Pair students and set a time limit of 3 minutes. Walk around the room, helping as needed.
- Call on a few students to tell the class about their reactions.

EXTENSION

- Ask students to think about an older person they know who has done something well for a long time.
- Model the activity by giving a personal example. (For example, *My father has been a lawyer for 40 years. He got his law degree in 1963.*)
- Pair students and have them take turns telling their partners about the person.
- Call on a few students to tell the class about the person they thought of.

Please go to www.longman.com/worldview for additional in-class model conversation practice.

HOMEWORK

- Assign *Workbook* page 82, Vocabulary Exercises 1 and 2, and page 84, Listening Exercises 5 and 6.

Reading

6 **Read the article. Then match the women's names with their jobs.**

1. Dodo Cheney _____   a. singer
2. Carmen Dell'Orefice _____   b. tennis player
3. Omara Portuondo _____   c. model

Life after 70

Today, not all people over 70 think they're old. People stay younger for longer. Three women who are over 70 and still going strong, are Omara Portuondo, Dodo Cheney, and Carmen Dell'Orefice. What do they do, and how long have they done it?

Cuban singer **Omara Portuondo** is one of the most popular jazz singers in the world. She has sung in clubs and cabarets for over 50 years and was on a Buena Vista Social Club album. Now she is 73 years old and is still one of the star singers at the famous Tropicana Club in Havana, Cuba.

Dodo (Dorothy) Cheney is an 86-year-old tennis champion. She has played tennis for more than 70 years. Now she plays in tournaments for people over 75 and she has won over 320 matches.

Carmen Dell'Orefice is 71 years old. She has been a model since she was 13. Her career started 58 years ago when a photographer saw her on a bus and asked to take her photo. Today she still works for the Ford modeling agency.

7 **Read the article again. Complete the information about the three women.**

1. Omara Portuondo is _____ years old.
2. She has been a singer for more than _____ years.
3. The kind of music Omara sings is _____.
4. Dodo Cheney is _____ years old.
5. She has been a tennis player for more than _____ years.
6. She has won more than _____ tennis matches.
7. Carmen Dell'Orefice is _____ years old.
8. She has been a model for more than _____ years.
9. She began working as a model after a _____ saw her on a bus.

8 *PAIRS.* **Discuss the questions.**

What's your reaction to the stories about the three women in the article?

When you are their age, will you have a job?

Grammar focus

1 **Look at the examples of the present perfect with _how long_, _for_, and _since_. Answer the questions.**

> How long **has** Dodo Cheney **played** tennis?
> She**'s played** tennis **for** 70 years.
> How long **has** Carmen Dell'Orefice **been** a model?
> She**'s been** a model **since** she was 13.

1. When did Dodo Cheney start playing tennis? _____ ago.

2. Does she play tennis now? _____

3. When did Carmen Dell'Orefice start working as a model? _____

4. Is she a model now? _____

2 **Look at the examples again. Circle the correct words to complete the rules in the chart.**

> **Present perfect: _how long/for/since_**
>
> Use the present perfect for actions that started in the **present / past** and continue in the **present / past**.
>
> Use **for / since** with a period of time (for example, _an hour, two months, 50 years_).
>
> Use **for / since** with a point in time (for example, _2:00 P.M., June 25, 1953_).
>
> **NOTE:** Use contractions with the subject pronouns and the verb _have_. For example, _**I've** been an engineer since 2002. **He's** worked in that office for two years._

> Grammar Reference page 148

3 **Read the information. Use the present perfect with _for_ or _since_ to write new sentences.**

1. He became a dancer when he was twelve. He is a dancer now.
   He's been a dancer since he was twelve.

2. He started teaching piano 38 years ago. He teaches piano now.

3. I started playing jazz in 1958. I play jazz now.

4. I have a guitar. I bought it in 2002.

5. They got married 50 years ago. They are married now.

6. She started playing tennis 70 years ago. She plays tennis now.

7. She started a new job on January 10. She works there now.

8. We started to study English last year. We study English now.

9. They live in Australia. They moved there eight years ago.

Grammar focus

LANGUAGE NOTES

- The focus in this unit is on the present perfect used to talk about actions that started in the past and continue in the present. For example, *I have known him for a long time.*

- *For* is used with periods of time. For example, *We've lived here for a year.*

- *Since* can be used with a point in time. For example, *We've lived here since last March.*

WARM-UP

Note: Skip this warm-up if you're doing this lesson (Lesson B) during the same class period as Lesson A.

- Books closed. Tell students they will listen to the article from the Reading section.

- Write *How long?* on the board. Tell students to listen and write down how long each woman has been in her job.

- 🎧 Play the audio from Lesson A, Reading, Exercise 6. (It models the grammar of the unit.)

- Call on a few students to tell you how long the women have been in their jobs. Write these cues on the board: (*Dodo/tennis player/for more than 70 years; Carmen/model/for 58 years; Omara/singer/for over 50 years*)

Exercise ❶

- Tell students to read the examples and study the bold-faced words. Point out or elicit that one of the statements uses *for* and the other *since*. Tell them to think about the difference between the two time expressions.

- Ask students to write the answers to the four questions that follow the examples.

- Go over the answers with the class.

Answer key

1. 70 years ago
2. yes
3. 58 years ago/when she was 13
4. yes

Exercise ❷

- Have students study the examples again. Tell them to circle the correct words to complete the rules in the chart.

- Have students compare their answers with a partner's.

- Go over the answers with the class.

- Ask a few questions to elicit the key points about the grammar: For example, *What's the form of the present perfect?* (*have* + past participle) *Which word is used with a point in time—for or since?* (*since*) *Which word is used with a period of time?* (*for*)

Answer key

past; present   for   since

LANGUAGE NOTES

- The auxiliary *has* is pronounced either as a weak form or as a contraction: For example, *How long has* /həz/ *Dodo Cheney played tennis? She's played tennis for 70 years.*

- Note the weak pronunciation of *for* in connected speech: *for* /fɚ/ *70 years.*

- Students often have problems with the pronunciation of the *-ed* ending in regular past participles. The rules are the same as for the pronunciation of the simple past tense *-ed* ending: It is pronounced as an extra syllable /əd/ only after the sounds /t/ and /d/ as in *wanted, needed.* Otherwise, the ending is pronounced as the sound /d/, as in *played* or /t/ as in *worked.*

Exercise ❸

- Before students begin Exercise 3, answer any questions they might have. You may also want to refer the class to the Grammar Reference for Unit 21 on page 148.

- Explain the task: Students will read the information and will write new sentences using the present perfect and *for* or *since.* Go over the example.

- Set a time limit of 10 minutes. Walk around the room, helping as needed.

- Have students compare their answers with a partner's.

- Go over the answers with the class.

Answer key

1. He's been a dancer since he was twelve.
2. He's taught piano for 38 years.
3. I've played jazz since 1958.
4. I've had a car since 2002.
5. They've been married for 50 years.
6. She's played tennis for 70 years.
7. She's worked there since January 10.
8. We've studied English since last year.
9. They've lived in Australia for eight years.

EXTENSION

- Have students work in pairs to write a description of a famous person. Remind them to use the present perfect and expressions with *for* or *since.* Demonstrate the activity. Give these descriptions: *He's (has) been an actor for at least 40 years. He was born in Scotland. He's (has) played James Bond several times. He's (has) been a British knight since 2000.*

- Have students guess the name of the famous person you described. (Sean Connery)

- Pair students and set a time limit of 5 minutes.

- Have volunteers read their descriptions and ask the class to guess the name of the person described.

Speaking

Exercise 4

This activity provides practice on asking questions with *how long* and using the present perfect with *for* and *since*. It also prepares students for Exercises 5 and 6.

- Explain the task: Students will fill in the *You* column with information about themselves. Point out that the question cues in the first column follow a pattern: One asks for some information, the next is a follow-up question and asks how long that information has been true. (For example, *Where do you live? How long have you lived there?*)

- Before answering the questions, tell students to write an additional question asking for information and the follow-up question at the end of the chart.

- Have students work individually to complete the *You* column in the chart. Set a time limit of 5 minutes. Walk around the room, helping as needed.

Exercise 5

- **Pairs.** Explain the task: Students will use the question cues to interview a partner and complete the last column of the chart. Go over the example, asking two volunteers to read the questions and answers.

- Pair students and set a time limit of 10 minutes. Walk around the room, helping as needed.

Exercise 6

Call on several students to tell the rest of the class one interesting fact about their partners.

TRB For additional interactive grammar practice, have students do the reproducible activity for this unit in the *Teacher's Resource Book.*

Writing

Exercise 7

- Assign the writing task for class work or homework.

- Explain the task: Students will use the questions in Exercise 4 as cues to write an article about someone they know well.

- Brainstorm names of people students might know well enough to write about.

- **TRB** Optionally, give students a copy of the model (see the *Teacher's Resource Book,* Writing Models). Ask them to read the model and notice the vocabulary and grammar from the unit.

- If students don't have the model, write the following on the board:

   My friend Asim is from Egypt. He has lived in the capital city, Cairo, for seven years. He works at the Egyptian Museum, where he has worked since 1999.

- Have a student read the sentences aloud. Answer any questions students might have.

- Walk around to make sure everyone understands the task.

For suggestions on how to give feedback on writing, see page xii of this *Teacher's Edition.*

CONVERSATION TO GO

At the end of class, call on two students to role-play the conversation.

HOMEWORK

- 📖 Assign *Workbook* page 83, Grammar Exercises 3 and 4, and page 84, Pronunciation Exercises 7, 8, and 9.

- 🔘 If students do not have the *WorldView Workbook,* assign listening homework from the Student CD. Write on the board:

   Track 47
   The article tells us only one woman's nationality. Who is she and where is she from?

- 🎧 Tell students to listen to the audio and write the answer to the question. Have them bring their answer to the next class.

   (Answer: *It's Omara Portuondo, and she's from Cuba.*)

Speaking

4 *BEFORE YOU SPEAK.* **Ask yourself the questions. Write your answers in the *You* column.**

YOU	YOUR PARTNER
Where / live? _I live in . . ._	
How long? _I've lived there . . ._	
Where / work?	
How long?	
What / interested in?	
How long?	
What / study?	
How long?	
What / favorite possession?	
How long?	

5 *PAIRS.* **Now ask your partner the same questions. Write the information about your partner in the chart.**

A: *Where do you live?*
B: *In Mexico City.*
A: *How long have you lived there?*
B: *Since 1998.*

6 **Tell the class one interesting fact about your partner.**

Writing

7 **Think about a person you know well. Answer the questions in Exercise 4 about this person. Then use your answers to write about the person. Use the present perfect with *for* and *since*.**

CONVERSATION TO GO

A: How long **have you been** married?
B: **For** two months!

Job share

Vocabulary Words related to tasks in an office
Grammar Modals for requests and offers
Speaking Making and responding to requests and offers

Getting started

1 **Complete the sentences with the verbs in the box.**

arrange	do	file	get	have	leave	make (2x)	~~send~~	sign

1. I need to __send__ a fax to Paula. Do you have her fax number?
2. Did you _____ the email from Sam?
3. Can I _____ a message for Ms. Parker, please?
4. Can you _____ the meeting notes, please? The folders are over there.
5. I'll be there in a minute. I have to _____ a call first.
6. Sorry, but I can't _____ the copying now. I'm too busy.
7. Can you _____ your name here, please? Right next to the *X*.
8. What time should we _____ the meeting?
9. Let's _____ a meeting for next Friday.
10. I need to _____ a reservation at La Scala for tomorrow at 7:30 P.M.

2 *PAIRS.* **Discuss. Which of the tasks in Exercise 1 have you done?**

Reading

3 **Look at the ad. What do you think** *job share* **means?**

4 **Read the ad. Answer the question.**

What are the three ways you can share a job?

JOB SHARE

Do you love your job but want to work only part-time? Then maybe a job share is right for you. With a job share, you and your job-share partner can share one full-time job. This can work different ways.

- You work in the morning, and your partner works in the afternoon.
- You work Monday to Wednesday morning, and your partner works Wednesday afternoon to Friday.
- You both work 20 hours per week and you arrange your own schedules.

Call Job Share today
at 1-800-JOB-1234

We'll find the right job-share partner for you!

Job share

OBJECTIVES

Students will:

- activate vocabulary related to tasks in an office
- do listening, speaking, and writing tasks related to making and responding to requests and offers
- focus on using modals for requests and offers
- practice weak pronunciation of *can, could, should,* and *would,* and linking these words to the next word in requests

BACKGROUND INFORMATION

In job-share arrangements, two people voluntarily share the responsibilities of one full position. This type of arrangement has become popular, especially for women with children. There are three types of job sharing that work well:

1. There is shared responsibility, and no real division of tasks. The two workers are interchangeable. This works in jobs where the work is continuous such as in a factory.

2. There is divided responsibility, and tasks can be divided cleanly, such as between projects or clients in marketing.

3. The responsibilities are completely different, but two workers each work part time and so account for one full-time position, for example, a file clerk and a production assistant.

WARM-UP: WHY JOB SHARE?

Students will discuss the advantages and disadvantages of job sharing.

- Tell students that this unit is about jobs and job sharing. Find out if students understand the meaning of the unit title, "Job share." Elicit that when people "job share," they split the hours and the tasks that one full-time employee would usually do.
- Brainstorm the advantages and disadvantages of job sharing. Elicit examples of each. (For example, Advantage: *Working parents can have more time with their children.* Disadvantage: *They make less money.*)

Getting started

OPTION: VOCABULARY PREVIEW

Have students look at the verbs in the box. Point out that these verbs are parts of verb-noun combinations referring to tasks in an office. Demonstrate the idea of verb-noun combinations, or collocations, by doing the first word *arrange* with the class. Ask: *What things might someone* arrange *at work?* (meetings, schedules, papers) Go over each verb in the box and ask leading questions to elicit nouns that go with each verb.

Exercise ❶

- Tell students to complete the sentences with the verbs in the box.
- Set a time limit of 2 minutes. Walk around the room, helping as needed.
- Have students compare their answers with a partner's.
- Go over the answers with the class.

Answer key			
1. send	4. file	7. sign	10. make
2. get	5. make	8. have	
3. leave	6. do	9. arrange	

Exercise ❷

- Pair students. Tell each pair to look at the list of tasks in Exercise 1 and identify which of the tasks they have done.
- Set a time limit of 1 minute.
- Call on some volunteers to tell the class which of the tasks they have done. Encourage them to say if they liked doing the tasks.

Reading

Exercise ❸

- Tell students to look at the ads. Ask: *What does the title "Job Share" mean?* (It means the sharing of tasks at work between two employees.)
- Ask them if they have shared any of their tasks at work with a coworker. Encourage them to share their experience with the class.

Exercise ❹

- Before asking students to read the ad, ask them what kind of information they expect to find in the ad. (*Possible answers:* More information about what "job share" is, number of work hours per week, skills needed for the position, the number to call for the job)
- Have the class read the ad. Set a time limit of 2 minutes.
- After 2 minutes, call on volunteers to answer the questions, using the information in the ad.

Exercise ❺

- **Pairs.** Explain the task: Students will look at the photos and discuss which jobs could be shared and which job would be difficult to share. Tell them to give reasons why a job would be difficult to share.
- Pair students and set a time limit of 3 minutes. Walk around the room, helping as needed.
- Call on a few students to say aloud their answers and their reasons.

Answer key

Possible answers:
All of the jobs could be shared if the tasks were divided evenly. For example, a taxi driver could split a shift with another person, a secretary could divide the schedule and/or the tasks, and a teacher could teach only certain classes. It would be more difficult for a musician to job share unless both musicians knew the programs equally well.

Listening

Exercise ❻

- Have students discuss potential problems when two people share a job. Elicit an example from the class. (For example, *Something doesn't get done because each thought the other would do it.*)
- Pair students and set a time limit of 3 minutes for the discussion. Walk around the room, helping as needed.
- Call on a few students to report their answers to the class.

Answer key

Possible answers:
miscommunication, tasks not completed, workers don't know the job equally well, inequitable schedule or conflicts over schedules

Exercise ❼

- Have students read the questions so they know what to listen for. Point out that they will be listening only for the main idea of the conversation.
- 🎧 Play the audio.
- Have students compare their answers with a partner.
- Go over the answers with the class.

Answer key

1. Administrative assistant
2. Marcy didn't finish all of her work. She wants Ken to finish it for her.

Exercise ❽

- Tell students they will listen again. This time, they will listen for more detailed information than in the previous exercise.
- Explain the task: As they listen to the conversation again, students will check the tasks that Marcy actually did.
- 🎧 Play the audio again.
- Have students compare their answers with a partner's.
- Go over the answers with the class.

Answer key

Check: answer the phones; do the copying; reply to emails

EXTENSION

- Tell students to imagine themselves in Ken's position. Have them discuss ways he could respond if the situation with Marcy continued to be a problem.
- Pair students and set a time limit of 3 minutes.
- Call on a few students to discuss Ken's options. (For example, *tell the supervisor or meet with Marcy to clearly define responsibilities.*)

◉ Please go to www.longman.com/worldview for additional in-class model conversation practice and supplementary reading practice.

HOMEWORK

- 📖 Assign *Workbook* page 85, Vocabulary Exercises 1 and 2, and page 87, Listening Exercises 5 and 6.

5 *PAIRS.* Look at the photos. Which of these jobs could two people share? Which jobs would be difficult to share?

Listening

6 *PAIRS.* Discuss. What problems can there be when two people share a job?

7 🎧 Ken and Marcy share a job at a modeling agency. Listen to their conversation. Then answer the questions.

1. What job do Ken and Marcy share?
2. What is the problem?

8 🎧 Listen again and check (✓) the tasks that Marcy did.

> ✓ answer the phones
> ___ send faxes
> ___ do the copying
> ___ reply to e-mails
> ___ call the photographer
> ___ call the new model
> ___ make a reservation for lunch

Grammar focus

1 Look at the examples. Write *R* next to the requests (asking people to do things for you). Write *O* next to the offers (saying you will do things for other people).

1. A: **Can you call** the restaurant, please? _R_
   B: Yes, of course.

2. A: **Could you do** this copying? ___
   B: Sorry, I'm afraid I can't.

3. A: **Would you like me to arrange** a meeting for you? ___
   B: Yes, please. I'd like to meet here at the office.

4. A: **Should I make** a reservation at Loon's? ___
   B: Yes, for 1:00, please.

5. A: **I'll send** this fax for you. ___
   B: Thanks!

2 Look at the examples again. Complete the rules in the chart with *can you, could you, I'll, should I,* and *would you like me to.*

Modals for requests and offers: *can you, could you, I'll, should I,* and *would you like me to*
To make a request, ask a question with _____ or _____ + the base form of the verb.
To make an offer, ask a question with _____ or _____ + the base form of the verb, or make a statement with _____ + the base form of the verb.
NOTE: *I'll = I will*

> Grammar Reference page 148

3 Complete the conversations with requests or offers. Use the words in parentheses.

1. A: _Would you like me to call_ (**would/call**) the airline for you?

   B: Yes, please. _____ (**could/make**) a reservation for me on the 10:00 A.M. flight?

2. A: _____ (**can/finish**) the report today?

   B: Sure. Then _____ (**should/leave**) it on your desk?

3. A: _____ (**will/arrange**) the meeting for you. Is Friday OK?

   B: Yes, fine. And _____ (**can/send**) an e-mail to Bernie about it?

4. A: _____ (**would/get**) a taxi for you?

   B: No. Don't worry. I can do that. But _____ (**can/check**) the fax machine, please? I'm expecting an important fax.

Grammar focus

LANGUAGE NOTES

- Use the modals *can* and *could* + the base form of the verb to make polite requests. For example, *Could you pass the salt, please? Can you please call Mr. Sanders?*
- Use *should I* and *would you like me to* + the base form of the verb to make offers in the form of questions. Use *I'll* to make an offer using a statement. Note that *I could* can also be used to make an offer.

WARM-UP

Note: Skip this warm-up if you're doing this lesson (Lesson B) during the same class period as Lesson A.

- Books closed. Tell students they will listen to the conversation between Marcy and Ken from the Listening section.
- Ask students to listen carefully for the questions Ken and Marcy ask each other. Ask: *Is the speaker asking the other person to do something or is he or she offering to do something for the other person?*
- 🎧 Play the audio from Lesson A, Listening, Exercise 7. (It models the grammar of the unit.)
- Call on a few students to give examples of Marcy's requests and Ken's offers. (For example, Marcy's requests: *Can you call the photographer? Could you call (Eric), too?* Ken's offers: *Would you like me to send them for you? Should I call her now?*)

Exercise ❶

- Have students read the five conversations, focusing on the bold-faced words. Point out or elicit that each dialogue starts with a question except the last one, which is a statement offering to do something and uses *I'll* + the base form of *send*.
- Tell students to look at the first conversation. Ask: *Is A making a request or an offer?* (a request) *What words are used to make requests and what words are used to make offers?*
- Have students label each of the examples either *R* for *request* or *O* for *offer*.
- Go over the answers with the class.

Answer key

1. R   2. R   3. O   4. O   5. O

Exercise ❷

- Have students study the examples again.
- Tell students to complete the rules in the chart with *can you, could you, I'll, should I,* and *would you like me to.*
- Have students compare their answers with a partner's.
- Go over the answers with the class.
- Ask a few questions to elicit the key points about the grammar: For example, *Which modals do we use to make requests?* (can you, could you) *Which do we use for offers?* (I'll, should I, would you like me to) *What form of the verb follows the modal or pronoun?* (base form)

Answer key

1. *can you* or *could you*
2. *should I* or *would you like me to, I'll* or *I will*

Exercise ❸

- Before students begin Exercise 3, answer any questions they might have. You may also want to refer the class to the Grammar Reference for Unit 22 on page 148.
- Explain the task: Students will use the words in parentheses to complete the conversations with requests or offers. Go over the example.
- Have students work individually to complete the task. Set at time limit of 3 minutes. Walk around the room, helping as needed.
- Have students compare their answers with a partner's.
- Go over the answers with the class.

Answer key

1. A: Would you like me to call
   B: Could you make
2. A: Can you finish
   B: should I leave
3. A: I'll arrange
   B: can you send
4. A: Would you like me to get
   B: can you check

EXTENSION

- Pair students. Tell them to express the requests and offers in Exercise 3 in another way. (For example, *Should I call the airline for you?*)
- Set a time limit of 3 minutes. Go over the answers with the class.

Pronunciation

> ### LANGUAGE NOTES
> - Modals often have a weak pronunciation when they come before another word. For example, *Can* /kən/ *you send these faxes? Should* /ʃəd/ *I make a reservation?*
> - Within a phrase, a consonant sound at the end of one word is usually linked to a vowel sound at the beginning of the next word. For example, *Should I call a taxi?*
> - *Could you* and *would you* are often blended together and pronounced as "couldja" and "wouldja" in informal conversation: *Could you* /kədʒə/ *do this copying? Would you* /wədʒə/ *like me to send this?* The /d/ at the end of the modal is blended with the /y/ at the beginning of *you* to make the sound /dʒ/.

Exercise ❹
- Tell students they will listen to expressions used in requests.
- 🎧 Play the audio. Call attention to the weak pronunciation of the modals and *you.*
- Point out the linking of the consonant sound /d/ at the end of *should* to the vowel sound of *I.*
- Call attention to the way *could you* and *would you* are blended and pronounced together as "couldja" and "wouldja." Demonstrate the difference by saying the words by themselves first and then linked together.

Exercise ❺
- Tell students that they will listen again. This time, they will listen and repeat.
- 🎧 Play the audio, stopping after each sentence to allow students to repeat chorally as well as individually.
- Encourage students to use polite intonation for the requests—with a high voice range and rising intonation at the end.

Exercise ❻
- **Pairs.** Explain the task: Students will work in pairs to practice the conversations in Exercise 3.
- Pair students. Assign A and B roles. Set a time limit of 2 minutes. Remind the pairs to switch roles afterward.

Speaking

Exercise ❼
Pairs. This exercise provides practice with using modals to make offers and requests.
- Explain the task: Students will role-play two situations. The supervisor will make requests, and the employee will make offers.
- Pair students. Tell Student A to turn to page 140, and Student B to page 141. Set a time limit of 10 minutes.
- Have volunteers perform their role-plays for the class.

TRB For additional interactive grammar practice, have students do the reproducible activity for this unit in the *Teacher's Resource Book.*

Writing

Exercise ❽
- Assign the writing task for class work or homework.
- Explain the task: Students will look at the To-Do list and identify four tasks they want to do and four tasks they don't want to do. Then they will write an email to their job-share partner, offering to do four tasks and requesting that the partner do the other four. For each task they should provide a reason.
- Demonstrate the activity with the first task *write a report.* Ask students who would like to write the report. Elicit a reason why (for example, *I enjoy writing.*). Write a sentence on the board using the reason. (For example, *I'll write the report because I enjoy writing.*)
- Brainstorm reasons for and against each task. (For example, *I like to write.* Or *I'm a terrible writer.*)
- **TRB** Optionally, give students a copy of the model (see the *Teacher's Resource Book,* Writing Models). Ask them to read the model and notice the vocabulary and grammar from the unit.
- If students don't have the model, write the following on the board:

  Hi, Jane.
  We have a lot of things to do next week, so I thought we should get organized and divide the work.

  I'll write the report on the conference because I attended most of the seminars. I'll also do the filing . . . Could you have lunch with Jeffrey Houston on Monday?

- Have a student read the sentences aloud. Answer any questions students might have.
- Walk around to make sure everyone understands the task.

For suggestions on how to give feedback on writing, see page xiv of this *Teacher's Edition.*

CONVERSATION TO GO
At the end of class, call on two students to role-play the conversation.

HOMEWORK
- 📖 Assign *Workbook* page 86, Grammar Exercises 3 and 4, and page 87, Pronunciation Exercises 7 and 8.
- 💿 If students do not have the *WorldView Workbook,* assign listening homework from the Student CD. Write on the board:

  Track 48
  Marcy makes a lot of requests from Ken. What does he say he <u>won't</u> do?

- 🎧 Tell students to listen to the audio and write the answer to the question. Have them bring their answer to the next class.

  (Answer: *He won't call the new model or the restaurant.*)

Pronunciation

4 🎧 **Listen. Notice the weak pronunciation of** *can, could, should,* **and** *would* **and the way these words are linked to the next word.**

Can you call the restaurant, please?

Could you do this copying?

Should I make a reservation?

Would you like me to arrange a meeting?

Can you send these faxes?

Could you answer the phone?

Should I call a taxi?

Would you like me to do the filing?

5 🎧 **Listen again and repeat.**

6 *PAIRS.* **Practice the conversations in Exercise 3.**

Speaking

7 *PAIRS.* **Role-play two situations. Take turns making requests and offers. Student A, look at page 140. Student B, look at page 141.**

A: Can you do the filing, please?
B: Yes, of course. I'll do it this afternoon.

Writing

8 Choose one of these jobs—travel office clerk, reporter for a TV station, restaurant manager, English teacher—or think of another job. Make a To-do list for the job. Look at the sample To-do list for ideas. Write a memo to your "job share partner." Ask him or her to do some things on the list. Offer to do other things on the list. Give reasons.

TO-DO LIST
(Administrative Assistant)

write a report
talk with your boss about a problem
have lunch with a new client
go on a business trip to Hawaii
do the filing
plan an office party
type a letter
go to a computer class

CONVERSATION TO GO

A: **Could you lend** me some money, please?
B: Sure. And I'll take you to the cash machine on the way home.

Changing customs

Vocabulary Things you customarily do
Grammar *used to/didn't use to*
Speaking Talking about past customs

Getting started

1 **Complete the questions with the correct words from the box.**

dinner	~~doors~~	food	games	home	horse
housework	long skirts	shoes	slippers		

1. Do men open _____*doors*_____ for women?

2. Do women wear _____ ?

3. Do families have _____ together every night?

4. Do women do all the _____ ?

5. Do people shop for _____ every day?

6. Do families play _____ together in the evening?

7. Do people stay _____ in the evening?

8. Do people travel by _____ and carriage?

9. Do people take off their _____ and put on
_____ when they go into a house?

2 🎧 **Listen and check your answers.**

3 *PAIRS.* **Take turns asking and answering the questions in
Exercise 1. Answer about people you know.**

A ___

B ___

C ___

Changing customs

OBJECTIVES

Students will:

- activate vocabulary related to things they customarily do
- do reading, speaking, and writing tasks related to talking about past customs
- focus on using *used to/didn't use to*
- practice pronunciation of *used to/didn't use to*

WARM-UP: ALL ABOUT SHOES

Pairs. Students will brainstorm words for different types of shoes.

- Tell students that this unit is about how customs change over time. Make sure everyone understands the meaning of *customs* in the unit title, "Changing customs," by asking volunteers to give examples. (For example, the customs of throwing rice at weddings, shaking hands when you meet someone.)
- Tell students that they will work in pairs to create a list of different types of footwear. Tell them to think of the most common types of shoes such as boots, sandals.
- Pair students and set a time limit of 3 minutes.
- After three minutes, ask a few volunteers to say aloud their answers. (Possible answers: *sandals, boots, high heels, slippers, sneakers, running shoes, cleats, loafers, platform shoes, pumps, clogs*)
- Write the students' answers on the board, and have students copy them in their vocabulary notebooks.

Getting started

CULTURE NOTES

- Some practices in the United States have changed since the women's movement in the 1960s. For example, today men don't necessarily open doors for women and are more likely to help with the housework.
- With the invention of refrigeration, people started to buy larger quantities of food at one time. In the United States, many people go grocery shopping just once a week.
- Families in the United States are very busy and don't always have dinner together. Many are too busy to do things together as a family.

OPTION: VOCABULARY PREVIEW

Write the following verbs and verb phrases on the board: *open, wear, have, do, shop, play, stay, travel by, take off, put on*. Brainstorm possible nouns for each of these verbs by asking questions. For example, for the verb *open*, ask: *What things can we open?* (doors, windows, books, boxes) Then have students look at the words in the box and ask which of these words can go with *open*. (doors) Continue brainstorming nouns for the rest of the verbs. Alternatively, have students complete the exercise in pairs.

Exercise ❶

- Explain the task: Students will complete the sentences with the words from the box. Go over the example.
- Set a time limit of 2 minutes. Walk around the room, helping as needed.
- Tell students they will check their answers in the next activity.

Exercise ❷

- Tell students to check their answers as they listen to the audio.
- 🎧 Play the audio. Encourage students to correct any wrong answers.
- Go over the answers with the class.

Answer key

1. doors	6. games
2. long skirts	7. home
3. dinner	8. horse
4. housework	9. shoes; slippers
5. food	

Exercise ❸

- **Pairs.** Explain the task: Students will take turns asking and answering the questions in Exercise 1.
- Pair students and set a time limit of 5 minutes. Walk around the room, helping as needed.
- Call on a few students to read their answers aloud.

Reading

Teaching Tip! Activating prior knowledge

Draw students' attention to the title of the article. Tell them to think of customs they know that involve shoes. (For example, *shoes tied to the cars of newlyweds, taking off one's shoes before entering a house*). This will help activate prior knowledge before reading the article.

FYI

Customs are practices carried out on a societal level, whereas *traditions* can be passed down within families, ethnic groups, or societies.

Exercise 4

- Have students look at the pictures. Ask them questions about each one. (For example, *Who is in the picture? What time period do you think it is?*)
- Have students look at the article. Ask them how many numbered paragraphs there are. (five) Tell them to write the number of the paragraph next to each picture.
- Set a time limit of 5 minutes. Walk around the room, helping as needed.
- Have students compare their answers with a partner's.
- Go over the answers with the class.

Answer key

Picture A: 2; Picture B: 5; Picture C: 1; Picture D: 3; Picture E: 4

Exercise 5

- Tell students that they will reread the article. Tell them to read the statements first before rereading the article so they know what information they need to confirm or refute.
- Then have them write *T* (True) or *F* (False) after each statement.
- Set a time limit of 5 minutes. Walk around the room, helping as needed.
- Have students compare their answers with a partner's.
- Go over the answers with the class.

Answer key

1. F   2. F   3. T   4. T   5. F

EXTENSION

Tell students to reread the statements in Exercise 5 and to change the false statements to make them true. (*Possible answers:* 1. A long time ago, people **used to** throw shoes at the bride and groom. 2. Soldiers in the ancient Roman army wore **different** sandals—depending on how important they were. 5. At Anglo-Saxon weddings, the groom touched the bride's head with **her** shoes.)

HOMEWORK

- Assign *Workbook* page 88, Vocabulary 1 and 2, and page 90, Listening Exercises 5 and 6.

Reading

4 **Read the article. Then match the paragraphs with the pictures.**

SHOES

Customs and Traditions Around the World

Maybe you don't think about shoes very often. You probably think shoes are boring, but there are very interesting old customs associated with shoes. Here are just a few of them.

D____

E____

1. A long time ago, people used to throw shoes at the bride and groom after the wedding because they thought it was good luck. Some people still tie shoes to the back of the newlywed couple's car.

2. In ancient Rome, a soldier's sandals used to tell everyone how important he was in the army: a captain or a foot soldier.

3. High heels and platform shoes are not new. Hundreds of years ago, people used to wear them in the street because the streets were full of garbage. The garbage didn't touch their feet, so their feet didn't get dirty.

4. In France, when Louis XIV was king, people thought red shoes were very special. Only the very rich aristocracy used to wear them when they visited the king.

5. Strange things happened at Anglo-Saxon weddings. The father of the bride used to give the bride's shoes to the groom. Then the groom used to touch the bride's head with these shoes. This meant that the father no longer owned his daughter—she now belonged to the groom.

5 **Read the article again and write *T* (true) or *F* (false) after each statement.**

1. In some countries, people still throw shoes at the bride at her wedding. F

2. All soldiers in the ancient Roman army wore the same sandals.

3. People wore high heels and platform shoes many years ago.

4. The very rich people wore red shoes when they visited King Louis XIV.

5. At Anglo-Saxon weddings, the groom touched the bride's head with his shoes.

Grammar focus

1 **Study the examples. Notice the difference between the sentences with *used to* and those in the simple past.**

used to	Simple past
(?) What **did** they **use to do** at weddings?	What **did** they **do** at your wedding?
(+) They **used to throw** shoes at the bride and groom.	They **threw** rice at my husband and me.
(–) Poor people **didn't use to wear** red shoes.	I **didn't wear** red shoes.

2 **Look at the examples again. Circle the correct words to complete the explanations in the chart.**

used to/didn't use to
Use *used to* to talk about something that happened in the past and **still happens / isn't still happening** in the present.
Use *used to* to talk about something that happened **only once / more than once** in the past.
Use the **past form / base form** of the verb after *used to*.

Grammar Reference page 148

3 **Complete the sentences with the correct form of *used to* and a verb from the box.**

~~drink~~ eat go open play walk wear

1. In the U.K. one hundred years ago, most people __didn't use to drink__ (not) coffee, but now a lot of people do.

2. _____ men _____ doors for women in your country fifty years ago?

3. People _____ (not) in restaurants very often, but now it's more common.

4. When you were a child, _____ girls _____ wear jeans to school?

5. One hundred years ago, a young man and woman _____ (not) for walks without a chaperon.

6. My grandmother _____ two miles to school every day.

7. _____ your parents _____ games with you when you were a child?

Grammar focus

LANGUAGE NOTES

- Use *used to* + the base form of the verb to talk about past habits or past situations that no longer exist in the present.
- *Used to* always refers to the past. There is no present tense form.
- *Used to* is usually used in sentences that contrast the past and the present. The time expressions *now, no longer,* and *not anymore* are used to emphasize the contrast.
- To form *Yes/No* questions, use *did* + subject + *use to.*
- To form the negative, use *didn't use to. Used to* is more common in affirmative statements than in negative statements or questions.

WARM-UP

Note: Skip this warm-up if you're doing this lesson (Lesson B) during the same class period as Lesson A.

- Books closed. Tell students they will listen to the article that they read in the Reading section.
- Write these sentences on the board and have students copy them: *People _____ shoes at the bride and groom. Hundreds of years ago, people _____ them in the street because the streets were full of garbage. The father of the bride _____ her shoes to the groom.*
- Tell students to listen to the audio and complete the sentences.
- 🎧 Play the audio from Lesson A, Reading, Exercise 4. (It models the grammar of the unit.)
- Ask volunteers to come up to the board to complete the sentences. Encourage students to correct their answers as necessary. (*Answers:* used to throw; used to wear; used to give)
- Ask: *Does the article talk about things people still do or about things people did before but don't do now?*

Exercise ❶

- Have students read the two sets of examples. Draw their attention to the bold-faced forms.
- Encourage students to compare the sentences using *used to* with the examples in the simple past tense. Point out or elicit that both sets of examples refer to the past.

Exercise ❷

- Have students study the examples again.
- Tell students to circle the words to complete the rules in the chart. Walk around the room, helping as needed.
- Have students compare their answers with a partner's.
- Go over the answers with the class.
- Ask a few questions to elicit the key points about the grammar. For example, *What form of the verb follows used to?* (the base form) *What tense is used to talk about something that happened only once in the past?* (the simple past)

Answer key

isn't still happening   more than once   base form

Exercise ❸

- Before students begin Exercise 3, answer any questions they might have. You may also want to refer the class to the Grammar Reference for Unit 23 on page 148.
- Explain the task: Students complete the sentences with the correct form of *used to* and a verb from the box. Go over the example.
- Have students complete the activity individually. Set a time limit of 5 minutes. Walk around the room, helping as needed.

Answer key

1. didn't use to drink
2. Did . . . use to open
3. didn't use to eat
4. did . . . use to wear
5. didn't use to go
6. used to walk
7. Did . . . use to play

Pronunciation

> ### LANGUAGE NOTES
>
> - The word *used* on its own is normally pronounced /yusd/. But in the expression *used to*, the two words are blended and pronounced together as a single word "useta." For example, *Women used to* /yustə/ *wear long skirts*. The voiced /z/ sound in *used* is pronounced as the voiceless /s/, and the word *to* is pronounced with its weak form /tə/.
> - The form *use to* in questions and negatives is also pronounced /yustə/. For example, *What did they use to* /yustə/ *do at weddings?*
> - Blending words together such as in the expression "used to" /yustə/ are common in conversation.

Exercise ❹

- Tell students that they are going to listen to the blended sound of *used to*.
- 🎧 Play the audio. Ask students to notice the way the words are blended together in *used to*.
- Point out the weak pronunciation of *to*: /tə/.
- To emphasize the difference in pronunciation, say the words *used* and *to* separately first and then in the blended form "useta."

Exercise ❺

- Tell students that they will listen again. This time, they will listen and repeat.
- 🎧 Play the audio again, stopping after each item to allow students to repeat chorally. The first two sentences are broken down into smaller parts to highlight the pronunciation of *used to*/*use to* and to make the sentences more manageable for students to say.

Speaking

Exercise ❻

This exercise provides practice with *used to* to talk about past customs. It also prepares students for Exercise 7.

- Have students look at the photos. Call on volunteers to say what the people are doing in the pictures.
- Explain the task: Students will use *used to*/*didn't use to* to write sentences about past customs in the United States.
- Have students do the activity. Set a time limit of 10 minutes. Walk around the room, helping as needed.
- After 10 minutes, call on a few students to report their answers to the class.

Exercise ❼

- **Groups of 3.** Explain the task: Students will talk about customs in their country that have changed over the past 50–100 years. Tell them to talk about the categories that are listed. Go over the example.
- Assign partners, and set a time limit of 10 minutes. Walk around the room, helping as needed.
- Call on a few students to report their ideas to the class.

EXTENSION

- Pair students. Tell the pairs to think of an invention that would change the way we do some everyday activities.
- Have each pair create an ad to sell their invention. The ad should contrast the way of life in the past and the way of life made possible with the invention. Remind students to use *used to*. For example, *Remember when you used to have to squeeze that toothpaste out of the tube? Those days are over with Autobrush.*
- Encourage students to draw a picture of their invention. Set a time limit of 10 minutes.
- Have volunteers share their ideas with the class.

TRB For additional interactive grammar practice, have students do the reproducible activity for this unit in the *Teacher's Resource Book.*

Writing

Exercise ❽

- Assign the writing task for class work or homework.
- Explain the task: Students will write a paragraph comparing their lives as children with their lives now. Remind them to use *used to*/*didn't use to*.
- Brainstorm ideas of things that they used to do or didn't use to do.
- **TRB** Optionally, give students a copy of the model (see the *Teacher's Resource Book*, Writing Models). Ask them to read the model and notice the vocabulary and grammar from the unit.
- If students don't have the model, write the following on the board:

  When I was a child, all I did was go to school every day and play after school. I also used to like a lot of junk food. . . . I used to go to the movies a lot, too.

- Have a student read the sentences aloud. Answer any questions students might have.
- Walk around to make sure everyone understands the task.

For suggestions on how to give feedback on writing, see page xiv of this *Teacher's Edition.*

CONVERSATION TO GO

At the end of class, call on two students to role-play the conversation.

HOMEWORK

- 📖 Assign *Workbook* page 89, Grammar Exercises 3 and 4, and page 90, Pronunciation Exercises 7 and 8.
- 🎧 If students do not have the *WorldView Workbook*, assign listening homework from the Student CD. Write on the board:

  Track 50
  What color shoes were popular when Louis XIV was king of France?

- 🎧 Tell students to listen to the audio and write the answer to the question. Have them bring their answer to the next class.

  (Answer: *red*)

Pronunciation

4 🎧 **Listen. Notice that *used to* and *use to* are pronounced the same way: "useta."**

used to	Women used to wear long skirts.
didn't use to	Poor people didn't use to wear red shoes.
What did they use to do at weddings?	They used to throw shoes at the bride and groom.

5 🎧 **Listen again and repeat.**

Speaking

6 *BEFORE YOU SPEAK.* **Look at the photos. Think about customs and lifestyles 50–100 years ago. Write three sentences about what people used to do. Write three sentences about what people didn't use to do.**

People used to have to go outside to get water.

spending
time at home

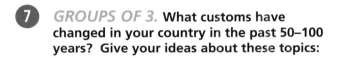

doing the
housework

7 *GROUPS OF 3.* **What customs have changed in your country in the past 50–100 years? Give your ideas about these topics:**

- clothes
- food and drink
- communication
- entertainment

- family life
- school
- transportation
- work

playing sports

working on
the farm

In the past, people didn't use to have cars. They used to travel by horse and carriage. Now most people travel by car or motorcycle.

Writing

8 **Write a paragraph about life when you were a child and your life now. Write about the things you used to do and no longer do—and about things you didn't use to do but you do now. Use *used to/didn't use to*.**

CONVERSATION TO GO

A: **Did** women **use to wear** jeans?
B: No. They always **used to wear** skirts or dresses.

Take a risk

Vocabulary Adventure sports
Grammar Present perfect vs. simple past
Speaking Talking about experiences

Lesson A

Getting started

1 Match the words with the photos.

1. rock climbing _A_
2. snowboarding ___
3. jet skiing ___
4. parasailing ___
5. snowmobiling ___
6. waterskiing ___
7. scuba diving ___
8. snorkeling ___
9. skateboarding ___
10. windsurfing ___

Pronunciation

2 🎧 Listen to the words in Exercise 1. Notice the number of syllables and the stress. Put each word in the correct group.

⬤ ○ ○ ○	⬤　　○　　○
	rock climbing

3 🎧 Listen and check your answers. Then listen again and repeat.

4 *PAIRS.* Discuss the questions.

Which sports do you do in the mountains?
Which do you do in the ocean?
Which do you do in the city?
Which of these sports have you tried?

A

B

C

D

E

Take a risk

OBJECTIVES

Students will:

- activate vocabulary related to adventure sports
- do listening, speaking, and writing tasks related to talking about experiences
- focus on the difference between the present perfect and the simple past
- practice putting stress on different syllables

WARM-UP: WHO CAN THINK OF THE MOST SPORTS?

Groups of 4. Students brainstorm the names of sports.

- Tell students that this unit is about sports. Explain that the title of the unit, "Take a risk," means "do something even though there is a chance something bad will happen."
- Tell students that they will think of as many sports as they can in 1 minute.
- Divide the class into teams of 4.
- After 1 minute, have a representative from each team write the names of sports on the board.
- The teams earn a point for each sport on their list that was not mentioned by the other teams. The team with the most points wins the game.

Getting started

OPTION: VOCABULARY PREVIEW

Encourage students to look closely at the names of the sports and find clues to the meaning of the words. For example, for *rock climbing*, point to Picture A and ask: *What's the girl doing?* (climbing) *What is she climbing?* (a huge rock/a rocky mountain) *So what do you think the sport is called?* (rock climbing) Continue asking guiding questions for the words in Exercise 1, at the same time pointing to details in the pictures for further clues to the meanings of the words. Alternatively, have students complete the exercise in pairs.

Exercise ❶

- Explain the task: Students will write the letters of the pictures next to the names of the sports.
- Set a time limit of 3 minutes. While students are working, walk around the room, helping as needed.
- Have students compare their answers with a partner's.
- Go over the answers with the class.

Answer key

1. rock climbing: A
2. snowboarding: C
3. jet skiing: G
4. parasailing: J
5. snowmobiling: H
6. waterskiing: F
7. scuba diving: E
8. snorkeling: I
9. skateboarding: D
10. windsurfing: B

EXTENSION

- Have students work individually. Tell them to rank the sports according to how dangerous they think they are: *1* = most dangerous, *10* = least dangerous.
- Pair students to compare their rankings.

Pronunciation

Exercise ❷

- Tell students that the circles represent the number of syllables. The big circles represent the syllables with the main stress.
- Ask students to count the number of syllables and write the name of each sport in the correct stress group.
- Model the activity. Write *rock climbing* on the board and count out the syllables on your fingers. Ask the class where the stress is on *rock climbing*. (***rock*** *climbing*) Mark the correct stress with large and small circles.
- 🎧 Play the audio, stopping after each item to give students time to write the word in the chart.

Exercise ❸

- Tell students they are going to check their answers and practice saying the names of some sports.
- 🎧 Play the audio, stopping after each word and asking students to repeat it chorally.

Answer key

●	•	•	•	●	•	•
snow	mo	bi	ling	rock	climb	ing
wa	ter	ski	ing	jet	ski	ing
scu	ba	di	ving	wind	sur	fing
pa	ra	sai	ling	snow	boar	ding
				snor	ke	ling
				skate	boar	ding

Exercise ❹

- Explain the task: Students will work in pairs and will decide where the sports in the chart are done. Ask them which of the sports they have tried.
- Pair students and set a time limit of 2 minutes.
- Go over the answers with the class. Ask volunteers to tell the class which sports their partners have tried.

Answer key

In the mountains: *rock climbing, snowboarding, snowmobiling*
In the ocean: *jet skiing, parasailing, waterskiing, scuba diving, snorkeling, windsurfing*
In the city: *skateboarding*

Listening

Exercise ❺

- Explain the task: Students will listen to interviews with Andy and Paula and answer the questions.

- Have students read the two questions so they know what to listen for.

- Ask students what they think Adventure Zone is. (a place to try adventure sports) Brainstorm reasons someone would go there. (to try a specific sport, to meet other adventurous people)

- 🎧 Play the audio.

- Have students compare their answers with a partner's.

- Go over the answers with the class.

Answer key

1. Andy   2. She's the new water sports instructor.

Exercise ❻

- Explain the task: Students will listen again to the interview with Andy and will check the sports he has tried under the heading *Tried it?* In the next column, they will write *Y* if Andy enjoyed it and *N* if he didn't.

- Go over the example.

- 🎧 Play the audio.

- Have students compare their answers with a partner's.

- Go over the answers with the class.

Answer key

	Tried it?	Enjoyed it?
snorkeling	✓	Y
waterskiing	✓	Y
parasailing	✓	N
scuba diving		
windsurfing		

⊚ Please go to www.longman.com/worldview for addional in-class model conversation practice and supplementary reading practice.

HOMEWORK

- 📖 Assign *Workbook* page 91, Vocabulary Exercises 1 and 2, and page 93, Listening Exercises 5 and 6.

Listening

5 🎧 Listen to the interviews with Andy and Paula, who just arrived at Adventure Zone. Answer these questions.

1. Which one is on vacation?

2. Why is the other one there?

6 🎧 Listen again to the interview with Andy. Check (✓) each sport he has tried. In the next column, write *Y* if he enjoyed it and *N* if he didn't.

	Tried it?	Enjoyed it?
snorkeling	✓	
waterskiing		
parasailing		
scuba diving		
windsurfing		

24

Grammar focus

1 Study the examples. Notice the difference between the sentences in the present perfect and those in the simple past tense.

Present perfect	Simple past
(?) **Have** you ever **tried** any dangerous sports?	What sport **did** you **try**?
(+) I've **gone** snorkeling.	I **went** snorkeling when I was a kid.
(−) I **haven't gone** windsurfing.	I **didn't go** windsurfing when I was in Puerto Rico.
I've **never gone** windsurfing.	

2 Look at the examples again. Circle the correct words to complete the rules in the chart.

Present perfect vs. simple past

Use the **simple past / present perfect** to talk about actions that happened at a specific time in the past (yesterday, last Saturday).

Use the **simple past / present perfect** to talk about things that happened at an unspecified time in the past, and when we don't know or it's not important when the action happened.

Grammar Reference page 148

3 Complete the conversations with the words in parentheses. Use the correct form of the present perfect or simple past.

1. A: ___Have you ever gone___ (**you/ever/go**) parasailing?

   B: No, I _____.

2. A: _____ (**you/watch**) that program about rock climbing last night?

   B: Yes, I _____. It _____ (**be**) really interesting.

3. A: _____ (**your sister/ever/take**) windsurfing lessons?

   B: No, she _____, but she once _____ (**try**) waterskiing.

4. A: _____ (**you/enjoy**) your adventure vacation last summer?

   B: No, I _____. It _____ (**be**) terrible.

5. A: I _____ (**never/do**) any adventure sports. How about you?

   B: Yes, I _____ (**go**) scuba diving for the first time last month.

   A: _____ (**you/like**) it?

   B: Yes, I _____ (**have**) a wonderful time.

4 *PAIRS.* Practice the conversations in Exercise 3.

Grammar focus

LANGUAGE NOTES

- Use the present perfect to talk about things that started in the past, continue up to the present, and may continue into the future. Use it to talk about things that happened at an unspecified time in the past.

- Use the present perfect to talk about things that have happened in a period of time that is not yet finished, such as *today, this month, this year*.

- Use the simple past to talk about things that happened at a specific past time. The time—such as *yesterday, last month, last year*—is often stated.

WARM-UP

Note: Skip this warm-up if you're doing this lesson (Lesson B) during the same class period as Lesson A.

- Books closed. Tell students they will listen again to the conversation that they heard in the Listening section.

- Write these sentences on the board and tell students to copy them: *I _____ snorkeling. I _____ to snorkel when I was a kid. But I _____ it on TV.*

- 🎧 Play the audio from Lesson A, Listening, Exercise 5. (It models the grammar of the unit.)

- Tell students to listen for the sentences on the board and to fill in the missing verb forms.

- Have volunteers come up to the board and fill in the missing verbs. (*'ve gone, learned, 've seen*)

- Ask: *Are the verb forms the same?* (no) *What's the difference in meaning between the second and third sentences?* (In the second sentence, the action—*learned*—is finished. In the third sentence, the action—*have seen*—happened at an unspecified time and may happen again.)

Exercise ❶

- Tell students to look at the examples and study the bold-faced words. Point out or elicit that both the present perfect and the simple past express things that happened in the past but their meanings are very different.

- Ask: *How are the simple past and the present perfect different?* (In the simple past, the action is completed at a specific time in the past. In the present perfect, the action started at an unspecified time in the past and may continue into the future.)

Exercise ❷

- Have students study the examples again.

- Tell students to circle the correct information to complete the rules in the chart.

- Have students compare their answers with a partner's.

- Go over the answers with the class.

- Ask a few questions to elicit the key points about the grammar: For example, *Which tense do we use when we don't know when an action happened?* (the present perfect) *Which tense do we use when we know exactly when an action happened?* (the simple past)

Answer key

simple past   present perfect

Exercise ❸

- Before students begin Exercise 3, answer any questions they might have. You may also want to refer the class to the Grammar Reference for Unit 24 on page 148.

- Explain the task: Students will complete the conversations using the cues in parentheses. Remind them to use either the present perfect or the simple past.

- Go over the example. Ask: *In what tense is "Have you ever gone"?* (the present perfect) *Why is that tense used in the question?* (because the time of the action is unspecified)

- Have students complete the exercise individually. Set a time limit of 5 minutes. Walk around the room, helping as needed.

- Have students compare their answers with a partner's.

- Go over the answers with the class.

Answer key

1. A: Have you ever gone
   B: haven't
2. A: Did you watch
   B: did; was
3. A: Has your sister ever taken
   B: hasn't; tried
4. A: Did you enjoy
   B: didn't; was
5. A: 've never done
   B: went
6. A: Did you like
   B: had

Exercise ❹

- Tell students that they are going to practice the conversations from Exercise 3.

- Pair students and set a time limit of 5 minutes. Walk around the room, helping as needed.

- Call on volunteers to read the conversations aloud.

Speaking

Exercise ❺

This exercise practices writing questions with the present perfect and *ever*. It also prepares students for Exercises 6 and 7.

- Explain the task: Students will think of four adventure sports and write questions about those sports using *Have you ever*.
- Have students look at the example. Point out that it begins with *Have you ever*, and is followed by the past participle of the verb *go* and then the adventure sport.
- Brainstorm verbs that might go with sports such as *go, be,* and *try*. Write the verbs on the board.
- Set a time limit of 5 minutes.

Exercise ❻

- Explain the task: Students will interview three other students and ask about the sports they chose in Exercise 5.
- Tell them to use the bulleted items to ask follow-up questions in their interviews. Remind them to take notes on each student's answers.
- Students will ask different follow-up questions depending on the answer to *Have you ever . . . ?* For example, if the answer is *yes*, the follow-up question might be *Did you enjoy it?* If the answer is *no*, the follow-up question might be *Would you like to try it?*
- Model the activity with a student. Ask: *Have you ever tried rock climbing? Did you enjoy it? Have you ever gone waterskiing? Would you like to try it? Have you seen it on TV?* Take notes on the student's responses on the board.
- Divide the class in groups of 4 and set a time limit of 12 minutes. Walk around the room, helping as needed.

Exercise ❼

Call on a few students to report on their interviews.

EXTENSION

- Do a whole-class survey. Elicit from the class the names of all the sports they had in their notes. Write them on the board.
- Read each of the sports aloud, and ask students to raise their hands if they have done the sport before. Make tally marks next to each sport.
- When the survey is complete, ask: *Why do you think (name of sport) is so popular? Do you think the choice of the sport depends on a person's gender or age?*

TRB For additional interactive grammar practice, have students do the reproducible activity for this unit in the *Teacher's Resource Book*.

Writing

Exercise ❽

- Assign the writing task for class work or homework.
- Explain the task: Students will write a paragraph to complete their application form for an Adventure Zone vacation.

- Brainstorm ideas for what they might include on the application.
- **TRB** Optionally, give students a copy of the model (see the *Teacher's Resource Book,* Writing Models). Ask them to read the model and notice the vocabulary and grammar from the unit.
- If students don't have the model, write the following on the board:

  I've gone snorkeling and scuba diving. I tried these sports when I was in Cancun in Mexico, and I really enjoyed them. I've gone jet skiing, too . . . .

- Walk around to make sure everyone understands the task.

For suggestions on how to give feedback on writing, see page xiv of this *Teacher's Edition.*

CONVERSATION TO GO

At the end of class, call on two students to role-play the conversation.

HOMEWORK

- 📖 Assign *Workbook* page 92, Grammar Exercises 3 and 4, and page 93, Pronunciation Exercises 7 and 8.
- Assign *Workbook* Self-Quiz 6.
- ⊙ If students do not have the *WorldView Workbook,* assign listening homework from the Student CD. Write on the board:

  Track 53
  What two sports does Andy want to try?

- 🎧 Tell students to listen to the audio and write the answer to the question. Have them bring their answer to the next class.

  (Answer: *scuba diving and windsurfing*)

FOR NEXT CLASS

- Tell students that the next class will be a review class covering Units 21–24.
- Have students review the material in the units to prepare for the activities in Review 6.
- **TRB** Make copies of Quiz 6 in the *Teacher's Resource Book.*

Unit no.	Review Grammar	Listen to Student CD	Study Grammar Reference
21	Present perfect: *how long/for/ since*	Track 47	Page 148
22	Modals for requests and offers	Track 48	Page 148
23	*used to/didn't use to*	Track 50	Page 148
24	Present perfect vs. simple past	Track 53	Page 148

Speaking

5 *BEFORE YOU SPEAK.* **Choose four adventure sports and write four more questions beginning with *Have you ever . . . .***

Have you ever gone waterskiing?

6 **Interview three students using your questions from Exercise 5. Take notes. Find out . . .**

- who has done these sports.
- who enjoyed/didn't enjoy them.
- who wants to try them.

- who has only watched them.
- what other sports they have done. (Were the sports dangerous?)

7 **Tell the class what you found out about one of your classmates' experience with sports.**

Writing

8 **Write a paragraph to complete your application form for an Adventure Zone vacation.**

APPLICATION

Where the fun never ends!

- **Please tell us about your experience with adventure sports.**
- **Which sports have you done?**
- **Which sports have you not done but want to try?**

CONVERSATION TO GO

A: **Have** you **ever done** any adventure sports?
B: Yes, I **went** snowboarding last week. It was fun!

Unit 21 Long life

1 🎧 Listen to the model conversation.

2 Write six statements about things you have done. Use the present perfect tense. Write some true statements, and make up some statements that are not true (but sound possible).

3 *GROUPS OF 3.* Take turns. Say one of your statements aloud. The others in the group say, "True" or "False." A correct guess = 1 point.

Points: _____

Who is the winner?

Unit 22 Job share

4 🎧 Listen to the model conversation.

5 Imagine that you are an administrative assistant in your language school. Make a list of six tasks that you need to do today.

TO DO

_____
_____
_____
_____
_____
_____

6 *PAIRS.* Role-play. You and your partner share the administrative assistant job. Combine the lists that you wrote in Exercise 5. Take turns. Offer to do some tasks. Ask your partner to do some tasks.

7 Change partners and repeat the role-play.

📼 You may wish to use the video for Units 21–24 at this point. For video activity worksheets, go to www.longman.com/worldview.

Unit 21: Long life

- Review the material presented in Unit 21
- Grammar practice: present perfect with *how long, for,* and *since*

WARM-UP

Books closed. Ask a few questions about how long students have done certain activities. For example, ask: *How long have you lived in this city? How long have you had your car?*

Exercise ❶

- Tell students they will listen to a conversation that models Exercise 3. Tell them to listen and decide whether the following statement is true or false: *The speaker has had a computer since last year.* (true)
- 🎧 Play the audio.

Exercise ❷

- Review the form of the present perfect: (*have/has* + past participle).
- Have students write six sentences about activities they have done using the present perfect tense. Tell them to include sentences that are not true.
- Set a time limit of 3 minutes. Walk around the room, helping as needed.

Exercise ❸

- Divide the class into groups of 3. Explain the task. The members of each group will take turns reading aloud their sentences. The other members will say if the sentence is true or false.
- 🎧 If needed, play the audio for Exercise 1 again.
- Remind each group to keep score. Walk around the room, helping as needed.

WRAP-UP

Invite students to share with the class any new information they learned about their group members.

Unit 22: Job share

- Review the material presented in Unit 22
- Grammar practice: modals for requests and offers

WARM-UP

Books closed. Ask a student this question: *Can someone give me a hand?* Wait for the student's response. If the student does not give the appropriate response, repeat the question, this time, adding more context: Pretend to lift something heavy (or any difficult task) and say: *Can someone give me a hand, please? I need help carrying this.* Ask: *What does "Can you give me a hand" mean?* (It is a request for help.)

Exercise ❹

- Tell students they will listen to a conversation that models Exercise 6. Tell them to listen and list at least three tasks that the two employees have to do. (*make copies, make coffee, return a phone call, send emails, make lunch reservations, do some filing*)
- 🎧 Play the audio.

Exercise ❺

- Encourage students to include on their lists tasks that they enjoy doing as well as ones they don't enjoy.
- Set a time limit of 2 minutes.

Exercise ❻

- Pair students. Explain the task. The partners will role-play the role of administrative assistants who share tasks. They will discuss how to divide the tasks.
- 🎧 If needed, play the audio again.
- As the pairs choose tasks, encourage them to explain why they prefer to do certain tasks rather than others. Walk around the room, helping as needed.

Exercise ❼

- Pair students with new partners and set a time limit of 4 minutes.
- Have the pairs role-play the same conversation.

WRAP-UP

Ask students to report to the class how they divided their workloads. Ask: *Did the pairs divide the tasks equally, or did some divide up the tasks according to the degree of difficulty or personal preferences? Did both partners think the division of tasks fair?*

Unit 23: Changing customs

- Review the material presented in Unit 23
- Grammar practice: *used to/didn't use to*

WARM-UP

Books closed. Invite students to share some things they used to do but no longer do now. For example, *I used to get nervous every time I went for a job interview. Now, I'm more relaxed.*

Exercise 8

- Tell students they will listen to a conversation that models Exercise 9.
- Write the following sentences on the board: 1. *Student A used to be short.* 2. *Student B used to talk in class a lot.* Have students listen to find out whether each sentence is true or false. (1. true; 2. false)
- 🎧 Play the audio.

Exercise 9

- Pair students. Explain the task. Each pair will play a game.
- Explain the mechanics for the game: Each pair needs a coin to toss and two markers. The markers can be any small object provided each student in the pair chooses a different marker. For example, they can be different coins, small pieces of paper with students' names, or small pieces of colored paper.
- Decide which side of the coin is worth one point for every correct sentence and which is worth two points.
- 🎧 If needed, play the audio for Exercise 8 again.
- Walk around the room, helping as needed.
- If time allows, have the pairs switch partners and play another round of the game.

WRAP-UP

Have students report to the class one activity that their partners used to do.

Unit 24: Take a risk

- Review the material presented in Unit 24
- Grammar practice: present perfect vs. simple past

WARM-UP

Books closed. Write a few activities on the board, such as *scuba diving, mountain climbing, skateboarding.* Take a quick poll about which activities students have done. (*Who has gone scuba diving? Who has gone mountain climbing? Who has skateboarded?*) Invite those who have to share their experience with the class.

Exercise 10

- Tell students they will listen to people take a survey. The survey models Exercise 12. Have students listen and find out which activity Mina has done. (*windsurfing*)
- 🎧 Play the audio.

Exercise 11

- Have students look at the list of adventure sports in the chart.
- Have them choose four sports and pretend that they have done these. Have them put check marks after the sports they choose.

Exercise 12

- Explain the task: Students will look for one person in the class who has done each activity.
- 🎧 Play the audio again for Exercise 10.

Exercise 13

- Have students compare their findings as a class.
- Invite volunteers to say which adventure sports they have actually done, if any.

Unit 23 Changing customs

8 🎧 Listen to the model conversation.

9 *PAIRS.* Take turns. Toss a coin (one side of the coin = one point, the other side = two points). Make sentences with a verb from the chart. Use *used to* + the verb to talk about something you used to do as a child, and say how it's different now. Keep score. The person with the most points is the winner.

Verb	_____'s points	_____'s points
be		
go		
have		
watch		
wear		
play		
think about		
TOTAL		

Unit 24 Take a risk

10 🎧 Listen to the model conversation.

11 Imagine that you are an extreme athlete. Put a check next to four sports in the second column in the chart. These are the sports you have done.

12 Walk around the room. Find out which sports your classmates have tried. Take turns. Ask *Yes/No* questions. When someone answers, "Yes, I have," write his or her name in the chart. Ask only one question each turn! Try to find one person for each sport.

Adventure sports	Your experience	Find someone who has gone...
1. snowboarding		
2. waterskiing		
3. scuba diving		
4. windsurfing		
5. skateboarding		
6. rock climbing		
7. jet skiing		
8. snowmobiling		

13 *PAIRS.* Compare your answers. Did you find the same people?

Real fighters

Vocabulary **Sports**
Grammar **could** and **be good at** for past ability
Speaking **Talking about ability in the past**

Getting started

1 Complete the chart with the missing words.

Person (noun)	Sport (noun)	Action (verb)
boxer	boxing	box
swimmer		
	running	
skier		
	diving	dive
		skate

2 *PAIRS.* Discuss the questions.

Which sports in Exercise 1 do you like to watch? Do you like to do any of these?

Do you know the names of any athletes who do the sports in Exercise 1?

What other athletes do you know? What sports do they do?

Reading

3 Look at the photos of the boxers. Guess who they are. What's the connection between them?

4 Read the article and check your answers to Exercise 3.

5 Read the article again. Write the events from Muhammad Ali's life on the timeline.

Float like a butterfly.
Sting like a bee.
Your hands can't hit
what your eyes can't see.

— *Muhammad Ali*

1942   1954   1960

Ali was born

Real fighters

OBJECTIVES

Students will:

- activate vocabulary related to sports
- do reading, speaking, and writing tasks related to talking about abilities in the past
- practice weak and strong pronunciations of *could* and strong pronunciation of *couldn't*

WARM-UP: CHARADES

Groups of 4. Students mime verbs used with sports.

- Tell students that this unit is about sports. Explain that the title of the unit, "Real fighters," refers to two people who became famous through the sport of boxing.
- Write these verbs on slips of paper: *box, swim, ski, run, dive, skate.*
- Tell students that they will take turns miming the verbs for the class to guess.
- Model the activity by miming a verb (for example, *dive*). Have the class guess the verb.
- Divide the class into groups of 4. Give each student a slip of paper and set a time limit of 1 minute.
- Call on a few volunteers to act out a verb, and have the class guess the sport.

Getting started

LANGUAGE NOTES

Review the spelling rules for adding *-ing* and *-er* to the base form of verbs:

- If the verb ends in a silent *e*, drop the *e* before adding *-ing.* Add only *-r* to form the *-er* ending.
- If a one-syllable verb ends in a consonant, a vowel, and a consonant (CVC), double the last consonant before adding *-ing* or *-er.* Do not double the last consonant if it is a *w, x,* or *y.*

OPTION: VOCABULARY PREVIEW

Remind students of the spelling rules for adding *–ing* and *–er* to the base form of verbs given in the Language Notes. Go over the example in Exercise 1. Write the word *box* on the board. Ask: *What kind of a word is* box? (an action word or a verb) *What ending do we add to refer to the person who boxes?* (*–er*) *What ending do we add to refer to the sport?* (*–ing*) Write the two spelling rules on the board and give examples for each.

Exercise ❶

- Explain the task: Students will complete the chart.
- Tell students to look at the words in each column. Ask what the words in each column have in common. (The nouns for people end in *–er,* the nouns for sports end in *–ing,* and the action words are in their base form.)

- Set a time limit of 5 minutes. While students are working, walk around the room, helping as needed.
- Have students compare their answers with a partner's.
- Go over the answers with the class.

Answer key

Person (noun)	Sport (noun)	Action (verb)
boxer	boxing	box
swimmer	swimming	swim
runner	running	run
skier	skiing	ski
diver	diving	dive
skater	skating	skate

Exercise ❷

- Tell students they will work in pairs to answer the questions.
- Pair students and set a time limit of 5 minutes. Walk around the room, helping as needed.
- Call on a few students to report their answers to the class.

Reading

Exercise ❸

- Tell students to look at the photos and answer the questions. Remind them that using visual clues can help them predict the content of a reading.
- Have students compare their answers with a partner's.
- Tell the class they will confirm their answers when they read the article.

Exercise ❹

- Tell students to read the article and confirm their answers to Exercise 3.
- Set a time limit of 5 minutes.
- Go over the answers to Exercise 3.

Answer key

1. The two boxers are Muhammad Ali and Laila Ali.
2. They are father and daughter.

[*See page T117 for Exercise 5*]

Exercise 5

- Explain the task: Students will reread the article and complete the timeline.
- Tell students that they should scan, or read quickly, to find the dates in the article and then locate the event.
- Set a time limit of 5 minutes. Walk around the room, helping as needed.
- Have students compare their answers with a partner's.
- Go over the answers with the class.

Answer key

1942	Cassius Clay was born.
1954	When he was twelve years old, he started boxing.
1960	He won the gold medal in boxing at the Olympics.
1964	He converted to Islam and changed his name to Muhammad Ali.
1984	Doctors found that Ali had Parkinson's disease.
1996	Ali lit the Olympic torch.

Exercise 6

- Explain the task: Students will read the poem and will discuss its meaning.
- Divide the class into groups of 3 and set a time limit of 3 minutes.
- Call on a few students to report their answers to the class.

◎ Please go to www.longman.com/worldview for additional in-class model conversation practice.

HOMEWORK

- 📖 Assign *Workbook* page 96, Vocabulary Exercises 1 and 2, and page 98, Listening Exercises 6 and 7.

Laila Ali is Muhammad Ali's daughter. In 1999, at the age of twenty, Laila began boxing. In four years, she won fourteen fights and proved that she could box. But she couldn't beat her father's reputation.

The Greatest

Muhammad Ali was "The Greatest." He was the first boxer to become the heavyweight champion of the world three times. Ali was born in 1942 and was named Cassius Clay. When he was twelve years old, he started boxing. Soon he was really good at boxing. He won the gold medal in boxing at the Olympics in 1960. In 1964, Clay converted to Islam and changed his name to Muhammad Ali.

People noticed more than Ali's boxing—they noticed his personality. He was smart, and he was good at getting media attention. He was famous for saying, "I am the greatest!" He was also a poet, and he could make up poems on any subject: himself, other boxers, and even politics.

As Ali got older, he began to have health problems. He couldn't speak very well or move quickly. In 1984, doctors found that he had Parkinson's disease. Although Ali wasn't able to box anymore, he still had many fans and he could still sign autographs. And he could still help people fight for a better world.

In 1996, the world watched Muhammad Ali light the Olympic torch in Atlanta, Georgia. He couldn't stop the shaking in his hands, but he showed once more that he was "The Greatest."

 GROUPS OF 3. Read the poem on page 116 by Muhammad Ali. He recited this poem to intimidate other boxers. What does it mean? Discuss.

1964   1984   1996

Grammar focus

1 Study the examples with *could* and *be good at*.

(+++)	Ali **could**		really well.	(+++)	Ali **was**	really		
(++)	They **could**		well.	(++)	They **were**			
(+)	Laila **could**	box	pretty well.	(+)	Laila **was**	pretty	good at	boxing.
(–)	We **couldn't**		very well.	(–)	We **weren't**	very		sports.
(– –)	He **couldn't**		at all.	(– –)	He **was**	no		

2 Look at the examples again. Circle the correct words to complete the rules in the chart.

Could and *be good at* for past ability
Could/couldn't is followed by **a noun / the base form of the verb**.
Be good at/not be good at is followed by **a noun / the base form of the verb**.

> *Grammar Reference page 149*

3 Complete the sentences about past ability with *could* or *be good at*. Use the words in parentheses.

1. Jane ___was really good at diving___, so she became a diving coach. (really good/diving)

2. Martin _____, so he joined the school swimming team. (swim/pretty well)

3. I _____ when I was young, but now I can play pretty well. (no good/playing the piano)

4. They _____, so they decided to take lessons. (play golf/not very well)

5. We _____, so we entered the salsa competition. (good/dancing)

6. My brother _____, so he used to go skiing every weekend. (really good/skiing)

7. She _____ before she hurt her knee. (run/fast)

8. I _____, so I didn't enjoy gym class at school. (not very good/sports)

9. He _____ when he got his first pair of boxing gloves. (box/not at all)

Pronunciation

4 🎧 Listen. Notice the different weak and strong pronunciations of *could*. Notice the strong pronunciation of *couldn't*.

Could you play the piano?	Yes, I could.
How well could you play?	I could play pretty well.
Could you ski?	No, I couldn't. I couldn't ski at all.

5 🎧 Listen again and repeat.

Grammar focus

LANGUAGE NOTES

- Use *could* to express ability in the past. *Couldn't* is the negative of *could*.
- *Be good at* is also used to talk about ability. Use *was* or *were* with *good at* to talk about past ability.
- To form the negative, use *wasn't/weren't + good at*. For example, *I wasn't good at boxing.*
- To make the negative form stronger, use *no* instead of *not*. For example, *I was no good at boxing.*

WARM-UP

NOTE: Skip this warm-up if you're doing this lesson (Lesson B) during the same class period as Lesson A.

- Books closed. Tell students they will listen to the article they read in the Reading section.
- Make two columns on the board: *could/couldn't* and *was good at*. Tell students to copy the words.
- Ask students to listen for and write down two things Muhammad Ali "could" do and two things he "was good at."
- 🎧 Play the audio from Lesson A, Reading, Exercise 4. (It models the grammar of the unit.)
- Call on students to tell the class their notes on Muhammad Ali's past abilities.

Exercise ❶

- Tell students to read the examples and study the bold-faced words. Point out the verbs and the adverbs in each.
- Tell students to study carefully how the verb in each sentence is formed.

Exercise ❷

- Have students study the examples again.
- Tell them to circle the words to complete the rules in the chart.
- Go over the answers with the class.
- Ask a few questions to elicit the key points about the grammar. For example, *What form follows could/couldn't?* (the base form of the verb) *What follows be good at?* (a noun) *What do the two structures describe?* (past ability)

Answer key

the base form   a noun

Exercise ❸

- Before students begin Exercise 3, answer any questions they might have. You may also want to refer the class to the Grammar Reference for Unit 25 on page 149.
- Explain the task: Students will complete the sentences with the words in parentheses.

- Go over the example. Ask students why they should use the expression *be good at.* (*diving* is a noun)
- Set a time limit of 10 minutes. Walk around the room, helping as needed.
- Have students compare their answers with a partner's.
- Go over the answers with the class.

Answer key

1. was really good at diving
2. could swim pretty well
3. was no good at playing the piano
4. couldn't play golf very well
5. were good at dancing
6. was really good at skiing
7. could run fast
8. wasn't very good at sports
9. couldn't box at all

Pronunciation

LANGUAGE NOTES

- *Could* has both a strong and a weak pronunciation.
- *Could* is usually unstressed and has its weak pronunciation when it is used in the middle of a sentence, for example, *I could* /kəd/ *play pretty well.* When it is used at the end of a sentence such as in short answers, *could* has a strong pronunciation, for example, *Yes, I could* /kʊd/. At the beginning of a *Yes/No* question, *could* can have either a weak or strong pronunciation, for example, *Could* /kəd/ *or* /kʊd/ *you ski?*
- When *could* comes before *you* in a question, the two words are often blended together and pronounced as "couldja" in informal conversation, for example, *How well could you* (/kədʒə/ *or* /kʊdʒa/) *play?*
- The negative *couldn't* always has a strong pronunciation, for example, *I couldn't* /kʊdnt/ *ski at all.*

Exercise ❹

- Tell students that they will listen to the different pronunciations of *could* and *couldn't.*
- 🎧 Play the audio. Call attention to the different colors used for the weak and strong pronunciations.
- Point out the blended pronunciation "couldja" in the three questions. Demonstrate the pronunciation by saying the words *could* and *you* by themselves first and then linking them together.

Exercise ❺

- Tell students that they will listen again. This time, they will listen and repeat.
- 🎧 Play the audio, stopping after each item and asking students to repeat it chorally.
- Ask pairs of students to say the questions and answers. Check their pronunciation.

Speaking

Exercise 6

This exercise will give students the opportunity to practice talking about past abilities. It also prepares them for Exercises 7 and 8.

- Explain the task: Students will add one past ability to the list and will complete the survey for themselves.

- Tell students to look at the examples in Exercise 1 and notice how the + and – signs are used. Point out that +++ means *really well*, whereas – – means *not at all*. Students will use + and – to indicate their past abilities.

- Model the activity by giving a personal example. For example, *Ten years ago I could swim really well.* Ask students what you should write under *how well*. (+++)

- Set a time limit of 5 minutes. Walk around the room, helping as needed.

Exercise 7

- Explain the task: Students will take turns interviewing a partner about their past abilities and will fill in the chart.

- Model the activity with a student. Write *swim* on the board. Read A's lines from the example and have the student read B's lines. Next to *swim*, write +.

- Pair students and set a time limit of 10 minutes. Walk around the room, helping as needed.

Exercise 8

- Copy the list from the chart on the board in a column (*swim, cook, drive, play an instrument, ride a bike, speak a foreign language*). Write headings across the top: +++, ++, +, –, – –.

- Call on students to report their partner's answers. Put tally marks under the appropriate headings.

TRB For additional interactive grammar practice, have students do the reproducible activity for this unit in the *Teacher's Resource Book*.

Writing

Exercise 9

- Assign the writing task for class work or homework.

- Explain the task: Students will write about a sport or other activity they could do in the past. They will describe the activity and how well they could do it.

- Brainstorm ideas of sports or other activities.

- **TRB** Optionally, give students a copy of the model (see the *Teacher's Resource Book*, Writing Models). Ask them to read the model and notice the vocabulary and grammar from the unit.

- If students don't have the model, write the following on the board:

  When I was a kid, I could sing really well. I could remember the lyrics of all the songs I liked, and I used to sing them all the time. I was also good at creating my own versions of songs—I sometimes created new lyrics, or did my own adaptations of the melody.

- Have a student read the sentences aloud. Answer any questions students might have.

- Walk around to make sure everyone understands the task.

For suggestions on how to give feedback on writing, see page xii of this *Teacher's Edition*.

CONVERSATION TO GO

At the end of class, call on two students to role-play the conversation.

HOMEWORK

- 📖 Assign *Workbook* page 97, Grammar Exercises 3, 4, and 5, and page 98, Pronunciation Exercises 8 and 9.

- 🔊 If students do not have the *WorldView Workbook*, assign listening homework from the Student CD. Write on the board:

  Track 54
  In what year did Cassius Clay become Muhammad Ali? Why did he change his name?

- 🎧 Tell students to listen to the audio and write the answers to the questions. Have them bring their answers to the next class.

  (Answers: *1964. He converted to Islam.*)

Speaking

6 *BEFORE YOU SPEAK.* **Complete the survey about your abilities ten years ago. Add one ability to the list. Use plus (+) and minus (–) signs as in Exercise 1 to show how well you could do each activity.**

PAST ABILITIES SURVEY

Ten years ago, could you . . .	YOU How well?	YOUR PARTNER How well?
swim?		
cook?		
drive?		
play an instrument?		
ride a bike?		
speak a foreign language?		
other? _____		

7 *PAIRS.* **Interview each other and complete the survey form. Give examples to show how well you could do each activity.**

A: *Could you swim ten years ago?*
B: *Yes, I could. I could swim pretty well.* (Or *I was pretty good at swimming.*)
I could swim a mile without stopping.

8 **Report your partner's answers to the class. Then discuss the results of the survey. Which things could everyone in the class do?**

Writing

9 **Write about a sport or another activity that you could do in the past. Describe the activity and give examples to show how well you could do it. Say whether you can still do it. Use *could* and *be good at*.**

CONVERSATION TO GO

A: Could you drive when you were in high school?
B: Yes, I could drive pretty well, but I couldn't afford a car!

UNIT 26

On the go

Vocabulary Travel
Grammar Present perfect: *yet, already*
Speaking Saying what you've done so far

Lesson A

Getting started

1 *PAIRS.* **Look at the picture. Find the words in the box.**

a bag/suitcase	a passport	a pillow	slippers
a teddy bear	a tennis racket	a ticket	a video

2 *PAIRS.* **Look at the picture again. Which things in the picture do you take with you when you travel? Which things do you leave at home? What other things do you take?**

On the go

OBJECTIVES

Students will:

- activate vocabulary related to travel
- do listening, speaking, and writing tasks related to talking about what they've done so far
- focus on using the present perfect with *yet* and *already*
- practice using contracted forms of *have* and *has*

WARM-UP: I NEVER LEAVE HOME WITHOUT . . .

Groups of 3. Students talk about what they always take with them when they leave home.

- Tell students this unit is about travel. Tell them the title of the unit, "On the go," is an expression that means "very busy or moving all the time." Here, it is used in the context of traveling.
- Write the following sentence stem on the board and ask students to complete it in their own words: *I never leave home without . . . .*
- Model the activity with a personal example. (For example, *I never leave home without my wallet.*)
- Divide students in groups of 3 and set a time limit of 2 minutes. Tell each group to finish the sentence.
- Call on a few students to report on their group members' answers. (For example, *Rosie never leaves home without her cell phone, and Paulo never leaves home without his car keys.*)

Getting started

OPTION: VOCABULARY PREVIEW

Write the words in Exercise 1 on the board. Read each word aloud and have students listen and repeat. Call on individual students to put a check next to the items that are needed when traveling. (bag/suitcase, passport, ticket) Point to each of the other words on the board and ask: *Where or when do you use/need this object?*

Exercise ❶

- **Pairs.** Tell students to look at the picture of the bedroom.
- Explain the task: In pairs, students will take turns finding the vocabulary words in the picture.
- Model the activity. Ask a student to point to *a bag* or *suitcase* in the picture.
- Pair students and set a time limit of 2 minutes. While students are working, walk around the room, helping as needed.
- Go over the answers with the class.

Answer key

The bag or suitcase is the brown open case on the bed. The teddy bear is the yellow stuffed animal on the chair in the corner. The passport is on the bed, to the right of the bag/suitcase. The tennis racket is on the floor of the closet/wardrobe. The pillow is at the head of the bed. The ticket is on the bed, just above the passport. The slippers are on the floor, near the foot of the bed. The video is on the dresser, next to the camera.

EXTENSION

Reinforce the vocabulary by calling out a word from Exercise 1. Tell students to point to the object in the picture.

Exercise ❷

- Explain the task: Students will look at the picture again and will answer the questions in pairs.
- Have students read the questions.
- Pair students and set a time limit of 3 minutes.
- Call on a few students to report their answers to the class.

EXTENSION

- Pair students. Tell them to list at least one thing they can do with each item.
- Encourage them to think of unusual as well as the typical uses of the item. (For example, *I can use the bag or suitcase to sit on.*)
- After 3 minutes, call on students to share their ideas.
- Have the class vote on the most creative use of an item.

Exercise ❸

- Explain the task: Students will write the letter of the phrase next to the sentence it completes. Encourage students to focus on the verb + noun combinations. The exception is *go online*, which is a verb + adverb combination.
- Go over the example.
- Have students work individually. Set a time limit of 3 minutes.
- Have students compare their answers with a partner's.
- Go over the answers with the class.
- Answer any questions students may have about the new vocabulary. Clarify meaning as necessary and/or allow students to use their dictionaries.

OPTION

Have students complete the task in pairs or small groups.

Answer key

1. b	3. e	5. h	7. f
2. a	4. g	6. d	8. c

EXTENSION

Check understanding of the vocabulary by asking volunteers to create their own sentences using the phrases in Exercise 3.

Listening

Exercise ❹

- Tell students to look at the picture of Melissa.
- Explain the task: Students will listen to a conversation between Melissa and her friend. Tell them to circle *a* or *b* to answer the questions.
- Before you play the audio, tell students to read the questions first so they know what information to listen for.
- 🎧 Play the audio.
- Have students compare their answers with a partner's.
- Go over the answers with the class.

Answer key

1. a	2. b	3. b

Exercise ❺

- Explain the task: Students will listen again and check the travel preparations Melissa has completed.
- Have the students read the To-do list so they know what to pay attention to when listening again.
- 🎧 Play the audio.
- Have students compare their answers with a partner's.
- Go over the answers with the class.

Answer key

Check: sell the car, get my vaccinations, renew my passport, buy an airline ticket, make a hotel reservation

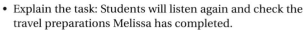 Please go to www.longman.com/worldview for additional in-class model conversation practice supplementary reading practice.

HOMEWORK

- 📖 Assign *Workbook* page 99, Vocabulary Exercises 1 and 2, and page 101, Listening Exercises 5 and 6.

3 Match the beginnings of the sentences on the left with the correct endings on the right.

1. Go to the embassy and **apply for** _b_

2. She'll have to **renew** ____

3. I'm waiting for the bank to **transfer** ___

4. Tell the doctor that you need to **get** ___

5. I'll fold the clothes, but you **pack** ____

6. I'll call the travel agency and **book** ____

7. I sometimes call the airline directly, but most of the time I **go**____

8. We plan to drive around the country so we're going to **rent** ____

a. **her passport** soon.

b. **a visa** to enter the country.

c. **a car**.

d. **a hotel** room.

e. **the money**.

f. **online** to buy my tickets.

g. **a vaccination** against cholera.

h. **the bags**.

Listening

4 🎧 **Melissa is getting ready to go on a trip. Listen to her conversation with a friend. Circle *a* or *b* to answer the questions.**

1. When is Melissa going to travel?
   a. next week   b. the week after next
2. Where is she going?
   a. to Cairo   b. to Quito
3. What is she going to do there?
   a. relax   b. work

5 🎧 **Listen again. Look at the list and check (✓) the travel preparations Melissa has completed.**

TO-DO LIST
- sell the car ✓
- transfer the money
- get my vaccinations
- renew my passport
- apply for a visa
- buy an airline ticket
- make a hotel reservation
- pack my bags

Grammar focus

1 **Study the examples of the present perfect with *yet* and *already*.**

> **(?)** **Have** you **sold** the car **yet**? Yes, I **have**. / No, **not yet**.
> **(+)** I've **already made** a reservation.
> **(–)** She **hasn't called** back **yet**.

2 **Look at the examples again. Complete the rules in the chart with *yet, not yet*, or *already*.**

> **Present perfect: *yet, already***
>
> Use the present perfect + _____ when an action is complete.
>
> Use the present perfect + _____ when an action is not complete, but we think it will happen.
>
> Use the present perfect + _____ to ask if an action is complete.

> *Grammar Reference page 149*

3 **Complete the phone conversation with *already* or *yet*.**

Mom: Hi, Melissa. Have you finished packing for your trip **(1)** _yet_?

Melissa: No, not **(2)** _____. But I've gotten my visa **(3)** _____.

Mom: Good. Have you sent me your new email address **(4)** _____?

Melissa: Yes, Mom. And I've **(5)** _____ sent you my new phone number at work.

Mom: Great. Have you called your grandfather **(6)** _____ to say goodbye?

Melissa: No, I haven't called him **(7)** _____. But I've **(8)** _____ called Aunt Rose.

Mom: OK. I've **(9)** _____ emailed my boss that I'll need to take the afternoon off to take you to the airport. He hasn't said OK **(10)** _____, but I'm sure he will.

Pronunciation

4 🎧 **Listen. Notice the contracted forms of *have* and *has*.**

I**'ve** already sold the car.	She**'s** already sold the car.
I**'ve** called my aunt.	She**'s** called her aunt.
I**'ve** gotten a visa.	She**'s** gotten a visa.
I**'ve** changed my email address.	She**'s** changed her email address.

5 🎧 **Listen again and repeat.**

6 *PAIRS.* **Look at Melissa's list on page 121. Take turns making statements about the things Melissa has done. Use contracted forms.**

Grammar focus

LANGUAGE NOTES

- Use the present perfect with *already* to talk about things that have happened before now. *Already* usually comes between *have* and the past participle. *Already* can also come at the end of the clause. For example, *We've already eaten. / We've eaten already.*

- Use the present perfect with *not yet* to talk about things that have not happened before now. *Yet* usually comes at the end of the clause; it can also come between *have not* and the past participle. For example, *We haven't eaten yet. / We haven't yet eaten.*

- Use *yet* in questions to ask if something has happened before now. For example, *Have you eaten yet?*

- Use *already* in a question to express surprise that something happened sooner than expected. For example, *Have they left already?*

WARM-UP

Note: Skip this warm-up if you're doing this lesson (Lesson B) during the same class period as Lesson A.

- Books closed. Tell students they will listen again to the conversation that they heard in the Listening section.

- Have students copy these: *Have you sold it _____? She hasn't called back _____. I've _____ bought my ticket.*

- Explain the task: Students will listen for the sentences and will complete them with *yet* or *already*.

- 🎧 Play the audio from Lesson A, Listening, Exercise 4. (It models the grammar of the unit.)

- Call on individual students to read aloud the completed sentences.

Exercise ❶

- Have students read the examples and study the bold-faced words. Point out or elicit that *yet* is used in the question and the negative statement, and *already* is used in the affirmative statement.

- Have students think what the meanings of *yet* and *already* are in present perfect structures.

Exercise ❷

- Have students study the examples again.
- Tell them to complete the rules in the chart.
- Have students compare their answers with a partner's.
- Go over the answers with the class.
- Ask questions to elicit the key points about the grammar: For example, *What word do we usually use in present perfect questions to ask if an action is complete?* (yet) *Where does the word go in the question?* (at the end)

Answer key

already	not yet	yet

Exercise ❸

- Before students begin Exercise 3, answer any questions they might have. You may also want to refer the class to the Grammar Reference for Unit 26 on page 149.

- Tell students to complete the conversation with *already* or *yet*.

- Go over the example.

- Set a time limit of 5 minutes. Walk around the room, helping as needed.

- Have students compare their answers with a partner's.

- Go over the answers with the class.

Answer key

1. yet	5. already	8. already
2. yet	6. yet	9. already
3. already	7. yet	10. yet
4. yet		

Pronunciation

Teaching Tip! Using visuals to teach contraction

To visually demonstrate the way two words are contracted, hold up a piece of paper with the full form *I have* or *She has* written out. Then fold the paper so that the *ha* in *have* or *has* is covered.

Exercise ❹

- Explain that English speakers generally use contractions rather than full forms when they speak. Tell students that they will listen to the pronunciation of contractions.

- 🎧 Play the audio.

- Demonstrate the difference between the full and contracted forms by saying some of the sentences twice, once with the full form and then with the contraction.

Exercise ❺

- Tell students that they will listen again. This time, they will listen and repeat.

- 🎧 Play the audio again, stopping after each item and asking students to repeat it chorally. Or divide the class and have half the class say the sentences on the left and the other half say the sentences on the right.

- Ask a few individual students to say the sentences. Check their pronunciation.

Exercise ❻

- Explain the task: Students will look at Melissa's list on page 121 and the items they checked for Lesson A, Listening, Exercise 5. They will take turns naming the things Melissa has done.

- Pair students and set a time limit of 2 minutes. Remind students to use contractions.

- Walk around the room, helping as needed.

- Call on several pairs to present to the class some of their statements about Melissa's plans.

Speaking

Exercise 7

This exercise provides opportunity for students to talk about things they have already done and prepares students for Exercise 8.

- **Groups of 3.** Explain the task: Students will imagine that they are going on a business trip with two other coworkers. Each coworker will check two things they have already done on their To-do lists.
- Have students read the To-do lists. Make sure they understand all the tasks on the lists.
- Divide the class in groups of 3. Assign or have them choose roles: Student A, Student B, or Student C.
- Have students work individually. Tell them to check off two things that they have done. Remind them not to show their lists to their classmates.
- Set a time limit of 2 minutes.

Exercise 8

- Explain the task: Students stay in their groups. They will discuss what they have and have not done on their lists, using *already, yet,* and *not yet.* Tell them to make a list of things that no one has done yet and decide who will do them and when.
- Model the activity with a student. Have the student read A's question in the example. Demonstrate how to answer, using the present perfect. (For example, *No, not yet. I'll do it tomorrow.*) Add a question (for example, *Have you gotten the visas yet?*), and elicit an appropriate response from the student (for example, *No, I haven't.*). If the answer is *no,* discuss who will do it and when. (For example, *Are you going to get the visas, or should I?*)
- Set a time limit of 10 minutes. Walk around the room, helping as needed.

Exercise 9

- Explain the task: Each group will choose a representative to report on their discussions.
- Go over the example.
- Call on a representative from each group to report on the things their group has and hasn't done.

TRB For additional interactive grammar practice, have students do the reproducible activity for this unit in the *Teacher's Resource Book.*

Writing

Exercise 10

- Assign the writing task for class work or homework.
- Explain the task: Students will write about an important goal and the things they have and haven't done yet to reach that goal.
- Brainstorm goals that students might have and possible steps for reaching those goals.
- **TRB** Optionally, give students a copy of the model (see the *Teacher's Resource Book,* Writing Models). Ask them to read the model and notice the vocabulary and grammar from the unit.
- If students don't have the model, write the following on the board:

    I'm going on vacation next week, and I still have lots of things to do! I'm going to Australia. I've never been there before, so I'm really excited about the trip. I've already bought my airline ticket and made a hotel reservation for the first week.

- Have a student read the sentences aloud. Answer any questions students might have.
- Walk around to make sure everyone understands the task.

For suggestions on how to give feedback on writing, see page xiv of this *Teacher's Edition.*

CONVERSATION TO GO

At the end of class, call on two students to role-play the conversation.

HOMEWORK

- 📖 Assign *Workbook* page 100, Grammar Exercises 3 and 4, and page 101, Pronunciation Exercises 7 and 8.
- 🌐 If students do not have the *WorldView Workbook,* assign listening homework from the Student CD. Write on the board:

    Track 56
    Where is Melissa going to live during her first week in Quito?

- 🎧 Tell students to listen to the audio and write the answer to the question. Have them bring their answer to the next class.

    (Answer: *She's going to stay at a hotel.*)

Speaking

7 *GROUPS OF 3.* **You all work for Matrix International. You're going on a business trip to Spain. Decide who are Students A, B, and C. Look at your To-Do list. Work alone. Check (✓) two things that you've already done.**

Student A TO DO	Student B TO DO	Student C TO DO
- arrange meetings in Spain	- make the hotel reservations	- buy a guidebook
- get the visas	- rent a car	- get travel insurance
- change some money	- get an international driver's license	- tell co-workers about the trip
- book a taxi to the airport	- go online to buy the airline tickets	- make dinner reservations for the first night

8 *GROUPS OF 3.* **Take turns. Ask each other *Yes/No* questions about the things on the list in Exercise 7. Check (✓) the completed activities. Write notes about when your partners will do the other ones.**

A: Have you made the hotel reservations yet?
B: Yes, I have. OR No, not yet. I'll do it tomorrow.

9 **Report to the class about some of the things your group has and hasn't done.**

John hasn't made the hotel reservations yet, but he's going to make them on Friday.

Writing

10 **Think of an important goal you have, such as graduating from school or living in another country. Write about things you have already done to reach your goal and things you haven't done yet.**

CONVERSATION TO GO

A: **Have** you **bought** the tickets **yet**?
B: No, I **haven't done** that **yet**, but I**'ve already done** everything else!

Behave yourself

Vocabulary Verbs and their opposites
Grammar Present factual conditional (*If* + simple present + simple present)
Speaking Talking about consequences

Getting started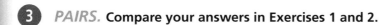

1 Match the verbs on the left with the verbs on the right that have the opposite or nearly opposite meaning.

1. cancel _b_
2. lose ____
3. borrow ____
4. refuse to ____
5. remember ____
6. push ____

a. agree to
b. schedule
c. pull
d. forget
e. lend
f. find

How do you behave?

1 If you forget a friend's birthday, do you:
   A send a card right away and say the mail is slow?
   B send a card and apologize for forgetting?
   C send no card and say it got lost in the mail?

2 Complete each sentence with a verb from Exercise 1.

1. I'm going to use the stairs. I _refuse to_ wait any longer for the elevator.
2. Can I _____ your pen, please?
3. You have to _____ the door away from you to close it.
4. Did he _____ his keys again?
5. I'm really pleased that they always _____ my birthday.
6. I'm sorry, but I have to _____ our meeting today.

3 *PAIRS.* Compare your answers in Exercises 1 and 2.

Behave yourself

OBJECTIVES

Students will:

- activate vocabulary related to verbs and their opposites
- do reading, speaking, and writing tasks related to talking about consequences
- focus on the present real conditional (*if* + simple present + simple present)
- practice different vowel sounds

WARM-UP: OPPOSITES ATTRACT!

Students participate in a speed drill focused on opposites.

- Tell students that this unit is about behavior and consequences. Explain that the title of the unit, "Behave yourself," is an expression used to tell someone to act properly.
- Explain that in this unit, students will focus on verbs that are opposite in meaning. To get them thinking about opposites, play a speed drill.
- Toss a ball or beanbag to a student and say a word that has an opposite such as *hot*. Elicit the opposite. (*cold*) That student can then say a word and toss the ball to another student. Repeat until all the students have had a chance to call out a word.

Getting started

OPTION: VOCABULARY PREVIEW

Tell students to look at the words in Exercise 1. Ask a leading question for each word to test students' understanding of the word. For example, for the word *cancel*, ask: *What things do you usually cancel?* (an appointment, a game, a date, an order) Write the answers for each word on the board. Encourage students to use their dictionaries, so they can answer your questions.

Exercise ❶

- Explain the task: Students will write the letter of each verb on the right next to its opposite—or nearly opposite meaning—on the left. Go over the example.
- Have students work individually to complete the exercise. Set a time limit of 2 minutes.
- Tell students they will check their answers in Exercise 3.

Exercise ❷

- Tell students to complete the sentences with the verbs from Exercise 1.
- Go over the example.
- Set a time limit of 2 minutes. While students are working, walk around the room, helping as needed.
- Again, tell students they will check their answers in the next exercise.

Exercise ❸

- Pair students. Have them compare their answers to Exercises 1 and 2.
- Set a time limit of 3 minutes.
- Go over the answers with the class.
- If time allows, find out if there were items partners disagreed on.

Answer key

Exercise 1

1. b	3. e	5. d
2. f	4. a	6. c

Exercise 2

1. refuse to	4. lose
2. borrow	5. remember
3. push	6. cancel

Reading

Exercise ❹

- Have students look at the reading. Ask: *What type of reading is it?* (It's a quiz.) *Where would you see this kind of quiz?* (in a magazine)
- Tell students to read the quiz and mark their answers.
- Set a time limit of 2 minutes. Walk around the room, helping as needed.
- Tell students to check the answer key at the bottom of the quiz to see if they have good manners. Remind students not to take the results too seriously. This is meant to be a fun activity—not a judgment on their characters!

Exercise ❺

- Tell students they will guess their partner's answers and then compare their results.
- Pair the students and set a time limit of 3 minutes.
- Call on a few students to talk about the differences in their reactions to the situations described in the quiz.

Pronunciation

> ### LANGUAGE NOTES
>
> - Students often have difficulty with the sounds /ɪ/ as in *give* and /ɛ/ as in *get*.
> - For the sound /ɪ/, the tongue is pushed forward a little and the mouth is slightly open. The lips are not spread.
> - For the sound /ɛ/, the tongue is raised high and pushed more toward the front of the mouth. The lips are spread in a smiling position. Tell students to focus on relaxing the muscles in their mouths (tongue and lips).
> - For the sound /ɛ/, the mouth is a little more open than for /ɪ/. For /ɛ/, the tongue is in a mid position, but slightly lower than for /ɪ/. The tongue does not glide up, as it does in pronouncing /ɪ/. The muscles of the lips and tongue are more relaxed for /ɛ/ than they are for /ɪ/.

Exercise ❻

- Tell students they will listen to the different pronunciations of *i* in *give* and *e* in *forget*.
- 🎧 Play the audio.
- Model the pronunciation of the two sounds, demonstrating the shape of the mouth.
- Point out the spellings. The sound /ɪ/ is usually spelled with the letter *i*. Spellings for the sound /ɛ/ usually include the letter *e*.

Exercise ❼

- Tell students they will listen again. This time, they will listen and repeat.
- 🎧 Play the audio again, stopping after each item to allow students to repeat chorally.
- Ask individual students to repeat. Check their pronunciation.
- If students pronounce the vowel /ɛ/ more like /ɪ/, remind them to open their mouths a little more. If students pronounce the vowel /ɪ/ more like /ɛ/, remind them to close their mouths just a little.

💿 Please go to www.longman.com/worldview for additional in-class model conversation practice.

HOMEWORK

- 📖 Assign *Workbook* page 102, Vocabulary Exercises 1 and 2, and page 104, Listening Exercise 5.

Reading

4 Do you have good manners? Take the quiz. Then check the answers in the key below.

5 *PAIRS.* Read the quiz again and guess your partner's answers. Compare your answers with your partner's answers. Who has better manners?

2 **If someone pushes a shopping cart in front of you in the supermarket, do you:**

A give the person an angry look but say nothing?

B ask the person to please stop?

C push the cart back at the person?

3 **If a friend gives you a gift you really don't like, do you:**

A take it but never use it?

B take it but use it only when your friend is there?

C take it but give it to someone else?

4 **If a friend borrows money from you and forgets to pay you back, do you:**

A tell your friend that you need some money and hope he or she remembers?

B ask your friend for the money?

C refuse to talk to your friend until you get the money?

5 **A friend cancels a night out with you, saying she has to work. If you see the friend later that evening at the movie theater, do you:**

A say nothing?

B ask your friend why she isn't at work?

C refuse to go out with your friend again?

Mainly A answers: You behave quite well but you aren't always honest.   Mainly B answers: You behave very well.   Mainly C answers: You don't behave very well at all. Try harder!

KEY

Pronunciation

6 🎧 Listen. Notice the different vowel sounds for /ɪ/ in *give*, and /ɛ/ in *forget*.

/ɪ/	g**i**ve	g**i**ft	**i**f	**i**t
/ɛ/	forg**e**t	fri**e**nd	rem**e**mber	n**e**ver

I give him a gift   If I remember, I give him a gift.

I send it later.   If I forget, I send it later.

I never give it away.   If I get a gift from a friend, I never give it away.

7 🎧 Listen again and repeat.

Grammar focus

1 **Study the examples of the present real conditional.**

If clause	Result clause
(+) If I **forget** a friend's birthday,	I **send** a card later.
(–) If I **don't remember** a friend's birthday,	I **don't send** a card.
(?) If you **forget** a friend's birthday,	**do** you **say** you are sorry?

2 **Look at the examples again. Circle the correct letters to complete the chart.**

Present real conditional
The action in the result clause _____ the action in the *if* clause.
a. depends on   b. doesn't depend on
Use the simple present in _____.
a. the *if* clause   b. the result clause   c. both clauses
NOTE: Use a comma after the *if* clause when the *if* clause comes first.

> *Grammar Reference page 149*

3 **Complete the present real conditional sentences with the correct forms of the verbs in parentheses.**

1. If he _forgets_ (**forget**) his wife's birthday, he __buys__ (**buy**) her flowers the next day.

2. If my sister _____ (**borrow**) my car, I _____ (**take**) the bus to work.

3. If the weather _____ (**be**) bad, they _____ (**not go**) away for the weekend.

4. If someone _____ (**speak**) very loudly on the train, I _____ (**get**) angry.

5. If he _____ (**not/come**) home at 10:00, his mother _____ (**call**) his friends.

6. If I _____ (**not/have**) enough money, I _____ (**borrow**) some from my friends.

7. If his friends _____ (**ask**) him, _____ (**he/lend**) them his car?

Grammar focus

LANGUAGE NOTES

- Use the present real conditional to talk about general truths and scientific facts.
- The *if* clause talks about the condition; the result clause talks about what happens if the condition occurs.
- Use the simple present tense in both clauses.
- Also use the present real conditional to talk about habits and recurring events.
- The word *if* usually has a weak pronunciation and is linked to the word after it. In the *if* clause, the voice goes up in pitch on the most important word and then falls just a little or falls and then rises slightly. In the result clause, the voice goes up on the important word and then falls to a low note, indicating that the speaker has finished the sentence.

WARM-UP

Note: Skip this warm-up if you're doing this lesson (Lesson B) during the same class period as Lesson A.

- Books closed. Tell students they will listen to the quiz they read in the Reading section.
- Tell them to listen for the word that begins the first four items in the reading.
- 🎧 Play the audio from Lesson A, Reading, Exercise 4. (It models the grammar of the unit.)
- Ask students what word they heard at the beginning of items 1 through 4. (*If*) Call on students to say what they remember about the sentences. Ask: *What verb tense follows* If *in these sentences?* (simple present)

Exercise ❶

- Have students read the three examples and study the bold-faced words.
- Ask: *What are the first clauses called?* (*if* clauses) *And the second clauses?* (result clauses)

Exercise ❷

- Have students study the examples again.
- Tell students to look at the examples and circle the letter of the correct information to complete the rules in the chart.
- Have students compare their answers with a partner's.
- Go over the answers with the class.
- Ask a few questions to elicit the key points about the grammar: *What tense is used in the* if *clause?* (the simple present) *What tense is used in the result clause?* (the simple present) *What do we use after the* if *clause when it begins a sentence?* (a comma)

Answer key

a. (depends on); c. both clauses

Exercise ❸

- Before students begin Exercise 3, answer any questions they might have. You may also want to refer the class to the Grammar Reference for Unit 27 on page 149.
- Explain the task: Students will complete the sentences with the correct forms of the verbs in parentheses.
- Have students complete the exercise individually. Set a time limit of 5 minutes. Walk around the room, helping as needed.
- Have students compare their answers with a partner's.
- Go over the answers with the class.

Answer key

1. forgets; buys
2. borrows; take
3. is; don't go
4. speaks; get
5. doesn't come; calls
6. don't have; borrow
7. ask; does he lend

EXTENSION

- Pair students. Tell them to write only the *if* clause for three present real conditional sentences. (For example, *If I save money regularly, . . . ; If it rains very hard, . . . ; If they are really busy, . . .*)
- Have them exchange sentences with a partner and complete each sentence. (For example, *If I save money regularly, I can travel during the summer. If it rains very hard, the basement gets flooded. If they are really busy, they eat out.*)

Speaking

Exercise ❹

This exercise will give students the opportunity to practice using present real conditionals. It also prepares them for Exercise 5.

- Explain the task: Students will work in pairs. They will create a quiz like the one in the Reading section. Remind students to focus on situations that may demonstrate good manners (for example, while shopping, in a restaurant, at home, with friends). Tell them to write three questions and three possible answers for each question.

- Pair students and set a time limit of 10 minutes. Walk around the room, helping as needed.

Exercise ❺

- Explain the task: Students will work in groups of 4. They take turns asking and answering the questions in their quizzes.

- Tell students that each student in the group should ask at least one question of the other pair of students.

- Have two volunteers read the example in the *Student Book* to model the activity.

- Divide the class into groups of 4. Set a time limit of 10 minutes.

- Call on a few students to report on the results of the quiz to the class.

EXTENSION

- To give the students more oral practice, subdivide each group of 4 so that one person from each previous pair is now paired with a new partner.

- Tell them to ask and answer all three questions in their partner's quiz.

TRB For additional interactive grammar practice, have students do the reproducible activity for this unit in the *Teacher's Resource Book.*

Writing

Exercise ❻

- Assign the writing task for class work or homework.

- Explain the task: Students will choose a situation from the quiz on pages 124–125 or their own quiz and write a paragraph describing what they do in that situation. They should also explain their behavior. Remind them to use the present real conditional.

- Using examples of situations from the quizzes, brainstorm reasons for behaving in a particular way.

- **TRB** Optionally, give students a copy of the model (see the *Teacher's Resource Book,* Writing Models). Ask them to read the model and notice the vocabulary and grammar from the unit.

- If students don't have the model, write the following on the board:

  If I forget a friend's birthday, I don't send a card because it takes a couple of days for the card to arrive. I call my friend right away or I send an email, and I apologize for forgetting.

- Have a student read the sentences aloud. Answer any questions students might have.

- Walk around to make sure everyone understands the task.

For suggestions on how to give feedback on writing, see page xiv of this *Teacher's Edition.*

CONVERSATION TO GO

At the end of class, call on two students to role-play the conversation.

HOMEWORK

- 📖 Assign *Workbook* page 103, Grammar Exercises 3 and 4, and page 104, Pronunciation Exercises 6 and 7.

- 🎧 If students do not have the *WorldView Workbook,* assign listening homework from the Student CD. Write on the board:

  Track 58
  Circle the letter of the answer you think is the worst or the rudest behavior.

  1. a   b   c
  2. a   b   c
  3. a   b   c
  4. a   b   c
  5. a   b   c

- 🎧 Tell students to listen to the audio and circle the letter of the answer to each item. Have them bring their answers to the next class.

  (Answers: *Most students will probably identify choice c in each item as the rudest behavior.*)

Speaking

4 *PAIRS.* **Think about situations that happen while people are shopping, at a restaurant, at home, or with friends. Write three questions. Begin each one with** *If . . . ?* **and give three choices in the result clause.**

1 If <u>The waiter or waitress brings you the wrong food</u> **, do you:**
A. <u>say nothing but feel angry</u> **?**
B. <u>remind the waiter or waitress what you ordered</u> **?**
C. <u>refuse to eat anything</u> **?**

2 If _____ **, do you:**
A. _____ **?**
B. _____ **?**
C. _____ **?**

3 If _____ **, do you:**
A. _____ **?**
B. _____ **?**
C. _____ **?**

4 If _____ **, do you:**
A. _____ **?**
B. _____ **?**
C. _____ **?**

5 *GROUPS OF 4.* **Take turns asking and answering the questions in your quiz. Do your classmates have good manners?**

Writing

6 **Choose a situation from the quiz on pages 124–125 or from your own quiz above. Write a paragraph describing what you do if you are in that situation. Also explain why you behave that way. Use the present real conditional.**

CONVERSATION TO GO

A: What **do** you **do if** your boss **asks** you to work late?
B: **If I want** to keep my job, I **stay** to finish the work!

Just the job for you

Vocabulary Job descriptions
Grammar *like* + verb + *-ing*, *would like* + infinitive
Speaking Talking about jobs and career preferences

Lesson A

Getting started

1 *PAIRS.* **Look at the photos. Use these phrases to make two sentences describing each job.**

- be active
- be creative
- earn a good salary
- have a lot of responsibility
- travel a lot
- work alone
- work inside
- work outdoors
- work with animals
- work with his/her hands
- work with people
- work with technology

A: *A farmer works outdoors.*
B: *A farmer also works with animals.*

farmer

computer trainer

chef

market researcher

mechanic

airline pilot

Just the job for you

OBJECTIVES

Students will:

- activate vocabulary related to job descriptions
- do reading, speaking, and writing tasks related to talking about jobs and career preferences
- focus on using *like* + verb + *-ing, would like* + infinitive
- practice different vowel sounds

WARM-UP: MORE JOB TALK

Groups of 3. Students talk about jobs.

- Tell students that this unit is about jobs and career preferences.
- Explain that the title of the unit, "Just the job for you," is an expression that means "the job is perfect for you."
- Tell students they will take turns saying one thing about a job they have now or a job they had before. If they have never had a job, they can describe a job a friend or a relative has or had.
- Clarify the task by giving a personal example. (For example, *My sister takes food orders and serves customers. She's a waitress.*)
- Divide the class into groups of 3 and set a time limit of 2 minutes.
- Call on a few students to describe a job.

Getting started

OPTION: VOCABULARY PREVIEW

Have students look at the phrases in Exercise 1. Ask: *What do you think these phrases describe?* (They describe some jobs.) Tell students that you will read aloud each of these descriptions and that they will call out a job that fits the description. Call out "be active" and ask the class what job can be described as active. (an athlete, a teacher, a farmer, a chef, a mechanic) Encourage students to explain why they think a job fits a particular description by giving further information about that job.

Exercise ❶

- Tell students to look at the photos.
- Explain the task: In pairs, students will take turns describing each job in the photos. They will each make one sentence about each job using the phrases.
- Go over the example.
- Pair students and set a time limit of 3 minutes. While students are working, walk around the room, helping as needed.
- Call on a few students to describe the jobs in the photos.

Answer key

(Possible answers)
A farmer works outdoors.
A farmer works with animals.
A computer trainer works with people.
A computer trainer works with technology.
A chef is creative.
A chef has a lot of responsibility.
A market researcher earns a good salary.
A market researcher works with people.
A mechanic works with his or her hands.
A mechanic works alone.
An airline pilot travels a lot.
An airline pilot has a lot of responsibility.

EXTENSION

- Expand on the list of phrases describing jobs. Ask the class to brainstorm other ways to talk about people's work. (For example, *entertain people, help people, use the Internet, have a stressful job, teach.*)
- Then ask volunteers to make sentences with the phrases. (For example, *An actor entertains people. A doctor helps people. A researcher uses the Internet. A professor teaches.*)

Pronunciation

LANGUAGE NOTES

- In American English, vowel sounds before *r* are pronounced with the tip of the tongue curled up toward the roof of the mouth and the body of the tongue pulled back slightly.

- Many students have trouble with the /ɚ/ sound in *work* and *earn,* often confusing it with other vowel sounds before *r*. To make the sound /ɚ/, the tongue is pulled back a little and bunched up. The tip of the tongue turns up, but does not touch the roof of the mouth. The lips are slightly rounded.

- The sound /ɚ/ is unstressed (shorter and weaker) in the last syllable of the words *computer* and *researcher*.

- The sound /ɚ/ can be spelled with almost any vowel letters + *r*, for example, *perfect, earn, first, work, turn*.

Exercise ❷

- Tell students that they will listen to the pronunciation of the sound /ɚ/.

- 🎧 Play the audio.

- Point out that even though the /ɚ/ sound is spelled with two or even three letters as in *work* or *earn*, it is pronounced as a single sound.

- Tell students to notice the different spellings of /ɚ/ in the words in this exercise.

Exercise ❸

- Tell students that they will listen again. This time, they will listen and repeat.

- 🎧 Play the audio again, stopping after each word and asking students to repeat chorally.

- Ask a few individual students to repeat. Check their pronunciation.

- If students have difficulty with the pronunciation of /ɚ/, use hand gestures to show the movement of the tongue. Hold one hand stretched out flat, with the palm up, and then curl your fingers up a little to show how the tongue curls up. Explain that the tongue curls up but does not touch the roof of the mouth.

Exercise ❹

- Have students look at the phrases. Explain that at least one word in each phrase has the sound /ɚ/ and another word has a different vowel sound before *r*.

- 🎧 Play the audio.

- You may want to point out that all vowels before the letter *r* have a different sound than when they come before other letters.

Exercise ❺

- Tell students they will listen again. This time, they will listen and repeat.

- 🎧 Play the audio again, stopping after each item to allow students to repeat chorally.

- Ask individual students to repeat. Check their pronunciation.

- Students may have difficulty with the vowel + /r/ sounds in *outdoors, more, career,* and *market*. To help them with these sounds, have them say the vowel sound without /r/ first. Then tell them to add a short /ɚ/ sound, moving the tongue up toward the hard roof of the mouth and rounding the lips slightly. Tell them to notice that the tongue does not touch the roof of the mouth.

Reading

Exercise ❻

- Tell students to look at the reading. Ask: *What type of text or reading material are these?* (They're newspaper want ads.)

- Tell students to read the ads and match them with the jobs in the photos on page 128. Go over the example.

- Have students compare their answers with a partner's.

- Go over the answers with the class.

Answer key

A. chef	C. mechanic
B. market researcher	D. computer trainer

Exercise ❼

- Have students read the want ads again. Tell them to choose a job they want to do and a job they don't want to do. If they don't want to do any of the jobs, they should choose a job that sounds the best of the choices available. This exercise will prepare them for Exercise 8.

- Set a time limit of 1 minute.

Exercise ❽

- Explain the task: Students will talk about the jobs they want to do and those they don't want to do from Exercise 7. They should give reasons for their choices.

- Divide the class into groups of 3 and set a time limit of 3 minutes. Walk around the room, helping as needed.

- Call on a few students to report their answers to the class.

- 🖥 Please go to www.longman.com/worldview for additional in-class model conversation practice.

HOMEWORK

- 📖 Assign *Workbook* page 105, Vocabulary Exercises 1 and 2, and page 107, Listening Exercises 5 and 6.

Pronunciation

2 🎧 **Listen. Notice the /ɚ/ sound.**

work   earn   learn   computer   perfect   researcher

3 🎧 **Listen again and repeat.**

4 🎧 **Now listen to these phrases. Notice that /ɚ/ sounds different from the other vowel + *r* in each phrase.**

work outdoors   earn more   computer software   the perfect career   market researcher

5 🎧 **Listen again and repeat.**

Reading

6 **Read the want ads and match them with the jobs in the photos.**

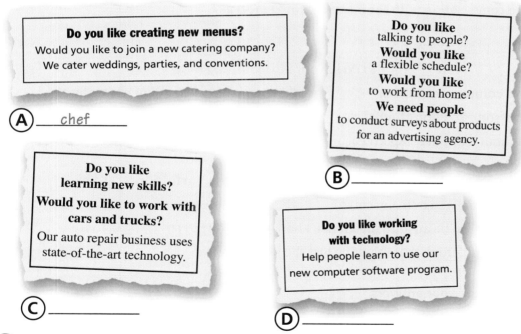

Do you like creating new menus?
Would you like to join a new catering company?
We cater weddings, parties, and conventions.

Ⓐ ___chef___

Do you like talking to people?
Would you like a flexible schedule?
Would you like to work from home?
We need people to conduct surveys about products for an advertising agency.

Ⓑ _____

Do you like learning new skills?
Would you like to work with cars and trucks?
Our auto repair business uses state-of-the-art technology.

Ⓒ _____

Do you like working with technology?
Help people learn to use our new computer software program.

Ⓓ _____

7 **Read the want ads again and choose:**

• a job you want to do
• a job you don't want to do

8 *GROUPS OF 3.* **Discuss your answers to Exercise 7. Explain the reasons for your choices.**

Grammar focus

1 Study the examples. Notice the difference between the sentences with *like* and those with *would like*.

like + verb + *-ing*	*would like* + infinitive
(?) Do you **like working** with people? (Yes, I **do**. / No, I **don't**.)	**Would** you **like to work** from home? (Yes, I **would**. / No, I **wouldn't**.)
(+) I **like learning** new skills.	**I'd like to be** a mechanic.
(–) I **don't like working** outside.	I **wouldn't like to be** a chef.

2 Look at the examples again. Circle the correct words to complete the rules in the chart.

like, would like

Use *like* + verb + *-ing* to talk about **a future possibility / present likes and dislikes**.

Use *would like* + infinitive to talk about **a future possibility / present likes and dislikes**.

Grammar Reference page 149

3 Complete the conversation with *(not) like* or *would (not) like*.

A: I **(1)** _'d like_ to get a new job.

B: What **(2)** _____ you _____ to do in your next job?

A: Well, I love computers, and I **(3)** _____ working with technology. I'm not really a "people person," so I don't think I **(4)** _____ to work with people all the time.

B: OK, how about computer repair? **(5)** _____ you _____ to learn how to fix computers?

A: That sounds interesting. I've never tried it, but I **(6)** _____ to fix things, I think.

B: OK, are you interested in fixing cars?

A: No, I **(7)** _____ to be an auto mechanic. I hate getting dirty. I **(8)** _____ to try computer repair. I think that might be just the job for me!

4 🎧 Listen and check your answers.

Grammar focus

LANGUAGE NOTES

- *Would like* is used as a polite way of saying *want*. *Would like* can be followed by a noun or by an infinitive. The focus in this unit is on *would like* + infinitive. For example, *I would like to get a better job*.

- *Would like* is also used to talk about a future possibility.

- The verb *like* can be followed by an infinitive or a gerund. *Like* followed by a gerund (verb + -*ing*) is used to talk about an activity that is true in the present.

WARM-UP

Note: Skip this warm-up if you're doing this lesson (Lesson B) during the same class period as Lesson A.

- Books closed. Tell students they will listen to the want ads that they read in the Reading section.

- Write these sentences on the board and tell students to copy them: *Do you like _____ new menus? Would you like _____ a new catering company?*

- Tell students to listen for the sentences and to complete them.

- ○ Play the audio from Lesson A, Reading, Exercise 6. (It models the grammar of the unit.)

- Go over the answers with the class by asking students to call out the missing words. (*creating, to join*)

Exercise ❶

- Have students read the examples and study the bold-faced words. Point out or elicit the different forms following the verbs. (verb + -*ing* after *like*, infinitive after *would like*)

- Tell students to think about the time the forms *like* + verb + -*ing* and *would like* + infinitive are used.

Exercise ❷

- Have students study the examples again.

- Tell them to circle the correct information to complete the rules in the chart.

- Have students compare their answers with a partner's.

- Go over the answers with the class.

- Ask a few questions to elicit the key points about the grammar. For example, *Does* like + verb + -ing *refer to the present or the future?* (the present) *What about* would like + infinitive? (the future)

Answer key

present likes and dislikes
a future possibility

Exercise ❸

- Before students begin Exercise 3, answer any questions they might have. You may also want to refer the class to the Grammar Reference for Unit 28 on page 149.

- Tell students to complete the conversation with *(not) like* or *would (not) like*.

- Set a time limit of 4 minutes. Walk around the room, helping as needed.

- Have students compare answers with a partner's. Point out that they will check their answers in the next activity.

Exercise ❹

- Tell students to check their Exercise 3 answers as they listen to the conversation.

- ○ Play the audio.

- Go over the answers with the class.

Answer key

1. 'd like	5. Would . . . like
2. would . . . like	6. like
3. like	7. wouldn't like
4. 'd like	8. 'd like

EXTENSION

If time allows, have students work in pairs and practice the conversation in Exercise 3.

Speaking

Exercise 5

This exercise provides an opportunity for students to practice using *would like*. It also prepares them for Exercise 9.

- Tell students to write down three jobs they would like to do and three jobs they wouldn't like to do. Remind them not to show their list to their classmates.

- Set a time limit of 2 minutes.

Exercise 6

- Tell students to imagine they are career counselors who help people decide on new careers based on their likes and dislikes. They will write questions for a classmate seeking career advice.

- Go over the examples.

- Tell students to write additional questions that ask about career preferences. Remind them to use *would you like* + infinitive, *do you like* + verb + *-ing*.

- Set a time limit of 3 minutes. Walk around the room, helping as needed.

- After 3 minutes, call on a few students to read their questions.

Exercise 7

- Explain the task: Students will take turns asking and answering the questions they wrote in Exercise 6. Tell them to listen carefully to their partner's answers because they will need this information for Exercises 8 and 9.

- Pair the students and set a time limit of 5 minutes. Walk around the room, helping as needed.

Exercise 8

- Tell students to write down three jobs they think their partner would like to do and three jobs they think their partner wouldn't like to do, based on their answers in Exercise 7.

- Set a time limit of 2 minutes.

Exercise 9

This is an activity that ties together Exercises 5 through 8.

- Explain the task: Students will take turns comparing their lists from Exercises 5 and 8. They should give reasons why they chose each job for themselves and for their partners, using the information they gathered in Exercise 7.

- Go over the example.

- Pair the students as they were for Exercise 7, and set a time limit of 10 minutes. Walk around the room, helping as needed.

- Call on a few students to report on their discussions.

- Find out how many students agreed with their partners' choices.

TRB For additional interactive grammar practice, have students do the reproducible activity for this unit in the *Teacher's Resource Book.*

Writing

Exercise 10

- Assign the writing task for class work or homework.

- Explain the task: Students will write a want ad.

- Brainstorm ideas for jobs and write them on the board.

- **TRB** Optionally, give students a copy of the model (see the *Teacher's Resource Book*, Writing Models). Ask them to read the model and notice the vocabulary and grammar from the unit.

- If students don't have the model, write the following on the board:

    Do you like working with animals?
    Do you like working outdoors?
    Would you like to work in a zoo?

For suggestions on how to give feedback on writing, see page xiv of this *Teacher's Edition*.

CONVERSATION TO GO

At the end of class, call on two students to role-play the conversation.

HOMEWORK

- 📖 Assign *Workbook* page 106, Grammar Exercises 3 and 4, and page 107, Pronunciation Exercises 7 and 8.

- Assign *Workbook* Self-Quiz 7

- 🎧 If students do not have the *WorldView Workbook*, assign listening homework from the Student CD. Write on the board:

    Track 62
    Circle the number of the job that someone could do at home. Then write the name of the job.

    1   2   3   4

- 🎧 Tell students to listen to the audio and write the answer to the exercise. Have them bring their answer to the next class.

    (Answer: *2; market researcher*)

FOR NEXT CLASS

- Tell students that the next class will be a review class covering Units 25–28.

- Have students review the material in the units to prepare for the activities in Review 8.

- **TRB** Make copies of Quiz 7 in the *Teacher's resource Book.*

Unit no.	Review Grammar	Listen to Student CD	Study Grammar Reference
25	*Could, be good at*	Track 54	Page 149
26	Present perfect: *yet, already*	Track 56	Page 149
27	Present real conditional	Track 58	Page 149
28	*Like* + verb + *-ing*, *would like* + infinitive	Track 62	Page 149

Speaking

5 *BEFORE YOU SPEAK.* **Write down three jobs you would like to do and three jobs you would not like to do. Write them on a piece of paper. Keep this list for later.**

6 **Look at the questionnaire for choosing a job. Add 3 more questions.**

7 *PAIRS.* **Take turns asking and answering your questions from Exercise 6.**

8 **Write down three jobs you think your partner would like to do and three jobs you think your partner would *not* like to do.**

9 *PAIRS.* **Take turns comparing your lists from Exercises 5 and 8. Explain why you chose each job for yourself and for your partner.**

I think you'd like to work as a mechanic. I chose that job for you because you like working with your hands and you like being active.

> Choosing a Job Questionnaire
>
> Do you like working with people?
> Would you like to travel?
> Do you want to work outdoors?

> Jobs my partner would like:
> 1.
> 2.
> 3.
>
> Jobs he or she wouldn't like:
> 1.
> 2.
> 3.

Writing

10 **Think of a job you would like to have. Write a want ad for that job. Use the want ads on page 129 as a model.**

CONVERSATION TO GO

A: Do you like working here?
B: No, I don't.
A: Would you like to work abroad?
B: Yes, I would.

Unit 25 Real fighters

1 🎧 Look at the picture and listen to the model conversation.

2 *PAIRS.* The people in the pictures are athletes. Find out how well they could do sports ten years ago. Student A, look at page 138. Student B, look at page 141.

3 Compare your charts. Are they the same? Who is the best athlete?

Unit 26 On the go

4 🎧 Look at the picture and listen to the model conversation.

5 *GROUPS OF 4.* Rafael is going on a trip. Look at the picture and the To-do list. You have one minute. Remember all the things Rafael has and hasn't done to prepare for his trip.

Close your book. Write sentences about what Rafael has and hasn't done. You have 5 minutes. The group with the most sentences wins.

Points: _____

Rafael has booked a hotel. He hasn't gotten a haircut yet.

📼 You may wish to use the video for Units 25–28 at this point.
For video activity worksheets, go to www.longman.com/worldview.

Unit 25: Real fighters

OBJECTIVES

- Review the material presented in Unit 25
- Grammar practice: *could* and *be good at* for past ability

WARM-UP

- Books closed. On the board write the following verb forms:

  could (not) + verb
  be good at + verb + *-ing*

- Ask some students to make sentences describing some of their past abilities or what they were good at in the past. Give a personal example: *In his younger years, my father could scuba dive, and my mother was very good at horseback riding.*

Exercise ❶

- Tell students they will listen to a conversation describing the abilities of a woman named Lise. Tell students to listen for the answer to this question: *What couldn't Lise do ten years ago?* (She couldn't swim very well. She was no good at diving.) *What could she do?* (She could skate.)

- 🎧 Play the audio.

Exercise ❷

- Explain the task: Students will work in pairs. Each student in the pair will have charts with different information about the abilities of the people in the picture. Students will ask and answer questions to complete their charts.

- Pair students. Have Student A go to page 138, Student B to page 141. Tell them to look at their charts.

- Tell them to look at the information they have and determine which information they need.

- Set a time limit of 5 minutes. Tell the pairs to take turns asking questions and to complete their charts with the symbols on the page.

- Walk around the room, helping as needed.

Exercise ❸

- After 5 minutes, have students compare their charts with their partners' to check their information. Tell them to correct any incorrect information.

- Tell students to discuss who they think should win Best Athlete. Set a time limit of 1 minute for the discussion.

- Invite pairs of students to say who they think should win Best Athlete and briefly explain why.

Unit 26: On the go

OBJECTIVES

- Review the material presented in Unit 26
- Grammar practice: present perfect with *yet* and *already*

WARM-UP

- Books closed. Ask students to name a few activities that they do at the end of a course or school year. Make a short list of these activities on the board.

- Invite volunteers to say which activities they have already done and which they haven't done yet.

Exercise ❹

- Tell students they will listen to a conversation that models Exercise 5. Tell them to listen to find out one thing the person has done and one thing he hasn't. (*He has gotten his passport and bought his airline ticket. He hasn't packed his suitcase or made a hotel reservation.*)

- 🎧 Play the audio.

Exercise ❺

- Divide the class into groups of 4. Explain the task: Students will look at the picture to make sentences about what Rafael has already done and hasn't done yet to prepare for the trip to Costa Rica.

- Have each group write a list of all the things that Rafael has done and the things that he hasn't done. Set a time limit of 5 minutes.

- Remind the groups to write their total points in the blank. After 5 minutes, ask each group for their total points to determine which group has the highest score.

WRAP-UP

- Tell the groups to exchange papers. Have the groups correct each other's answers, awarding one point to each sentence that is correct in content as well as in grammar.

- Have students return the papers and compare their scores with other groups in the class.

Unit 27: Behave yourself

- Review the material presented in Unit 27
- Grammar practice: present real conditional (*If* clause)

> **WARM-UP**
>
> Books closed. Ask students what they do if they are sick and can't go to class.

Exercise 6

- **Groups of 4.** Tell students to read the situations in the chart. Ask them if they have been in any of these situations.
- Have each group discuss a possible problem for each situation. Tell them to write the problems in the second column.

Exercise 7

- Tell students they will listen to different people's answers to the question: *What do you do if you lend a friend $100, and he or she forgets about it?* Tell students to listen to the two people's answers. (*remind the person directly; remind the person by email; ask the person to pay back; just forget about it.*)
- 🎧 Play the audio.

Exercise 8

- Divide the class into groups of 4.
- Have students read through the list of situations.
- Tell the groups to discuss the best thing to do in each situation. Encourage them to try to convince one another that their idea is the best thing to do. Have them write the agreed suggestion on a piece of paper.
- Set a time limit of 6 minutes. Walk around the room, helping as needed.

Exercise 9

Have groups report their suggestions to the class. Encourage them to explain why they chose each suggestion as the best thing to do.

Unit 28: Just the job for you

- Review the material presented in Unit 28
- Grammar practice: *like* + verb + *-ing; would like* + infinitive

> **WARM-UP**
>
> Books closed. Ask students what kinds of things they would like to do in a job.

Exercise 10

- Tell students they will listen to a conversation that models Exercise 11. Tell them to listen and find out what Mark likes to do as a teacher and what he doesn't like to do. (*He likes working with children, working outside, and being active. He doesn't like doing paperwork.*)
- 🎧 Play the audio.

Exercise 11

- Pair students. Ask them to read each person's profile of likes and dislikes.
- 🎧 If needed, play the audio for Exercise 10 again.
- Set a time limit of 8 minutes. Tell each pair to work together to suggest possible jobs for each candidate.

Exercise 12

Invite partners to report to the class their job choices for each person. Encourage them to explain why they think their suggestions are good for the person.

Unit 27 Behave yourself

6 GROUPS OF 4. Look at the situations. Think of problems that may happen for each situation. Complete the chart.

Situation	Problem
1. You lend your friend $100.	
2. It's your friend's birthday.	
3. You borrow your friend's bicycle.	
4. Your friend gives you a gift.	
5. You and your friend have a date to go to dinner.	

7 🎧 Listen to the model conversation.

8 GROUPS OF 4. Discuss each situation. Agree on the best thing to do for each.

9 Report back to the class. Choose a situation. What is the best thing to do?

Unit 28 Just the job for you

10 🎧 Look at the job profiles and listen to the model conversation.

Name: Mark
What would you like to do?
- work with children
- be active
- work outside
Is there anything you don't like?
- doing a lot of paperwork
Jobs: _____ Coach _____

Name: Sun-Ju
What would you like to do?
- work with my hands
- work alone
- be creative
Is there anything you don't like?
- working from 9 to 5 every day
Jobs: _____

Name: Bruno
What would you like to do?
- work with technology
- earn a good salary
- work inside
Is there anything you don't like?
- traveling a lot
Jobs: _____

11 PAIRS. Look at the job profiles again and discuss what each person would like to do in his or her next job. Think of two jobs that each person could do.

12 Report to the class. What's the best job for each person? Explain why you chose it.

World of Music 4

This Used to Be My Playground
Madonna

Vocabulary

1 Match the expressions with their meanings.

Expression

1. Don't look back. _c_
2. Keep your head held high. ___
3. This was my childhood dream. ___
4. Don't hold onto the past. ___
5. Life is short. ___
6. No regrets. ___
7. This is our pride and joy. ___
8. My heart is breaking. ___

Meaning

a. Be proud of yourself.
b. I wanted this when I was very young.
c. Don't think about the past.
d. I'm very sad.
e. We're very proud of this.
f. Live in the present.
g. Use your time carefully, because you won't live forever.
h. Don't feel bad about past events.

> **The 90s**
>
> In the 1990s, **Madonna** became not just a pop superstar but a movie star as well. "This Used to Be My Playground" is from one of her movies, A League of Their Own.

2 The title of the song is "This Used to Be My Playground." What is a playground? What do you think the song will be about?

Listening

3 🎧 Listen to the song. Circle *a* or *b* to answer the questions.

1. What is the singer thinking about?
   a. She's remembering the past.
   b. She's thinking about the future.

2. Who is she talking to in the song?
   a. someone she met a long time ago
   b. someone she met recently

4 🎧 Listen to the song again. Complete the lyrics on page 135 with the words you hear.

5 *PAIRS.* Compare your answers in Exercise 4.

World of Music 4

OBJECTIVES

- Introduce the song "This Used to Be My Playground" by Madonna
- Vocabulary practice: common expressions and their meanings
- Express personal reactions to the message of the song

BACKGROUND INFORMATION

Madonna recorded "This Used to Be My Playground" in 1992 for the movie *A League of Their Own*. The movie is about the first professional women's baseball league in the United States, which was formed during World War II. Madonna also starred in the movie with Tom Hanks, Geena Davis, and Rosie O'Donnell.

WARM-UP

- Books closed. Ask students if they know that Madonna has acted in movies. Invite students to name some movies Madonna starred in. (*Evita, A League of Their Own, Swept Away*)
- Ask them if they have seen any of Madonna's movies and if they like Madonna as an actor. Ask: *Do you think Madonna is a good actor? Do you like her better as an actor or as a singer?* Encourage students to explain their answers.
- Ask them if they have seen or are familiar with the movie, *A League of Their Own.* If none of them have seen the movie, encourage them to watch it when they have a chance.
- Tell students they will listen to one of Madonna's songs, "This Used to Be My Playground," which was the theme song of the movie *A League of Their Own.*

The 90s

- Ask this question: *What do you remember about the 90s?* (*Possible answers:* economic boom, rapid advances in technology, wealth for many, materialism)
- Remind students that one of the singers who became very popular during the 90s was Madonna. Ask them to name some songs by Madonna. ("Material Girl," "Like a Prayer," "Papa Don't Preach," "What It Feels Like for a Girl," "This Used to Be My Playground")
- Encourage students to sing some lines from any Madonna songs they know.
- Ask them if they like Madonna and explain why they like her.

Vocabulary

Exercise ❶

- Tell students to read the sentences under "Expression" and those under "Meaning." Explain the task: Students will choose the meaning that best explains each expression.
- Elicit, or explain, any unfamiliar vocabulary and answer any questions students might have.
- Set a time limit of 5 minutes for students to do the exercise.
- After 5 minutes, have students check their answers as a class. Tell students that the expressions are used in the lyrics of the song they will hear.

Answer key		
1. c	4. f	7. e
2. a	5. g	8. d
3. b	6. h	

Exercise ❷

- Tell students to look at the title of the song. Discuss the meaning of *playground.*
- Ask: *What do you think the song is about?* (Possible answer: *It's about the past.*) Encourage students to predict what the song is about based on the title and the expressions in Exercise 1. Accept any logical answers.

Listening

Exercise ❸

- Tell students to read questions 1 and 2. Have them listen to the song and answer the questions.
- 🎧 Play the song.
- Tell students they will check their answers in Exercise 5.

Exercise ❹

- Explain the task: Students will listen to the song again and will complete the lyrics.
- Have students read through the song lyrics. Clarify the meanings of any unfamiliar vocabulary.
- 🎧 Walk around, helping as needed. You may need to play the song again to give students more time to complete the exercise.

[See page T135 for Exercise 5]

Exercise ❺

- Pair students. Have them compare their answers. Encourage them to change any incorrect answers.

- Answer any questions students might have about Exercise 4.

- Tell students to go back to their answers to Exercise 3. Ask if they need to change their answers to the questions.

- Give students time to review their answers. Then check the answers to Exercises 3 and 4 together.

Answer key

Exercise 3

1. a   2. a

Exercise 4

Stanza 1: dream, ran, friend
Stanza 2: back, head, life, heart, past
Stanza 3: wish, hope, your face, place, never say
Stanza 4: playground, world
Stanza 5: were
Stanza 6: free, were

OPTION

Play the song again and have students sing along.

Speaking

Exercise ❻

- Ask students to read the lyrics again and underline some of the expressions about the past, such as *don't look back, live and learn, say good-bye to yesterday, no regrets.* Clarify the meanings of these expressions.

- Divide the class into groups of 3. Tell each group to discuss the answers to the questions.

- Set a time limit of 5 minutes for the discussion. Walk around the room, helping as needed.

- After 5 minutes, invite students to share their answers to the questions.

This Used to Be My Playground

[Chorus]
This used to be my playground.
This used to be my childhood _____ .
This used to be the place I _____ to.
Whenever I was in need of a _____ .
Why did it have to end?
And why do they always say:

Don't look _____ .
Keep your _____ held high.
Don't ask them why,
Because _____ is short.
And before you know,
You're feeling old,
And your _____ is breaking.
Don't hold on to the _____ .
Well, that's too much to ask.

[Chorus]

No regrets,
But I _____ that you were
here with me.
Well then there's _____ yet.

I can see your _____
in our secret _____ .
You're not just a memory.
Say good-bye to yesterday
Those are words I'll _____ .

This used to be my _____ .
This used to be our pride and joy.
This used to be the place we ran to
That no one in the _____
could dare destroy.

This used to be our playground. (used to be)
This used to be our childhood dream.
This used to be the place we ran to.
I wish you _____ here with me.

This used to be my playground. (Ah, ah, ah)
This used to be my childhood dream.
This used to be the place we ran to.
The best things in life are always _____ .
Wishing you _____ here with me.

Speaking

6 **GROUPS OF 3. Discuss these questions.**

1. What feeling do you get from this song? Why do the music and words make you feel that way?

2. Look at some expressions from the song. Do you think these expressions give good advice? Why or why not?

   a. Don't look back.

   b. Keep your head held high.

   c. Life is short.

   d. No regrets.

Unit 2, Exercise 6
Student A

Make these phone calls to Student B. Apologize and make an excuse.

I'm afraid I can't come to work. I have a terrible headache.

1. You have a headache, and you can't go to work. Call your boss.
2. You want to watch a baseball game tonight, but your friend wants you to go to a movie with him/her. Call your friend, Student B, and make an excuse for not going to the movies.
3. Your boss wants you to go out for dinner with a client, but you have a dentist appointment at 6:00. Call your boss, Student B.

Answer these phone calls from Student B. Listen to his/her problems. Show sympathy.

That's too bad.

4. You're an English teacher. Student B is your student.
5. You're a manager in an office. Student B is an employee in your department.
6. You're going to move into your new apartment tomorrow. Student B is your friend.

Review 1, Exercise 10
Student A

Dario is going on a trip. Take turns asking questions to fill in his schedule.

Where is he going to go on Saturday? What's he going to do on Sunday?

Dario's Travel Schedule		8 days/7 nights
Day	**Where**	**What**
Sat.	fly into the city	visit a museum
Sun.	drive down the coast	
Mon.		
Tues.		attend a festival
Wed.	drive to the mountains	
Thurs.		
Fri.		buy souvenirs at a market
Sat.		✕✕

Unit 6, Exercise 8

Read the email messages and write replies to each one.

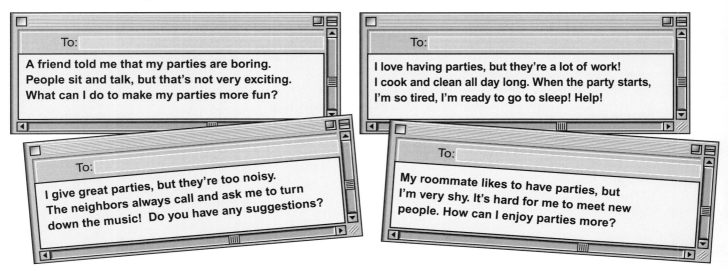

To:
A friend told me that my parties are boring. People sit and talk, but that's not very exciting. What can I do to make my parties more fun?

To:
I love having parties, but they're a lot of work! I cook and clean all day long. When the party starts, I'm so tired, I'm ready to go to sleep! Help!

To:
I give great parties, but they're too noisy. The neighbors always call and ask me to turn down the music! Do you have any suggestions?

To:
My roommate likes to have parties, but I'm very shy. It's hard for me to meet new people. How can I enjoy parties more?

Unit 7, Exercise 6
Student A

Student A, begin. Look at these pictures of your colleagues from another office. Give each person a name. Then describe each one to your partner. Your partner will show you the person in the picture on page 33. Is your partner correct?

A: My colleague, Sandra Vazquez, is going to arrive on Saturday. Can you meet her at the airport?
B: Sure. What does she look like?
A: She . . .

Now, switch roles. Look at page 33.

Review 2, Exercise 8
Student A

Student A, begin. Describe the person in your picture A. Then Student B will describe the person in his or her picture A. Is it the same person? Then Student B continues with picture B.

Picture A   Picture B   Picture C   Picture D

Unit 2, Exercise 6
Student B

Answer these phone calls from Student A. Listen to his/her problems. Show sympathy.

That's too bad.

1. You're a supervisor. Student A is your employee.
2. You want to go to the movies tonight. Student A is your friend.
3. You're a supervisor. Student A is your employee.

Make these phone calls to Student A. Apologize and make an excuse.

I'm sorry, but I can't come to class today. I have a fever.

4. You can't go to your English class because you have a fever. Call your teacher, Student A.
5. You have a sore throat and cough. There's an important meeting at work. Call your boss, Student A, and apologize for not going to the meeting.
6. Your friend, Student A, wants you to help him move into a new apartment, but you don't want to. Call your friend and make an excuse.

Review 1, Exercise 10
Student B

Dario is going on a trip. Take turns asking questions to fill in his schedule.

What's he going to do Saturday? Where is he going to go on Sunday?

Dario's Travel Schedule		8 days/7 nights
Day	**Where**	**What**
Sat.	fly into the city	visit a museum
Sun.		go swimming
Mon.	go on safari	
Tues.		
Wed.		go hiking
Thurs.	take a bus to the lake	
Fri.		buy souvenirs at a market
Sat.	fly home	

Review 7, Exercise 2
Student A

Look at the chart. Ask questions to find out how well each athlete could do sports ten years ago. (Don't look at your partner's chart.)

Athlete	Sport	10 years ago
Lise	🏊	–
	🤿	– –
	🏃	+
Ho-Jin	🤼	
	🏋	
	🚣	
Flavia	🚣	+ +
	🏊	+
	🥊	– –
Simon	🏃	
	🚣	
	🏋	

Symbol	Meaning	
+++	could . . . really well	be really good at . . .
++	could . . . well	be good at . . .
+	could . . . pretty well	be pretty good at . . .
–	couldn't . . . very well	be not very good at . . .
– –	couldn't . . . at all	be no good at . . .

Unit 7, Exercise 6
Student B

Student B, look at these pictures of your colleagues from another office. Give each person a name. Then describe each one to your partner. Your partner will show you the person in the picture on page 33. Is your partner correct?

B: My colleague, Carlos Lopez, is going to arrive on Saturday. Can you meet him at the airport?
A: Sure. What does he look like?
B: He…

Review 2, Exercise 8
Student B

Student A will describe the person in his or her picture A. Then you will describe the person in your picture A. Is it the same person? Then continue with picture B.

Picture A   Picture B   Picture C   Picture D

Unit 6, Exercise 6

Look at the costs in the worksheet. Put a check (✓) next to your suggestions.

Party Planning Worksheet

		Cost	Check (✓)
Location	At school/home/the office	$0	
	Hotel	$150	
Food and beverages	Snacks (chips, cheese, sandwiches, soft drinks)	$75	
	Buffet dinner with soft drinks	$150	
	Formal dinner with soft drinks and wine	$275	
	Dessert buffet	$100	
	Ice cream	$50	
	Cookies	$30	
Music	Band	$150	
	DJ	$75	
	CD player	$0	
Entertainment	Photographer	$75	
	Games	$100	
	Celebrity guest	$300	
	Total:		

Review 4, Exercise 13
Student A

Student A, you're at the supermarket. Call Student B to ask what you should buy.

Switch roles. Student A, look at the food in the picture. Tell Student B what food you have at home and suggest what he or she needs to buy.

Unit 18, Exercise 7

There were 16 people in the picture on page 85. Try to answer these questions about each person:

- What were they doing?
- What were they wearing?
- Where were they in the picture?

A man was chasing his dog. He was wearing a red jacket.

Unit 22, Exercise 7
Student A

Use the phrases to make your requests and offers.

Requests	Offers
Can you...?	Would you like me to...?
Could you...?	Should I...?
	I'll...

A: Can you do the filing, please?
B: Yes, of course. I'll do it this afternoon.

- **Situation 1**
  You're an executive at a television station. Student B is your assistant. Ask Student B to:
  a. send a fax.
  b. make a dinner reservation at the Lemon Tree Restaurant.
  c. type a letter.

- **Situation 2**
  You're a shoe salesperson in a department store. Student B is the store manager.
  a. You're waiting on a customer. Your boss asks you to do something. Offer to do the task after you finish with the customer.
  b. You hurt your back on the weekend. You think Bob (another salesperson) can help. Offer to ask Bob.
  c. You're going to the sandwich shop for lunch. Your boss asks you to do something. Offer to do the task after lunch.

Review 7, Exercise 2
Student B

Look at the chart. Ask questions to find out how
well each athlete could do sports ten years ago.
(Don't look at your partner's chart.)

Athlete	Sport	10 years ago
Lise	(swimming)	
	(sailing)	
	(running)	
Ho-Jin	(wrestling)	+ +
	(skiing)	+
	(rowing)	–
Flavia	(rowing)	
	(swimming)	
	(shooting)	
Simon	(running)	+ +
	(rowing)	+
	(skiing)	–

Symbol	Meaning	
+++	could . . . really well	be really good at . . .
++	could . . . well	be good at . . .
+	could . . . pretty well	be pretty good at . . .
–	couldn't . . . very well	be not very good at . . .
– –	couldn't . . . at all	be no good at . . .

Unit 22, Exercise 7
Student B

Use the phrases to make your requests and offers.

Requests	Offers
Can you . . . ?	Would you like me to . . . ?
Could you . . . ?	Should I . . . ?
	I'll . . .

A: Can you do the filing, please?
B: Yes, of course. I'll do it this afternoon.

- **Situation 1**
  You're an administrative assistant at a television
  station. Student A is your boss. Use this information
  when your boss makes a request:
  a. The fax machine is broken. Offer to send
     an email instead.
  b. The Lemon Tree Restaurant is closed.
     Offer to try some other restaurants.
  c. You're busy typing a report. Your boss
     asks you to do something. Offer to do the
     task after you finish the report.

- **Situation 2**
  You're the manager of a department store. Student A
  is a salesperson in the shoe department. Ask Student
  A to:
  a. put the shoes back in the storeroom.
  b. help you move a large box.
  c. put *Sale* signs on certain shoe racks.

Unit 9, Exercise 7
Students B and C

You are customers at Rosie's Restaurant. Look at the menu. Decide what you would like and give your order to your waiter/waitress.

Waiter: Would you like to order?
Customer: Yes. I'd like the chicken in herb sauce.

Rosie's Restaurant

Appetizers	Cup	Bowl
Tomato soup	$3.25	$4.00
Chicken soup	$3.25	$4.00
Soup of the day	$3.25	$4.00

Entrées	
Pasta with tomato sauce	$8.95
Pasta with garlic sauce	$9.95
Chicken in herb sauce	$12.95
Shrimp with vegetables	$15.95

Side dishes	
French fries	$2.25
Garden salad	$2.95
Mixed vegetables	$2.75
Rice	$2.25

Desserts	
Ice cream	$3.00
Chocolate or vanilla	
Cake	$4.25
Cheesecake	$5.00

Review 4, Exercise 13
Student B

Student B, look at the food in the picture. Tell Student A what food you have at home and suggest what he or she needs to buy.

Switch roles. Student B, you're at the supermarket. Call Student A to ask what you should buy. Write a shopping list.

Review 1, Exercise 10
Student C

Dario is going on a trip. take turns asking questions to fill in his schedule.

Where is he going to go on Sunday? What is he going to do on Saturday?

Dario's Travel Schedule		8 days/7 nights
Day	**Where**	**What**
Sat.	fly into the city	
Sun.		
Mon.		see elephants and lions
Tues.	visit the countryside	
Wed.		
Thurs.		do water sports
Fri.	return to the city	
Sat.		

Grammar reference

Unit 1

Simple present and adverbs of frequency

- Use **how often** to ask about frequency.
  How often *do you go to the movies?*
  How often *does Mary visit you?*
- Use adverbs of frequency (**never, sometimes, usually, often, always**) with the present tense to say how often something happens.
  Do they **always** *go out on Saturday?*
  She **usually** *goes to a café.*
  Peter doesn't **often** *watch TV.*
  We **sometimes** *get takeout.*
  I **never** *work late.*

Notes:

- Adverbs of frequency go after the verb **be**, but before all other verbs.
  It's **always** *noisy.*
  John **often runs** *after work.*
- The adverb **sometimes** can also go at the beginning of a sentence.
  Sometimes *we get takeout.*

Unit 2

Linking words: *and, but, so*

- Use the words **and**, **but**, and **so** to connect ideas.
- Use **and** to connect similar ideas.
  I have a headache, **and** *my stomach hurts.* (I have two problems.)
- Use **but** to connect different ideas.
  I have a headache, **but** *my stomach feels okay.* (I only have one problem: a headache.)
- Use **so** to show a result.
  I took some aspirin, **so** *I feel better.* (I feel better because I took aspirin.)

Unit 3

Simple past: regular and irregular verbs

- Use the simple past to talk about completed actions in the past, often with a specific time reference (*in 1990, yesterday, last year,* etc.).
- Add **–d** or **–ed** to regular verbs to form the simple past in affirmative statements.
  A television station **hired** *her.*
  She **wanted** *to be famous.*

- Some verbs are irregular in the simple past. (See the list on page 150.)
  She **got** *a job in television.*
  People **began** *to notice her.*

Negative	Subject + **didn't** + base form of the verb She **didn't finish** college. Her parents **didn't have** a lot of money.
Question	**Did** + subject + base form of the verb **Did** people **like** her television program? **Did** she **make** movies?
Short answers	**Yes** + subject + **did** **Yes**, she **did**.
	No + subject + **didn't** **No**, she **didn't**.

Unit 4

Be going to for future

- Use **be going to** to talk about future plans.

Affirmative	Subject + **be going to** + base form of the verb I**'m going to see** the Rocky Mountains. It**'s going to be** crowded there.
Negative	Subject + **be** + **not** + **going to** + base form of the verb You**'re not going to travel** with me. I**'m not going to take** a lot of stuff.
Question	**Be** + subject + **going to** + base form of the verb **Is** the weather **going to be** sunny? **Are** the markets **going to be** open?
Short answers	**Yes** + subject + **be** **Yes**, it **is**.
	No + subject + **be** + **not** **No**, it **isn't**.

Notes:

- The form of **be** must agree with the subject.
  I **am going to** *travel.*
  You **aren't going to** *snorkel.*
  She's **going to** *speak English.*
  We're **going to** *go on a safari.*
  They're **going to** *sightsee.*
- You can use the present continuous **going to** instead of **going to go** to talk about traveling.
  We're **going to go** *to India.*
  We're **going to** *India.*

Grammar reference

Unit 5

Modals: *should* and *shouldn't* for advice

• Use *should* to give and ask for advice.

Affirmative	Subject + **should** + base form of the verb You **should** shake hands. She **should** take a gift.
Negative	Subject + **shouldn't** + base form of the verb We **shouldn't** take our shoes off. They **shouldn't** arrive late.
Question	**Should** + subject + base form of the verb **Should** we shake hands? **Should** she use first names?
Short answers	**Yes** + subject + **should** **Yes**, you **should**.
	No + subject + **shouldn't** **No**, she **shouldn't**.

Unit 6

Expressions for making suggestions

Use *why don't, let's (not), maybe . . . could,* and *how about* to make suggestions.

• *Why don't* + subject + base form of the verb
  Why *don't* we have a party?
  Why *don't* you come?

• *Let's (not)* + base form of the verb
  Let's take something.
  Let's not make salad.

• *Maybe* + subject + *could*
  Maybe you *could* take drinks.
  Maybe he *could* get ice.

• *How about* + verb + *–ing*
  How about playing some games?
  How about listening to some music?

Unit 7

Be and *have* with physical descriptions

• Use *be* to talk about people's ages.
  I'm 34. How old *are* you?

• Use *be* to talk about people's height.
  You *are* short, and he *is* average height.

• Use *be* to talk about people's weight.
  She *is* slim, but her sisters *are* heavy.

• Use *have* to talk about people's eyes.
  Ben and Jeff *have* green eyes, but Ann *has* blue eyes.

• Use *have* to talk about people's hair.
  She *has* long hair, but he *has* short hair.

• Use *have* to talk about people's facial hair.
  Keith *has* a moustache, but he *doesn't have* a beard.

Exception: Use *be* with *bald*.
Ken has thick hair, but his father *is* bald.

Unit 8

Say and *tell*

• *Say* and *tell* are irregular verbs in the simple past.
  say → *said*   tell → *told*

• Always use an object pronoun (*me, you, him, her, it, us, them*) or a noun with *told*.
  I *told you* that I saw the movie.
  You *told me* that you didn't like it.
  He told *John* about making movies.

• Never use an object pronoun or noun with *said*.
  She *said* that she loved Dr. No.
  We *said* that Halle Berry was a great actress.

• Use the present after *say* or *tell* and the past after *said* or *told*.
  She *says* that Casablanca *is* a good movie.
  She *said* that she *liked* black-and-white films.
  He *tells* me that Star Wars *is* his favorite movie.
  He *told* me that he *loved* the special effects.

Note: You don't have to use the word *that* with *say* or *tell*.
She said she liked black-and-white films.
He told me he loved the special effects.

Unit 9

Would like/like, would prefer/prefer

- Use **like** and **prefer** to talk about the things you usually like.
  I **like** shrimp.
  He **likes** going out to dinner.
  We **prefer** red wine to white.
  She **prefers** small restaurants to large ones.
- Use **would like** and **would prefer** to talk about the things that you want at this moment or in the future.
  Would you like a drink?
  I**'d like** a glass of water, please.
  Would you prefer the chicken or the shrimp?
  We**'d prefer** the chicken tonight, thanks.

Notes:
- Use the contraction **'d** for **would** in affirmative sentences.
  I**'d like** the fish.
  We**'d prefer** red wine.
- Use **prefer** to show a choice between two things.
  Prefer is usually used in negative sentences.
  I **prefer** juice to soda.

Unit 10

Will for predicting

- Use **will** and **will not (won't)** to make predictions about the future.

Affirmative	Subject + **will ('ll)** + base form of the verb People **will** travel more. We**'ll** take vacations to the moon.
Negative	Subject + **will not (won't)** + base form of the verb People **won't** use cars as much. We **won't** pollute the environment.
Question	**Will** + subject + base form of the verb **Will** types of transportation change? **Will** the population of the world increase?
Short answers	**Yes** + subject + **will** **Yes**, it **will**.
	No + subject + **won't** **No**, it **won't**.

- Also use **I think** and **I don't think** with **will/won't** to make predictions about the future.
  I think we**'ll** use the Internet more.
  I think people **won't** write letters anymore.
  I don't think there **will** be hotels in space.
  Do you think we**'ll** fly private jets instead of driving cars?

Note: When using **I think** with **will/won't**, be careful to form negatives and short answers correctly. (**Think** is in the present.)

I don't think **I'll** go.
X I think I won't go.

Do you think **we'll** survive?
Yes, I do.
X Yes, I will.

Unit 11

Have to/don't have to

- Use **have to** to say that something is necessary.
  I **have to** get up early to go to work. (It's necessary.)
  I **don't have to** get up early on Sundays. (It's not necessary.)
  Do you **have to** use a computer at work?

Affirmative	Subject + **have/has to** + base form of the verb I **have to** work a lot. She **has to** travel for her job.
Negative	Subject + **don't/doesn't have to** + base form of the verb Doctors **don't have to** sell things. The salesperson **doesn't have to** type.
Question	**Do/Does** + subject **have to** + base form of the verb **Do** you **have to** work on weekends? **Does** your boss **have to** review your work?
Short answers	**Yes** + subject + **do/does** **Yes**, she **does**.
	No + subject + **don't/doesn't** **No**, she **doesn't**.

Note: Use **do/does** (not **have/has**) in short answers.

Do you have to work late?
Yes, I **do**.
X Yes, I have.
No, I **don't**.
X No, I haven't.

Grammar reference

Unit 12
Present perfect for indefinite past: *ever, never*

• Use the present perfect to talk about events that happened at an unspecified time in the past.

Affirmative	Subject + **have/has** + past participle I **have traveled** a lot. He **has spent** time outdoors.
Negative	Subject + **haven't/hasn't** + past participle We **haven't worked** on a farm. She **hasn't grown** food.
Question	**Have/has** + subject + past participle **Have** you **lived** overseas? **Has** it **rained** a lot?
Short answers	**Yes** + subject + **have/has** **Yes**, I **have**. **Yes**, it **has**.
	No + subject + **haven't/hasn't** **No**, I **haven't**. **No**, it **hasn't**.

• Use *ever* to make a question with the present perfect.
*Have you **ever** traveled overseas?*
• Use *not* or *never* to make a negative statement with the present perfect.
*No, I have**n't**. I have **never** traveled overseas.*

Note: To form the past participle of regular verbs, add *–d* or *–ed* to the base form of the verb. There is a list of irregular verbs on page 150.

Unit 13
Review: possessive *'s*

• Use *'s* after people's names or singular nouns to show possession.
*They're the family**'s** photos.*
*It's not Lisa**'s** jewelry box.*
*Where is James**'s** watch?*
• Use *'* after regular plural nouns to show possession.
*That is my grandparents**'** trunk.*
*The boys**'** photos are in the album.*
• Use *'s* after irregular plural nouns.
*The children**'s** toys are upstairs.*
*Where are the women**'s** dresses?*

Possessive adjectives

• Use possessive adjectives (**my, your, his, her, its, our, their**) to replace a possessive noun in a sentence.
This is Paul's guitar. → *This is **his** guitar.*
That is the dog's bed. → *That is **its** bed.*

Note: it's = it is; its = possessive adjective

Possessive pronouns

• Use possessive pronouns (**mine, yours, his, hers, ours, theirs**) to replace a possessive adjective and the noun it describes.
They're my books. → *They're **mine**.*
It's our house. → *It's **ours**.*

Belong to

• Use the verb **belong to** to talk about things that a person has or owns.
*The book **belongs to** me.* (I own the book.)
*The dolls **belong to** Cindy.* (Cindy owns the dolls.)

Unit 14
Adverbs of manner; comparative adverbs

• Use adverbs of manner to tell how an action is done.
*You asked **rudely**, but I answered **politely**.*
• Many adverbs of manner are formed by adding *–ly* to an adjective.
proud → proudly
polite → politely
kind → kindly
suspicious → suspiciously
• Use **more/less** + adverb of manner + **than** to compare two actions.
*Mapela talks **more quickly than** Haneko.*
*Haneko talks **more slowly than** Mapela.*

Notes:

• For adjectives ending in *–y*, change the *y* to *i*, then add *–ly*.
happy → happ**ily**
angry → angr**ily**
• **Well** is the adverb form of **good**.
*Mahala is a **good** singer.*
*Mahala sings **well**.*

Unit 15

Verbs for *likes/dislikes* + noun/verb + *–ing*

- Use a noun or the base form of a verb + *–ing* after *like*, *love*, and *hate*.
  *I **like** jogging.*
  *You **love** jogging, but you **hate** swimming.*
  *We **don't like** aerobics.*
  ***Do** they **like** sports?*
  *Yes, he **loves** playing tennis, and she **loves** golf.*

Unit 16

Quantifiers: *some, any, much, many, a lot of*

For count and non-count nouns

- Use *some* in affirmative statement when you don't know the exact quantity or if quantity isn't important.
  *I have **some** bread.*
  *She bought **some** apples.*
- Use *any* in negative statements and questions.
  *He didn't get **any** cheese.*
  *Did we buy **any** oranges?*
- Use *a lot of* in affirmative and negative statements and questions to talk about a large quantity.
  *Do you eat **a lot of** fresh fruit?*
  *We eat **a lot of** fresh fruit.*
  *I don't eat **a lot of** fruit, but I eat **a lot of** vegetables.*
  *She eats **a lot of** apples.*

For count nouns

- Use *many* in negative statements and questions.
  *I don't eat **many** vegetables.*
  *How **many** tomatoes are there?*
  *Are there **many** apples?*

For non-count nouns

- Use *much* in negative statements and questions.
  *I don't spend **much** money.*
  *How **much** milk is there?*
  *Is there **much** yogurt?*

Unit 17

Modals: *have to/had* to for present and past necessity

Present

- Use *have to* to say that something is necessary.
  *I **have to** go to work today.* (Work is required. I don't have a choice.)

*I **don't have to** go to work today.* (Work isn't required. It is Sunday, and the office was closed.)

Past

- Use *had to* to say that something was necessary in the past.
  *I **had to go** to work yesterday.* (Work was required. I didn't have a choice.)
  *I **didn't have to** go to work today.* (Work wasn't required. It was a holiday, and the office was closed.)

Unit 18

Simple past and past continuous

- Use the past continuous to talk about a past action that was happening over a period of time.
  *The police **were working** all night.*
- Use the simple past to talk about a completed past action.
  *A witness **saw** the crime.*
- Use the simple past and past continuous together in one sentence if the first action was still going on when the second action happened.
  *The man **was running away** when the police **arrived**.*
  (First, the man started running away. He was still running away. Then the police arrived.)
  *I **was reading** when I **heard** a noise.*
  (First, I started reading. I was still reading. Then I heard a noise.)

Unit 19

Because, for, and infinitives of purpose

- Use the words *because*, *for*, or an infinitive verb to answer the questions *why* and *what for*.
- Use *because* followed by a clause to talk about purpose.
  *I went to the bank **because** I needed money.*
  *She bought a sandwich **because** she was hungry.*
- Use *for* followed by a noun to talk about purpose.
  *I went to the bank **for** a new checkbook.*
  *She bought a sandwich **for** a snack.*
- Use an infinitive verb (sometimes followed by a noun) to talk about purpose.
  *I went to the bank **to get** some money.*
  *She bought a sandwich **to eat**.*

Grammar reference

Unit 20
Indefinite and definite articles: *a/an, the*

- Use *a/an* the first time you talk about something.
  *A young couple has **an** old house.*
- Use *the* to talk about the same thing again.
  ***The** couple turns **the** house into a hotel.*
- Use *the* when there is only one example of something.
  ***The** moon goes around **the** Earth.*
- Use *the* with superlative adjectives.
  *The Mousetrap is **the** most famous murder mystery.*
- Use *the* to talk about something specific.
  *I don't like **the** ice cream at that restaurant.*
  *Did you enjoy **the** music at the show?*
- Don't use *the* to talk about things in general.
  I like ice cream. It's my favorite dessert.
  ✗ I like the ice cream.

Unit 21
Present perfect: *how long/for/since*

- Use the present perfect to talk about actions or states that started in the past and continue into the present.
  I've lived here for a long time. (I came here a long time ago, and I still live here.)
  We've known each other since 1992. (We met in 1992, and we still know each other.)
- Use *how long* with the present perfect to ask about length of time.
  How long have you had your dog?
  How long has she studied French?
- Use *for* to talk about length of time.
  I've had him for two years.
  She has studied it for four months.
- Use *since* to say when the action started.
  I've had him since last March.
  She has studied it since January.

Unit 22
Modals: requests and offers

- Use *will* in affirmative statements to offer to do things for people.
  I'll send the faxes for you.
  I'll help you after lunch.
- Use *should* and *would you like me to* in questions to offer to do things for people.

Should I send the faxes for you?
Would you like me to help you after lunch?
- Use *can* and *could* to ask people to do things for you.
  Can you photocopy this, please?
  Could you answer the phone?

Unit 23
Used to/didn't use to

- Use *used to* followed by the base form of the verb to talk about things that generally happened in the past, but that don't happen now.

Affirmative	Subject + ***used to*** + base form of the verb *I **used to** drink a lot of coffee (but now I don't).*
Negative	Subject + ***didn't use to*** + base form of the verb *Women **didn't use to** wear pants in public (but now they do).*
Question	***Did*** + subject ***use to*** + base form of the verb ***Did** families **use to** spend more time together?*
Short answers	***Yes*** + subject + ***did*** ***Yes**, they **did**.*
	No + subject + ***didn't*** ***No**, they **didn't**.*

Unit 24
Present perfect vs. simple past

- Use the present perfect (*have/has* + past participle) to talk about events up to now. It isn't important when the events happened.
  I've gone rock climbing with my friends.
  (refers to some time in the past; it doesn't matter when)
  Have you ever been to Switzerland?
  (refers to any point in the past)
  Sophie has never gone snorkeling.
  (refers to all time in the past)
- Use the simple past to talk about completed actions in the past, often with a time reference.
  I went rock climbing a lot when I was younger.
  (refers to a past action; I don't go anymore)
  Did you go to Switzerland?
  (refers to a specific time or trip in the past)
  Sophie didn't go snorkeling when we were in Cancun.
  (refers to a specific time or trip in the past)

Unit 25

Could and be good at for past ability

• Use **could/couldn't** to talk about abilities in the past.

Affirmative	Subject + **could** + base form of the verb He **could** hit a baseball really far. We **could** ski fast.
Negative	Subject + **couldn't** + base form of the verb They **couldn't** run very quickly. I **couldn't** dive.
Question	**Could** + subject + base form of the verb **Could** you wrestle when you were younger? **Could** she win competitions?
Short answers	**Yes** + subject + **could** **Yes**, she **could**.
	No + subject + **couldn't** **No**, she **couldn't**.

• Also use **be/not be good at** + a noun to talk about abilities in the past.
Ali **was good at** boxing.
The swimmer **wasn't good at** skiing.
Were you **good at** sports?
• Use adverbs of degree to (**really, pretty, very well, at all**) emphasize past abilities.

He	**could** swim **really well**. **was really good at** swimming.
She	**could** swim **pretty well**. **was pretty good at** swimming.
We	**couldn't** swim **very well**. **weren't very good at** swimming.
You	**couldn't** swim **at all**. **were no good at** swimming.

Unit 26

Present perfect: yet, already

• Use **already** with the present perfect when the action is completed. (It is not important when it happened.)
I've **already** received the visas in the mail. *(Here they are.)*
She's **already** packed her bags. (The bags are ready.)

• Use **not yet** when the action is not completed but you think that it will happen.
I haven't found my passport **yet**. (But I will.)
We haven't rented a car **yet**. (We don't have one now, but we will get one.)
• Use **yet** to ask if an action is complete.
Has she left **yet**? (Is she still there or did she leave?)
Have you called your sister **yet**? (Do you still need to call or did you finish calling?)

Unit 27

Present real conditional (If + simple present + simple present)

• Use the present real conditional to talk about things that are usually true.
If I **forget** a friend's birthday, I say I'm sorry.
If I **need** a ride to work, my dad drives me.
If she **doesn't have** money, I lend it to her.
Does he get angry **if** she forgets their anniversary?

Note: The **if** clause can go before or after the main clause. Use a comma to separate the two clauses *only* when the **if** clause comes first.

If it rains, I take the bus.
I take the bus **if** it rains.

Unit 28

Like + verb + –ing, would like + infinitive

• Use **like** + verb + **–ing** to talk about your present likes and dislikes.
I **like** learning new skills.
I **don't like** working outside.
Do you **like** helping people?
• Use **would like to** + the base form of the verb to imagine future possibilities.
I'd **like to** be a teacher.
I **wouldn't like** to be a farmer.
Would you **like** to write books?

Grammar reference

Irregular Verbs

Simple present	Simple past	Past participle	Simple present	Simple past	Past participle
be	was/were	been	ride	rode	ridden
become	became	become	read	read	read
begin	began	begun	run	ran	run
break	broke	broken	say	said	said
build	built	built	see	saw	seen
buy	bought	bought	sell	sold	sold
catch	caught	caught	send	sent	sent
choose	chose	chose	shake	shook	shaken
come	came	come	show	showed	shown
cost	cost	cost	sing	sang	sung
do	did	done	sit	sat	sat
draw	drew	drawn	sleep	slept	slept
drink	drank	drunk	speak	spoke	spoken
drive	drove	driven	spend	spent	spent
eat	ate	eaten	stand	stood	stood
fall	fell	fallen	swim	swam	swum
feel	felt	felt	take	took	taken
fight	fought	fought	teach	taught	taught
find	found	found	tell	told	told
fly	flew	flown	think	thought	thought
forget	forgot	forgotten	throw	threw	thrown
get	got	gotten	understand	understood	understood
give	gave	given	wear	wore	worn
go	went	gone	win	won	won
grow	grew	grown	write	wrote	written
hang	hung	hung			
have	had	had			
hear	heard	heard			
hurt	hurt	hurt			
keep	kept	kept			
know	knew	known			
leave	left	left			
lend	lent	lent			
lose	lost	lost			
make	made	made			
mean	meant	meant			
meet	met	met			
pay	paid	paid			
put	put	put			
quit	quit	quit			

Vocabulary

Unit 1
get takeout
go for a walk
go out for dinner
go to the beach
go to the gym
go to the movies
meet friends
rent a video
sleep late
stay home
watch TV
work late

Unit 2
arm
back
ear
eye
foot
hand
head
leg
mouth
nose
stomach
throat
a cold
a cough
a fever
a headache
a sore throat
a stomachache
I hurt my . . . .
My . . . is/are sore.

Unit 3
be born
find a job
get married
give money to charity
go to school
graduate from school
grow up
have children
work hard

Unit 4
Australia
Africa
Asia
Canada
England
Europe
India
Ireland
Italy
Korea
North America
South Africa
coast
countryside
market
monuments
mountains
safari

Unit 5
arrive on time
bow
exchange business cards
give a gift
kiss
shake hands
take a flowers
take your shoes off
use first names/last names
visit someone's home
wear a suit

Unit 6
a birthday party
a costume party
a going-away party
afford
buy
cost
pay
rent
spend

Unit 7
age
elderly
middle-aged
young
height
average height
short
tall
weight
average weight
heavy
slim
hair
black
blond
brown
curly
dark
bald
beard
long
mustache/moustache
sideburns
straight

Unit 8
action movie
comedy
science fiction movie
romantic film
actress
actor
director
special effects
scenery
amazing
black-and-white film
classic
excellent
exciting
fantastic
fast
good
interesting
slow

Unit 9
customer
waiter
menu
appetizer
entree
side dish
cappuccino
coffee
espresso
tea
dessert

Vocabulary

cheesecake
chocolate ice cream
raspberry sorbet
fork
glass
knife
napkin
pepper
salt
spoon
garden salad
herbs
mixed vegetables
olives
pasta
rice
sauce
shrimp
soup of the day
tomatoes

Unit 10

climate
communication
economy
government
politics
population
prediction
space
technology
transportation

Unit 11

arrange meetings
communicate
give presentations
make decisions
make money
meet with clients
travel
type letters and contracts
wait on customers
work as a team
work long hours

Unit 12

build a house
catch a fish

cook for a group
grow food
have an adventure
make clothes
spend time
start a business
take care of animals
teach a class
travel abroad
use a computer
work on a farm
write an article

Unit 13

ballet shoes
baseball glove
camera
doll
jewelry box
photo album
pin
shawl
toy truck
watch
fall apart
fall out
give away
pass on
put away
throw away
take out
try on

Unit 14

absent-minded
ashamed
bad-mannered
calm
embarrassed
forgetful
loud
polite
proud
relaxed
rude
suspicious
trusting
upset

Unit 15

aerobics
baseball
basketball
biking
golf
hockey
jogging
karate
skiing
soccer
swimming
tennis
volleyball

Unit 16

bread
chocolate
cookies
fruit
juice
lettuce
onions
oranges
salt
strawberries
vegetables
water
yogurt

Unit 17

break
casual
commute
downsize
flextime
formal
full-time
part-time
supervisor
telecommute

Unit 18

police officer
intruder
suspect
victim
witness

confess
get arrested
investigate
question
report

Unit 19

clothing store
coffee house
convenience store
drugstore
hair salon
newsstand
restaurant
blouse
blow-dry
bottle of aspirin
candy bar
cup of coffee/tea
haircut
magazine
perfume
sandwiches
shampoo
socks
T-shirt

Unit 20

actors
applaud
audience
chairs
composer
costumes
musical
performers
play
playwright
opera
scenery
seats
spectators
theater

Unit 21

a couple of days/weeks/
    months/years
a long time
ages

more than five days/
    weeks/months/years
noon
New Year's Eve
over ten days/weeks/months/years
the day before yesterday
two days/weeks/months/years ago

Unit 22

arrange a meeting
do the copying
file the notes
get an email
have an appointment
leave a message
make a reservation
send a fax
sign your name

Unit 23

do housework
have dinner
open doors
play games
put on your slippers
shop for food
stay home
take off your shoes
travel by horse and carriage
wear skirts

Unit 24

jet skiing
parasailing
rock climbing
scuba diving
skateboarding
snorkeling
snowboarding
snow mobiling
waterskiing
windsurfing

Unit 25

boxer/boxing/box
diver/diving/dive
runner/running/run
skater/skating/skate

skier/skiing/ski
swimmer/swimming/swim
wrestler/wrestling/wrestle

Unit 26

a pillow
slippers
a teddy bear
a tennis racket
a ticket
a video
apply for a passport
book a hotel room
get a vaccination
go online
pack a bag
renew a visa
rent a car
transfer money

Unit 27

agree to
borrow
cancel
find
forget
lend
lose
pull
push
refuse to
remember
schedule

Unit 28

be active
be creative
conduct surveys
earn a good salary
have a lot of responsibility
help people learn
travel a lot
work alone
work inside
work outdoors
work with animals
work with his/her hands
work with people
work with technology

Student Book Audioscript

Unit 1   It's the weekend!

Listening, Exercises 4 and 5, page 3

H = Host   Y = Yuka   M = Marcelo

H: Good morning! This morning on "Life Around the World," we'll look at how people in different countries spend their weekends. We have some visitors with us in the studio today. Yuka is here from Kyoto, Japan. How are you today?

Y: Fine, thanks.

H: Tell us about your typical weekend. What's your favorite part?

Y: Mmm . . . that would be Friday nights.

H: Oh! Do you stay home on Friday nights?

Y: No, never. I usually work until 6:00 or so, and then I go home to eat.

H: What do you usually have?

Y: Well, I never cook on Fridays because I'm tired after work. I usually get a takeout bento from a convenience store.

H: What's a bento?

Y: Oh, it's prepared food. It has different kinds of vegetables and fish and rice . . . all in a box.

H: Is it good?

Y: Yes, and it's easy.

H: What do you do after dinner?

Y: I usually get together with friends and go to the movies. I love movies.

H: Yeah. Me, too! And onto our next guest. . . . Marcelo, you're from Brazil, right?

M: Yes, from Santos.

H: And what's your favorite day of the weekend?

M: I love Sundays. I usually sleep late in the morning. Then my wife and I always go for a walk on the beach in the afternoon. We often meet friends there.

H: At the beach?

M: Yes. Everybody goes there. The beach is always crowded on Sundays. It's the place to go!

H: Interesting!

M: After that, we sometimes go out for lunch.

H: How often do you go out on Sunday nights?

M: Sunday nights? We usually stay home on Sunday nights.

H: I see. Thanks! And now, Emma, from London. . . .

Pronunciation, Exercises 6 and 7, page 3

I never work on Saturday.

I usually go to the gym.

What do you do on Sunday?

We go for a walk on the beach.

She always gets takeout on Fridays.

She goes to the movies with her friends.

Unit 2   Excuses, excuses

Getting started, Exercise 2, page 6

1. eye
2. arm
3. back
4. hand
5. head
6. nose
7. mouth
8. stomach
9. ear
10. throat
11. foot
12. leg

Listening, Exercises 5 and 6, page 7

R = Roger   T = Tony

Conversation 1

R: Art Science Enterprises . . .

T: May I speak to Roger, please?

R: This is Roger.

T: Hello, Roger. This is Tony. I'm really sorry, but I'm not feeling very well. I have a fever, so I can't come to work today.

R: That's OK, Tony. Don't worry. I hope you feel better. But let me know if you can't come in tomorrow.

T: OK. Thanks, Roger. Bye.

Conversation 2

T: Hello, Roger? It's Tony. I'm afraid I can't come to work today. I have a bad cough, and my throat is very sore. I'm just going to stay in bed, I think.

R: That's OK, Tony. Hope you get better soon.

Conversation 3

T: Roger, it's Tony. Listen, I'm sorry, but I have a stomachache.

R: That's too bad!

T: Yeah, I think it was something I ate. It's probably just a 24-hour thing. I can't come in today, but I'll probably be there tomorrow.

R: OK. Umm, give me a call tomorrow and let me know how you are.

Conversation 4

T: Roger . . .

R: Tony . . . hmm, let me guess. You hurt your back, and you can't move.

T: How did you know?

R: Relax, Tony . . . . Stay in bed . . . . Take as long as you like. In fact, don't come back on Monday. You're fired. You don't work here anymore. A client saw you yesterday on your cell phone . . . at a hotel in Cancun . . . on vacation.

Pronunciation, Exercises 4 and 5, page 8

I'm sorry, but I have a cold.

I have a cough, and my throat is sore.

I'm really sorry, but I'm not feeling very well.

I have a fever, so I can't come to work.

Unit 3   A life of achievement

Reading from pages 10–11 for the Optional Grammar Warm-up

Note: See the Reading on *Student Book* pages 10–11 for the text of the audio.

Pronunciation, Exercise 4, page 13

Oprah lived in Mississippi.

She wanted to be famous.

She loved reading.

She studied hard.

But she decided to leave school.

She worked for a TV station.

She also acted in several movies.

She finished her first film in 1985.

She started her own TV show.

Millions of people watched it.

She used her success to start a charity.

The charity collected millions of dollars.

Pronunciation, Exercise 5, page 13

lived	decided	started
wanted	worked	watched
loved	acted	used
studied	finished	collected

Unit 4   Travel with English

Pronunciation, Exercise 2, page 14

England	Asia
Italy	Europe
Korea	Australia
Canada	Ireland
India	Africa

Pronunciation, Exercise 3, page 14

Column 1	Column 2	Column 3
England	Italy	Korea
Asia	Canada	Australia
Europe	India	
Ireland	Africa	

Reading from page 15 for the Optional Grammar Warm-up

Note: See the Reading on *Student Book* page 15 for the text of the audio.

Review 1   Units 1–4

Unit 1, It's the weekend!, Exercise 1, page 18

S = Suki   R = Roland   J = Jorge

S: Roland, do you always go to the gym on weekends?

R: No, I usually try to go, but I don't always. Do you?

S: No, I never go to the gym on weekends! That's when I relax.

R: OK, thanks.

S: Jorge, do you always go to the gym on weekends?

J: Yes, even if I'm really tired, I always go. It's important to stay in shape.

S: Great. Jorge . . .

J: Now let me ask you something. Do you usually go out to eat on the weekends?

S: Definitely! I usually have pizza on Friday night, and I like to go to different restaurants on Saturday.

J: OK, usually goes out to eat on weekends . . . Suki. Thanks!

Unit 2, Excuses, excuses, Exercise 4, page 18

A: OK, it's our turn. One space . . . I'm sorry, I can't come to work today. I have a sore throat.

B: That's OK. I'll see you tomorrow.

C: Now it's our turn. We move two spaces . . . I'm afraid I hurt my arm, so I can't come to work today.

D: I'm sorry! I hope you feel better.

B: OK, our turn!

Unit 3, A life of achievement, Exercise 6, page 19

A = Arnold   Y = Yoko   C = Chen

A: OK, here's my first statement: I visited the U.S. when I was ten years old.

Y: I don't know . . . It's possible . . . I guess I'll say *true*.

A: What do you think, Chen?

C: Well, I remember that you went to the U.S. last year, and I think it was your first time. So I'm going to say *false*.

A: Chen, you're right. I visited the U.S. last year for the first time. You get a point.

C: Yoko, now you read one of your statements . . .

Unit 4, Travel with English, Exercise 9, page 19

A: Where is he going to go on Saturday?

B: Saturday? Umm, he's going to fly into the city. But what is he going to do there?

C: He's going to visit a museum.

B: OK. . . . What about on Sunday? Where's he going to go?

A: He's going to drive down the coastline . . . .

World of Music 1   River Deep, Mountain High

Listening, Exercises 2 and 3, pages 20–21

When I was a little girl I had a rag doll;
The only doll I've ever owned.
Now I love you just the way I loved that rag doll;
But only now my love has grown.
And it gets stronger in every way,
And it gets deeper let me say,
And it gets higher day by day.

[Chorus]

Do I love you? My, oh, my!
River deep, mountain high
If I lost you would I cry?
Oh how I love you baby, baby, baby, baby.

When you were a young boy did you have a puppy
That always followed you around?
Well, I'm gonna be as faithful as that puppy
No, I'll never let you down.

'Cause it goes on and on like a river flows.
And it gets bigger, baby, and heaven knows,
And it gets sweeter, baby, as it grows.

[Repeat chorus]

I love you, baby, like a flower loves the spring.
And I love you, baby, like a robin loves to sing.
And I love you, baby, like a schoolboy loves his pie.
And I love you, baby, river deep, mountain high.

[Repeat chorus]

Unit 5   Culture shock

Listening, Exercises 3 and 4, page 23

W1 = businesswoman 1

M1 = businessman 1

M2 = businessman 2

W2 = businesswoman 2

W1: Hello, I'm here to talk about doing business in the U.S. First, does anyone have any questions?

M1: I do. I want to ask about meetings. When should we arrive?

W1: For business appointments, you should definitely arrive on time or possibly five minutes early.

M2: Should we exchange business cards when we first meet people?

W1: Actually, the first thing you should do is shake hands. At some point later, you can exchange business cards. Sometimes people exchange cards right away, and sometimes a little later, and sometimes they exchange cards at the end of their meeting. I guess it's not clear, but people usually exchange cards at some point during their meeting.

W2: I understand people are usually informal. Should we use first names?

W1: Hmm. That depends. If it's not clear, you should begin with the person's last name— call them Mr. or Ms. Smith. Or wait until they call you by your first name, and then you can do the same.

M2: What about social situations? What should we do if we're invited to someone's home?

W1: I'm glad you asked that question. When you go to someone's home for dinner, you should take some flowers or a small gift. But there's one big difference from Japan . . . you shouldn't take your shoes off. If you do, you'll be the only person in the room with no shoes.

M1: And what should we wear?

W1: For business meetings, you should of course wear a suit. For dinner parties, you should ask your host. Most people from the U.S. are informal outside of work!

Pronunciation, Exercises 5 and 6, page 25

You should arrive on time.

You shouldn't take your shoes off.

Should I take a gift?

Yes, you should.

Shouldn't I wear a suit?

No, you shouldn't.

Pronunciation, Exercise 7, page 25

1. You shouldn't arrive early.
2. You should ask questions.
3. Shouldn't I use first names?
4. You should take flowers.
5. Should I shake hands with everyone?

Unit 6   Party time!

Listening, Exercises 5 and 6, page 27

PP = Party planner   C = Client

PP: Hi. Nice to see you again. So, you're having another office party. Do you want to do it the same way as last year, or do you want to try something different? How about having a theme party? We could have . . .

C: No, I'd rather have a simpler party . . . we can't really afford anything fancy this year. Umm . . . how about looking at how much we spent last year and then we can decide together what to do?

PP: OK. First things first: Where do you want to have it? Why don't we rent the ballroom at the Sheraton again?

C: No, let's have it at the office this year. We don't need to pay for a big room when we have the uh, you know . . . our conference room. It's a good size for a party.

PP: Yes, that's fine. So how about the music?

C: Well, the music was great last year, but maybe you could get a DJ this time. Uh, we can't really afford a band.

PP: And how about food? Maybe we could do a dessert buffet—you know, have people serve themselves from a selection of cakes, pastries, and cookies. Dessert buffets are very popular this year. Are you interested?

C: Yeah, let's do that. Umm . . . how much does it cost?

PP: I'm sure we can give you a good price . . . .

A: Let's have a party next weekend.

B: Good idea. Why don't we get a band?

A: We can't afford it. How about getting a DJ?

B: OK. What about food?

A: Maybe we could order pizza.

B: I don't like pizza. Why don't we just have snacks?

Unit 7   First impressions

Listening, Exercises 3 and 4, page 31

A = Amy   C = Cristina

A: Hello. Hi, Cristina. It's Amy.

C: Oh, hi. What's up?

A: Listen, my friend Maurice asked me for your phone number. I think he wants to ask you out.

C: Really? Hmm, Maurice. Maurice, Maurice, . . . What does he look like?

A: He's in my English class. And you met him at the party the other night. You know, he's tall?

C: Oh, right. He's tall and has blond hair? And really nice hazel eyes?

A: No, he doesn't have blond hair or hazel eyes. He has brown hair—curly brown hair—and brown eyes.

C: OK. And he's a little heavy?

A: Heavy? No, he isn't heavy at all. He's quite slim. Very athletic-looking.

C: I still can't picture him. And I met him at the party?

A: Yes, remember? He was there with my friend, Julia.

C: Right. Julia. Julia, Julia . . . What color hair does she have?

A: Black. She has long, straight black hair.

C: Long hair? Wait, I must be thinking of someone else. How tall is she?

A: Well, she's pretty short. Shorter than I am, anyway.

C: OK, I think I know who Julia is. But wait, I still don't remember Maurice. Does he have a mustache?

A: No, he doesn't.

C: How old is he?

A: I don't know. In his late 20s. Probably around 28.

C: I still don't know who he is.

A: Well, he's really nice. And he's definitely interested in you.

C: OK. If you think he's nice, sure, give him my phone number. Maybe we can all meet for coffee or something. And could you email me his photo before we meet?

A: Sure thing. I'll see you later.

C: OK, bye.

Pronunciation, Exercises 4 and 5, page 33

She's tall and slim.

I'm not tall or slim.

He's average height and has black hair.

He isn't short or heavy.

He has curly brown hair and hazel eyes.

He doesn't have a beard or mustache.

She has long black hair and brown eyes.

She doesn't have blond hair or blue eyes.

Unit 8   At the movies

Reading from page 35 for the Optional Grammar Warm-up

Note: See the Reading on *Student Book* page 35 for the text of the audio.

Pronunciation, Exercises 5 and 6, page 37

a classic black-and-white film

the best science fiction movie

an interesting story

a slow start

exciting special effects

an excellent actress

He said that he liked *Star Wars*.

She told us she loved old films.

Review 2   Units 5–8

Unit 5, Culture shock, Exercise 1, page 38

A: Are you ready? Here's the first clue: When you do this, you shouldn't be late.

B: When you go to a job interview?

A: No. Here's the next clue: You should take a small gift.

C: When you go to a surprise birthday party?

A: No. Here's another clue: You should say that the food is delicious.

D: I know! You should do all those things when you go to a friend's home for dinner!

A: Yes, that's right!

Unit 6, Party time!, Exercise 5, page 38

A: OK, I'll go first . . . . Let's have the party outside!

B: Good idea. How about having a band?

C: Sure. And why don't we get some balloons?

A: Balloons are a good idea. Maybe we could serve hamburgers.

B: Yeah, let's have a barbecue.

C: I love barbecues . . .

Unit 7, First impressions, Exercise 7, page 39

A: OK, I'll describe my first picture. It's a woman. She's short, and she has a medium build. She has black hair. She's middle-aged, I think, maybe about 40 years old. She has brown eyes. What about yours?

B: Well, it's also a woman. She's middle-aged. She's a little bit heavy. She's medium height. She has brown hair and blue eyes.

A: OK, so it isn't the same person . . .

Unit 8, At the movies, Exercise 9, page 39

A: What kind of movies do you like?

B: I like action movies.

A: What's your favorite action movie?

B: Well, I like the Bond movies, especially the new ones.

A: Why do you like them?

B: The stories are good, and I like the special effects.

Unit 9   What would you like?

Listening, Exercises 4 and 5, page 41

W = Waiter   C1 = Customer 1   C2 = Customer 2

W: Good evening. Welcome to the Shrimp Boat. Would you like a table for two?

C1: Yes, please.

W: Would you like to sit here by the window or outside on the patio?

C2: It's chilly, darling. I'd prefer to sit inside.

C1: We'd like to sit inside, by the window.

W: Right this way. . .

W: Are you ready to order now, or would you like a few more minutes?

C2: Actually, we have a few questions. What's the Shrimp Savoy?

W: That's very good . . . . It's shrimp in an herb sauce with tomatoes and olives.

C1: Mmm! And the Shrimp Plaza, what's that?

W: That's delicious. Do you like olives?

C1: Yes, I do.

W: Well, it's shrimp in a delicious black olive sauce with tomatoes and herbs.

C2: And could you tell me about the Shrimp Ritz?

W: Oh, that's our signature dish. It's shrimp in a tomato sauce, with herbs and olives. Delicious!

C1: OK. I really like olives, so I'd like the Shrimp Plaza.

W: And what would you like?

C2: I'd like the Shrimp Ritz.

W: And would you prefer rice or pasta?

C1: I'd like rice.

C2: I'd prefer pasta.

W: Would you like an appetizer to start? We have three choices: the shrimp cocktail, the garden salad, or a great soup of the day. It's a shrimp soup with . . .

C1, C2: . . . tomatoes, olives, and herbs?

Pronunciation, Exercises 4 and 5, page 43

What would you like?
I'd like the shrimp.
Would you like salad?
Yes, thanks. I would.
Would you prefer rice or pasta?
I'd prefer pasta.

Unit 10   Big issues

Pronunciation, Exercises 2 and 3, page 44

climate	population
prediction	communication
transportation	economy
politics	government

Reading from page 45 for the Optional Grammar Warm-up

Note: See the Reading on *Student Book* page 45 for the text of the audio.

Unit 11   Hard work

Reading from page 49 for the Optional Grammar Warm-up

Note: See the Reading on *Student Book* page 49 for the text of the audio.

Pronunciation, Exercises 4 and 5, page 50

have to   have to work
I have to work long hours.
Does he have to work hard?

has to   has to drive
He has to drive a lot.
He has to pick up the pizza.

Unit 12   Island life

Reading from page 53 for the Optional Grammar Warm-up

Note: See the Reading on *Student Book* page 53 for the text of the audio.

Pronunciation, Exercise 5, page 55

Have you ever	Have you ever lived overseas?
Has he ever	Has he ever grown vegetables?
Have you ever	Have you ever spent time outdoors?
Have they ever	Have they ever used a computer?

Review 3   Units 9–12

Unit 9, What would you like?, Exercise 1, page 56

A: Would you like the menu?
B: Yes, please.
A: Are you ready to order?
B: Yes, I'd like to start with an appetizer.
A: What would you like? We have soup or shrimp cocktail.
B: Umm, Can you tell me about them?
A: Sure. The soup today is chicken with vegetables. The shrimp cocktail is shrimp with lemon and cocktail sauce.
B: I see. OK. I'd like the soup . . .

Unit 10, Big issues, Exercise 5, page 56

A: I predicted that cars won't need gasoline in 20 years. Did you make that prediction, too?
B: Well, I think that it will happen, but I don't think that it will happen in 20 years. The technology won't be ready then. I wrote that we'll have cars that don't use gasoline in 100 years. By then, we'll have the technology.
A: OK, we have the same prediction, just not at the same time, so we don't get any points. What's your prediction for 50 years?
B: Well, I think that in . . .

Unit 11, Hard work, Exercise 9, page 57

A: OK. Guess what job I'm thinking of.
B: Do you have to work outside?
A: Yes, I do.
C: Do you work inside, too?
A: Yes.
B: OK—outside and inside. Do you have to work with people?
A: Yes.
C: Do you have to use a computer?
A: No, not usually.
B: Do you work with food?
A: Yes, I do.
C: Are you a grocery store owner?
A: No, I'm not.
B: Do you have to drive a car?
A: Yes.
B: I know! You're a delivery person!
A: That's right!
C: OK, we had to ask seven questions to guess the job . . . .

Unit 12, Island life, Exercise 11, page 57

A: Have you ever cooked for a large group?
B: No, I haven't.
A: Oh, too bad.
B: Have you ever taken care of animals?
A: Yes, I have.
B: Great. So I can write your name there . . . . Thanks.

World of Music 2   Wonderful Tonight

Listening, Exercises 2 and 3, pages 58–59

It's late in the evening
She's wondering what clothes to wear.
She puts on her makeup
and brushes her long blonde hair.
And then she asks me, "Do I look all right?"
and I say, "Yes, you look wonderful tonight."

We go to a party
and everyone turns to see
this beautiful lady,
who's walking around with me.
And then she asks me, "Do you feel all right?"
and I say, "Yes, I feel wonderful tonight.

I feel wonderful because I see the love light in your eyes,
and the wonder of it all, is that you just don't realize,
how much I love you."

It's time to go home now
and I've got an aching head.
So I give her the car keys
and she helps me into bed.

And then I tell her,
as I turn off the light,
I say, "My darling, you were wonderful tonight!
Oh, my darling, you were wonderful tonight."

Unit 13   Keepsakes

Getting started, Exercise 3, page 60

1.	ballet shoes	I
2.	baseball glove	E
3.	camera	A
4.	doll	H
5.	jewelry box	F
6.	photo album	C
7.	pin	B
8.	shawl	J
9.	toy truck	G
10.	watch	D

Listening, Exercises 6 and 7, page 61

M = Mr. Freeman   L = Lisa

M: Oh, look. It's the old trunk. I haven't seen this in years. Your mother put a lot of keepsakes in here when we moved.

L: What's inside? Can we open it?

M: Yeah, let's take a look.

L: What's that?

M: Let's see . . . Oh, look at all this stuff. Your mom didn't want to throw these things away.

L: What's that, Dad?

M: This is your grandmother's jewelry box.

L: Oh, it's so pretty! Is there anything in it?

D   No, it's empty. Your grandmother passed her jewelry on to your mother. Hasn't Mom ever shown you her mom's jewelry?

L: No, I don't think so. I'll ask her later . . . . Dad! What's this?

M: That's Grandpa's watch. He wore it all the time. Look! It still works!

L: Ooo, look! An old photo album!

D   That's mine. It has pictures from when I was in school.

L: Be careful, Dad! The album is falling apart.

M: You're right. The pages are falling out. Let's put it away. We can look at it later.

L: OK . . . Oh, look! A baseball glove! Cool!

M: Wow! That belongs to your mother! She loved playing baseball when she was a little girl. Your uncles say she was pretty good.

L: Can I use the glove?

M: Try it on. Does it fit?

L: Yeah!

M: OK, great. We can play some baseball this afternoon.

L: I want to show this to Mom! This is so cool!

Pronunciation, Exercises 8 and 9, page 61

Take it out.
Don't give it away.
It's falling apart.
I'll try it on.
Let's throw it away.
Wait! Something is falling out.

Unit 14   Tales of Nasreddin Hodja

Getting started, Exercise 2, page 64

1. upset   a. unhappy
2. embarrassed   b. ashamed
3. calm   a. relaxed
4. suspicious   b. not trusting
5. proud   b. pleased with yourself
6. polite   a. kind
7. absent-minded   a. forgetful
8. rude   b. bad-mannered
9. loud   b. noisy

upset	polite
embarrassed	absent-minded
calm	rude
suspicious	loud
proud	

Reading from page 65 for the Optional Grammar Warm-up

Note: See the Reading on *Student Book* page 65 for the text of the audio.

Pronunciation, Exercises 5 and 6, page 67

angrily	quietly
suspiciously	comfortably

Pronunciation, Exercises 7 and 8, page 67

happily	nervously
politely	hungrily

Unit 15   Popular sports

Getting started, Exercise 3, page 68

go biking, go jogging, go skiing, go swimming
play basketball, play golf, play hockey, play soccer, play tennis, play volleyball
do aerobics, do karate

aerobics	hockey	soccer
basketball	jogging	swimming
biking	karate	tennis
golf	skiing	volleyball

Listening, Exercise 5, page 69

A = Anchor   CB = Carol Brand

A: . . . And finally, a new report from the Canadian Fitness Institute, or CFI, shows some interesting results. The institute conducted a survey of Canadian men and women who participate in some kind of sport. Carol Brand, you helped analyze the results of the study. What can we learn from it?

CB: Well, we can really look at the kind of exercise that Canadians like doing.

A: So, which sport do Canadians like playing the most?

CB: That's an interesting one. The two most popular sports are golf and hockey. A total of fifteen percent of the people in the study really love playing one of these two sports.

A: And I suppose that hockey was the most popular?

CB: Surprisingly, no, it wasn't. Golf was the most popular sport in the study; eight percent play golf, while only seven percent play hockey.

A: That *is* surprising! . . . Well, what other sports do people like playing?

CB: Well, baseball is pretty popular . . . six percent say they play baseball. The next one is swimming—five percent of the people in the study say that they like swimming.

A: Hmm. So we have two team sports—hockey and baseball—and two individual sports—golf and swimming.

CB: That's right. And two other popular sports are also team sports: volleyball and basketball.

A: How many people play those sports?

CB: Those two are equal: three percent of the people in the study love volleyball and three percent love basketball.

A: So we see how Canadians like to get their exercise! Are there other things that we can learn from this study? For example, . . .

Listening, Exercise 6, page 69

CB: Another thing the report shows is that men and women like playing different sports.

A: Really? Well, do men and women both like playing golf and hockey, the two most popular sports in Canada?

CB: According to the study, a lot of men play both of those sports, but most women don't like playing golf or hockey very much. But, can you guess which sport women do more often than men?

A: Uh, volleyball?

CB: That's a good guess, but men and women were actually almost equal in volleyball. No, the sport that is most popular with women is swimming. Six percent of women say that they like swimming, compared to only four percent of men.

A: I bet that more men prefer baseball.

CB: You're right. Men seem to like team sports a lot. Baseball and basketball are both much more popular with men than with women. Eight percent of men play baseball, compared to only three percent of women. And five percent of men play basketball, but only two percent of women do!

A: That's very interesting. For more results of CFI's study, you can visit our web page . . . .

Pronunciation, Exercises 5 and 6, page 71

Do you like skiing?

Yes, I love skiing.

Do you like playing golf?

No, I hate playing golf.

Women liked swimming, and men liked basketball.

My sister likes doing aerobics, and my brother likes playing soccer.

Unit 16 Food for thought

Getting started, Exercise 2, page 72

1. bread	B	8. oranges	J
2. chocolate	M	9. salt	K
3. cookies	D	10. strawberries	I
4. fruit	E	11. vegetables	C
5. juice	G	12. water	F
6. lettuce	L	13. yogurt	H
7. onions	A		

bread	lettuce	vegetables
chocolate	onions	water
cookies	oranges	yogurt
fruit	salt	
juice	strawberries	

Pronunciation, Exercise 4, page 72

| soup | good | cookies | juice |
| sugar | food | fruit | |

Pronunciation, Exercise 5, page 72

Column 1	Column 2
soup	sugar
food	good
fruit	cookies
juice	

Listening, Exercises 9 and 10, page 73

I have good news today for all you chocolate lovers. Recent studies say chocolate is good for you! But how much chocolate should you eat? Well, not much—a maximum of three chocolate bars a month. Eating twenty chocolate cookies a day is definitely not a good idea, but remember: chocolate eaters live longer than non-chocolate eaters.

And the same is true for salt. Another recent study says salt eaters live longer. Now there's a change! Do you have any salt in the house these days?

Another myth from the past is that bread and potatoes make you fat. A new study says, "Eat a lot of bread and potatoes. You'll lose weight and get thinner." Ha! They don't know how many potatoes I can eat.

Do you remember the saying "An apple a day keeps the doctor away?" Well, dentists might not agree. They now say there is a lot of acid in fruit. It's bad for your teeth, so don't eat much fruit—or at least brush your teeth after you eat it!

Finally, doctors used to say that you shouldn't drink coffee or tea, but now it's OK. Coffee is an anti-depressant: a few cups of coffee a day can make you happy. And . . . a little tea can help you think. So there's a little food for thought! Happy eating!

Review 4 Units 13–16

Unit 13, Keepsakes, Exercise 1, page 76

One special keepsake is my grandfather's watch . . . . It's an old-fashioned watch, you know, a round pocket watch. And it still works! My grandmother gave it to me after my grandfather died. And it's important to me because his father gave it to him. So it's very old. Someday, I'm going to pass it on to one of my children. It's gold on the outside . . .

Unit 14, Tales of Nasreddin Hodja, Exercise 6, page 76

A: OK, I'll go first. Hmm, *happily*. Let's see. . .
One day a young man walked happily down the road. He was happy because he was going to visit the most beautiful woman in the village. Now it's your turn.

B: OK. I got *absent-mindedly*. Umm . . . He absent-mindedly looked up at the sky while he was walking. Suddenly he saw something shocking.

C: My turn. Umm, *calmly*. . . . The man took a deep breath. He calmly started to walk backwards.

D: OK . . . *quickly*. Umm, then he turned around. He started to walk more quickly . . .

A: Great! My turn again . . . Umm, ...

Unit 15, Popular sports, Exercise 10, page 77

A: So, which resort do you want to go to?

B: I love skiing, so I'd like to go to the Blue Mountain Club.

C: I hate skiing. I don't like cold weather.

A: What do you like doing?

C: I love doing aerobics . . . but I also like doing karate.

A: I love doing sports outside . . .

C: Then we can go to the Sports Plus Club. They have golf!

B: I don't know. I don't really like playing golf. But I like biking! What about . . .

Unit 16, Food for thought, Exercise 12, page 77

A: Hello?

B: Hi. It's me. I'm at the supermarket, and I'm not sure what we need. Do we have any bread?

A: Yes, but not a lot. Can you get some more?

B: Sure. Wait a second, I have to write it down . . . How about fruit? Do we have any fruit?

A: Well, we have a lot of oranges and a few strawberries. But we don't have any apples or bananas.

B: OK. We need apples and bananas. And do we have any vegetables?

A: Vegetables? Let's see . . . there are a lot of onions . . .

B: So I'll get some lettuce and tomatoes, and we can make a salad.

A: That sounds good. OK, we also . . .

Unit 17   A nice place to work

Listening, Exercises 6 and 7, page 79

I = Interviewer   T = Tom

I: We're in New York to learn about new office practices in the U.S. Tom Banks works for a large computer firm here in the city. He's been in the computer field for more than twenty years. Tom, how have office practices changed?

T: Well, one change is how we dress. Twenty years ago, I had to wear a suit every day. But—oh, about ten years ago—the company introduced casual Fridays . . .

I: Casual Fridays?

T: Yes. On Fridays, we don't have to wear a suit. We can wear "business-casual" clothes. We have to wear clothes that look good—we can't wear sneakers or jeans—but we don't have to wear suits and ties anymore on Fridays.

I: So, do you like wearing casual clothes to work?

T: Yes, it's much more comfortable. And I don't have to spend so much money on expensive suits.

I: That's great! And work relationships? How different are they?

T: Today, our relationships are much less formal. In the past, we had to call our supervisors by their titles and last names— you know, "Mr. or Ms. So and So." But today, we don't have to use last names. We call one another by our first names—even the CEO of the company!

I: Is your work schedule different?

T: Oh, yes. That's changed a lot, too. Today, I have to work longer hours! But it's flexible. In the past, we had to work from 9:00 to 5:00 every day, but now I don't have to. Now, we have flextime, so I can work from 11:00 to 7:00 if I want to, and I don't have to go into the office every day. I can work at home some of the time and telecommute.

I: So, what do you think about these new office practices?

T: They're great. The company had to change to keep its good employees. This was a great company when I started here twenty years ago. But you know what? It's even better now!

Pronunciation, Exercises 4 and 5, page 81

I had to wear a suit to the office.
I had to work from 9 to 5.
But now I don't have to.
I don't have to wear a suit to work.
I don't have to go to the office every day.
I can work from 11 to 7 if I want to.
But I have to work longer hours!

Unit 18   Hollywood mystery

Reading from page 83 for the Optional Grammar Warm-up

Note: See the Reading on *Student Book* page 83 for the text of the audio.

Pronunciation, Exercises 4 and 5, page 85

We were playing video games.
My parents were standing in the study.
They were waiting for the police.
Our housekeeper was working in the kitchen.
A man was running away.
He was wearing sneakers.

Unit 19   Bargain hunters

Pronunciation, Exercises 5 and 6, page 87

newsstand   coffee house   hair salon

Pronunciation, Exercise 8, page 87

drugstore   haircut   convenience store
clothing store   candy bar

Listening, Exercises 10 and 11, page 87

Well, this is what happened . . . I went to the television station and met the other contestants. We got our lists. There were seven items on the list. They said we had four hours to shop. I left the station and started shopping.

First, I went to the newsstand for a magazine. It was $3.95. So far, so good.

Then, I went to the drugstore because I had to get a bottle of a hundred aspirin. I found a bottle for $4.99. That was OK, but I was worried because the most expensive items were still to come.

After the drugstore, I went to the hair salon to get a shampoo, haircut, and blow-dry. I looked great, but it cost $35.00! It was my most expensive purchase so far. My total was $43.94. Was that low enough? I hoped so!

One of the things on my list was a cup of coffee. Since I needed time to think, I went to a coffee house next. I bought a cup of coffee for $2.50. I drank my coffee and planned my next stop.

After that, I went to a clothing store because a blouse was next on my list—a pink blouse. Luckily, there was one left. And it was on sale! It was only $24.99. Things were looking good!

Next, I went to a convenience store to buy a candy bar. It cost 65 cents, so my total didn't go up much. But I felt good because I was almost done. Only one more stop to go.

I saved the best for last—lunch at a Chinese restaurant. The food was great, but I ate fast because I wanted to see the check. It was $7.50. I rushed back to the station. The other contestants were there, and we all showed our totals. And guess what! I spent the lowest amount—$79.58—and I won!

Unit 20   A long run

Reading from page 91 for the Optional Grammar Warm-up

Note: See the Reading on *Student Book* page 91 for the text of the audio.

Pronunciation, Exercises 4 and 5, page 93

The Mousetrap is the longest-running play.
A couple has an old house.
They turn the house into a hotel.
You have to see the play.
The ending is very surprising.

Review 5   Units 17–20

Unit 17, A nice place to work, Exercise 1, page 94

A: So, you're interested in a job as a salesperson in my bookstore. Do you have any experience?

B: Well, I worked in another bookstore.

A: Really? What did you do?

B: I had to wait on customers. It was a very busy store, so I had to help a lot of people.

A: In our store, you also have to look up titles on the computer. Do you know how to do that?

B: Yes, I did that all the time.

Unit 18, Hollywood mystery, Exercise 5, page 94

A: What were you doing at 9:30?

B: I was at the video store with my friend. We were looking for a movie to watch.

A: Which movie did you choose?

B: We chose . . . um . . . *Daredevil*.

A: Who paid for the movie?

B: I did.

A: OK, what did you do after that?

B: Well, we left the video store. My friend was driving, and I was pointing directions . . . .

Unit 19, Bargain hunters, Exercise 9, page 95

A = Ari   J = Jenny   R = Roberto   D = Darcy

Ari: I'm going to the newsstand to buy a magazine.

J: Ari is going to the newsstand to buy a magazine, and I'm going to the convenience store for some gum.

R: OK, Ari is going to the newsstand to buy a magazine. Jenny is going to the convenience store for some gum, and I'm going to the drugstore because I need aspirin.

D: Ari is going to the newsstand to buy a magazine. Jenny is going to the convenience store for some gum. Roberto is going to the drugstore because he needs aspirin, and I'm going to the hair salon to get a haircut.

R: Ari, you go again.

Ari: All right . . . I'm going to the newsstand to buy a magazine. Jenny . . . .

Unit 20, A long run, Exercise 11, page 95

A: My turn first, right? Um, the woman's name is Maria. She's a famous actress.

B: OK . . . Maria's in a popular play. The play is a love story . . . . Your turn now.

C: Everyone in the audience loves the play. They clap for a long time at the end.

A: Hmm. . . . The man in the audience is Tony. This is the first time he's seen the play.

B: He is looking at Maria. He thinks she is beautiful.

C: When the play is over, Tony . . .

World of Music 3   Matter of Time

Listening, Exercises 2 and 3, pages 96–97

Speak softly.
Don't wake the baby.
Come and hold me once more,
Before I have to leave.
Hear there's a lot of work out there.
Everything will be fine.
And I'll send for you, baby,
Just a matter of time.

Our life,
The only thing we know.
Come and tell me once more,
Before you have to go.
But there's a better world out there,
Though it don't feel right.
Will it feel like our home?
Just a matter of time.

And I hope this song we sing's
Not another empty dream.
There's a time for you and me,
In a place living happily.

[repeat]

Walk quietly.
Don't make a sound.
Believe in what you're doing,
I know we can't be wrong.
Don't worry about a thing,
We'll be all right.
And we'll be there with you,
Just a matter of time.

And we'll all be together,
Just a matter of time.
Matter of time
Matter of time

We'll be together,
In a matter of time.
You and me,
In a matter of time.
Feel like a home,
Matter of time.

Unit 21　Long life

Pronunciation, Exercises 3 and 4, page 98

thirty-first	there
three	more than
month	the day

Pronunciation, Exercise 5, page 98

When did you start work there?

> In 2002.
> When I was 23.
> The beginning of the month.
> More than three months ago.
> On Thursday, the 30th.

Reading from page 99 for the Optional Grammar Warm-up

Note: See the Reading on *Student Book* page 99 for the text of the audio.

Unit 22　Job share

Listening, Exercises 7 and 8, page 103

K = Ken　　M = Marcy

K: Hi. So, how were Monday and Tuesday?

M: Busy. Someone wanted one of our male models immediately for a jeans ad—you know, that new guy, Eric. I had to answer the phone every two minutes, and hundreds of people left messages. On top of that, Ed kept giving me faxes to send, copying to do, emails to reply to . . . It was crazy.

K: Wow! So how much did you get done?

M: Not much. I did the copying and the emails, but I didn't have time to send these faxes yesterday, and I think they're important.

K: Well, would you like me to send them for you?

M: Please. And can you call the photographer? Ed wants to have a meeting with her. He asked me to do that yesterday, too.

K: OK. When?

M: Tonight, I think . . . . Yeah, about 8:00.

K: Tonight? OK. Should I call her now?

M: Yeah, that'd be great. And Ed wants a lunch meeting at Loon's Restaurant with Eric, the new model. Could you call him, too? I forgot. Uh, I have his phone number here somewhere. Ah, here it is. Oh, no! And I didn't make a reservation at the restaurant! Oops!

K: Look. I have my own work to do for Ed today. I can't do your work, too. I'll arrange the meeting with the photographer, but can you make the other calls before you go?

M: Sorry. I can't now. I'm meeting my girlfriend for lunch and I'm already late. Oh—I almost forgot. Ed wants to see you right away. He has a few extra things he needs you to do today.

K: What?

Pronunciation, Exercises 4 and 5, page 105

Can you call the restaurant, please?
Can you send these faxes?
Could you do this copying?
Could you answer the phone?
Should I make a reservation?
Should I call a taxi?
Would you like me to arrange a meeting?
Would you like me to do the filing?

Unit 23　Changing customs

Getting started, Exercise 2, page 106

1. Do men open doors for women?
2. Do women wear long skirts?
3. Do families have dinner together every night?
4. Do women do all the housework?
5. Do people shop for food every day?
6. Do families play games together in the evening?
7. Do people stay home in the evening?
8. Do people travel by horse and carriage?
9. Do people take off their shoes and put on slippers when they go into a house?

Reading from page 107 for the Optional Grammar Warm-up

Note: See the Reading on *Student Book* page 107 for the text of the audio.

Pronunciation, Exercises 4 and 5, page 109

used to	Women used to wear long skirts.
didn't use to	Poor people didn't use to wear red shoes.

What did they use to do at weddings?
They used to throw shoes at the bride and groom.

Unit 24   Take a risk

Pronunciation, Exercise 2, page 110

rock climbing	waterskiing
snowboarding	scuba diving
jet skiing	snorkeling
parasailing	skateboarding
snowmobiling	windsurfing

Pronunciation, Exercise 3, page 110

Column 1	Column 2
parasailing	rock climbing
snowmobiling	snowboarding
waterskiing	jet skiing
scuba diving	snorkeling
	skateboarding
	windsurfing

Listening, Exercises 5 and 6, page 111

D = Dave   A = Andy   P = Paula

D: Hi, everyone. Welcome to Adventure Zone! I'm Dave . . . . Now, let's find out which sports you want to do on your vacation. OK, and . . . what's your name?

A: Andy Jenkins.

D: OK, Andy. Jenkins, Jenkins . . . yes. Here you are on the list. Have you done any adventure sports before?

A: Yes, I've gone snorkeling—I learned to snorkel when I was a kid, and I love it. And I've been waterskiing and parasailing, but only once.

D: Waterskiing and parasailing? When did you do that?

A: On my vacation in Puerto Rico last year.

D: And what did you think of them?

A: Well, I really enjoyed waterskiing. But I didn't like parasailing very much.

D: So, what do you want to try this time?

A: Scuba diving. I've never done it before. But I've seen it on TV, and it looks great. And I've never been windsurfing, either. I'd like to try that, too.

D: OK! And you're . . .?

P: Paula Benson.

D: Paula Benson . . . uh, I can't find your name.

P: But I'm not . . .

D: Not on the list. I know. That's all right. Have you ever done any of these sports, Paula?

P: Yes, but . . .

D: Like what?

P: I've done all of them, lots of times, but . . .

D: And you enjoyed them all?

P: Yes, I did, but I'm not here . . .

D: OK. But surely there's something you haven't done?

P: No, I've done everything. Look, I'm not here on vacation. I'm the new water-sports instructor.

D: Oh . . .

Review 6   Units 21–24

Unit 21, Long life, Exercise 1, page 114

A: OK, are you ready? Here's my first statement: I've had a computer since last year.

B: I think that one's true. Your homework is always done on the computer.

C: Well, I think it's false. You always check your email at school, so I don't think you have a computer at home.

B: So, is it true or false?

A: It's true . . . I've had a computer since last year. Barbara, you said true, so you get a point.

C: But what about checking your email at school?

A: Oh, I just do that when I have extra time before class. I check it at home, too.

B: OK, now it's my turn. Ready?

Unit 22, Job share, Exercise 4, page 114

A: OK, let's look at our to-do list. How should we divide the work?

B: Well, I can make copies. Is that OK with you?

A: That sounds good. Umm . . . would you like me to make the coffee?

B: Yes, thanks. And I'll return Ms. Boon's phone call.

A: Oh, good. I hate returning phone calls. Could you write the email messages?

B: Sure, no problem. So, I'll make copies, return Ms. Boon's call, and send emails. Could you make the lunch reservations?

A: Yeah, I'd be happy to. And what else is on our list?

B: Well, let's see, we have to do the filing . . .

Unit 23, Changing customs, Exercise 8, page 115

A: My turn first. Oh, good, I get two points for this sentence. OK, the first verb is *be*. Let's see . . . As a child, I used to be very short. I finally started to get taller when I was about 12. Now I'm one of the tallest people I know. So, write down two points for me . . . OK, your turn!

B: OK. Oh, I only get one point for my sentence. OK, well, *be*. Umm, I used to be very shy as a child.

A: Really?

B: Yes, really. I used to be very shy, and I didn't use to speak in class at all.

A: Well, now . . .

B: Now I'm not shy, and I talk in class all the time. Write down one point for me. Here, it's your turn again.

A: Thanks. Two points again! OK, the next verb is . . . .

Unit 24, Take a risk, Exercise 10, page 115

Conversation 1

C = Celia   E = Eli

C: Eli, have you ever gone snowboarding?

E: No, I haven't.

C: Oh, too bad. Your turn now.

E: OK. Have you ever gone windsurfing?

C: Yes, I have.

E: Great! I'll write down your name . . . Celia . . . OK, thanks. Bye!

C: Bye!

Conversation 2

E = Ellie   M = Mina

E: Hey, Mina, have you ever gone windsurfing?

M: Yes, I have!

E: Oh, good. Let me write your name . . . Mina.

Unit 25   Real fighters

Reading from page 117 for the Optional Grammar Warm-up

Note: See the Reading on *Student Book* page 117 for the text of the audio.

Pronunciation, Exercises 4 and 5, page 118

Could you play the piano?
Yes, I could.
How well could you play?
I could play pretty well.
Could you ski?
No, I couldn't. I couldn't ski at all.

Unit 26   On the go

Listening, Exercises 4 and 5, page 121

K = Katia   M = Melissa

K: Hi, Melissa. How's it going?

M: Don't ask! I'm going crazy. There's so much to do!

K: When are you leaving?

M: In a week. By this time next week, I'll be in Quito.

K: Wow! You must be excited. Last time we spoke, you were trying to sell the car. Have you sold it yet?

M: Yes, thank goodness. Someone bought it yesterday, so now I need to call the bank and transfer the money. And I've gotten all my vaccinations.

K: Good for you. Did they hurt?

M: Yes—they were horrible, but at least I don't have to worry about them anymore. Oh, and my new passport has arrived.

K: Great! What about the visa?

M: No, not yet. I couldn't apply for it without the passport. But I talked to someone at the embassy in New York. She promised to take care of it quickly, but she hasn't called back yet.

K: And what about your ticket?

M: Yeah, I've already bought my airline ticket . . . and I went online and made a hotel reservation for the first week.

K: So what else do you have to do?

M: Just pack my bags, I haven't done that yet . . . but I can't until the last minute, anyway.

K: And when do you start your new job?

M: The week after next.

K: So that's it! You're really going!

M: Yes . . . I hope I'm doing the right thing and that I have no regrets!

Pronunciation, Exercises 4 and 5, page 122

I've already sold the car.

She's already sold the car.

I've called my aunt.

She's called her aunt.

I've gotten a visa.

She's gotten a visa.

I've changed my email address.

She's changed her email address.

Unit 27   Behave yourself

Reading from pages 124–125 for the Optional Grammar Warm-up

Note: See the Reading on *Student Book* pages 124–125 for the text of the audio.

Pronunciation, Exercises 6 and 7, page 125

| give | gift | if | it |
| forget | friend | remember | never |

I give him a gift.	If I remember, I give him a gift.
I send it later.	If I forget, I send it later.
I never give it away.	If I get a gift from a friend, I never give it away.

Unit 28   Just the job for you

Pronunciation, Exercises 2 and 3, page 129

| work | learn | perfect |
| earn | computer | researcher |

Pronunciation, Exercises 4 and 5, page 129

work outdoors	the perfect career
earn more	market researcher
computer software	

Reading from page 129 for the Optional Grammar Warm-up

Note: See the Reading on *Student Book* page 129 for the text of the audio.

Grammar focus, Exercise 4, page 130

A: I 'd like to get a new job.

B: What would you like to do in your next job?

A: Well, I love computers, and I like working with technology. I'm not really a "people person," so I don't think I'd like to work with people all the time.

B: OK, how about computer repair? Would you like to learn how to fix computers?

A: That sounds interesting. I've never tried it, but I'd like to fix things, I think.

B: OK, are you interested in fixing cars?

A: No, I wouldn't like to be an auto mechanic. I hate getting dirty. I'd like to try computer repair. I think that might be just the job for me!

Review 7   Units 25–28

Unit 25, Real fighters, Exercise 1, page 132

A: What could Lise do ten years ago? Could she swim?

B: No, she couldn't swim very well.

A: OK . . . How about diving?

B: She was no good at diving—she couldn't dive at all!

A: OK . . . And could she skate?

B: Well, she was pretty good at skating.

A: Uh-huh.

B: All right, what about . . .

Unit 26, On the go, Exercise 4, page 132

A: Let's see, he hasn't packed his suitcase yet.

B: Right. But look—he's already gotten his passport.

A: Yes, what else? Has he made a hotel reservation?

C: No, look here. See? He hasn't made it yet.

B: Hmm. What else? Has he bought his airline ticket yet?

D: Look here. I think it's a printout . . . .

Unit 27, Behave yourself, Exercise 7, page 133

A: Here's a situation for you. What do you do if you lend your friend $100, and he or she forgets about it?

B: Well, if my friend forgets that he owes me money, I usually remind him.

A: Really? You do that? What about you, Grace? What do you do?

C: Hmm, that's a difficult situation. I don't tell my friend directly. I just remind him by email. And what do you usually do?

A: If it's a hundred dollars, I ask my friend when she can pay me back. If it's a small amount, say a dollar or two, I just forget about it. But she can never borrow money from me again.

Unit 28, Just the job for you, Exercise 10, page 133

A: Mark says he likes working with children. Maybe he can be a teacher.

B: Right, but he says he'd like to work outside and be active. Teachers usually work inside.

A: Sometimes they do a lot of paperwork, too. Mark doesn't like doing paperwork.

B: That's true. So what can he do?

A: Well, how about being a coach? Like a soccer coach or basketball coach?

B: Good idea. That's very active.

A: And he can work outside.

B: Great. He can be a coach. Now we need to think . . . .

World of Music 4　This Used to Be My Playground

Listening, Exercises 3 and 4, pages 134–135

[Chorus]
This used to be my playground.
This used to be my childhood dream.
This used to be the place I ran to
Whenever I was in need
Of a friend.
Why did it have to end?
And why do they always say:

Don't look back,
Keep your head held high.
Don't ask them why
Because life is short.
And before you know,
You're feeling old,
And your heart is breaking.
Don't hold on to the past.
Well, that's too much to ask.

[Chorus]

No regrets,
But I wish that you
Were here with me.
Well, then there's hope yet.
I can see your face
In our secret place.
You're not just a memory.
Say goodbye to yesterday
Those are words I'll never say.

This used to be my playground.
This used to be our pride and joy.
This used to be the place we ran to
That no one in the world could dare destroy.

This used to be our playground. (used to be)
This used to be our childhood dream.
This used to be the place we ran to.
I wish you were here with me.

This used to be my playground. (Ah, ah, ah)
This used to be my childhood dream.
This used to be the place we ran to.
The best things in life are always free.
Wishing you were here with me.

Workbook Audioscript

Based on the Student Audio CD

Unit 1

Listening, Exercises 5 and 6, page 14

Script same as *Student Book* Listening, Exercises 4 and 5, page T154

Pronunciation, Exercises 7 and 8, page 14

Script same as *Student Book* Pronunciation, Exercises 6 and 7, page T154

Unit 2

Listening, Exercises 5 and 6, page 17

Script same as *Student Book* Listening, Exercises 5 and 6, page T154

Pronunciation, Exercises 7 and 8, page 17

Script same as *Student Book* Pronunciation, Exercises 4 and 5, page T155

Unit 3

Listening, Exercises 5 and 6, page 20

Note: See the Reading on *Student Book* pages 10 and 11 for the text of the audio.

Pronunciation, Exercises 7 and 8, page 20

Script same as *Student Book* Pronunciation, Exercise 5, page T155

Unit 4

Listening, Exercises 6 and 7, page 23

Note: See the Reading on *Student Book* page 15 for the text of the audio.

Pronunciation, Exercises 8 and 9, page 23

Script same as *Student Book* Pronunciation, Exercise 2, page T155

Unit 5

Listening, Exercises 5 and 6, page 28

Script same as *Student Book* Listening, Exercises 3 and 4, page T156

Pronunciation, Exercise 7, page 28

Script same as *Student Book* Pronunciation, Exercise 7, page T156

Unit 6

Listening, Exercises 5 and 6, page 31

Script same as *Student Book* Listening, Exercises 5 and 6, page T157

Pronunciation, Exercises 7 and 8, page 31

Script same as *Student Book* Pronunciation, Exercises 4 and 5, page T157

Unit 7

Listening, Exercises 5 and 6, page 34

Script same as *Student Book* Listening, Exercises 3 and 4, page T157

Pronunciation, Exercises 7 and 8, page 34 (Student CD Track 63)

tall and slim
short and heavy
a beard or mustache
black hair and brown eyes

Unit 8

Listening, Exercises 5 and 6, page 37

Note: See the Reading on *Student Book* page 35 for the text of the audio.

Pronunciation, Exercises 7 and 8, page 37

Script same as *Student Book* Pronunciation, Exercises 5 and 6, page T157

Unit 9

Listening, Exercises 5 and 6, page 42

Script same as *Student Book* Listening, Exercises 4 and 5, page T158

Pronunciation, Exercises 7 and 8, page 42

Script same as *Student Book* Pronunciation, Exercises 4 and 5, page T158

Unit 10

Listening, Exercises 5 and 6, page 45

Note: See the Reading on *Student Book* page 45 for the text of the audio.

Pronunciation, Exercises 7 and 8, page 45

Script same as *Student Book* Pronunciation, Exercises 2 and 3, page T158

Unit 11

Listening, Exercises 5 and 6, page 48

Note: See the Reading on *Student Book* page 49 for the text of the audio.

Pronunciation, Exercises 7 and 8, page 48 (Student CD Track 64)

1. I have to work long hours.
2. Does he have to work hard?
3. He has to drive a lot.
4. He has to pick up the pizza.
5. We have to meet clients.
6. Do you have to travel to meet them?
7. Yes. And I have to give a lot of presentations.
8. We have to communicate well.

Unit 12

Listening, Exercises 5 and 6, page 51

Note: See the Reading on *Student Book* page 53 for the text of the audio.

Pronunciation, Exercises 7, 8, and 9, page 51

Script same as *Student Book* Pronunciation, Exercise 5, page T159

Unit 13

Listening, Exercises 6 and 7, page 56

Script same as *Student Book* Listening, Exercises 6 and 7, page T160

Pronunciation, Exercises 8 and 9, page 56

Script same as *Student Book* Pronunciation, Exercises 8 and 9, page T160

Unit 14

Listening, Exercises 5–8, page 59

Note: See the Reading on *Student Book* page 65 for the text of the audio.

Pronunciation, Exercises 9 and 10, page 59

Script same as *Student Book* Pronunciation, Exercises 5–8, page T160

Unit 15

Listening, Exercises 5 and 6, page 62

Script same as *Student Book* Listening, Exercise 5, page T161

Pronunciation, Exercises 7 and 8, page 62

Script same as *Student Book* Pronunciation, Exercises 5 and 6, page T161

Unit 16

Listening, Exercises 5 and 6, page 65

Script same as *Student Book* Listening, Exercises 9 and 10, page T162

Pronunciation, Exercises 7 and 8, page 65 (Student CD Track 65)

1. good   food
2. fruit   soup
3. sugar   cookies
4. good   soup
5. fruit   juice

Unit 17

Listening, Exercises 5 and 6, page 70

Script same as *Student Book* Listening, Exercises 6 and 7, pages T162–T163

Pronunciation, Exercises 7 and 8, page 70

Script same as *Student Book* Pronunciation, Exercises 4 and 5, page T163

Unit 18

Listening, Exercises 5 and 6, page 73

Note: See the Reading on *Student Book* page 83 for the text of the audio.

Pronunciation, Exercises 7 and 8, page 73

Script same as *Student Book* Pronunciation, Exercises 4 and 5, page T163

Unit 19

Listening, Exercises 5 and 6, page 76

Script same as *Student Book* Listening, Exercises 10 and 11, page T163

Pronunciation, Exercises 7 and 8, page 76

Script same as *Student Book* Pronunciation, Exercises 5–8, page T163

Unit 20

Listening, Exercises 5 and 6, page 79

Note: See the Reading on *Student Book* page 91 for the text of the audio.

Pronunciation, Exercises 7 and 8, page 79

Script same as *Student Book* Pronunciation, Exercises 4 and 5, page T163

Unit 21

Listening, Exercises 5 and 6, page 84

Note: See the Reading on *Student Book* page 99 for the text of the audio.

Pronunciation, Exercises 7 and 8, page 84

Script same as *Student Book* Pronunciation, Exercises 3 and 4, page T164

Unit 22

Listening, Exercises 5 and 6, page 87

Script same as *Student Book* Listening, Exercises 7 and 8, page T165

Pronunciation, Exercises 7 and 8, page 87

Script same as *Student Book* Pronunciation, Exercises 4 and 5, page T165

Unit 23

Listening, Exercises 5 and 6, page 90

Note: See the Reading on *Student Book* page 107 for the text of the audio.

Pronunciation, Exercises 7 and 8, page 90 (Student CD Track 66)

1. Women used to wear long skirts. They didn't use to wear pants.
2. Poor people didn't use to wear red shoes. Rich people used to wear red shoes.
3. What did they use to do at weddings?
4. They used to throw shoes at the bride and groom. They didn't use to throw rice.

Unit 24

Listening, Exercises 5 and 6, page 93

Script same as *Student Book* Listening, Exercises 5 and 6, page T166

Pronunciation, Exercises 7 and 8, page 93

Script same as *Student Book* Pronunciation, Exercise 2, page T165

Unit 25

Listening, Exercises 6 and 7, page 98

Note: See the Reading on *Student Book* page 117 for the text of the audio.

Pronunciation, Exercises 8 and 9, page 98 (Student CD Track 67)

1. She couldn't skate well.
2. I could ride a bike when I was five.
3. He could swim well ten years ago.
4. Couldn't you cook at all?
5. I could speak English before I came here.

Unit 26

Listening, Exercises 5 and 6, page 101

Script same as *Student Book* Listening, Exercises 4 and 5, page T167

Pronunciation, Exercises 7 and 8, page 101 (Student CD Track 68)

1. He's renewed his passport.
2. She's bought her airline ticket.
3. I've made a hotel reservation for next week.
4. He's changed his phone number.
5. I've called my mother.
6. She's promised to take me to the airport.

Unit 27

Listening, Exercise 5, page 104

Note: See the Reading on *Student Book* pages 124–125 for the text of the audio.

Pronunciation, Exercises 6 and 7, page 104 (Student CD Track 69)

1. If I remember, I give him a gift.
2. If I forget, I send it later.
3. If I get a gift from a friend, I never give it away.

Unit 28

Listening, Exercises 5 and 6, page 107

Note: See the Reading on *Student Book* page 129 for the text of the audio.

Pronunciation, Exercises 7 and 8, page 107 (Student CD Track 70)

1. outdoors   learn
2. more   repair
3. repair   perfect
4. work   earn
5. career   earn
6. market   computer
7. perfect   researcher
8. computer   learn

Workbook Answer Key

Unit 1

Vocabulary, Exercise 1

1. g   **3.** d   **5.** b   **7.** c
2. h   **4.** a   **6.** f   **8.** e

Vocabulary, Exercise 2

1. go out for dinner   **4.** sleep late
2. go to the movies   **5.** go to the gym
3. watch TV   **6.** stay home

Grammar, Exercise 3

1. Movie theaters are **always** crowded on Friday nights.
2. I **usually** meet my friends at about 9:00.
3. He **often** works late.
4. I'm **always** happy to get takeout.
5. They **never** stay home on Saturday nights.
6. My family is **often** busy on the weekend.

Grammar, Exercise 4

1. Joanna and her friends always go to the movies on Friday nights.
2. She never works late on Friday nights.
3. She always goes to the gym on Friday nights.
4. She never sleeps late on Saturdays.
5. She sometimes goes for a walk on Saturdays.
6. She sometimes gets takeout on Saturdays.
7. She usually goes to the beach on Sundays.

Listening, Exercise 5

Friday, May 24
6:00 leave work
6:30 get takeout
7:00 have dinner
7:30 meet friends
8:00 go to the movies

Sunday, May 26
10:00 get up
12:00 go to the beach
1:00 meet friends
2:00 go out for lunch

Listening, Exercise 6

1. never ~~always~~   **5.** often ~~always~~
2. never ~~sometimes~~   **6.** sometimes ~~never~~
3. usually ~~always~~   **7.** usually ~~sometimes~~
4. usually ~~often~~

Pronunciation, Exercise 7

1. I <u>never</u> <u>work</u> on <u>Saturday</u>.
2. I <u>usually</u> <u>go</u> to the <u>gym</u>.
3. <u>What</u> do you <u>do</u> on <u>Sunday</u>?
4. We <u>go</u> for a <u>walk</u> on the <u>beach</u>.
5. She <u>always</u> gets <u>take</u>out on <u>Fridays</u>.
6. She <u>goes</u> to the <u>movies</u> with her <u>friends</u>.

Unit 2

Vocabulary, Exercise 1

```
          ¹b ²a  c  k
             r
 ³s  t  o  m  a  c ⁴h
                   e
 ⁵f  o  o ⁶t        a
          ⁷h  a ⁸n  d
       ⁹e  a  r     o
          o     s      ¹⁰l
          a    ¹¹e  y   e
¹²m  o  u  t  h         g
```

Vocabulary, Exercise 2

1. C   **3.** B   **5.** F
2. E   **4.** D   **6.** A

Grammar, Exercise 3

1. and   **4.** but   **7.** but   **10.** so
2. but   **5.** so   **8.** so
3. so   **6.** and   **9.** but

Grammar, Exercise 4

A	B	C
1. b	**1.** c	**1.** b
2. c	**2.** a	**2.** a
3. a	**3.** b	**3.** c

Listening, Exercise 5

✓ a fever   ___ a bad cold
✓ a sore throat   ✓ a cough
___ a sore arm   ✓ a sore back
✓ a stomachache   ___ a headache

Listening, Exercise 6

3 That's too bad!
4 Relax, Tony. Stay in bed.
1 That's OK, Tony. Don't worry. I hope you feel better.
2 That's OK, Tony. Hope you get better soon.

Pronunciation, Exercise 7

1. I'm sorry, but I have a cold.
2. I have a cough, and my throat is sore.
3. I'm really sorry, but I'm not feeling very well.
4. I have a fever, so I can't come to work.

Unit 3

Vocabulary, Exercise 1

1. e   **3.** c   **5.** d   **7.** h
2. g   **4.** f   **6.** a   **8.** b

Vocabulary, Exercise 2

1. grow up
2. have children
3. graduate from school
4. get married
5. go to school
6. find a job
7. work hard
8. give money to charity

Grammar, Exercise 3

1. was
2. took
3. won
4. went
5. did not/didn't expect
6. did not/didn't pay
7. were
8. realized
9. asked
10. put
11. was born
12. grew up
13. died
14. was not/wasn't
15. graduated

Grammar, Exercise 4

Yesterday, Phil Easton **got** up at 6:00. He **left** for work at 6:45. He **had** coffee and **read** the morning newspaper on the train. He **arrived** at work at 7:30. He **started** his computer and **answered** his email. At 9:00, Phil **met** with his team. Then he **got** on the phone with the managers in Europe. At 12:00, he **ate** lunch in the company cafeteria. After lunch, he **spoke** to the people in his department. At 3:00, he **put** on his coat and **went** out for a short walk. Then he **was** back on his computer. He **did** research and **wrote** reports. At 6:15, he **shut** down his computer. He **caught** the 6:30 train home. What **did** he do on the train? He **slept**!

Listening, Exercise 5

_5_ She acted in *The Color Purple*.
_2_ She became a newscaster.
_1_ She left college.
_4_ She started *The Oprah Winfrey Show*, now called *Oprah*.
_7_ She began a magazine called *O*.
_3_ She had her first TV talk show.
_6_ She started a charity called Oprah's Angel Network.

Listening, Exercise 6

1. F 1954
2. F didn't have
3. F liked/loved
4. F didn't graduate from/left
5. T
6. F 1984
7. T
8. F didn't have
9. F women
10. T

Pronunciation, Exercise 7

/t/ or /d/	/ɪd/
lived	wanted
loved	decided
worked	acted
finished	started
watched	collected
used	

Unit 4

Vocabulary, Exercise 1

Vocabulary, Exercise 2

Australia	North America	Europe
Africa	Asia	

Vocabulary, Exercise 3

1. lake
2. safari
3. coast
4. monuments
5. countryside
6. festivals
7. mountains

Grammar, Exercise 4

1. What flight is Peter going to take?
2. Is he going to rent a car in Vancouver?
3. What is he going to do in Vancouver on Monday and Tuesday?
4. Is he going / Is he going to go home on Friday?
5. How are Helen and Mark going to get to Tofino?
6. Are they going / Are they going to go to the beach in Tofino?
7. How long are they going to stay in Tofino?
8. When are they flying / going to fly home?

Grammar, Exercise 5

1. He's going to take GlobalAir Flight #122.
2. (Yes, he is.) Yes, he's going to rent a car.
3. He's going to tour downtown on Monday. He's going / He's going to go to Stanley Park, and he's going to visit Granville Island on Tuesday.
4. No, he isn't. He's going / He's going to go home on Saturday.
5. Helen and Mark are going to fly to Vancouver. They're going to take a ferry to Victoria. They're going to drive to Tofino.
6. (Yes, they are.) Yes, they're going to go to the beach in Tofino.
7. They're going to be in Tofino for five days.
8. They're going to fly home on Saturday.

Listening, Exercise 6

November	Canada
December	Australia
January	India
February	South Africa
March	Ireland

Listening, Exercise 7

1. a
2. b
3. b
4. a
5. b
6. a

Pronunciation, Exercise 8

Eng•land It•a•ly Ko•re•a Can•a•da In•di•a
A•sia Eu•rope Aus•tra•lia Ire•land Af•ri•ca

Unit 5

Vocabulary, Exercise 1

1. c	**3.** f	**5.** h	**7.** e
2. d	**4.** b	**6.** a	**8.** g

Vocabulary, Exercise 2

1. use someone's first name
2. arrive on time
3. shake hands
4. visit someone's home
5. give a gift
6. take off your shoes
7. exchange business cards
8. wear a suit

Grammar, Exercise 3

1. You should listen to your teacher and classmates.
2. You shouldn't talk on your cell phone.
3. You should do your homework.
4. You shouldn't arrive late.
5. You should ask questions when you don't understand.
6. You shouldn't leave class without permission.
7. You shouldn't eat in class.
8. You should arrive to class on time.
9. You should speak English.

Grammar, Exercise 4

1. should	**5.** should	**9.** should
2. should	**6.** Should	**10.** shouldn't
3. shouldn't	**7.** should	**11.** shouldn't
4. should	**8.** should	

Listening, Exercise 5

1. b   **2.** b   **3.** a   **4.** a   **5.** b

Listening, Exercise 6

You shouldn't take your shoes off.

Pronunciation, Exercise 7

1. should	**4.** Shouldn't	**7.** Shouldn't
2. shouldn't	**5.** shouldn't	**8.** should
3. Should	**6.** should	**9.** Should

Unit 6

Vocabulary, Exercise 1

1. e   **2.** a   **3.** f   **4.** c   **5.** b   **6.** d

Vocabulary, Exercise 2

1. rent	**3.** pay	**5.** spend
2. afford	**4.** buy	**6.** cost

Grammar, Exercise 3

B: Why don't you	**B:** Why don't we
B: how about	**A:** How about
A: Maybe I could	**B:** But let's not, Let's
A: let's	**A:** How about
B: Maybe you could	**B:** Why don't I

Grammar, Exercise 4

Hi, Jun.

We need to plan Hui's going-away party. How about **having** it on May 28? His last day in the office is May 31.

Let's not **use** the lunchroom. It's small. Why don't we **use** Conference Room C? It's bigger than the other conference rooms. Maybe you could **reserve** it for May 28 from 3:00 to 4:00.

What about the food? How about **getting** crackers and cheese and fruit? It's after lunch, so we don't want too much food. Why don't we **talk** to Amy? She got really good stuff for our last office party. She also knows Hui well, so she can give us some ideas for a gift. Let's **set** up a meeting with her for early next week. Maybe you could **email** her.

One more thing. Why don't I **tell** Hui that a few of us are going to take him out for lunch on May 30? That way, the party on the 28th will be a big surprise. (Let's **take** him out to lunch on the 30th, too, though!)

Listening, Exercise 5

Picture b

Listening, Exercise 6

His company can't afford a fancy party.

Pronunciation, Exercise 7

A: Let's have a (party) next weekend?
B: Good (idea). Why don't we get a (band)?
A: We can't (afford) it. How about getting a (DJ)?
B: (OK). What about (food)?
A: Maybe we could order (pizza).
B: I don't (like) pizza. Why don't we just have (snacks)?

Unit 7

Vocabulary, Exercise 1

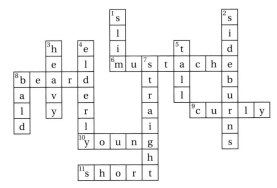

5 down: tall	11 across: short
1 down: slim	7 down: straight
8 down: bald	2 down: sideburns
8 across: beard	10 across: young
6 across: mustache	3 down: heavy
4 down: elderly	9 across: curly

Vocabulary, Exercise 2

1. the boy   **2.** the woman   **3.** the man

Grammar, Exercise 3

1. is	**5.** is	**8.** is	**11.** is
2. is	**6.** is	**9.** is	**12.** has
3. has	**7.** has	**10.** is	**13.** has
4. is			

Grammar, Exercise 4

1. 's young	**8.** 's young
2. 's tall	**9.** 's
3. he's	**10.** she's tall
4. 's slim	**11.** is
5. he's	**12.** has long brown hair
6. has blond hair	**13.** has hazel eyes
7. has blue eyes	

Listening, Exercise 5

1. doesn't have	**3.** brown	**5.** tall
2. brown	**4.** quite slim	**6.** late

Listening, Exercise 6

She has long straight black hair, and she's pretty short.

Pronunciation, Exercise 7

1. and **2.** and **3.** or **4.** and

Unit 8

Vocabulary, Exercise 1

```
A L B R I G F B H O O Y B T K
C O M E D Y A L A C T O R U S
C D E H E L N L O Y S L E A P
T D I R E C T O R T L R U L N
A E R S R E A T G O O D A D G
H E O T B I S H F G W O C E M
O R M E A W T N M N T V T W O
W P A M A Z I N G A E O I N D
C E N M B O C L S I M W O A I
A L T O N E X C E L L E N T E
R I I N T E R E S T I N G J O
E S C I E N C E F I C T I O N
```

Vocabulary, Exercise 2

1. comedy	**5.** actor	**9.** romantic
2. good	**6.** slow	**10.** fantastic
3. amazing	**7.** action	**11.** director
4. excellent	**8.** science fiction	

Grammar, Exercise 3

1. said	**4.** said	**7.** told	**9.** said
2. told	**5.** said	**8.** said	**10.** told
3. told	**6.** told		

Grammar, Exercise 4

1. Adam said his favorite movie of all time was *Casablanca.*

2. Matt said (that) he loved science fiction movies.

3. Sue said (that) she really liked romantic comedies.

4. Jane said (that) she wanted to rent a Kurosawa film.

5. Jeff said (that) *The Matrix Reloaded* had amazing special effects.

6. Ben said (that) they planned to go to the movies this weekend.

7. Inez said (that) the scenery in *Lawrence of Arabia* was fantastic.

Listening, Exercise 5

Tomás: D   Reiko: E   Mariana: A

Listening, Exercise 6

1. ~~good~~ amazing
2. ~~excellent~~ interesting
3. ~~boring~~ slow
4. ~~exciting~~ excellent
5. ~~amazing~~ good
6. ~~movies~~ films

Pronunciation, Exercise 7

1. a <u>c</u>lassic <u>b</u>lack-and-white fil<u>m</u>
2. the be<u>s</u>t <u>sc</u>ie<u>nc</u>e fi<u>ct</u>ion movie
3. <u>i</u>nterestin<u>g</u> <u>s</u>tory
4. a <u>s</u>low <u>s</u>tart
5. ex<u>c</u>iting <u>s</u>pecial effe<u>ct</u>s
6. an ex<u>c</u>ellent a<u>ct</u>ress
7. He said that he li<u>k</u>ed *Star Wars*.
8. She to<u>l</u>d us she lo<u>v</u>ed old <u>f</u>il<u>m</u>s.

Unit 9

Vocabulary, Exercise 1

1. napkin	**5.** menu
2. cappuccino	**6.** shrimp
3. sauce	**7.** mixed vegetables
4. raspberry sorbet	

Vocabulary, Exercise 2

1. napkin	**5.** menu
2. raspberry sorbet	**6.** shrimp
3. Mixed vegetables	**7.** sauce
4. cappuccino	

Grammar, Exercise 3

1. prefer
2. prefer
3. 'd prefer / would prefer
4. prefers
5. 'd prefer / would prefer
6. 'd prefer / would prefer
7. Would . . . prefer

Grammar, Exercise 4

1. Would you like	**5.** We'd like
2. I like	**6.** I'd like
3. I'd like	**7.** He likes
4. Do you like	

Listening, Exercise 5

Picture a

Listening, Exercise 6

1. a   **3.** b   **5.** b   **7.** b
2. a   **4.** b   **6.** b   **8.** b

Pronunciation, Exercise 7

1. would you
2. I'd
3. Would you like
4. would
5. Would you
6. I'd prefer

Unit 10

Vocabulary, Exercise 1

1. technology
2. transportation
3. space
4. communication
5. climate
6. government
7. population
8. politics
9. economy

Vocabulary, Exercise 2

1. technology
2. climate
3. population
4. space
5. economy
6. communication
7. government
8. politics
9. transportation

Grammar, Exercise 3

1. will be 8 billion
2. will have the strongest economy
3. will be one world government
4. will get hotter
5. will speak Spanish
6. will work everywhere
7. will drive flying cars
8. will take vacations on space stations

Grammar, Exercise 4

1. They don't think that businesses will use paper anymore.
2. They don't think (that) people will work in offices.
3. They think (that) everyone will communicate with handheld computers.
4. They don't think (that) we will have paper money anymore.
5. They think (that) the world economy will be strong.

Listening, Exercise 5

1. a   **3.** a   **5.** a   **7.** b
2. b   **4.** a   **6.** b

Listening, Exercise 6

1. won't   **3.** won't   **5.** won't
2. will   **4.** won't   **6.** will

Pronunciation, Exercise 7

1. a   **3.** c   **5.** c   **7.** b
2. b   **4.** a   **6.** c   **8.** a

Unit 11

Vocabulary, Exercise 1

1. work long hours
2. meet with clients
3. arrange meetings
4. give presentations
5. travel
6. communicate
7. work as a team
8. type documents

Vocabulary, Exercise 2

1. work long hours
2. travel
3. give presentations
4. work as a team
5. arrange meetings
6. meet with clients

Grammar, Exercise 3

1. (a) have to, (b) don't have to, (c) have to Picture _B_
2. (d) has to, (e) Does . . . have to, (f) has to Picture _C_
3. (g) do I have to, (h) have to, (i) have to Picture _A_

Grammar, Exercise 4

1. Sue doesn't have to type reports.
2. Jodie and Russ have to give presentations.
3. Tony has to answer email.
4. Arnie and Sue have to pick up visitors at the airport.
5. Betsy and Jodie don't have to arrange meetings.
6. Arnie and Russ don't have to answer email.
7. Jodie doesn't have to call clients.

Listening, Exercise 5

1. a   **3.** b   **5.** b   **7.** b
2. b   **4.** a   **6.** a

Listening, Exercise 6

don't have to give me

Pronunciation, Exercise 7

1. I have to
2. Does he have to
3. He has to
4. He has to
5. We have to
6. Do you have to
7. I have to
8. We have to

Unit 12

Vocabulary, Exercise 1

1. grow
2. catch
3. build
4. have
5. make
6. spend
7. take care of
8. teach

Vocabulary, Exercise 2

1. spends time
2. catch fish
3. built a house
4. grows food
5. teaches a class
6. took care of animals
7. make clothes
8. have an adventure

Grammar, Exercise 3

1. Has Anna ever used a computer?
2. Has Flavia ever taught swimming?
3. Has Anna ever gone on camping trips?
4. Has Flavia ever written emails?
5. Has Anna ever taken care of children?
6. Has Flavia ever made travel reservations?
7. Has Anna ever sent packages overseas?
8. Has Flavia ever cooked dinner for a family?

Grammar, Exercise 4

1. No, she hasn't. She's never used a computer. / She hasn't ever used a computer.
2. No, she hasn't. She's never taught swimming. / She hasn't ever taught swimming.
3. Yes, she has. She's / She has gone on camping trips.
4. Yes, she has. She's / She has written emails.
5. Yes, she has. She's / She has taken care of children.
6. Yes, she has. She's / She has made travel reservations.
7. No, she hasn't. She's never sent packages overseas. / She hasn't ever sent packages overseas.
8. No, she hasn't. She's never cooked dinner for a family. / She hasn't ever cooked dinner for a family.

Listening, Exercise 5

He's worked on a farm.
He's lived overseas.

Exercise 6

1. spent time outdoors
2. worked on a farm
3. lived overseas
4. cooked for large groups

Pronunciation, Exercise 7

1. Have you ever   Have you ever lived overseas?
2. Has he ever   Has he ever grown vegetables?
3. Have you ever   Have you ever spent time outdoors?
4. Have they ever   Have they ever used a computer?

Pronunciation, Exercise 9

you + ever: *w*
he + ever: *y*
they + ever: *y*

Unit 13

Vocabulary, Exercise 1

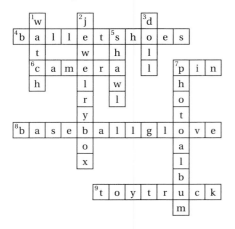

Vocabulary, Exercise 2

1. give . . . away
2. put away
3. fall apart
4. try . . . on
5. pass, on
6. fall out
7. throw . . . away
8. Take . . . out

Grammar, Exercise 3

1. Daniel's, his
2. Bo's, his
3. Irina's, hers
4. Hee-Sook's, hers

Grammar, Exercise 4

1. them
2. her
3. us
4. him
5. me
6. you

Grammar, Exercise 5

1. **B:** Mine, yours
2. **B:** theirs, ours
3. **B:** hers
  B: his

Listening, Exercise 6

a. 2   **b.** 1   **c.** 4   **d.** 3

Listening, Exercise 7

1. c   2. d   3. b   4. a

Pronunciation, Exercise 8

1. Take it <u>out</u>.
2. Don't give it <u>away</u>.
3. It's falling <u>apart</u>.
4. I'll try it <u>on</u>.
5. Let's throw it <u>away</u>.
6. Wait! Something is falling <u>out</u>.

Exercise 9

1. Take it out.
2. Don't give it away.
3. It's falling apart.
4. I'll try it on.
5. Let's throw it away.
6. Wait! Something is falling out.

Unit 14

Vocabulary, Exercise 1

1. e   2. f   3. a   4. d   5. b   6. c

Vocabulary, Exercise 2

1. suspicious
2. absent-minded
3. upset
4. embarrassed
5. proud
6. bad-mannered
7. relaxed

Grammar, Exercise 3

1. He walked around the city happily.
2. She displayed her painting proudly.
3. I waited for the news calmly.
4. They sat in the restaurant and ate dinner quietly.
5. We looked at the man with the large bags suspiciously.
6. She answered the questions nervously.
7. Every hour, the bells rang loudly.

Grammar, Exercise 4

1. more easily than
2. more politely
3. faster than
4. more comfortably
5. more slowly
6. more carefully

Listening, Exercise 5

1. b   2. a

Listening, Exercise 6

1. H   2. A   3. H   4. A   5. A

Listening, Exercise 7

1. a   2. b

Listening, Exercise 8

1. rude   3. politely   5. angrily
2. quickly   4. loudly   6. badly

Pronunciation, Exercise 9

1. angrily   5. happily
2. suspiciously   6. politely
3. quietly   7. nervously
4. comfortably   8. hungrily

Unit 15

Vocabulary, Exercise 1

1. d   4. g   7. a   10. l
2. h   5. b   8. f   11. g
3. i   6. k   9. c   12. j

Vocabulary, Exercise 2

with one other person	with a team	alone
karate tennis golf	basketball hockey soccer volleyball	aerobics biking jogging skiing swimming

Grammar, Exercise 3

1. loves playing, hates going
2. likes doing, loves playing
3. loves doing, likes going
4. likes playing, loves going
5. hates playing, loves going
6. doesn't like doing, likes playing
7. loves playing, hates going
8. likes playing, loves going

Grammar, Exercise 4

Evan likes **playing** soccer. He's on a team, and they play every Sunday. He loves **going** to games, especially soccer and tennis matches.

Mark **does** karate. He's really good, and he's in great shape. He loves **jogging** and aerobics and he **goes** swimming in the university pool almost every day. He hates **watching** sports on TV, though.

Zach doesn't like **playing** team sports, but he likes **watching** baseball on TV. He really likes **bicycling** and swimming on the weekends. In the winter, he loves **going** skiing. This winter, we're going to . . .

Listening, Exercise 5

Check: basketball, hockey, swimming, golf, volleyball

Listening, Exercise 6

More popular with men	More popular with women	Equally popular with men and women
golf hockey baseball basketball	swimming	volleyball

Pronunciation, Exercise 7

1. Do you like skiing?
2. Yes, I love skiing.
3. Do you like playing golf?
4. No, I hate playing golf.
5. Women liked swimming, and men liked basketball.
6. My sister likes doing aerobics, and my brother likes playing soccer.

Unit 16

Vocabulary, Exercise 1

1. salt   7. cookies
2. lettuce   8. oranges
3. fruit   9. yogurt
4. chocolate   10. bread
5. water   11. juice
6. vegetables   12. onions
The word in the box is **strawberries**.

Vocabulary, Exercise 2

1. juice, water   5. salt
2. oranges   6. chocolate
3. lettuce   7. **A:** vegetables
4. cookies   **B:** onions

Grammar, Exercise 3

1. many   6. some
2. much   7. much
3. some   8. a few
4. few   9. any
5. much

Grammar, Exercise 4

1. How much salt did she put in the soup?
2. How many apples / How much fruit do you eat a day?
3. How many potatoes / vegetables should I get?
4. How much chocolate / candy did he eat yesterday?
5. How many strawberries do we need for the cake?
6. How much coffee do they drink every day?

Listening, Exercise 5

1. F   2. F   3. T   4. T   5. F   6. F

Listening, Exercise 6

1. a   2. a   3. b   4. b   5. b

Pronunciation, Exercise 7

1. different
2. same
3. same
4. different
5. same

Unit 17

Vocabulary, Exercise 1

1. d
2. a
3. f
4. h
5. g
6. i
7. j
8. c
9. e
10. b

Vocabulary, Exercise 2

1. break
2. downsize
3. part-time
4. full-time
5. formal
6. casual
7. flextime
8. commute
9. supervisor
10. telecommute

Grammar, Exercise 3

1. **A:** Did . . . have to get up
   B: did
2. **A:** Do . . . have to work
   B: do
3. **A:** Did . . . have to wear
   B: didn't
4. **A:** Does . . . have to wear
   B: do
5. **A:** Does . . . have to drive
   B: doesn't
6. **A:** had to leave
   B: have to do

Grammar, Exercise 4

1. No, they had to wear dresses or skirts.
2. They had to arrive for work 10 minutes early.
3. Employees had to take a 15-minute break in the afternoon.
4. Employees didn't have to work overtime.
5. Part-time employees had to work on Saturdays.
6. Men had to wear suits and ties.

Listening, Exercise 5

1. ~~new~~
2. ~~12~~ 10
3. ~~can~~ can't
4. ~~has to~~ doesn't have to
5. ~~cooler~~ more comfortable
6. ~~more~~ less

Listening, Exercise 6

1. had to
2. don't have to
3. have to
4. had to, don't have to
5. don't have to
6. had to

Pronunciation, Exercise 7

1. to, to
2. to
3. TO
4. to, to
5. to, to
6. to, TO
7. to

Unit 18

Vocabulary, Exercise 1

1. c
2. a
3. b

Vocabulary, Exercise 2

1. was arrested
2. reported
3. intruder
4. Police officers
5. suspect
6. victims
7. witness
8. investigating
9. questioning
10. confessed

Grammar, Exercise 3

1. It was raining when Vincent left the house.
2. Peter was talking to Tim when they saw an accident.
3. Charles was taking a bath when the phone rang.
4. Terry and Gene were watching TV when everything went black.

Grammar, Exercise 4

1. was shining
2. was walking
3. saw
4. was standing and watching
5. was yelling
6. was crying
7. was doing
8. ran
9. heard
10. looked
11. started
12. realized
13. were making

Listening, Exercise 5

Richard Price—living room—watching TV
Camille Price—parents' bedroom—reading a book
Brad Price—Brad's bedroom—playing video games
Martha McGuire—kitchen—cleaning up

Listening, Exercise 6

Mr. Price: was running away from, was wearing a blue jacket
Mrs. Price: was running on, was wearing a baseball cap
Brad: was wearing white sneakers, was running away from
Martha: was running into, was holding something

Pronunciation, Exercise 7

1. We were
2. My parents were
3. They were
4. Our housekeeper was
5. A man was
6. He was

Unit 19

Vocabulary, Exercise 1

1. **a.** cake	**b.** coffee	coffeehouse
2. **a.** haircut	**b.** blow-dry	hair salon
3. **a.** aspirin	**b.** perfume	drugstore
4. **a.** socks	**b.** blouse	clothing store
5. **a.** magazine	**b.** candy bar	newsstand

Vocabulary, Exercise 2

(See Exercise 1 Answer Key)

Grammar, Exercise 3

1. Josh went to the post office for some stamps.
2. Luz woke up late because her alarm clock was broken.
3. Allie went online to order the latest Harry Potter book.
4. I made an appointment at the salon for a haircut.
5. We went shopping after work because we had to buy a present.
6. Cara bought a new dress to wear to the party.

Grammar, Exercise 4

1. j 2. h 3. a 4. i 5. f 6. c 7. e 8. d 9. g 10. b

Listening, Exercise 5

magazine
bottle of aspirin
shampoo, haircut, and blow-dry
cup of coffee
blouse
candy bar
lunch at a Chinese restaurant

Listening, Exercise 6

newsstand: $3.95
drugstore: $4.99
hair salon: $35.00
coffeehouse: $2.50
clothing store: $24.99
convenience store: 65¢
Chinese restaurant: $7.50

Pronunciation, Exercise 7

1. **news**stand
2. **cof**feehouse
3. **hair** salon
4. **drug**store
5. **clo**thing store
6. **hair**cut
7. **can**dy bar
8. con**ven**ience store

Unit 20

Vocabulary, Exercise 1

1. operas, musicals, plays
2. actors, performers
3. chairs, seats
4. composers, playwrights
5. audience, spectators
6. costumes

Vocabulary, Exercise 2

1. operas
2. plays
3. audience
4. musicals
5. playwrights
6. composers
7. spectators
8. seats
9. costumes
10. chairs

Grammar, Exercise 3

1. a   4. an   7. a
2. the   5. a   8. a
3. the   6. The   9. The

Grammar, Exercise 4

1. a   7. a   12. an
2. a   8. The   13. a
3. the   9. the   14. an
4. the   10. the   15. a
5. the   11. the   16. a
6. the

Listening, Exercise 5

1. ~~an opera singer~~ **a composer**
2. ~~costume~~ **mask**
3. ~~dancer~~ **opera singer**
4. ~~doesn't love~~ **loves/is in love with** *or* ~~Raoul~~ **the Phantom**
5. ~~the Phantom~~ **Raoul** *or* ~~goes with~~ **doesn't go**

Listening, Exercise 6

1. b   2. a   3. a   4. b

Pronunciation, Exercise 7

1. *The Mousetrap* is **the** longest-running play.
2. **A** couple has **an** old house.
3. They turn **the** house into **a** hotel.
4. You have to see **the** play.
5. **The** ending is very surprising.

Unit 21

Vocabulary, Exercise 1

1. ages
2. New Year's Eve
3. more than three years
4. noon
5. a couple of months
6. the day before yesterday

Vocabulary, Exercise 2

1. ages
2. noon
3. a couple of months
4. more than three years
5. the day before yesterday
6. New Year's Eve

Grammar, Exercise 3

1. How long has he worked in Chicago?
2. Have you lived overseas for a long time?
3. How long has she studied fashion design?
4. How long have they known about it?
5. Has he had a computer since he was in college?
6. How long have you been married?
7. Has she always driven the same car?

Grammar, Exercise 4

1. have been   9. since
2. since   10. has been
3. For   11. since
4. have dominated   12. have earned
5. have brought   13. since
6. have won   14. have competed
7. since   15. have remained
8. have been

Listening, Exercise 5

1. **a.** jazz singer
   b. 73
2. **a.** tennis player
   b. 86
3. **a.** model
   b. 71

Listening, Exercise 6

1. over
2. more than
3. over, over
4. since
5. 58 years ago

Pronunciation, Exercise 8

voiceless *th* sound /θ/	voiced *th* sound /ð/
thousand	that
Thursday	they
thirty	then
twentieth	their
think	

Unit 22

Vocabulary, Exercise 1

1. a letter
2. a message
3. problems
4. the copying
5. a letter
6. an email
7. a fax
8. a meeting
9. some information

Vocabulary, Exercise 2

1. got
2. sign
3. make
4. did
5. sent
6. arranged
7. filed
8. left
9. have

Grammar, Exercise 3

1. Would you like me to
2. Could you
3. Should I
4. I'll
5. Should I
6. Can you

Grammar, Exercise 4

1. **A:** Can you / Could you
   B: should I / would you like me to
2. **A:** Can you / Could you
   B: I'll
3. **A:** Can you / Could you
   B: Should I / Would you like me to
4. **A:** Can you /Could you
   B: I'll
5. **A:** Can you / Could you
   B: Should I / Would you like me to
6. **A:** Can you / Could you
   B: I'll
7. **A:** Can you / Could you
   B: Should I / Would you like me to
8. **A:** Can you / Could you
   B: Should I / Would you like me to

Listening, Exercise 5

Check:
send faxes
call the photographer and arrange a meeting with her
call the new model
make a reservation for lunch

Listening, Exercise 6

Ken: send them
Marcy: call the photographer
Ken: call her now
Marcy: call him, too
Ken: arrange the meeting, make the other calls

Pronunciation, Exercise 7

1. Can you
2. Can you
3. Could you
4. Could you
5. Should I
6. Should I
7. Would you like me to
8. Would you like me to

Unit 23

Vocabulary, Exercise 1

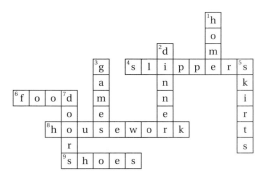

Vocabulary, Exercise 2

1. wear
2. play
3. open
4. shop for
5. have
6. put on
7. do
8. stay
9. take off

Grammar, Exercise 3

1. used to eat meat
2. used to wear glasses
3. used to read books
4. used to have long hair
5. used to cook
6. used to ride a bicycle/ride a bike

Grammar, Exercise 4

1. **A:** **(1)** did you use to play
   B: **(2)** used to play; **(3)** didn't use to play
2. **A:** **(4)** didn't use to eat out / didn't use to eat in restaurants
   B: **(5)** used to do
3. **A:** **(6)** did you use to eat
   B: **(7)** never used to eat
4. **A:** **(8)** did you use to wear
   B: **(9)** didn't use to wear

Listening, Exercise 5

1. c   2. d   3. a   4. b

Listening, Exercise 6

1. a   2. b   3. b   4. a

Pronunciation, Exercise 7

1. used to wear, didn't use to wear
2. didn't use to wear, used to wear
3. did they use to do
4. used to throw, didn't use to throw

Unit 24

Vocabulary, Exercise 1

1. snowboarding
2. skateboarding
3. scuba diving
4. snorkeling
5. rock climbing
6. waterskiing
7. windsurfing
8. parasailing
9. jet skiing

Vocabulary, Exercise 2

adventure

Grammar, Exercise 3

1. Has Nicole ever gone scuba diving?
2. When did she receive her certification?
3. How long has she taught at Adventure Zone?
4. Has Aidan ever taught water-skiing?
5. When did he live in Key West?
6. Has he ever won any competitions?
7. When did he teach at Adventure Zone?

Grammar, Exercise 4

1. Yes, she has.
2. She received her certification in 1999.
3. She has taught at Adventure Zone since 2000.
4. Yes, he has.
5. He lived in Key West from 2001 to 2003.
6. Yes, he has.
7. He taught at Adventure Zone from 2001 to 2004.

Listening, Exercise 5

A. 4 **B.** 5 **C.** 3 **D.** 1 **E.** 2

Listening, Exercise 6

1. b **2.** b **3.** a **4.** b **5.** a **6.** a **7.** b

Pronunciation, Exercise 7

rock climbing
jet skiing
snowmobiling
scuba diving
skateboarding
snowboarding
parasailing
waterskiing
snorkeling
windsurfing

Unit 25

Vocabulary, Exercise 1

boxing   running   diving   skating
swimming   skiing   wrestling

Vocabulary, Exercise 2

1. wrestle
   wrestlers
2. ski
   skiers
3. box
   boxers
4. skate
   skaters
5. run
   runners
6. dive
   divers
7. swim
   swimmers

Grammar, Exercise 3

1. Sam was really good at skiing.
2. Avril and Carol were pretty good at swimming.
3. Tomas and I were good at wrestling.
4. Fumi was not / wasn't very good at skating.
5. Yong-Jin was not / wasn't good at boxing.

Grammar, Exercise 4

1. Sam could ski really well.
2. Avril and Carol could swim pretty well.
3. Tomas and I could wrestle well.
4. Fumi couldn't skate very well.
5. Yong-Jin couldn't box well.

Grammar, Exercise 5

1. Justin was really good at math and science. Rebecca was really good at English and social studies.
2. Justin was pretty good at English and social studies. Rebecca was pretty good at math and science.
3. Justin was not / wasn't good at art. Rebecca was not / wasn't good at music.

Listening, Exercise 6

1. a **3.** a **5.** b
2. c **4.** b **6.** a

Listening, Exercise 7

1. f **3.** a **5.** d **7.** b
2. e **4.** g **6.** h **8.** c

Pronunciation, Exercise 8

1. couldn't **3.** could **5.** could
2. could **4.** Couldn't

Unit 26

Vocabulary, Exercise 1

1. pillow
2. slippers
3. vaccination
4. bag
5. teddy bear
6. tennis racket
7. video

Vocabulary, Exercise 2

Rent (a car)
renew (your passport)
Book (a hotel)
apply (for a visa)
get (your ticket)
go (online)
transfer (money)
pack (your suitcase)

Grammar, Exercise 3

1. Have you rented a car yet?
2. Has Adrian booked the hotel yet?
3. Have you canceled the newspaper delivery yet?
4. Have you asked Sarah to feed the cat yet?
5. Has Adrian bought a new suitcase yet?
6. Has Adrian packed yet?
7. Has Adrian cleaned the apartment yet?
8. Have you paid the bills yet?
9. Have you arranged for a taxi to the airport yet?
10. Has Adrian gotten a haircut yet?

Grammar, Exercise 4

1. Yes, I have. I've already rented a car.
2. Adrian hasn't booked the hotel yet.
3. I haven't canceled the newspaper delivery yet.
4. I haven't asked Sarah to feed the cat yet.
5. Yes, he has. He's already bought a new suitcase.
6. Adrian hasn't packed yet.
7. Adrian hasn't cleaned the apartment yet.
8. Yes, I have. I've already paid the bills.
9. I haven't arranged for a taxi to the airport yet.
10. Yes, he has. He's already gotten a haircut.

Listening, Exercise 5

transfer money __2__
get her new passport __4__
make a hotel reservation __7__
buy her airline ticket __6__
sell the car __1__
get her vaccinations __3__
pack her bags __8__
get her visa __5__

Listening, Exercise 6

1. Have you, yet
2. I've gotten
3. hasn't called, yet
4. I've already bought
5. haven't, yet

Pronunciation, Exercise 7

1. He's renewed
2. She's bought
3. I've made
4. He's changed
5. I've called
6. She's promised

Unit 27

Vocabulary, Exercise 1

1. **a.** remember   **b.** forget
2. **a.** schedule   **b.** cancel
3. **a.** lose   **b.** find
4. **a.** lend   **b.** borrow
5. **a.** agree to   **b.** refuse to
6. **a.** push   **b.** pull

Vocabulary, Exercise 2

1. pulled
2. remember
3. schedule
4. agreed to
5. pushed
6. lend
7. refused to
8. forgot
9. borrow
10. lost
11. find
12. cancel

Grammar, Exercise 3

1. She takes the train if she misses the bus.
2. He gets annoyed if he has to wait for a long time.
3. They go out to eat if they work late.
4. If the stores have sales, they become very crowded.
5. If I take a long flight, I fly business class.
6. If we want to relax, we go to the park.
7. If she doesn't understand something, she asks questions.
8. If you need supplies, you have to fill out a request form.

Grammar, Exercise 4

1. If the weather is good, they go to the beach.
2. If they get personal phone calls at work, their boss gets angry.
3. If it rains, the children play indoors.
4. I call the technology department if my computer doesn't work. *Or* If my computer doesn't work, I call the technology department.
5. If he gets good grades, his parents are happy.
6. If he has to give presentations, he gets nervous.

Listening, Exercise 5

1. If you forget
2. Is someone pushes
3. If a friend gives you
4. If a friend borrows money
5. If you see the friend

Pronunciation, Exercise 7

1. **If** I **remember**, I **give him** a **gift**.
2. **If** I **forget**, I **send it** later.
3. **If** I **get** a **gift** from a **friend**, I **never give it** away.

Unit 28

Vocabulary, Exercise 1

1. hands
2. inside
3. outdoors
4. alone
5. people
6. animals
7. technology

Vocabulary, Exercise 2

1. conducts surveys
2. helps people learn
3. earns a good salary
4. is creative
5. is active
6. travels a lot

Grammar, Exercise 3

a. Do
b. do
c. Would
d. 'd
e. Does
f. does
g. Would
h. would
i. Do
j. does
k. doesn't
l. Would
m. would

Grammar, Exercise 4

1. Do you like having a lot of responsibility?
2. Would you like to own your own business?
3. Would you like to work from home?
4. Do you like working with your hands?
5. Do you like to fix things?
6. Would you like to earn a good salary?
7. Do you like cooking?
8. Do you like being creative?
9. Would you like to learn the secrets of the great chefs?

Listening, Exercise 5

1. a   **2.** a   **3.** b   **4.** b

Listening, Exercise 6

1. Do you like creating
2. Would you like to join
3. Do you like talking
4. Would you like to work
5. Do you like learning
6. Would you like to work
7. Do you like working

Pronunciation, Exercise 7

1. Different
2. Different
3. Different
4. Same
5. Different
6. Different
7. Same
8. Same

PRONUNCIATION TABLE

(Adapted from the *Longman Dictionary of American English*)

VOWELS

Symbol	Key Word
i	beat, feed
ɪ	bit, did
eɪ	date, paid
ɛ	bet, bed
æ	bat, bad
ɑ	box, odd, father
ɔ	bought, dog
oʊ	boat, road
ʊ	book, good
u	boot, food, student
ʌ	but, mud, mother
ə	banana, among
ɚ	shirt, murder
aɪ	bite, cry, buy, eye
aʊ	about, how
ɔɪ	voice, boy
ɪr	beer
ɛr	bare
ɑr	bar
ɔr	door
ʊr	tour

CONSONANTS

Symbol	Key Word
p	pack, happy
b	back, rubber
t	tie
d	die
k	came, key, quick
g	game, guest
tʃ	church, nature, watch
dʒ	judge, general, major
f	fan, photograph
v	van
θ	thing, breath
ð	then, breathe
s	sip, city, psychology
z	zip, please, goes
ʃ	ship, machine, station, special, discussion
ʒ	measure, vision
h	hot, who
m	men, some
n	sun, know, pneumonia
ŋ	sung, ringing
w	wet, white
l	light, long
r	right, wrong
y	yes, use, music